SLAVERY
AT SEA

THE NEW BLACK STUDIES SERIES

Edited by Darlene Clark Hine
and Dwight A. McBride

*A list of books in the series appears
at the end of this book.*

SLAVERY AT SEA

Terror, Sex, and Sickness in the Middle Passage

SOWANDE' M. MUSTAKEEM

University of Illinois Press

URBANA, CHICAGO, AND SPRINGFIELD

∞ This book is printed on acid-free paper.

Library of Congress Cataloging-in-Publication Data
Names: Mustakeem, Sowande' M., author.
Title: Slavery at sea : terror, sex, and sickness in the
    middle passage / Sowande' M. Mustakeem.
Description: Urbana : University of Illinois Press,
    2016. | Series: The new Black studies series |
    Includes bibliographical references and index.
Identifiers: LCCN 2016020895 (print) | LCCN
    2016020650 (ebook) | ISBN 9780252098994
    (e-book) | ISBN 9780252040559 (hardcover : alk.
    paper) | ISBN 9780252082023 (pbk. : alk. paper)
Subjects: LCSH: Slave ships—Atlantic Ocean. | Slave
    trade—Atlantic Ocean Region. | Slaves—Violence
    against—Atlantic Ocean. | Slaves—Health and
    hygiene—Atlantic Ocean. | Women slaves—
    Atlantic Ocean Region.
Classification: LCC HT1332 (print) | LCC HT1332 M87
    2016 (ebook) | DDC 306.3620966—dc23
LC record available at https://lccn.loc.gov/2016020895

*For the centuries of women, men, children, and sages
whose collective lives will be infinitely remembered*

Contents

Acknowledgments

This book is marked by death on all sides through many forms and unexpected moments. Writing about slavery and terror while living with the unending cycles of death does not make for an easy living. Through the losses, I unknowingly found greater perspective over time on how best to navigate and transmit the coexisting worlds of the living and dead. This project and my own intellectual evolution have greatly expanded through a winding path connected to a diverse and large collective of people who each helped to make me a better historian, intellectual, and, most of all, an active and informed thinker about the world. I acknowledge and take full responsibility for any missing names or errors and ask that they be attributed to the erratic mind of an academic caregiver and not my heart.

The earliest support came in my undergraduate years at Elon University, when I knew less of what I envisioned for myself as my history professor, Dr. Mary Jo Festle, saw a spark of passion within me and nurtured my growing understanding of black history, gender, and civil rights, but also how to begin to walk the path of a historian—appreciating the ability to see all sides of humanity while discovering the best ways to document and mark time. Her incredibly meticulous and supportive teaching and mentoring still shape my approach to the ongoing evolution in the world of teaching and scholarship. The adventurous scholar I am, curious about the world's deeply vast ways was also encouraged in me at a young age by a great many, including: Dr. Wilhemina Boyd, Professor Anne Cassebaum, Dr. Joan Gunderson, Dr. Chalmers and Pam Brumbaugh, Professor Tom Henricks, Tait Arendt, Dr. Angela Lewelyn Jones, Dr. Thomas Erdmann, Professor Iris Chapman, Dr. Leo Lambert, Mrs. Sara Peterson, Professor Helen Mackay, Professor Prudence Layne, Janice Ratliff, Robert Springer, Dr. L'Tanya Richmond, and Father Dwight McBride, along with connections and vital friendships forged among many, most especially Susie Mahoney and Shellie Johnson, two near and dear sisters on my path. I am eternally grateful for the space granted at Elon University enabling me to actualize a quest for deeper understanding of a gendered historical past through African and African American Studies.

My time in graduate school greatly expanded my view of untapped possibilities while also electrifying the collegial ties, pursuit of ideas, accountability, and ongoing meanings of community that solidified my own understanding of a scholar's role for the present, future, and past. This crystallized first at Ohio State University in the Department of Black Studies, where I gained my deepest immersion in the actual discipline, its origins, its fights, its legacies, its needs, and political evolutionary struggles that many committed to the production of knowledge must endure for the uplift of many others. This greater appreciation for self, identity, and the understanding of on-the-ground scholar-activism began from the moments, conversations, laughs, and cries shared with my beloved professor, teacher, and mentor, the late Dr. William E. Nelson Jr. His absolute unwavering support on all my still budding ideas is the reason my future study of the Middle Passage exists today. I am also grateful for the very meaningful interactions shared with Drs. James Upton, Linda James-Myers, Magbaily Fyle, Leslie Alexander-Austin, and Lupenga Mphande, who through conversations, readings, and classes each helped to expand my wonders of the African diaspora and its future meanings. I also learned all over again the value of inspiration that exists at all levels, but through that I learned most about the power of open love, support, and unending laughs shared with Mrs. Shirley Turner and Ms. Jeanie, who both equally made my days in Ohio that much more cozy and always appreciated.

The external learning on the role of the black scholar at Ohio State University came through my lifelong ties within the Black Graduate Student Caucus that permanently forged my understanding that "being here is not enough," but instead it is the work that we do as a collective for the uplift of many. For this and much more I wish to thank the circle of fellow graduate students who the and still now further enrich my life in many ways: Erik Wilson and Damian Wilson, Charlie "CP" Pryor and the Pryor family, Leon Stevenson and family, Michael "Mike J" Jackson, John Nathaniel Singer, Esther Jones Cowan, Jelani Favors, Alvin Conteh, Christine Platt Patrick, Staceyanne Headley, Corey Posey, Veianca Millet, Ezemenari Obasi, Talitha LeFlouria, Travis Simmons, Javonne Stewart, Vincent and Tanisha Briley, April Peters Hawkins, Rich Milner, Derrick White, Cicero Fain, and Ernest Perry. I am even more grateful for the Black Graduate Caucus for strengthening our ties. I also thank my many Ohio families who supported me through this project, including my cousins Angela "Angie" Terry, Daniel Chadwick, Rodney Chadwick, and Aunt Mary and Uncle Lowell Terry, for making me and my friends always feel welcome and truly at home during time off. My other family and, most of all, Dr. Moriba and Barbara Kelsey and the surrounding tight-knit Columbus ASCAC community, who each lifted me up close and from afar amid my expansion and always reminded me of the bright future ahead, I thank you from the bottom of my heart.

Once enrolled, ironically at the suggestion of Dr. Mary Jo Festle, in the Comparative Black History (CBH) doctoral program in the History Department at Michigan State University, my intellectual pool expanded on even more profound levels. Within the confines of East Lansing my life changed most professionally through incredible support both institutionally and personally in every direction on my path, facilitating optimal growth to take full bloom. Those of us within the CBH program were extremely fortunate to have had the chance to study and learn from rigorous intellectuals and institution builders who exposed us at every level to the necessity of knowledge production, mentoring, conferences, supporting peers, and being thorough in our scholarship. This came especially from the many opportunities we were offered to travel to national conferences, visit archives, participate in study-abroad programs, and receive historical grants, and from the belief that the future of our own work truly matters. Professor Darlene Clark Hine showed, taught, and lifted each of us to our future potentials through these years. I owe a great debt to her, along with many others, including Peter Beattie, Laurent Dubois, and Jeffrey Wray, for furthering my intellectual advancement. To be a part of the continued institutional building and expansion, with this book being published in the New Black Studies Series edited by Dr. Darlene Clark Hine and Dr. Dwight McBride, is truly an honor.

This book and its development leading to what follows in published form has been made possible due to the tireless commitment of two professors, mentors, and close friends—Dr. Daina Ramey Berry and Dr. Pero Dagbovie—who individually and in tandem worked with and for me as a young aspiring historian, showing me even more concretely how to establish a viable career with rigorous and relevant scholarship. My love of history, the commitment to the scholarship, the archiving and telling the most deeply rich and researched stories of the lives of enslaved women and men, being always forward thinking, extending and forging generational legacies came most through one of the rarest gifts I gained when I chose to go to Michigan State University. When I was Daina's first PhD student, she poured every bit of effort into me to prepare me for the future, but she also inspired me, believed in me, restored my faith in the utility of academia as a black female scholar, showed me how to be in the archives, shared her family with me across the globe, and most of all exposed and connected me to the networks and opportunities that enable generational legacies that will extend well beyond both and all of us. The conversations and work we do are building a future still unseen, and I thank you infinitely for believing in me and for believing with me that the Middle Passage had a deeper history still untold. To Pero, I say it all the time: thank you for keeping me encouraged to stay focused, remained grounded, stay on the grind and active in producing scholarship that extends the legacy that Carter G. Woodson bestowed upon those of us who follow. My publishing record reflects the many conversations and nudges over the years; thank you for showing and telling me how stay active and relevant. You are a true and trusted friend, inspiration, and always intellectually supportive force that I am eternally proud to have on my path and merely a moment's call away.

My love of deeper reading and insightful questions came from the profound intellectual brilliance I was surrounded by in Michigan with Kennetta Hammond Perry, Eric Duke, Christina Cadora Webb, Meredith Roman, Mike Pfister, Marcie Cowley, Fumiko Sakashita, Ronald DeSuze, Mary Clingerman, Mary Phillips, Kafentse Chike, Osie Lee Gaines III, Taki Grant, Frank Alveranga, John Grant, Marshanda Smith, Ken Marshall, Dawn Curry, Mona Jackson, Rashida Harrison, Matt Pettway, Jennifer Barclay, Nik Ribianzsky, David Carletta, Piril Atabay, Keina J. Staley, Carlos Aleman, Jason Friedman, Lauren Anderson, Kelly Palmer, Amy Hay, Dan and Jamie Dalrymple, Nothkula Cele, Ryan Pettigrill, Ted Mitchell, Bethany Hicks, Ibra Sene, Asaan Starr, Alberto Nickerson, Leslie and Eric Washington, Bayyinah Jeffries, Darcia Grant, Harry Odamtten, Daniel Davis, Lindsey Gish, Chantalle Verna, Austin Jackson, Walter Sistrunk, and Brittany O'Neal.

This project spans various parts of the Atlantic because of the many conferences from which this book has received amazing support and excitement about the need for this area of historical scholarship. It would have not been possible without the array of libraries and archives whose collections I benefited from enormously across different parts of the country and diverse corners of the world, including the Duke University Special University Collections, the Rhode Island Historical Society, the South Carolina Historical Society, the Medical University Archives of the University of South Carolina, the John Carter Brown Library, the South Carolina Department of History and Archives, the South Caroliniana Library, the Gilder Lehrman Institute of American History, the New York Public Library, New York Academy of Medicine, the New York Historical Society, Liverpool Record Office, National Maritime Museum in London, University of Liverpool Sydney Jones Library, National Archives of UK Public Record Office, Royal College of Surgeons, Wellcome Medical Library, Royal Bank of England Archives, and the National Maritime Museum in Liverpool.

Even more, this book and its process has endured it own fascinating and sometimes uncertain journey to publication, and I am ever more fortunate that this project landed at the University of Illinois Press. Most of all I am grateful for continued interest expressed from Larin McLaughlin, who then passed it on to one of the kindest, most diligent, professional, and biggest champion editors I have ever met in an editor with Dawn Durante. She embodies what a real editor is by being truly thorough, transparent, empathic, passionate, and she remained enthusiastic about our partnered ideas on seeing this book and its future potential through to publication. Thank you a million times over to Jennifer Holzner for her incredibly artistic eye in helping to produce what I am more than certain will become an unforgettable book cover. Thank you also to Tad Ringo, Kevin Cunningham, Roberta Sparenberg, Laurie Matheson, and the entire UIP staff for fully believing in this book and its future promise.

My move to St. Louis has connected me to an incredible circle of support, love, and universal compassion on multiple levels of my life. My path is truly enhanced in connecting with and learning deeply from Victor Farwell; I thank you for lifting me even higher toward ascension and destined greatness. Along with him I am forever grateful to Jason Edwards, Matthew Wilke, Gayle Farwell, Jennifer Harpring, Walter Beckham, Selena Johnson, Simone Phillips, Joan Ferguson, Anahata Roach, John and Linda Vlasick, Beth Thater Thoesel, Allison Vandersand, Adam Richard, Justina Sharp, Travis Stephenson, Joseph Leaderbrand, Duane "Jingo" Williams, Cindy Lewis, Christie Lewis Agate and family, Shannon Dial, Cassie Overturf, Larry Tucker, Glenn Williams, Mark Lewis, Brandon Bokern, Jessica Caimi, Courtney DeLaria, Kira Gill, Anika and Will Townsel, Tiffany Monique, Tia Gaines, James Cassidy, Tiffany Barber, Broderick Pritchard, John Cobb, Dino Chase, Brad Stephens, Bradford James, Aaron Jacobs, Moondog Guebert, P. J. Heydt, Zach Jennings, Barrington Gates, Christian Paul, Aaron Perks, Tyrone Swinton, Val Hartwig, Don Tinsley, Valerie Myers, Alexis Tucci, Filomena Consiglio, Sarah Hayes, Kaci Morgan, T, James "Needles" Biko, Patrick O'Neill, James Savens, Christine Hughes, Stephanie Williams, Eric Littles, Jessica and Chris Clark and family, Aaron Blinkley, Anthony Hann, Michael Miller, Samantha Lee Braswell, Kat Welsh, and Robbie Luepker.

My family has proved to be a major source of strength through often unbearable times sincerely thank the many who have loved me both close and from afar throughout the years and trials, including Evelyn Lynch, Deardria Nesbit, Doris and Dot Black, the Harris-Eades family, the Hsi family, Missie Shealey, Janiyah Grant, Mike Shealey, Kelley Alexander, Miriam Phields, Uncle Sly Sanders and family, Uncle Kenny and Aunt Shirley Wood, Kenny Wood Jr. and family, my Mustakeem family in Atlanta, Vivian, Gene, and Teddy Buckingham and family, Grandpa "Dad" Preston Benton and the entire

Benton family, Kenneth Butler and family, Selma Harkness, Euzelle and Bert Wood, Woody Wood, Diane Wood, Rose and Uncle Bill Salisbury, the Justice family, the Terry family, Conchita and Jai Battle, and the multitude of cousins, aunts, and uncles everywhere who loved me enough to allow the studies to come first. As time has gone by with this book's evolution, I have also sadly lost a number of family, friends, and other people close to me whose energy and presence still shape this project in meaningful ways, including Grandma Marjorie Wood, Grandma Lena Benton, Grandma Helen Leggette, Queen Nzinga Heru, Shawn Yates, Bob Donaldson, Jamel Houseworth, Daina Howell, Keith Wood, Dean James E. McLeod, beloved historian Stephanie Camp, and more recently Jarrett Cochese Greene.

The greatest muses in my life are my students, because they hold the vision for social change and correcting humanity in the near and far future toward greatness. I have been fortunate to have taught many years' worth of students who inspired the work, questioned greater transparency on academia and the writing process, and demanded to know why certain people and marginalized narratives were left out of the dialogue even in twenty-first-century historical narratives. I am especially grateful for the first students I learned from amid their own education at Ohio State University: Jamie Columbine, Ricardo Reis, and Brandi Hogan. Later at Michigan State University: Meagan Mason, Ileana Cortez, Ashley Eigner, Jenae Chinn, Eric Washington, Oke Chukwu, Jamal Williams, Jessica Shawver, Raven Jones, and Courtney Griffith. At Washington University in St. Louis, my cup runneth over with those I can only thank through mere words: Lauren Henley and family, Jasmine Knowles, Atima Lui, Jyotsna Ramachandran, Chyna Bowen and family, Susan Kunihiro and family, Josh Smith, Ashley Fox, Tiffany Anne Johnson, Ryan Forman, Will Hawley, Rachel Margolin and family, Melanie Gatewood, Georgia McCandlish, Briana Prickens, Leslie Salisbury, Dylan Simonsen and family, Kawana Tharps, Ahkianne Wanliss, Yasmin Boakye, Sujay Kulsthrestha, Sara Harris, Ali Karamustafa, Josh Aiken, Ezinne Arizor, Michele Hall, Harry Kainen, Nelson Nwumeh, Beth Pearl-Barr and family, Lori Schlatter, Ben Shanahan, Olivia Suber, Justin and Julian Nicks, Rachel Hoffman, Alex Novelli, Brandon Wilson, Chandler Malone, Jared Skoff, Katie Yun, Lee Winter, Olivia Marcucci, Rori Bridge, Shira Weissmann, Tobeya Ibitayo, Reuben Riggs-Bookman, Julie Kennedy, Courtney Gray, Candice Harden, Latrionna Moore, James Mason, Chris Halline, Hallie Dobkien-Gellar, Courtney Amegashie, Ari Salzberg, Scotty Jacobs and family, Jamal Sadrud Din, Jessica Simon, Liam O'Donnell, Lori Schlatter, Samuel Lai, Satchel Siegel, Jason Silberman, and Zoe Sissac, among a multitude of many others who will always matter to me.

I have likewise amassed a collective of newer friends, colleagues, mentors, neighbors, and lifelong friends across the world through the decades and meaningful periods of my life who have established irreplaceable ties, who continued to call, and who also have kept me focused and motivated on the end goal. I thank especially Nzinga Kemp and Roshmond Patten, Holly Smith, Teishan Latner, Eric Kimball and family; Shellie and Anthony Pighet; Richard Mizelle, Rashaad Johnson, Jeff Fortin, Elizabeth Stordeur Pryor, Sharita Jacobs, Nadia Brown, J. T. Roane, Bryan Sinche, Kevin Dawson, Brandon Winford, Jessica Millward, Jessica Johnson, Jamie Thomas, Sharla Fett, Thomas Foster, Keona Irving, Maurice Hobson, Scot Brown, David Goldberg, Zebulon Miletsky, Michele Reid, Abou Bambara, Tiffany Gill, Meghan Ferrence, Shirletta Kinchen, Treva Lindsey, Amrita Chakbarti Myers, Stacey Robertson, James Conway, Reggie Ellis, Thabiti Willis, Jakobi Williams, Amilcar Shabazz, Christina Davis, Jonathan Smith, Nadia Brown, Cheryl Laird, Amani Marshall, Persavia Praylow, Bryan Yates, Curtis Austin, Sherwin Bryant, Walter Rucker, Karcheik Sims-Alvarado, Katrina Thompson, Fatima Muse, Justin Hansford, Stephan Bradley, Charles Berry, Mr. Bill Durbin, Mr. Freeman and family, Meche and Joe Jackson and family, and my extended family Adell and Christine Patton.

I also have become known for forging circles of friends wherever I go, and that has proved a great source of strength and beauty through adversity, most especially through the ties that will always connect me with my dear sister-friends Makiba Foster, Danice Brown, Michelle Adewumi, Korina Jocson, and Sasha Turner Bryson. Thinking on the necessity of these ties within and beyond home, I brought together several "sista-scholars" for our generation, and I am eternally grateful for the late-night calls, the tears, the grind-out conversations, and the belief continually shared that our work will soon collectively matter. Thank you for our unbreakable connection: Lashawn Harris, Kennetta Hammond Perry, Deirdre Cooper Owens, Sasha Turner Bryson, and Talitha LeFlouria.

At Washington University in St. Louis, I have been truly blessed. I am much more clear in my place, purpose, and future contributions that have been and continue to be supported. But most of all, I have learned hands-on from an amazing array of scholars, friends, and colleagues over the years who demonstrated and taught me the necessity of mentor relationships and the spirit of true friendship and fantastic colleagues to work and live among: Andrea Friedman, Iver Bernstein, Gerald Early, David Konig, Daniel Bornstein, Anjanette Wells, Lorena Walsh, Jason Purnell, Darrell Hudson, Jeffrey McCune, Leah Merrifield, Jill Stratton, Harvey Fields, Matt Devoll, Bill Tate, Garrett Duncan, Carol Camp Yeakey, Rudolph Clay, Sheri Notaro, Janary Stanton, Margaret Williams, Pete Benson, Sheryl Peltz, Raye Mahaney, Linda Nicholson, Rebecca Wanzo, Bill Maxwell, Shefali Chandra, William Tate, Kimberly Norwood, Ron Himes, Samba Diallo and Wilmetta Toliver-Diallo, Venus Bivar, Ignacio Nacho Sanchez, Lori Watt, Daniel Bornstein, Alex Dube, Kenneth Ludmerer,

Steven and Liling Miles, Heidi Kolk, Jenni Harpring, J. Dillon Brown, and Joe Lowenstein. The incredible junior faculty members at my university keep me both grounded and truly invigorated, including sharing intellectual space with Jonathan Fenderson, Douglas Flowe, Michelle Purdy, Monique Bedasse, Lerone Martin, Amber Musser, Anika Walke, Trevor Sangrey, Ebony Duncan, Vernon Mitchell, Diana Montano, Jordache Ellapen, and Maryan Soliman. I also remember and hold dear the years shared with the growing momentum of earlier intellectual exchanges forged then with and among other invigorating colleagues, including Sonia Lee, Yuko Miki, Paul Ramirez, Billy Acree, Derek Pardue, and Ignacio Infante.

There is a special group of leaders, friends, and exceptional models who represent still unimagined possibilities of collegiality and visionary support as they generously shared with and through me institutional support, incredible mentoring, and friendship through partnerships on new ideas. I thank you most of all to Vice Provost Adrienne Davis; you are a model of grace, empathy, incredible awareness and support, and insight on the future and its needs, and we are all, especially myself, much better because of your presence and vitality. My path has been incredibly supported by a great many in various corners, but my expansion has been unparalleled through the enduring connections and incredible collegial ties shared and maintained with Tim and Ann Parsons, Hillel and Debbie Kieval, Jean Allman, Peter Kastor, Dean Jen Smith, Assistant Vice Provost Rochelle Smith, Gerald Early, Rafia Zafar, Shanti Parikh, and Christine Johnson, each of whom has shown and taught me how to be even sharper in the prose of life as a scholar, leader, and friend. My many ideas would likewise have not ever taken shape in various ways without the forceful support and dynamic partnering put into motion with Jonathan Fenderson, Dean Mary Laurita, Makiba Foster, Sheretta Butler-Barnes, Paul Steinbeck, and Douglas Flowe through various exhilarating projects; they each reinforce the power of the collective toward igniting innovative real change.

Over the years I have learned the true value of mentors and mentoring, and they come in many forms at moments when we most need them. This project has grown exponentially over the years because of the unparalleled power of legacy, friendship, and mentoring. I am particularly indebted to conversations, conference commentary, and strategic guidance offered on my way forward from Marcus Rediker, Douglas Egerton, Vincent Brown, Richard Follett, Barbara Krauthamer, Jim Downs, Robin D. G. Kelley, Ed Baptist, Ben Vinson, Marcus Cox, Clarence Lang, Jeffrey Bolster, Glenn Gordinier, Ann Little, Christopher Brown Jr., Tera Hunter, Todd Savitt, David Barry Gaspar, David Roediger, Vincent Harding, Leslie Harris, Jennifer Morgan, Herman Bennett, Stephanie Smallwood, Peter Weinstein, Jane Landers, Wilma King, Heather Thompson, Kali Gross, Cheryl Hicks, and Khalil Muhammad.

I end in thanking both of my parents for this path, my father, Mohammed "M" Mustakeem, and my mother, Velma J. Mustakeem, for making this entire path and soul contract possible. My mother, my best friend, I thank for her unwavering support, and for incredible and rather uncanny understanding of the academic and writing process beyond her own stroke survival. She continues to show me and the world around her strength, love, compassion, endurance, and zest for life that shines through her brilliance and greatness of her own daily miracles, which I am blessed to bear witness to and help facilitate. Thank you for another lifetime of memories, laughter, and for nurturing the nerd within me toward absolute greatness. May the future and days ahead become even brighter for us both.

SLAVERY
AT SEA

Introduction

Middle Passage Studies and the Birth of Slavery at Sea

In a 1734 published account, British seaman William Snelgrave detailed his experiences while employed in the African slave trade. During his stay at Jaqueen, west of Benin in the Gold Coast region, a linguist brought him two black females for purchase, requesting that he "not let them be redeemed by any one that should offer to do it."[1] Snelgrave obliged the proposal and inspected both women, estimating one was "fifty, and the other about twenty Years old." Variables he used to calculate the bondwomen's ages go unrecorded, although his estimations hinged on their displayed bodies—namely, their capacity for future childbearing. During initial assessments he determined the older female "was past her Labour" and, as he declared, "not for my purpose." He chose instead to buy the younger female, believing she offered greater long-term productive and reproductive value. Snelgrave's refusal of the older captive prompted an immediate reaction from the interpreter: "It would highly oblige the King" that he purchase both females. Yet Snelgrave suspected that the coastal men "made use of the Kings Name, to get rid of an old Woman," leading him to cease negotiations.

Shortly after the failed proposition, Snelgrave gained insight into the circumstances surrounding the rejected older woman.[2] Disappointed with the female's inability to secure a buyer, the ruler's aide "ordered her to be destroyed" through forcible death. "The Woman's Hands being tied behind her, and her Feet across," several designated men put her "into the *Cannoe*, and carried [her] off about half a Mile from the Shore." They steered into deeper waters, casting the enslaved woman overboard, after which they witnessed some "voracious Fishes" begin to "tear her to pieces in an instant." Her seaborne execution reaffirmed racial and cultural biases that Snelgrave harbored against Africans given what he characterized as "the Barbarity of those people." The next day, however, he received a letter from his chief mate explaining that instead of falling victim to the jaws of traveling sharks, "the Woman was on board our Ship."

Traveling back from the coast, one of Snelgrave's officers "spied something floating on the Sea" alerting his attention. "[He] perceived [it] to be a human Body lying on its back," seeing the mysterious individual "now and then spurting Water out at the Mouth." Realizing the person "was still living, he ordered [it] to be taken into the Boat" and out of the water beneath. Several crewmen moved the female into the dinghy, untied the rope restricting her movement, and "chafed her Limbs, and rolled her Body about" until she successfully "discharged a good quantity of salt Water out of her Mouth." The sailors, unaware of the death sentence imposed on shore, remained perplexed with how "she had escaped the Sharks" routinely pervasive within open seawaters. The bondwoman's escape, facilitated by his own crew, forced Snelgrave to grow apprehensive "if the King of Dahome' should come to know" about her near missed tragedy.[3] He immediately ordered his first mate "to charge our People to keep the thing secret." After concluding affairs on shore, Snelgrave rejoined the vessel, conducted an immediate body examination to locate any lingering injuries or ailments, and, more critically, he probed how the bondwoman became enslaved. Relying on an interpreter, he queried her relationship with the local ruler, to which she responded that "she would never confess the reason of the King's displeasure against her." Soon after, the unnamed captive altered her story, declaring "she knew not that she had in any respect offended him." Still unclear is whether this captive was unaware of committing any previous wrongdoing or if her response was perhaps a protective measure used in lieu of possibly facing her accusers. The interpreter, fully cognizant of the prevailing circumstances, shared with Snelgrave that the female's removal "was on account of her assisting some of the King's Women in their Amours."[4]

Snelgrave remained uncertain about the bondwoman's movement into slavery, yet his curiosity did not hinder him from capitalizing on her unexpected inclusion as part of the ship's cargo. The crew maintained secrecy of her stowage, confining her within the hold and forcing her to journey across the Atlantic, leaving untold the experiences she endured and bore witness to on ship. Once docked overseas, this female captive, formerly cast and treated as worthless, was sold to an acquaintance of Snelgrave in Antigua. Bartered, sold, and exiled into a foreign space, she, much like scores of other slaves, never gained an opportunity to share her personal testimony of captivity. Historical details illuminating who this victim was, her life in Africa, the experiences she endured at sea, negotiations conducted for her overseas sale, or even how and if she survived enslavement in an unfamiliar environment are unrecorded. The fate of the younger female offered with the transported bondwoman is also obscured. What was the relationship of these two females? How long and with how many slave traders were they marketed? Did the king's aide impose the bondwoman's sentence, or was the operation perhaps a sole endeavor instigated by the linguist? Why was her execution left to be carried out at sea as opposed to on land? Direct evidence explaining what landed either of these women into slavery, along with the range of personal sufferings they endured is veiled. Their story, however, provides a glimpse into the unpredictable and often dangerous environments that slaves and sailors confronted. At the same time, invocation of these unnamed females, whose lives were tragically altered through the financial decisions of others, invites us to reckon more closely with complex factors of age, gender, value, and disposability of the black body amid the legal trade and traffic of people as commercial goods.

* * *

Historians have long been interested in the containment of black bodies and how freedom struggles inform dynamics between slaves and slaveholders. Tracing the movement of bondpeople in, out, and through the watery space of the Atlantic Ocean, this book explores the social conditions and human costs embedded in the world of maritime slavery. It does not compare plantations with slave ships or attempt to suggest any spatial hierarchies of trauma. Instead it broadens the gaze of captivity toward the interior and rather contentious seaborne spaces occupied by bondpeople, surgeons, and sailors. Cargo ships are not often studied as central sites of slavery. However, this book aims to show how the Middle Passage comprised a violently unregulated process critically foundational to the institution of bondage that interlinked slaving voyages and plantation societies.

A wealth of studies centered on plantations and slave communities continue to flourish in exposing the intricacies of domestic slavery across the Atlantic world. Yet the fundamental nature of shipboard captivity and its many terrors still has not been fully interrogated. For more than a century, beginning with W.E.B. Du Bois's seminal 1896 work, *The Suppression of the African Slave Trade to the United States of America, 1638–1870*, early slave trade scholars who followed explored the social and economic histories contained in the commercial traffic of bondpeople out of Africa, to which Eric Williams, Walter Rodney, Lorenzo Greene, Darold Wax, Daniel Mannix, and Malcolm Cowley, among a host of other historians, collectively expanded the intellectual scope of the slave trade in profound ways.[5] Philip D. Curtin's 1969 publication of *The Atlantic Slave Trade: A Census* sparked the most momentous redirection in slave trade scholarship. Relying on statistical models to quantify the movement of slaves out of Africa and into the Americas—infamously known as "the numbers game"—Curtin estimated that eleven million Africans were displaced across slave societies. The number-centered methodology, while useful, comprised the most dominant approach in slave trade historiography for over five decades.[6]

Quantifying slaving voyages and bondpeople is the most primary method for accessing the slave trading past, evident in the ongoing and rather exciting expansion of the Trans-Atlantic Slave Trade Database.[7] In an attempt to recover the wooden world of slave ships and the personal narratives lost behind the numbers, a small yet growing body of scholarship—which I refer to as "Middle Passage studies"—has begun to deepen the analysis of slavery by recentering the forcible sale and oceanic transport of African captives into the New World. Therein, Middle Passage studies within this book gives birth to a world of intellectual expansion still unseen in the historiography that poses more invasive new questions to extract the deeper and more painfully violent narratives of slave trading during the legal slave trading period.[8] Marcus Rediker and Stephanie Smallwood produced pathbreaking works examining the magnitude of the Middle Passage as symbiotic to slave societies and the modern world. Rediker unravels the series of multifaceted human dramas involving crewmen, slaves, and abolitionists to argue that slaving voyages devastated the lives of purchased captives while slave ships became the primary instrument fueling globalization and capitalism. Whereas Smallwood frames the slave trade through the intricate process of commodification into which bondpeople were cast on different sides of the Atlantic, astutely revealing that "[t]he most powerful instrument locking captives in as commodities for Atlantic trade was the culture of the market itself."[9] Seeing a pressing need for a more engaged treatment of seafarers within the slaving industry, Emma Christopher chronicles the complex lives of slave ship sailors to forge much greater insight into the meanings of whiteness, power, and the fragility of their own freedom as laborers within histories and memories of the slave trade.[10] Eric Taylor, on the other hand, traces an incredible number of ship revolts to show how these resistive measures comprised the most contentious interactions between crewmen and adult black males on slaving voyages.[11]

This book builds on the momentum of scholarship moving the Middle Passage from the periphery to consider how slavery functioned outside the locus of plantations. Looking beyond crowded cities, distant farms, murky swamps, and mountainous regions, it constructs a historical cultural womb of consciousness fueled by a commercial industry anchored on terror. Going further, it introduces the concept of "slavery at sea" into the lexicon of studies of slaving voyages, and makes meaning of the process. Doing so, this study examines the Middle Passage and, more importantly, the social space of ships and the ocean as epicenters in the making and unmaking of transported slaves. The Atlantic slave trade and, more specifically, the oceanic transport of African captives served as the lifeline of the evolving New World economy, based largely upon the labor of enslaved populations. These variegated seaborne pathways operated as the primary isolated channel through which bondpeople arrived into the Americas. How do we best frame, define, and make meaning of the Middle Passage to better understand its central importance in the cycle of Atlantic slavery? *Slavery at Sea* departs from most studies by integrating questions that probe the spectrum of human bondage through a multifocal lens extended toward sex, terror, the body, illness, and death. Delving even deeper, Middle Passage studies here interlinks the land and the sea by giving historical treatment to the scores of people directly affected by the fire of global financial interest ignited for slave labor. Left undefined and disjointed from Atlantic slave societies, the slave ship experience is remembered as a colorful mark in the triangular mapping of trade routes of goods, a chapter in history, an event, or at best a short trip that some slaves took. We therefore know far less about what power looked like up close and personal amid the trade and traffic of the most highly demanded eighteenth-century Atlantic good—African people—with considerably minimal attention to the gendered nature of this violent enterprise as well as the deeply painful legacies of loss and degradation permanently steeped in the memories of those made slaves and carried into the Americas.

Slavery is routinely understood through the prism of workplaces, fields, households, and landed sites of exploitation hinged upon the production of labor. Boundaries and the manipulation of space(s) continue to generate scholarly interest; however, the Atlantic Ocean remains tangential and largely invisible to these conversations.[12] Viewing these far-reaching oceanic bodies of water as more than highways and routes for the transport of goods, both human and material, this book widens the optic to include and recast the sea as a viable and transformative space of history. The Atlantic Ocean was more than just a space; it became an agent that imposed significant impact on people, further bridging the relationship of man and the sea.[13] As crewmen manned ships traveling into and between distant locales, the sea became a constant "zone of death."[14] The ocean was not just *where* the story of slavery transpired as black bodies were ferried beyond coastal ways and into unknown lands, but as this book reveals, it also became a central conduit for *how* bondage unfolded and consequentially devastated lives. Slave vessels were intimately private spaces, public only to those aboard. Yet the sea represented an important open arena of struggle for power and agency as captives jumped to their deaths and sailors flung slaves overboard knowing about, and in many respects relying upon, the presence of sharks and other dangerous sea creatures lurking beneath.[15]

Deepening our understanding of the Middle Passage as an embodied and far-reaching experience, *Slavery at Sea* historically traces it as a tangible experience of bondpeople rather than a cultural artifact of the African Diaspora. The Atlantic slave trade serves as the most iconic marker of struggle, oppression, unity, strength, and perseverance in the African Diaspora, but it is never thoroughly engaged for what really happened. As such, this horrific period in time continues unchallenged, untouched, and thus left as a bloodied yet sanitized chapter in global history. The Middle Passage likewise has long occupied an enduring focal point of diasporic cultural memory, evidenced by nations, poets, historians, and literary scholars who rely heavily on the symbolic nature of the slave trade as a useful departure for discussion of cultural idioms and emerging political ideologies that took shape within and beyond antebellum slavery. As such, imaginations of the slave ship experience continue to be invoked, redefined, and broadened to fit this middle ground of history, although often extending far from its conceptual origin. The pooling of distant monies for the buying and selling of black bodies set into motion an economy of violence systematically fueled through tightened entrepreneurial networks that proved enormously assistive in distribution needs. What was this system, and, more germane to this study, what were the human costs and consequences of these financial decisions?

To better understand the financial roots deeply tied to the massive traffic of black bodies for capital gain, the transatlantic slave trade is historically framed within this book as an industry and thus an institutional system that facilitated successful operation of the "human manufacturing process." Manufacturing processes are fundamentally understood as the mass production of goods that are (1) put together, (2) packaged, (3) delivered, and (3) sold. Applying this same formulaic understanding to examination of the slave trade and its four-century-long operation more concretely centers how this intercontinental enterprise contributed to the construction of a black labor force and the calculated terrain of brutal experiences bondpeople confronted prior to their landed displacement into the Americas. This process, which every slave endured, was operationalized through woven threads of power, exploit, and deprivation maintained by slave ship workers. Therein, within the sequential process of slavery at sea, captives faced and were refined, or rather manufactured, through three key phases: warehousing, transport, and delivery. From this socioeconomic lens, the movement of money—investment in ships and ship building materials; wages; and other financial incentives used to entice and employ captains and crews, inland capturers, coastal traders, and surgeons—served as initial down payments. Collectively the process financed and thus sponsored a global vortex of trade and terror internationally linked between Europe, Africa, the Caribbean, and the Americas not only through its laborers but most especially through the transport of human goods contained at its core and demanded by diverse Atlantic customers. By keeping the gaze upon merchants, investors, and currency, the many global laborers physically tasked with fulfilling these envisioned dreams of slave trading wealth remain trivialized along with the power these key players personally exacted in the lives of bondpeople.

Slavery at Sea centers the terrain of political struggle not only on oceangoing ships but also on the diverse and vulnerable bodies of captives continuously unmade by their transporters and the human manufacturing process. The hostile management of slaves is regularly associated with planters, overseers, slave drivers, and patrols; however, the production of black laborers was far from a land-based phenomenon. It is not enough to say that Africans were captured, transformed into commodities, shipped out of Africa, sold to interested buyers, and turned into slaves once moved into plantations. The human manufacturing process and, more importantly, the interior holds of merchant ships served as vital sites of power sailors used to dehumanize captives, enforce dependency, inflict pain, establish authority, and prohibit any sense of control over one's personal life in the near and far future. This level of mistreatment under the guise of refinement closely mirrored the tactic of what is known to many as "seasoning," a brutal yearlong intensive process routinely understood throughout the West Indies to enforce bondpeople's rapid adjustment to plantation slavery.[16] However, unbound by labor outputs and any immediate land-based laws of social order at sea, the totalizing of slavery began much earlier at the hands of slave ship workers through terror-centric means unimagined on land.

Sailors relentlessly unmade bondpeople's bodies through physical, emotional, and psychological conditioning, making intimately clear the dynamics of power.[17] Exploring the cyclical assaults on slaves' personhood uncovers the politics of the making and unmaking of black bodies for the first time, showing more holistically how men, women, the sick, weak, and unborn became paradigmatic to this foundational moment of conquest and debasement. This process of unmaking, which no captive was able to circumvent once forced into the slaving industry, produced a dramatic climate of terror in the world of slavery at sea that resulted in mental disorientation, familial and communal separation, malnourishment, lack of sanitation and cleanliness, severe isolation, debilitating diseases, miscarriages, sexual abuse, psychological instability, and bearing witness to physical violence committed against kin and shipmates. Equally salient to the slaving process was the refinement of manufactured slaves that it created. To be sure, testimonies that follow expose how slaves were broken and unmade through the relentless veins of violence anchored at its maritime core; doing so lays bare the formative and permanent stripping of their freedom. Carrying these deep psychological scars on land once imported overseas, the effects of the Middle Passage filtered within and beyond the ocean, irrevocably transforming bondpeople's lives as well as the societies and communities into which they were imported. One cannot make sense of the behaviors widespread throughout Atlantic slave societies—reproductive agency, maroonage, resistance to familial separation, suicide, violent rebellions, or even poisoning—without examining how these insubordinate patterns took shape through early manifestation at sea.

Enslaved Africans were the primary commodities of the slave trade; however, narratives of terror and strife as well as the types of people directly and personally affected by oceanic transport are largely unknown as intimate voices of the slave trade.[18] This book unveils multitudes of slaves whose stories of sorrow, saga, and triumph remain untold and thus unfamiliar to many. Dramatic scenes of degradation widespread on slave ships included more victims than adult black men, typically cast as representatives of all slaves purchased and sold to foreign buyers. The counting of bodies leaves silent the deeper interrogation of how gender informed the treatment of all transported slaves. As such, the metanarrative of black men, or rather the privileging of black masculinity within histories of the slave trade, symbolically confines black women and girls to plantations, marking slave ships as untraditional spaces where bonded females are rarely found, unexplored, forgotten, and therefore left out of the central story. Gendering the history of the slave trade solely through women's experiences still does not fully encapsulate the sufferings of the sold and unprotected. By "mining the forgotten," this book reconfigures a much larger human spectrum intentionally more inclusive of girls, boys, nursing mothers, infants, teenagers, elderly males and females, the diseased, as well as disabled slaves, similarly purchased and boarded on ships alongside healthy adult males.[19] The human stories of slavery at sea included more than just slaves, extending further to employed slave trade workers. Widening the gaze to center the violent entanglement of slaves, sailors, and surgeons holistically on ships and showing more of the overlooked, forgotten, and the many unremembered whose lives help to fully humanize the histories of slavery's horrors.

As slave transporters and working-class laborers of the sea, sailors served the most fundamental role in the transoceanic history of the slave trade, granting buyers access and furthering slave economies through the constant import of black bodies. Without them the commerce of African captives and exploitation of labor-based profit could not have transpired. The grueling labor and constant exposure of mariners' own lives to the unending risks of slaving allowed for the continuation of this global enterprise. Much like plantation overseers, the contributions of sailors to slavery remains relegated within the obscured margins and footnotes of history. Therefore, I remain especially indebted to the work of Emma Christopher, Marcus Rediker, and Jeffrey Bolster for the valuable insight they provide to better explore the largely invisible world of sailors and shipping.[20] The inner lives of seafarers are most times inaccessible due to the predominance of illiteracy, but also due to the construction of narratives that silence the labor that seamen performed in the movement and brutal management of bondpeople.

*   *   *

The forced mobility of slaves is often cast and claimed as solely a part of African American history, yet the reliance on and allocation of terrorizing violence for the sake of economic gain spanned more than four centuries and included a multiplicity of nations. The stories that follow emerge from the annals of the British and American slave trade during the peak and final century of the legal slave trading period of the eighteenth century, making what some would cast as simply a British Atlantic story. To be sure, the transoceanic movement of slaves superseded all national and landed boundaries, marking it as a painful and rather shameful aspect of history that many nations, countries, and states seldom choose to commemorate. This book does not intimately detail commercialized networks of slave trading in Central and Latin America, nor does it recount the forcible movement of slaves transported through the Indian Ocean or sub-Saharan networks. When carefully read through the lens of terror, however, parallels persist in the patterns of captivity and the relentless quest for power and wealth that put a premium on the Atlantic import of exploitable healthy black bodies at any human cost. Disaggregating the Middle Passage from an isolated event, but instead as an intricate part of a massively global human manufacturing process predicated on a continuum of abuses that every bondperson forced to chart the Atlantic confronted, it complicates the history more directly to account for diversity across gender, age, health, and the multiplicity of sufferings. Doing so reaffirms that not all slaves endured the transatlantic passage in the same way. By delving into the often volatile maritime world when the legal slave trade operated as a fashionable way of traffic, *Slavery at Sea* provides a more textured understanding of how human power, human pain, and economic greed enacted cycles of tragedies that spanned centuries, memory, time, and space.

Entrepreneurial ventures based upon African human capital served as crucial components to the evolving institution of slavery taking shape across the Caribbean and the Americas. The seventeenth century witnessed a gradual increase of involvement, particularly for the British, as merchants pooled resources to create joint stock companies—the Royal African Company, the Dutch West Indies Company, and the French Guinea Company—setting government-sanctioned monopolies into motion. Yet this period constituted a mere testing ground for slave sales. The eighteenth century bore witness to a dramatic transformation in commercial slavery across the Atlantic that created a spiraling intensification for African laborers. This explosion of interest resulted in the shipment of men, women, and children that underwent a quantum leap in numbers with more than six million captives being deposited into various Atlantic ports and slave societies.[21] During the opening decades of the century, charter companies proved ill equipped to fulfill the vast demand for bondpeople amid the decline of monopolistic control. As such, the downfall of monopolies and loss of trade control to a growing base of private traders meant the slave trade operated as the least regulated branch of commercial interests until its legal demise in the nineteenth century.[22] Merchants, brokers, and planters throughout the Atlantic world, including Rio de Janeiro, New Orleans, Antigua, South Carolina, Costa Rica, Barbados, Virginia, and St. Thomas, among many others, constituted the human web of commerce openly invested in the export and import of black bodies.

The main actors of *Slavery at Sea* are those who physically traveled the dangerous pathways of the sea—sailors, captives, and surgeons. By viewing the waterways as seminal spaces where history was made and slaves were produced, we can generate new questions of traditional sources. Surviving slave trade records are most times disjointed, fragmented, scattered, and disparate at best as they evoke greater violence on the lives and suffering of bondpeople through the omissions, silences, and limited access to their personal stories.[23] To say that the continuation of the Atlantic slave trade inscribed a bloodied mark of mistreatment in human history is by no means novel. Within this book I attempt to provide a sensitive and comprehensive understanding of the operation of unabated power, deprivation, and violent exploit through the Middle Passage. The primary sources used for this study are grouped into four broad categories, which I label personal, professional, financial, and public. I have done a careful reading of an array of records to pose an entirely new set of critical questions and provoke an uncomfortably closer gaze into the continuum of torture, abuse, and survival that bound slaves and sailors together on ships.

Personal sources of the slave trade, including diaries and published accounts, offer an uncanny engagement with the varied thoughts and observations of seamen and surgeons. Illiteracy was widespread among working-class seafarers, therefore discovery of a diary maintained by a slave ship sailor is an incredibly rare find. The notion of inscribing one's innermost thoughts without restriction into an object protected and locked away has significance in the depth of personal reflection the writer shares. A seaman's diary offers an intimately unfiltered gaze on the self, sea, and boarded slaves, although it contains far fewer details than historians would hope for in extrapolating greater details on the oceanic slaving process. The fleeting, almost subtle, commentaries on marine life regarding shipboard duties, fishing and food supply, weather patterns, and any insubordinate behaviors that slaves acted out during the passage have proven useful to this study. In much the same way, accounts that ship captains and surgeons published respectively helped to extend a deeper gaze into the process of coastal trade conducted with local African rulers; the types of slaves offered, bought, and refused; along with addressing the more common aspects of life on a slave ship, including sexual assaults and the violent deaths of slaves. Widespread publication and construction of these narratives emerged for reasons many times unknown. Providing the literate world access to the business and fatal dangers of the slaving industry, these recollections comprise permanent records that shape where, how, and if certain details of the trade are revealed or instead withheld.

Correspondences exchanged between the many men employed as professionals throughout the trade—merchants, brokers, and surgeons—make up the professional sources used in this book. The roles that many of these people served were vastly different; however, their future reputations and social status hinged upon particular slaving needs and concerns carefully described in handwritten letters. As the primary investors, merchants orchestrated the trade from afar by employing, and thereby entrusting, sea captains and their crew with full control in securing the most ideal slaves to generate lucrative profits overseas. Although they relied on the personal choices and decisions that sailors made in completing a slaving voyage, these entrepreneurs expressed specific commands on a ship crew's behaviors, specified slave preferences, and outlined the methods of necessary treatment and management of purchased captives. More than mere words, their demands legitimized a foundation of behaviors influential with how sailors transformed and thus broke bondpeople down through violence, separation, and extreme deprivation for frugal business purposes. Another category of professional sources equally germane to this project are the letters that various brokers from locally respected slave trading firms wrote. These men were tasked with marketing ships' arrivals and gathering crowds for auction sales, yet they also reported on the current progress of the trade, which is useful in tracing the social and financial value of slaves carried into port, sold and unsold. We therefore gain a better sense of the constant movement of ships and slaves. The cursory attention these sources call to bondpeople's bodies enables a bifocal-like gaze on their health—physical and psychological—while intimating how the terrorizing traumas of slavery at sea manifested in the behaviors of captives during market inspections and shoreline sales.

Slave ship surgeons similarly penned letters beneficial in uncovering details of the Middle Passage. Amid reports of personal tensions and abuses confronted with sea captains, these correspondences reveal the internal dynamics of shipboard authority relative to insurrections, the disciplining of slaves, dietary practices, medical outbreaks, and explanations of other human losses faced during a ship's passage. To gain greater access to the medical stories of slavery at sea, these letters are viewed alongside medical logs, a series of mortality lists, and a range of eighteenth-century medical literature. Surviving medical logs portray captives' treatment on slave ships through daily entries remarking on sickness, medical pain, and death as well as curative methods, including food and drinks, used to attempt to recover the health of ailing slaves. The listings of deaths that British surgeons were required to submit at the conclusion of a slaving voyage are valuable in foregrounding the range of illnesses and other ways bondpeople died on slaving voyages. These observations reaffirm that death pervaded slave ships not only through revolts but also through untreatable diseases, psychological shock, gynecological concerns, and suicidal means. Reading these slave trade records in tandem with eighteenth-century medical literature—books, pamphlets, and dissertations—I employ a nuanced approach to speculatively reconstruct how bondpeople perished from a range of contagious, debilitating, and deadly illnesses by examining shipboard diseases in conjunction with bodily symptoms and modes of treatment frequently used on land during this period of human trafficking.

Financial sources provide more than crude and cold numbers used to assess a bondperson's value and success in distant market sales. Ship logs and ship manifests form a crucial component of records that merchants required to better reflect on their expenses and strategies for future involvement in the trade. These dual sources enable us to look beyond prices and the circulation of monies to extract daily insights into how sailors attempted to preserve and manage boarded slaves. Through these queries we gain additional evidence on illness, insubordinate slaves, and the use of shipboard surveillance and violence. Cargo receipts and account sales likewise permit scholars to gain sustained exposure to a vast array of captives, including nursing women, infants, and elderly bondwomen forced into the trade. Even more than the incredible opportunities to tease out gender and age, brief notes that invoke sickness, blemishes, and missing limbs among newly imported captives enable a more textured depiction of slaves' bodies. We may not always have visual descriptions of how they entered the trade; however, the representation of their bodies—enfeebled, weakened, and many times traumatized—allows us the rare opportunity to interrogate their physical condition as they arrived into port. Therein, within this study *the body* is read as a text to better understand the tangible effects of slavery at sea. Doing so permits greater access to the different types of captives, family dynamics, illnesses, and body structures. It also encourages a reassessment of the meaning of "prime slaves" given the presence of "refuse slaves," a category that included the young, very old, diseased, and disabled. Those deemed undesirable for laboring needs were unable to be sent back to Africa; therefore, their representation in auction sales nudges close consideration into how the influx of newly arriving slaves—both prime and refuse slaves—were treated and became absorbed into local communities of slaves and slaveholders.

The primary base of records incorporated throughout this book includes two sets of public sources: newspapers and the curiously underutilized volume of testimonies given before the British House of Commons during the closing decade of the eighteenth century by a broad range of slave trade actors. As sailors traveled in and out of different seaports, they recounted details of violent dangers common in the African slave trade that circulated throughout the pages of local and international newspapers. While many times sensationalizing details to arouse sympathy toward the losses of white men, these stories provide distant, unfamiliar, and mere sketches of shipboard rebellions and deaths confronted by captives and their guards. The most extensive source used to penetrate the experiential and sensory experiences generally unknown on slave ships lies in the scores of people, intricately familiar and many times central to the trade as active participants, who gave testimonies within the legal arena of courts. Scribbled notes that many of them jotted down and gathered together to assist in their public reflections are not as easy to locate; however, through the recalled memories of former slave trade participants, the questions asked and themes addressed become more expansive. The woven tapestry of narratives that emerged facilitate an in-depth exposure to the treatment of the aged and refused, violent marking of slaves, variations of suicide, mistreatment of children, moments of psychological breakdowns, funerary practices on slave ships, dietary habits, ship toxicity, the birthing of slaves, musical expressions of sorrow, as well as the drastically emotional process of separation through slave auctions. Anchored within the power of these testimonies—public or private—is not only the freedom that many who testified shared in never having to account for devastating lives while growing the wealth of others but also the crucial choices and calculations intricately bound to the performance of remembering and disremembering events, people, and moments of violent eruptions in which sailors and surgeons served as witnesses and participants.

Throughout these compiled sources, the various individuals who through their employed participation placed themselves as both subjects and narrators of an active slaving past become more present. Transmitting often murky details, they constructed narratives, perpetuated silences, and provided insight and biases on distant places and foreign people. Although fraught with inconsistencies, embellishments, and ethnic and racial stereotyping, these varied archival sources provide fertile opportunities to widen the spectrum of bondage to include the world of slavery at sea. Jamaica Kincaid's critique of colonialism in constructing narratives of oppressed people within the Caribbean in many ways parallels the retelling of the history of the transatlantic crossing. She questions, "For isn't it odd that the only language I have in which to speak of this crime is the language of the criminal who committed the crime? And what can that really mean? For the language of the criminal can contain only the goodness of the criminal's deed. The language of the criminal can explain and express the deed only from the criminal's point of view. It cannot explain the horror of the deed, the injustice of the deed, the agony, the humiliation inflicted on me."[24]

Historians are bound to the testimonies, memories, and selected narratives put forth by the very individuals who determined captives' financial and social value while violently imposing the boundaries of life and death within which slaves were held. The voices of those enslaved therefore do not always exist where we would like. We instead gain momentary access to their bondage through their bodies, behaviors, and other characteristics that slave traders chose to record. Often renamed as mere units of sale, bondpeople were dehumanized, violently marked, and permanently remembered according to the numbers designating their inclusion among a vessel cargo, being renamed "No. 26," "No. 58," "No. 2," or by any other shrewd calculative tactic used to define, mark, and keep record of all stowed ship goods, including bondpeople. Once transported, delivered, and sold to awaiting buyers, the import of men, women, children, the elderly, disabled, and diseased—unable to be sent back—came to represent the backbone of slavery across the Americas. Viewing them only in terms of the skills they possessed and the labor and wealth that buyers believed they could generate from their bodies, we miss the opportunity to engage and understand the terrorizing process of transport bondpeople confronted and, more precisely, how they arrived broken and unmade. Ship commanders and their crews decided how best to constrain, manage, and treat valuable black bodies, whereas consumers across the Americas engaged in the bidding and buying process. These same buyers, lured by the coming of new laborers and dreams of unforeseen wealth, were unable and unwilling to see how the many injuries and scars—visible and invisible—that captives incurred through slavery at sea were sponsored and thus fueled by their own money and aggressive market demands.

*   *   *

This book reconceptualizes the Middle Passage as central to the operation of the Atlantic human manufacturing process. It traces the often unfamiliar world of slavery at sea from the point of capture through the massive import of bondpeople into distant slave societies. The first chapter, "Waves of Calamity," explores the transformation of human beings into chattel property amid business ventures conducted on the African side of the Atlantic. It foregrounds the complicated system of racial and cultural biases, cooperation, and trickery acted out between African merchants, brokers, and foreign white sailors to show how such connections fueled an evolving commercial enterprise hinged upon the buying and selling of black bodies. These entrepreneurial pursuits produced an unstable environment that led to a range of brutally shrewd tactics used to forcibly move slaves into the domain of coastal sales, thereby initiating their entrance into the first phase of the human manufacturing process through capture and warehousing that soon followed. Ship captains and physicians scrutinized and sorted through countless bodies to fulfill distant demands in securing the prime slaves, therefore chapter 2, "Imagined Bodies," analyzes the range of captives representative of the human merchandise made available to foreign buyers. Employing a less traditional lens, this discussion highlights

critical factors of age, gender, health, and diverse bodily configurations represented among offered slaves. Even more, it problematizes the idea that every
bondperson generated exploitable value—financial or social—by widening the
range to include the fate of the sold and unsold.

Sea captains employed precautionary measures to secure the most viable
captives, yet chapter 3, "Healthy Desires, Toxic Realities," moves into the second phase of the human manufacturing process—transport—that bondpeople
entered once sold into West African markets. This chapter reveals the landscape
of unhealthy conditions bondpeople faced while locked within the bowels of
slave vessels. Many captives boarded ships already distressed by intense starvation and the trauma of bondage. Going further, the discussion points to the
nutrient-deprived sea diets, lack of cleanliness, and dangerous weather patterns,
all of which jeopardized the health of boarded slaves and led to the continued
erosion of their bodies. Crewmen relentlessly sought to exert complete control over the lives of slaves lodged within a vessel's hold. Chapter 4, "Blood
Memories," addresses the violent legacies the Middle Passage ushered in by
chronicling open battles and the counter-resistive measures that sailors used
against bondpeople. The mere threat of armed slaves played upon racialized
fears while tearing away the veneer of control mariners imagined over their
captives. Violence on ships comprised more than rebellions and black male
insurgents. This chapter reinserts black women into these deadly interactions
while sharpening the focus to reveal how drastically hostile ship behaviors
manifested not only through physical combat but also through poisoning,
sexual terror, abortion, and the murders of enslaved infants.

Bondpeople regularly drew upon violence as an open mechanism to obtain
their freedom. Chapter 5, "Battered Bodies, Enfeebled Minds," focuses on those
females and males who did not engage in bloodied clashes, choosing instead to
direct their personal struggles with alienation and mistreatment toward their
own bodies through suicide. This chapter examines how bondpeople attempted
to cope psychologically with the shock of enslavement. The varied physical
and cultural behaviors some slaves acted out reveals how self-sabotage operated in the social spaces of ships and the sea. Fusing the importance of the
psyche, violence, and the physical body, chapter 6, "The Anatomy of Suffering,"
examines how the cumulative effects of slavery at sea affected bondpeople's
overall well-being, making them even more vulnerable to the specter of disease
and mortality. Centering bodily pain and the physical decline some captives
underwent within the socio-medical history of slaving voyages, it goes further
to trace how sailors and surgeons sought to counter many of these medical
outbreaks.

The seventh chapter, "A Tide of Bodies," traces the import of slaves through
the third and final phase of the Atlantic human manufacturing process: product
delivery. It does so by reconsidering the complexities of domestic slave markets

to analyze how slaves arrived into New World slave societies following their oceanic transport. Once imported and docked into distant seaports, the Middle Passage may have physically ended for bondpeople; however, the layered cycles of violence, deprivation, and death confronted at sea forced them to arrive pre-conditioned by the terrorizing dynamics of shipboard captivity maintained by the various workers tasked with their transport and preservation. Broadening the categorical view of newly arrived Africans beyond the general rubric of prime, young, male, and presumably healthy allows us to more fully consider the diversity of human commodities made available within eighteenth-century Atlantic slave markets. This chapter therefore traces how factors such as gender, age, trauma, illness, and disabilities influenced local markets and in some case prompted planters to forgo final slave sales. Most would agree that the Atlantic slave trade represented the largest forced migration of a group of people in recorded history. Viewing slaving voyages merely through the lens of supply, demand, and the triangular movement of goods bypasses the very process that not only landed Africans into slave societies but also created a massive influx of diverse personalities, diseases, psychological traumas, and bruised and disabled black bodies imported into the Atlantic plantation complex. Taken together, this book shows the refinement and consequential effects imposed on captives through the human manufacturing process that magnified most aptly through slavery at sea. The stories of incredible suffering, pain, and resiliency that follow collectively remind that the Middle Passage was not about the final destination but rather the violent production of slaves through the journey.

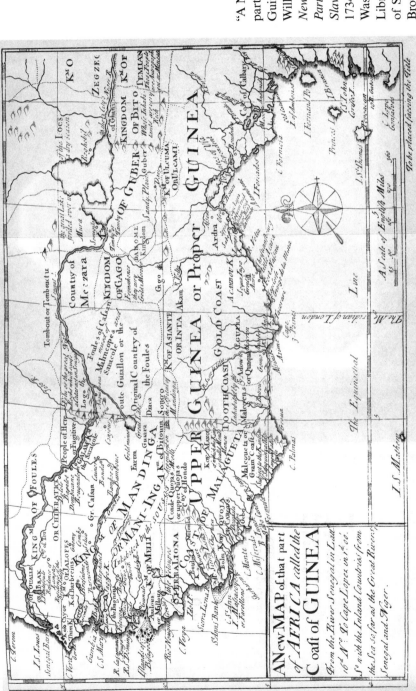

"A New Map of that part of African called Guinea." Original in William Snelgrave, *A New Account of Some Parts of Guinea and the Slave Trade* (London, 1734). Courtesy of Washington University Libraries, Department of Special Collections Brown.

1 Waves of Calamity

In 1770, at the age of thirteen, West African Quobna Ottobah Cugoano spent time visiting an uncle living near his home in Agimague.[1] While there he befriended "some of the children of my uncle's hundreds of relations," and occasionally they ventured into surrounding areas to amuse themselves. "I refused to go with the rest," Cugoano recalled one afternoon, being rather apprehensive that "something might happen to us" during their escapade. "You are afraid to venture your carcase," a friend jeered. Although concerned, Cugoano joined as they set out for their usual site in a nearby wooded area. However, this day proved far different than the rest. Less than two hours into their recreation, "troubles began, when several [African] ruffians came upon us suddenly," demanding that the children "committed a fault against their lord, and we must go and answer for it ourselves before him." Cugoano and his friends "attempted in vain to run away, but pistols and cutlasses were soon introduced, threatening, that if we offered to stir we should all lie dead on the spot." Obeying the deadly warning, the children were divided among the gathered men and transported away.

During the evening following a perilous trek, the kidnapped band of captives were "separated into different houses with different people." Little did Cugoano know that this would be the last time he would see his former playmates. Inquiring about their whereabouts the next day, his captors explained that they went "to the sea side to bring home some rum, guns and powder" for later use. "My hopes of returning home again were all over," Cugoano concluded, and as sadness weighed heavier from the circumstances, he refused all offered food and drink. Unlike his friends, Cugoano was kept in the unfamiliar village six additional days. Traveling to Cape Coast with a new abductor one morning, he observed that the man "carried a large bag with some gold dust" to allegedly help "buy some goods at the sea side to take with him to Agimague." As the two neared the coast, Cugoano saw several white people interspersed throughout the crowds, which invoked an immediate anxiety "that they would eat me," most likely influenced by circulating descriptions associating white foreigners with cannibalism.[2] No matter the stories formerly heard, once on the shoreline he saw with his own eyes the consequences of financial greed manifested as he and his former playmates were divided, sold, and displaced, thereby joining scores of other Africans forced into the coastal-wide market of slave sales within West Africa as buyable goods. "Many of my miserable countrymen," Cugoano recalled seeing them "chained two and two, some handcuffed, and some with their hands tied behind."

Amid transfer to a separate holding, Cugoano watched his transporter "take a gun, a piece of cloth, and some lead" off his person, after which the man explained that he must leave Cugoano alone. "This made me cry bitterly," Cugoano professed as he once again faced abandonment. Yet his cries went unanswered. Several men moved him to a nearby prison, where he remained locked for three days until sold. "There was nothing to be heard but rattling of chains, smacking of whips, and the groans and cries of our fellowmen." Records bury the day-to-day scenes of degradation that Cugoano saw, felt, heard, touched, or even smelled during his confinement. Most evident to contemporary readers is that as the smolder of captivity ignited and other slaves became increasingly resistant, Cugoano feared his own life witnessing them "lashed and beat in the most horrible manner."

As a teenage captive, Cugoano's anxieties of sensational violence expanded even further once he was sold onto a foreign ship. He tried soliciting help from other captives while lodged in the bowels beneath, but as he recollected, "I could find no good person to give any information of my situation to Accasa at Agimague." Hearing unfamiliar languages, clarification or really any sort of communication proved impossible with his shipmates. The permanence of Cugoano's displacement and the inability to find help grew in his mind, forcing him to reason, "I was thus lost to my dear indulgent parents and relations, and they to me."[3] His story offers a rare glimpse into the lived experience of the slave trade, firmly nudging the need to expand narratives of the Middle Passage beyond adult slaves. Kidnapped and propelled into bondage at a young age, Cugoano's testimony makes more real the manipulatively violent tactics used to prey on everyday people, including teenagers and children, in providing a steady supply of bodies and cash flow while also exposing firsthand the intricate web of negotiations and shrewd deals used to solidify the fate of captured slaves, shifting them in, out, and through multiple hands actively fueling the slaving process.

An unprecedented number of foreign traders poured into West Africa during the eighteenth century, drawn by the pursuit of profit and willing to expand the base of partnerships forged in the commercial slaving enterprise. These ventures, although risky both financially and physically, represented a critical aspect of overseas expansion as investors hired sailors, sending them across and into distant spaces for the procurement of slaves. The continuous and rather explosive rise of white buyers willing to exchange monies and seemingly luxurious goods for live black bodies ushered in an unstable period of vulnerability. Financial desires and laboring expectations were remotely envisioned yet locally mapped into and onto the lives of an incalculable many. As Cugoano's story reveals, the systematic process of slaving relied upon a tightened network of diverse individuals whose business dealings facilitated entrepreneurial needs between arriving foreigners and local black slave traders. Their long-term goals in the trafficking of people may have drastically differed; however, this intercontinental commercial enterprise relied on the routine use of brutality in constructing and supplying a massive black labor force. Moreover, negotiations made through these Atlantic financial collaborations conveyed a perceived global entrepreneurial right anchored on the ability to amass wealth off the innocent lives of others as fully expressed through continuation of the Middle Passage.

More than any customers, this chapter argues that foreign white traders may have come into a ready system of servitude already existent throughout West Africa; they came as business partners in the human manufacturing process with a shared commercial vision that over time manifested in the evolution of race and chattel slavery. International interests, demand for particular slaves, and, most of all, ready money created a violently fragile environment within the fabric of many local and inland West African societies, making everyone ready targets, regardless of gender, age, class, or status. Scholars have made too little of the sequence of violence, the brutal patterns used to capture slaves—warfare, impromptu raids, and targeted attacks waged on individuals and families—that led to the displacement of bondpeople across the Atlantic. The future and continuous flow of currency to and between inland capturers, African and mixed-race coastal men, and white traders hunting for sellable slaves made them immune to the daily distributions of violence. As such, their employed trade participation shattered most concerns about the gambling of strangers' lives and permanent dismantling of families and communities, which they not only perpetuated but also financially benefited from.

This chapter explores the first phase in the operation of the Atlantic human manufacturing process—warehousing—showing how the coming of white slave traders solidified business ties linked to a continuum of unparalleled disruption that enacted relentless assaults on slaves' lives, health, and bodies. The letters that merchants inscribed to ship captains prominently reveal the vulnerabilities and blatant expectations that investors held regarding crewmen's behaviors, shipboard management, the complex sphere of business conducted with local African traders, and the necessary use of violent tactics on a ship's passage. Although they relied on the personal choices and decisions that sailors made in completing a slaving voyage, these directives show more closely how distant financial dealings and local monies sanctioned a business plan anchored on terror. Beyond mere expressions of micromanagement, these handwritten letters functioned akin to contracts that legitimized the use of terrorizing behaviors and extreme deprivation in the commercial treatment of goods for frugal business purposes. By obliging the norms of this entrenched social network and operative slaving system, this made much easier the process of trade for arriving commanders in their dealings with local rulers, future business relations, and the reign of terror used to gather and supply healthy live black bodies. Therein, the conversations, movement of monies, employment of workers, and brokering of deals—both actualized and imagined—began the initial unmaking of black lives. For the many bondpeople at the center, permanent exile into the slaving industry signaled the formative making of slaves into goods and their unmaking through the severance of freedom.

Ordered Desires

Merchants in distant corners of the Atlantic financed and orchestrated the economic pursuits of slavery, indelibly shaping the future lives of seamen, surgeons, and, most important, Africans.[4] As businessmen, many of these individuals held certain expectations concerning their involvement in the risky business of slave trading and, most especially, preventing costly failures in the manufacturing process. English participants typically pooled their resources, "taking shares in a venture, buying or leasing a ship, and loading it with their own goods," aiming to fully maximize potential opportunities for future slaving wealth.[5] Their financial ties to the trade depended heavily on sailing vessels traveling to West Africa and the crewmen employed to facilitate operation of these financial dreams. Recognizing the uncertainty of profits and losses, some investors took shares in different slaving voyages to prevent massive deficits that might emerge from one single investment.[6] They sought economic security; however, many investors found that the sale of black people became a substantial gamble with unpredictable outcomes.

Heightened interests in gaining wealth through distant slaving activities enforced reliance on the labor and seafaring expertise that mariners held in the industries of trade and shipping.[7] After securing investments and insurance from local entities, merchants located and sought the services of sea captains whom they entrusted to lead different voyages to West Africa. Lower wages coupled with innumerable dangers on and off ship required crewmen to place their lives at constant risk, making work aboard slave vessels one of the least desired forms of employment. Unattractive in many respects, sailors found a constant supply of laboring opportunities within the maritime world of slaving. Through their employment they served as human conduits active in and centrally responsible for slaves' transport and preservation through the Middle Passage. Oceanic ventures fueled through the manufacturing of slaves required necessary interactions of hired captains to navigate and establish financial linkages with and to distant locales and differing populations of people aligned and interwoven as global workers in the pursuit of profit expansion. This symbolized that once hired, the expectations and agreements involved implied willingly immersing themselves directly in the hazards of seafaring and slaving at all costs. Most times historically unremembered as middlemen having little or no affect on bondpeople's lives, slave ship sailors physically enabled the movement of money, goods, slaves, and vessels for their hierarchical tier of employers spread across the Atlantic.

Working relationships that financiers cultivated with ship commanders relied in large part on their shipping familiarity and personal connections to enable West African trade. Owners of the vessel *Corsican Hero* expressed to a hired captain, "You have been so often at Affrica its needless to Recommend particular care in the treatment & usage of your Slaves as its as much your Interest as Ours to bring a good & healthy Cargo—to Markett."[8] The Vernon brothers, two Rhode Island merchants, wrote similar instructions to Thomas Rogers of the sloop *Wydaw*. Once docked on the African coast, the Vernons encouraged immediate disposal of goods carried from their home port to attract and entice more slave sales. Knowing Rogers had "a general knowlidge of the Affrican Trade," they declared their intentions were "not [to] attempt to give you any particular directions nor confine you" within any particular "strict order in that respect" of slave trading practices. Instead, Rogers was permitted to "Trade up & down y'e Coast," but only "as long as you find profit."[9] Serving a critical role operating as middlemen within the vast trade network, ship commanders received orders that may have conveyed a sense of free rein over their coastal ventures. However, for financiers the primary motive centered on accumulation of wealth through the bartering of goods and negotiations for slaves.

Well aware of the prevalence of alcoholism and the potential damages capable of drastically affecting a ship's transport, some investors spoke out against practices of inhumane treatment. Sea captain John Duncan received instructions warning, "be carefull to keep up good harmony & agreement amongst your officers & crew" during coastal business endeavors.[10] Long voyages demanded from sailors a posture of sustained cohesion with shared maritime duties and, most especially, representing themselves in a solidified fashion in the sight of boarded slaves. It was also not uncommon for commanders to receive instructions addressing matters of alcohol use and physical violence. Spirited drinks were common staples consumed at sea. Owners of the vessel *Ranger* gave Captain Spoors instructions encouraging "a little Brandy now and then may be very proper for the Seamen" during a ship's passage, although reiterating, "tis not our meaning to encourage Drunkenness or inattention to the Duty of the

Ship."[11] Knowing the consequences of overindulgence and the loss of efficient oversight, commanders were encouraged to maintain complete order. During January 1783, Charles Wilson, master of the brig *Madampookata*, prepared to depart for the coast of Angola. Prior to his travels, his Liverpool financier, Leyland, Penny and Co., advised, "You cannot too forcible impress on the minds of your officers (who are unacquainted with the African Trade) how necessary it is to establish among the Crew, a steady uniform discipline." In the financier's view, Wilson must "above all guard against Drunkenness," because they often discovered it "is the source of every tumult disorders" aboard different ships. To guard against such outbreaks, the company cautioned, "When you dispose of Liquor to the Sailors, let it be only in small quantities at a time."[12] Merchants etched correspondences detailing expectations of shipboard unity and careful handling of transported captives, yet left unto themselves amid an isolating sea culture, slave ship captains and hired crews created societies governed by their own constructed rules and evolving laws of order.

Unity among sailors was fundamental to the successful operation of any slaving endeavor. On July 2, 1787, financier Robert Bostock addressed orders to Captain Peter Reme insisting on the need for cohesion, instructing that he should "take Care to use your people with great Humanity," and make sure "not to beat nor Abuse them as you see many Voyages over set by ill treatment [that] causes them to run away." Strained relationships were a customary facet of sea life, emerging not only on the passage from Africa but also during other legs of the infamous triangular route. Perhaps distressed by relentless patterns of uncivil shipboard behaviors, a year later Bostock became even more explicit in the orders of employed sailors. Once in command of the sloop *Kite*, Stephen Bowers received several conditions concerning his voyage to Africa. "It is my particular Request and desire," Bostock explained, "that you treat your People with Great Humanity" while at sea. To achieve these demands, he commanded that Bowers "not beat nor abuse them," or, as he added, "Suffer your Mate or Mates to do it but that you keep a proper order and Command" over the vessel's crew.[13] Sailors served an invaluable role helping to satisfy merchants' overseas ventures, where any episodes of internal conflicts proved particularly damaging to their future lucrative desires. Therefore, to warn against any such infractions, explicit orders were frequently circulated.

Rules of Engagement

Despite prevailing expectations merchants held in regulating sea captains traveling across the Atlantic, business operated in a much different fashion once landed in West Africa. Slave sales depended on the cooperation mariners forged with local natives, regardless of their geographic location. One of the most important tactics helpful in solidifying relations and establishing a continuous coastal presence was the construction of trading posts, including castles, forts, and factories.[14] These physical sites varied in architecture and design, but together the resulting creations transformed the face of coastal West Africa, marking the evolutionary hold of outside nations in local slave trading affairs. Each individual site drastically altered the natural and communal surroundings, permanently marking a presence through social, physical, and cultural means. Bound by their own constructed walls, from the perspective of foreign traders the primary intention of these locales was to defend against outside enemies and natural elements, serve the needs of their inhabitants, and protect their material and financial interests.[15]

Unlike other parts of the world, these physical spaces manufactured for trade and slaving have a long and rather complicated history within western Africa. The Portuguese initiated construction of trading posts in 1482 with the erection of the castle São Jorge da Mina. Contemporarily known as Elmina Castle, this historical structure was solely dominant over the trade until 1637, when the Dutch seized control, securing it as their headquarters until 1814. During the early part of the seventeenth century, one castle, two forts, and one factory were reportedly built in western Africa as slaving interests continued to take shape. The middle part of this period, from 1646 to 1710, experienced the most significant increase in coastal alterations through construction of many of these sites. By the peak of the trade, posts were exchanged through several international hands resulting in two castles, twenty-two forts, and an incredible number of factories established during this fertile period.[16]

Following the waning success of the Royal African Company in the first two decades of the eighteenth century, private slave dealers created much more personalized transactions outside of company-imposed restrictions. The primary incentive guiding Europeans' arrival in Africa was the procurement of slaves, although this depended greatly on observing necessary preliminary customs. Relations forged with coastal Africans served as one of the most fundamental aspects of the trade. Upon arrival, ship captains typically waded into designated locales, casting their anchors close to a mile offshore due to the difficulties of docking larger vessels directly on land.[17] "As soon as the Natives perceive a ship on their Coast," one trader reported, "they make a smoke on the Sea-shore, as a Signal for the ship to come to and anchor."[18] The presiding commander, once anchored along with one of his officers, traveled to the coast by a small boat to inform local slavers of their arrival in hopes of establishing preliminary negotiations.[19] Locating the local king or principal men associated with slaving affairs, they discussed their trade intentions in hopes of solidifying their own financial foothold.

Word of the presence of white traders typically spread throughout shoreline communities. The establishment of good relations with local leaders and the allocation of gifts were critical to future slave sales; therefore, to better facilitate the process of gaining trade approval, some captains invited kings aboard their vessels. Within some customary practices, "a day or two after" a ship's port arrival into western Africa, "the king comes on board in his canoe, with a band of music, to break trade, as it is called." Practices varied considerably across the coast, but traditions frequently involved the distribution of gifts, known as *dashes,* to African rulers. Once final terms of agreement were completed and deemed beneficial to both parties, sea captains received permission to partake in slave negotiations.[20] "When the king breaks trade with the ship," one captain explained, "the assortment and quality of his cargo are sufficiently well known to all the [African] traders."[21] Knowledge of the various commodities lodged aboard foreign vessels helped to expedite slave sales while sparking greater desire for the import of material goods from distant locales into Africa.[22]

Vendible items were indigenous to African cultural practices, yet they served different functions in the slave trade. For some sailors they operated as a form of bribery to local chieftains, serving most times as a gesture and formal bid to enter coastal sales.[23] During the process, "gifts were offered and accepted, drinks and smokes exchanged, food cooked, and consumed together."[24] Prolonging their coastal stays and the process of trade, these initial encounters exposed crewmen to various aspects of African culture, which proved useful for later shipboard interactions.[25] Utilization of local resources and entrance into the complicated system of African trade required several important costs that all seamen were expected to oblige. Any disregard of these practices resulted in the inability of trade or the hindrance of formulating critical ties to obtaining desired slaves. Many distant entrepreneurs were well informed of the dynamics of the coastal African trade; therefore, mariners were expected to board items deemed most useful for a ship's oceanic voyage and coastal negotiations for ease of future trading. Often gathered from overseas travels and distant trading posts, materials such as "iron, copper and brass bars . . . used as currency, silks from India, refined metal ware and textiles from England," in addition to "the best of European drinks," were used in hopes of further enticing slave sales.[26] These tangibles served a multiplicity of purposes necessary within the vortex of trade; however, the importation of diverse commodities especially helped to cement relationships and assist in obliging customary trade policies.

The preliminary coastal practices that sailors engaged in with Africans demonstrated entrepreneurial intentions while also proving emblematic of a range of other factors. They attested foremost to the budding growth of slave demands taking place across the waterways. For Africans the presence of foreign traders and their willingness to offer various tokens formally acknowledged their arrival in coastal communities. The central role local leaders held in facilitating the slaving machine created what may have seemingly appeared prestigious positions by serving as "protector[s] or landlords" to arriving Europeans.[27] Offering monies and goods further revealed the posture of humility

Africans required of arriving white traders in order to merely gain entrance into conversations with local slave brokers. At the same time, these mannerisms exposed the incredible cross racial dependence confining sailors to the rules and customs of local black traders for the acquisition of human cargoes.

Diversity of localized reins of control occasionally fostered frustration among traveling seamen. Stereotypes involving West Africans' cultural inferiority repeatedly circulated in the European reading public. For seamen, the waterways of the Atlantic Ocean encompassed a similar and rather unique highway of information shaping the prejudices many of them carried into their interactions with Africans.[28] These token actions may have obliged customary practices required to gain access to their most valued commodities—slaves, yet, "whites were irritated at the universal demand for dashes, or bribes, as a preliminary to the trade and the need to indulge other native customs."[29] Maintaining a degraded view of shoreline cultures, seamen occasionally harbored feelings of resentment. Perhaps the most deep-seated hostility driving their frustrations was the inability to control negotiations from other competing nations. Despite these ill-harbored views, it proved far more practical to oblige customary practices given the financial stakes at hand.

After gaining approval from African elites to proceed with trade, sailors entered another set of negotiations. This took place with "people on the Sea Coast [who] act commonly as brokers" within coastal operations.[30] Serving as middlemen, many were generally responsible for supplying local demands for slaves. Some were appointed by regional rulers; in other cases the increase of relationships between mariners and African women throughout the eighteenth century produced mixed-race children who often served seminal roles in these transactional capacities.[31] Regardless of their racial background, in many cases the middlemen were most "trusted" by traveling seamen if merely because of their ability to execute commercial needs. One captain explained his inability to gain satisfactory business with "Natives of the Inland parts." Despite his frustrations, he found "the Natives here on the Sea side are much civilized" due in his estimation to regular contact and "conversing with the Europeans." "Here we can venture on Shore amongst the Natives, without any hazard."[32] The extent that some Europeans were interested in working with racially mixed coastal dwellers in contrast to African brokers is unknown; in a broader sense, however, for some sailors, skin color and acculturation toward European customs facilitated a greater sense of ease and comfort in the business process.

While operating as intermediaries between traders and arriving seamen, coastal retailers ensured their own benefit. Functioning akin to wholesale dealers, they worked with nearby commercial networks to help gather desired captives. Occasionally, some traveled inland, "where they know there are Slaves ready for sale" who had been previously captured and brought from the hinterland.[33] Histories of these men are rather murky, yet they served a critical link in controlling the inventory of captives carried from the interior and funneled to awaiting sea captains while also assessing the slaves' viability for commercial sale. While conducting business, a coastal man typically "takes what commodities he pleases for his Negro which he has to sell" in exchange for having "the choice of his goods" offered by ship commanders.[34] These imported goods not only determined the fate of available slaves, but they also facilitated tangible access to a range of desired human commodities. Recognizing the power at their disposal, some West African merchants used foreign interest in slaves toward their economic advantage by keeping some on hand and increasing prices. However, any captives unsold and still under the command of these shrewd entrepreneurs meant not only "the expence of feeding them, but there is also the risk of mortality."[35] Therefore, it proved lucrative and far less demanding for merchants to rid themselves of slaves held on hand to reduce accruing any further expenses and to satisfy white demand.

Both shoreline traders and seamen felt they had the upper hand within conducted sales. Belief of cultural inferiority and financial mismanagement shaped many seafarers' approach to their dealings within West Africa.[36] In November 1763, surgeon and slave trader Archibald Dalzel wrote from Annamaboe discussing the practices of his "black neighbours," the Fante people, whom he regularly observed during his stay on the Gold Coast. Recounting the current process of trade, he surmised, "What is likewise a bad Circumstance for us, [is] they think it meritorious to Cheat a White Man that lives in their power" within the surrounding coastal community. Continuing further, he explained, "If we catch them Stealing anything, we can exercise their own laws against them," which in all probability was worse if it had to do with matters of human property.[37] Dalzel's correspondence illustrates the bias of judgment prevalent among different Europeans in regular contact with coastal Africans during the era of slave trading. His characterization of locals likewise fueled a sense of protection operative among many white foreigners who felt equipped through the exploit of local judicial powers.

Unfavorable views held about African financial responsibility were far from uncommon. While preparing to travel to West Africa, on June 19, 1788, ship captain Stephen Bowers received instructions regarding coastal slaving operations that forewarned, "You are not to trust any Goods to the Natives on any Account whatsoever on forfeiture of your commissions & privilleges." Part of many investors' concern rested with how "trusting of Goods to them has been the totall defeat of many a Voyage on Account of there Defaults of payments."[38] Such warnings expose the racialized biases pervasive in the web of Atlantic slaving ventures. The "trusting" of goods involved distributing commodities without receiving the fair exchange of available captives. Yet and still, dashes were requirements and points of access seamen were unable to alter and thus forced to oblige in the pursuit of captives.

Because of these commonly held skewed perceptions, many ship masters employed different tactics to guard against any type of coastal infractions. "Everything the Europeans deal[t] in," one trade participant explained, relied often on fraudulent tactics used against local natives.[39] Ship commanders were unable to change the delicate trading process, being greatly dependent upon local residents to gain access to desired slaves. However, they fully understood how imported foreign goods would conceivably pique the interest of natives, helping ease the flow of coastal transactions. Occasionally they attempted to assert control through the quality of various material items carried for the purchase of bondpeople. In some instances, captains knowingly distributed tainted commodities in exchange for slaves. "There are so many methods in almost every article, by which they can deceive the Negroes" through the process of trade.[40] Direct evidence illuminating the historical origin of these practices is obscured; however, sailors harbored deep-seated ideas of African inferiority that crystallized most during conducted business. Dishonest strategies included altering liquor with water by "making three cases out of two, and putting in Cayenne pepper into the mouth of the bottle to make it taste strong."[41] Interestingly, many Africans shared the same sense of racial mistrust, although surviving sources render it close to impossible to determine the regularity nor how they sought to manage and thus counter fraudulent practices used by foreigners against them. White traders also attempted to use language and business variance among Africans for their slaving benefit. It was far from extraordinary to find "bottles that contain but half of the contents of the samples" while other times "mixing water with their brandy after the bargain has been made."[42] These incidents would invariably foster racial mistrust upon discovery of the manipulated items. Yet, they were bound within a financial gridlock where if coastal Africans or sailors accused either side of treachery, it could prove damaging to future business on which sailors and coastal brokers were greatly dependent and continually lured by the prospect of profitable slaving endeavors.

In addition to the tricks employed with liquor, some traders used deceptive practices with firearms. Guns were one of the most highly prized goods filtered into West Africa. The seventeenth century established early desires for these metal pieces, particularly among the ruling elite, for which interests peaked in the eighteenth century.[43] Europe reportedly imported between 283,000 and 394,000 guns into Africa per year.[44] In supplying increased demands for guns the intention was not to empower Africans, but rather to rid themselves of ill-equipped metal pieces. There coexisted "a demand for slaves on one side, and, on the other, a monopolist interest among African chiefs in obtaining European consumer goods, especially firearms."[45] To assist in fulfilling slaving requests, the greatest irony lied with some locals' willingness to exchange captives for guns with "their barrels burst, and thrown away." Given one trader's confession of witnessing "many of the Natives with their thumbs and fingers off," further questioning revealed that their digits were frequently "blown off by the bursting of their guns."[46] The desire for guns permitted access to technological advancements, but during the slave trade it fostered a much more potent perception of immediate strength and power, and the ability to claim a life by waging terrorizing control within local communities and during moments of warfare. Many white seafarers exploited these interests, funneling scores of guns into western Africa under the auspices of equal trade. Contemporary scholars know very little about the relationship of gun demands and bodily harm among traders or captives emerging from these inferior weapons. Central to these transactions were not only the personal costs of trade, but moreover the valued emphasis placed on items originating outside of Africa that perpetuated and further eroded the valuation of human life in exchange for direct access to material goods and increased wealth.

Inner Spaces, Outer Boundaries

With sailors from different nations simultaneously docked into ports across western Africa, aggressive competition for exclusivity of choice in slave sales emerged. Negotiations and exchange of goods fueled the complicated system of coastal sales, igniting the structural process responsible for the buying and boarding of slaves. The business of slaving varied in different regions according to the desires and policies of presiding rulers. Consistent movement of captives through various slaving spaces within and beyond the coastal shoreline further positioned local ruling groups, slaveholding classes, and merchants as crucial intermediaries determining the contours of access white traders gained to available captives. "When Europeans demanded laborers or slaves, the African merchant had to comply or lose his business."[47]

The increase of demands from across the Atlantic bolstered the entrepreneurial need to supply laboring bodies, setting into motion the expeditious manner in which bondpeople were secured and made available. As a consequence, "a new division of labor grew up around slave catching, maintenance, and transport."[48] Marching captives toward the sea line, interior traders, most times black, provided the crucial link necessary in fulfilling these foreign orders, although surviving sources leave unclear their personal lives. How were these traders recruited? What kind of daily lives did they live? Were there any gendered differences? Did any of them perhaps fall prey to the vicious cycle of bondage? Many of these people were understood by many as "people that live in the Up Country" who, in operating at the discretion of merchants and leaders, were primarily responsible for the capture and the often treacherous transport of newly captured slaves.[49] Being located in a central position and intimately familiar with areas between the interior hinterlands and the coastal shore made capture much more feasible, thereby enforcing greater dependence upon traders' participation. Interlinked within the cross-racial assemblage of slave trade workers, their roles in the cycle of captivity were pivotal, having full autonomy over who, how, and if certain people were carried into coastal market sales. Lured by the possibility of wealth, interior capturers rarely gave much regard to dismantling communities, nor did they make considerable efforts to keep family units intact. Instead, couples, parents, children, and siblings were routinely torn apart and sold to awaiting sea captains. On some occasions, enslaved families "were divided, some in one ship, and some in another," to create greater diversity and, most of all, to reduce any instances of revolts waged by those from the same community.[50]

Procurement of bondpeople did not occur in a peaceful manner; instead, it operated in a haphazard and unexpected fashion while people were engaged in a variety of activities.[51] Raids instigated against an entire village or community helped to effectively supply a broad range of captives. One surgeon shared the story of a female "brought on board very big with child" while the ship *Alexander* was docked at Bonny. Taking notice of her pregnant state, he asked how she came to be sold into slavery and learned that while "returning home from a visit she was seized" in a rather abrupt manner. "After passing through several hands of different traders," her captors carried her "down to the waterside and sold [her] to a voyage," where a sea captain immediately bartered for her inclusion among his vessel's cargo. In another instance, traders forced a man described as "advanced in years" into captivity from an abduction that occurred when "he and his son were planting yams in their field" in their community. So intensely engaged in their agricultural endeavors and unaware of events brewing within their proximity, "they were seized by professed kidnappers, and sold."[52] Immersed in their daily lives and oblivious to distant and local economic decisions crucial to their future fate, traders preyed upon the vulnerability of individuals and families, violently transforming the interior communities of Africa into a predatory environment. Through the process, abducted groups of strangers forced across distant lands represented crucial bargaining tools that inland capturers used to maintain their own position and wealth within the trade.

Incidents of kidnapping were considerably widespread. By the eighteenth century, 70 percent of purchased slaves were snatched from their homes and communities.[53] While asleep in their beds, two black women were taken by surprise one evening. Suddenly dragged out of their houses, they were confronted by several "war-men," who tied them up and immediately forced them in a coffle bound for the coast.[54] A similar example of extreme violence took place on the coast of Bonny Point where a young female came out of the woods to bathe one morning. On approaching the water, two men grabbed her, "secured her hands behind her back, beat her, and ill-used her, on account of the resistance she made."[55] Within the interior of Africa, the methods of capture differed for various bondpeople, yet their stories—invisible within most contemporary sources—collectively expose the often reckless brutality regimented through beatings and even rape with the overarching intention to dehumanize captives and force them into the evolving system of Atlantic slavery. Driven by means of profit and social capital, inland traders relied on intense aggression to fulfill local demand. In turn they developed a callous disregard of how, in taking away the livelihood of other Africans, their efforts fueled greater demand and expectation for the continued disruption of vulnerable lives and everyday society.

Escalating value placed upon black bodies created a threatening environment in which every person in African society, regardless of status, became a potential target. As foreign traders, many sailors worked to satisfy international investors, rendering them largely unmoved by the circumstances that landed slaves into bondage. When a ship arrived on the African coast, some mariners went beyond formalities with local rulers by offering coastal residents unsolicited gifts to encourage them to bring bondpeople. Slave trader James Towne recalled the case of a male captive who was formerly engaged as an enslaver and consequently forced into bondage. During his ship confinement, the captured man described how he became enslaved while on the Galenas River, relaying that four black men "took and plundered him of what he had, stripped him naked, brought him on board" a nearby ship, and sold him.[56] Lack of further details about this bondman's case raises several questions: How long did he serve in the role of trader? Were his captors from a neighboring community or his own? Was he transporting any captives who were taken and similarly sold? These queries go unanswered, yet the enslaved man's experience conclusively suggests that, much like competing European nations, rival local traders in West Africa worked to supply slaves, often at the expense of their own lives.

Criminal charges also ushered many people into captivity, which in turn helped to grow a slaving regime. Slave trader John Douglas testified, offering brief details regarding a male captive abruptly taken and sold "together with his father, mother, and three sisters."[57] We cannot know whether this bondman or any members of his family personally confronted such criminal charges; however, others fell victim to the use of manipulative tactics forcing them into captivity. An enslaved black man referred to as Cape Mount Jack was similarly deceived into bondage and boarded onto a slaver off the Windward Coast. Vaguely familiar with English, he explained how he became a part of the vessel's cargo and that one evening he was "invited to drink with some of his neighbours." After partaking in the festivities, he was beginning to leave when "two of the people" he dined with "got up to seize him" and prevented his departure. "He would have made his escape," but as the bondman noted, he was "stopped by a large dog."[58] Circumstantial reasons leading to this man's capture and sale beyond the lure of profit are unresolved. His forcible inclusion into bondage underscores how even customary social interactions were manipulated to traders' advantage, placing people and everyday modes of life at risk of unending disruption.

Similar to their African counterparts, foreign ship captains also employed dishonest strategies to acquire black bodies. These practices established a critical platform that increased the level of violence operative between various coastal regions. Due to an ongoing system of compulsory servitude, many white foreigners therefore saw themselves as "participants in a legitimate commerce, rather than receivers of stolen human property."[59] Contextualizing these realities, slave trader John Bowman recounted how a captain he worked for used him to acquire additional slaves through ulterior means while docked in West Africa. He gave directions for Bowman "to proceed up to the factory" in order to "settle myself as a trader amongst the inhabitants." Once a familiar face in the local community, his primary orders were to spark discord among the locals. To achieve this, the presiding commander prompted him to "encourage the town's people by supplying them with powder, ball, and ammunition, to go to war," making a concerted effort "to give them all the encouragement that laid in my power to get Slaves."[60] Sailors frequently resided within coastal African communities, often for extended periods of time. Their presence, while under the guise of solidifying future business networks, sometimes secretively proved detrimental to local residents unaware that the perpetuation of wars among neighboring regions came from scheming external forces in the slaving process.

Along with firearms, alcohol was another tactic implemented to gain bondpeople. One ship captain ordered a member of his crew to travel ashore and invite "two [African] gentlemen traders" back to the vessel. Bringing the two men aboard as requested, "the Captain took them down into the cabin, and made them drink to such an excess" that it rendered them both "unable to stand." While they lay intoxicated, the ship's crew "employed in getting sail upon the vessel, and making all ready" for their immediate departure. Amid the duties, "the captain called me down into the cabin and pointed to the sail case," telling the sailor to look in and "see what a fine prize he had got." Obliging the commander's orders, he recounted, "I was much surprized to find there the two men I had brought on board, whom he had made drunk, and concealed therein." For close to three hours both men "were still laying fast asleep"; after waking, they were immediately "ordered upon deck, put in irons, and sent forward amongst the men Slaves" already lodged aboard. Sober and fully cognizant of the social trickery used to force them into bondage, the two men reportedly "made lamentations, and were sorry that white men should be such great rogues to take them from their own country," because in their estimation "they were free men."[61]

The process, reasons, and distances that scores of African women, men, and children were forced to travel to the coastal line for sales to foreign traders came with varying motivations. Pulled from often disparate places, they were marched to the coast; bound within barracoons, pens, and slave dungeons; and boarded onto ships in different ports such as Gambia, Senegal, Hausaland,

Dahomey, Fante, Bonny, Benin, and Ga, among many other corners of the interior and exterior of West Africa. "They were taken from about a score of principal markets, and from smaller ones, on a 3,000 mile coast line between Senegal in the north and Angola in the south."[62] Precisely determining the means by which many captives landed in shoreline auctions remains uncertain owing to the paucity of sources that detail the full scope of bondpeople's forced migration through diverse hands in and out of local and overseas slave markets across a four-century operation. The evolving trilateral relationships between chiefs, sailors, and inland capturers was fundamentally predicated on securing black bodies to appease foreign demand. Most often these men were concerned less with where slaves were from and more with how and if they could extract any value through their purchase and future sale. The multitudes of people taken from their homes and communities and sold as commercial goods into predetermined deals were far from culturally homogenous; they represented diverse groups that span the historical DNA of blackness, including Fante, Bakongo, Yoruba, Ewe, Akan, Melimba, Woloof, Angola, Whydah, and Igbo, among many others.

Delving into the ethnic and cultural origins of females and males forced into the global traffic of purchased slaves, these geographical conclusions often map and (re)assign ethnic understandings onto their history.[63] Ethnicity in studies of the slave trade is most times based on two primary factors: a captive's point of departure from Africa and, most of all, the behaviors that slaves acted out during bondage. Surviving sources leave muted how bondpeople culturally and ethnically defined themselves amid the calculated groupings imposed on them by local and foreign traders. Gwendolyn Midlo Hall aptly reminds, "There is no detailed, existing body of knowledge about historical African ethnicities either in Africa or in the Americas."[64] Local wars, personal feuds, kidnappings, and raids facilitated the enforcement of captives into foreign hands. To be sure, inland capturers navigated the interior hinterlands of western Africa, employing routes and winding pathways that scholars may never come to fully recover and retrace the definitive point of a captive's origin.

Conclusion

The specialized commerce of slavery that transpired across much of coastal West Africa from the fifteenth through the nineteenth centuries was far from haphazard. An influx of white traders transformed West African societies, enabling the buying and selling of people as commercial goods. Explosive value centered on black bodies; the results were direct yet wide reaching, leading to the production of terrorizing environments—capture, kill, or be killed—that emerged across many West African societies. This in turn enabled the permanent stripping of a person's freedom through his or her enforcement into slavery and coastal stowage.

Slave demands were based on the importation of black people, to which the disaggregation of the women, men, children, and elderly is vitally necessary to better understand the human merchandise that slave ship sailors were employed to sort through, buy, transport, and deliver as cargo to awaiting buyers. Driven by incentives of financial growth and employment gain, sailors' economic motives bore significant influence on West Africa by fracturing normal modes of respect for human life, lured by the prospect of a steady cash flow. The arrival of foreign sailors ushered in a tumultuous landscape that resulted in scores of African people being either sold or killed and thus initiating the unmaking of black bodies. As a consequence, captives were unable for the first time to assert full control over their lives, families, or the violence sweeping their communities.

The global nature of the human manufacturing process required a much higher body count, which forced incredible reliance on inland capturers to supply an array of bodies. Slave markets operative within coastal West Africa represented the first phase of a host of transactions centering on bondpeople, transforming captives into chattel property on the African side of the Atlantic. By foregrounding the integrated lives of sailors, slaves, and surgeons, we gain closer insight into the array of Middle Passage workers globally interlinked through threads of power, exploitation, and deprivation they enacted through the slave trade, while making more real the foundational consequences of investments and demands made for autonomous yet imagined black bodies who merchants collectively envisioned expectations and financial dreams for slaves' laboring futures.

Overseas demands for West Africans set into motion diverse and rather creative strategies and tactics used to procure and make available different types of people to fuel the engine of slave commerce. As this chapter attempted to reveal, foundations of the slave trade, both internal and external to Africa itself, comprised an intricate amalgamation of men, money, and power. Superficially this history could be left at a mere clash of forces or unending debates that leave conversations simply as accusations of black and white complicity or the perpetuation of racial extermination. The ongoing multi-century-spanning slaving enterprise, when viewed as the locus of the human manufacturing process, was intimately tied to the sponsoring and subsequent endorsement of not just a commercial enterprise but also the buying and selling of slaves with a coastline of options most times devoid of regulated legal consequences. The conclusion of coastal transactions and displacement of captives on ships propelled the refinement process as sea captains and surgeons sorted through available live bodies to fulfill demand in obtaining both quality and desirable slaves.

2 Imagined Bodies

On May 4, 1789, merchant Robert Bostock penned a letter to sea captain Edward Williams outlining his slaving expectations, specifying, "I hope you will be very carefull about your Slaves," and directed that Williams "take none on Board but what is Healthy & Young." Several years later, on May 31, 1799, the commander of the vessel *Earl of Liverpool* received similar instructions: "You will be attentive in the choice of your Negroes, and do not receive any with bodily imperfections." After strongly urging avoidance of captives "exceeding twenty years of Age," the ship's owners recommended, "If Females are scarce you may buy Boys in the Place of them."[1] Black bodies continued to be collectively viewed as viable sources of commercial profit within and beyond western Africa during the eighteenth century, particularly among European and American merchants, who crafted orders articulating specific preferences in an attempt to predict the possibilities of sale in distant Atlantic markets. Working in tandem with market forces and planters' interests, investors projected onto the slaving process translating their version of ideal slaves they envisioned most valuable and therefore satisfactory to the rigors of plantation labor.

The transatlantic trade represented a vitally important pipeline for cheap labor filtered across the Atlantic world. Instigations of violence waged within and across parts of western Africa enabled, and in many ways invigorated, the myriad lucrative opportunities used to obtain slaves. What were the varying notions of social value assigned to those permanently made a part of the global system of slave trading? Moreover, how were these masses of black bodies treated once on the coast? Theoretically, all slaves held economic promise for buyers; however, quality assurances for exported captives were nonexistent within this vast commercial enterprise. White ship captains assessed bond-people's potential value and exploitable use in the near and far future through the landscape of their captive bodies. The range of distant orders and bodily configurations represented during coastal inspections made necessary the probing of differences. In attempting to precisely identify the ethnic variations and skilled labor that existed among offered slaves, scholars often miss much broader opportunities to interrogate the meanings of black bodies within slavery prior to their plantation displacement. Shifting the view toward the first phase of the human manufacturing process through warehousing, this chapter broadens the lexicon of the slave trade to include females, males, children, and elderly captives. Doing so shows the demographic categories routinely used in the calculus of slavery that likewise engender probing the fate of the sold and unsold. The primary thrust of this discussion overturns categories that classify all purchased captives as either "adult men" or "adult women." It introduces the notion of imagined bodies, or rather these perfect laboring bodies, financially conceived overseas through the articulated desires of merchants and buyers and set into motion through on-the-ground negotiations and deals made by slave ship sailors on the African side of the Atlantic.

Looking beyond quantity and more toward the quality of human commerce, valuations of slaves were measured heavily against the white gaze and the possibility of financial interest. Forcible inclusion of some slaves and the subsequent disregard of others problematizes this idea of valuable bodies, underscoring the need for more critical questions about the types of people involved—most especially across gender, age, and health—to better gauge the barometer of slaves: those perceived as formidable or sometimes undesirable. Serving as custodians physically tasked with fulfilling overseas demands for idealized slaves, captains, mates, and surgeons were expected to secure captives consistent with the values, skills, and lucrative desires crucial to their own economic well-being and future position within the trade. Amid the specter of slave sales, they enacted far more power than traditionally imagined through the choices and decisions made that led to the building of a slave regime—ideal or not—exported across and into the Atlantic and unable to be sent back. Transformed into commodities once aggressively placed at the center of coastal market transactions and forced into the warehousing phase of the human manufacturing process, bondpeople's lives were marked and unmade further through the social calculations made of their bodies and permanent restrictions implemented following sales to foreigners. Conversely, this chapter also uncovers the human costs, or rather the consequences of rejections perilously imposed against another group of slaves left and lost in the history simply as "refuse."

The Vast Array of Human Merchandise

Cemented within the minds of many investors, merchants, seamen, and planters was the acquisition of "prime slaves." Traders assessed the bodies of offered slaves, focusing most often on securing those with supreme qualities. But what did "prime" look like? How were these configurations understood? Healthy slaves represented the primary physical marker of high quality. Conventional wisdom likewise underscores bondpeople's skill sets; white traders assumed that a person's birthplace gave some indication of the knowledge and laboring capabilities he or she could carry and generate within Atlantic slave societies. However, two of the most pertinent factors foreign traders emphasized through their specificities were about gender and age. With social value and productive output always at the forefront, these determinants influenced the effect certain captives had in commanding the highest prices while fundamentally helping to appeal to a broader spectrum of buyers within the business of slave dealing.

Eighteenth-century market demands and plantation needs varied across time and space as Atlantic slaveholders expressed desires for different bondpeople, although concentrating primarily on the import of bondmen. Black men held the highest demand within coastal markets, forcing African suppliers to funnel more adult males into overseas exports than women and children.[2] Following the arrival of several lower-quality cargoes carried into South Carolina, merchant John Guerard wrote to Mr. William Toliff on September 29, 1753, regarding future imports: "In your next orders lay the [ship] Master under a Positive Injunction (instead of recommending) to purchase as many Young healthy Likely men as Possible" during coastal sales. Guerard emphasized the procurement of "as few females as he can," to which he added, "What he is Obliged to take of the Last sex Let them be young" in age. At the conclusion of his letter, Toliff reiterated his preference for "as many men Boys of 14 to 16 Years of Age as possible" during market selections.[3]

Bondmen garnered significant interest among distant merchants across the Americas; however, countless other captives were similarly assessed and forced into the vast network of slave commerce. Descriptors interchangeably used throughout slave trade documents make contemporary understandings of the inclusion of different captives somewhat difficult to discern. Scholars are therefore left to interpret the broad groupings assigned to purchased slaves. Six categorical labels routinely used to classify bonded males were "men," "men-boys," and "boys"; female labels included "women," "women-girls," and "girls." Adult captives made up the majority of ships' cargoes to satisfy distant agricultural needs biased toward the young and healthy, which furhter nudges a necessary reevaluation into how blackness and age was defined in the context of slave trading.[4]

Sailors were customarily encouraged to exert sufficient care in coastal sales. Ship commander Charles Knealy received instructions regarding future purchases, indicating that close to half should "consist of Prime Men Negroes from 15 to 25 yrs old" and "Boys" should range from "10 to 15" years old. "Women," on the other hand, needed to fall between "10 to 18" years in age.[5] Gendered demands varied according to local prices and availability. On July 17, 1755, South Carolina merchant Henry Laurens wrote with the hope of obtaining "likely healthy People" imported for market sales. Of those most favored, he requested "two thirds Men from 18 to 25 Years Old"; in addition, for "the other young Women from 14 to 18 the cost [was] not to exceed Twenty five Pounds Sterling per head" on average.[6] Opinions on captives' ages differed among investors, traders, and slaveholders, projecting their own needs and desires through an economic lens. Perhaps of even greater magnitude is how foreign traders used bondpeople's physical stature—height, youthful looks, breasts, size of genitals, and gray hair—to determine the categories within which they were not only assessed, but financially and socially valued. Therefore, besides mere supply, many of these speculations paralleled the reproductive and breeding regimes manipulated and orchestrated through the bodies of those already enslaved in distant plantation societies.

Adult women held a vital place within the chain of black laborers, representing indispensable sexual assets within the economy of slavery. All captives were inspected under the premise of securing healthy bodies and sound minds, but bondwomen were evaluated according to two additional qualifications: displays of beauty and the sexual/reproductive capacities they conceivably possessed. Anyone deemed contrary to these desires proved not only useless and undesirable, but essentially riskier investments. During negotiations, ship commanders were expected to give "a certain quantity of goods for slaves"; in some cases final sales were made "according to their appearance" relative to the favorability of interested buyers.[7] In 1722, British merchant Humphrey Morice gave specific orders for the purchase of two males to every one female, adding that if women were procured, "see they are good & Beautifull, never y'e worse."[8] Seamen were expected to judge the value of black females according to how aesthetically pleasing they were. Although these decisions relied heavily upon their personal opinion, Morice's instructions underscore how notions of beauty might have been more pronounced within the African Atlantic auction block than historically understood.[9]

No matter the destination, the importation of black women to distant plantation societies hinged upon a future life based fundamentally on the unending cycle of childbearing and child care. Prior to the conclusion of negotiations, crewmen scrutinized the attractiveness of available black women while maintaining a keen eye toward their future reproductive potential once landed and sold to interested planters. Widespread assumptions of African savagery influenced and thereby justified many financial transactions made for bondpeople. Ideals of desirability filtered these coastal decisions affecting the forthcoming cycle of sexual exploitation, breeding, and procreation. These crewmen, forcibly separated from landed populations, often for months at a time, made choices, decisions, and final selections of black females that, while aiming to satisfy distant buyers, were intimately tied to their personal attraction, tastes, and sexual appetites.

For bondwomen, their physical body parts and in many instances their breasts became the primary features slave traders often drew upon to base their final decisions of sale. Centering his entrepreneurial decision on the black anatomy, one merchant ordered crewmen's avoidance of Africans with "Long, Tripeish Breasts" and most especially those with "Navells sticking out."[10] The former description affirms the use of breasts as indicators of age and value; the latter presumably applied to those with a hernia or even pregnant women. After boarding twenty-one female captives from Bassa aboard a slaver in 1787, the presiding commander relayed that "the Women in general having good Breasts were strong and well."[11] The reproductive gaze held of black women was far from uncommon. A ship captain looking to board more females sent a crewman on shore. Logging his daily business interactions, he wrote: "Yellow Will brought me a woman slave, but being long breasted and ill made, refused her, and made him take her on shoar again," presumably to the original seller. For this woman, cast as old, disfigured, and unattractive, his refusal signaled a worthlessness and lack of value that he believed her future would generate. Assessments of the physicality of females' bodies differed under the gaze of interested strangers. Manipulative examinations of their contoured flesh—their vaginas, hips, thighs, and stomachs—violated the personhood of scores of female slaves. Inspecting the shape, size, and perceived firmness or sagginess of a woman's breasts, mariners speculated upon the protruding frontal parts of their confined bodies to assess their worth; commercially defining someone as "strong" or "weak" they sought to predict a female's age and future ability to procreate and nurse over a remaining lifetime in slavery.

Shifting views of breeding and procreation within distant slave societies centered on the bodies of African women, making claims and imposing racialized power and authority for the purposes of financial gain. Although largely conceived for the plantation system, sexualizing of females' bodies emerged on the African side of the Atlantic as crewmen and local coastal merchants strategically engaged in and agreed upon the final terms of sales. Regardless of age, notions of sexuality were continually placed into and onto the lives of bonded females through the critical eyes of capturers, negotiating brokers, and purchasing sailors lured by discerning the potential these women's bodies overtly displayed. Their flesh and, more importantly, their wombs represented a form of capital that seamen and awaiting planters actively exploited. Variations persisted widely on the type of female captives most suitable for these socially financial ventures. Working in tandem with these sexually structured ideas, complex ideals of patriarchy centralizing the reproductive roles black women were expected to work within and thus satisfy were originally envisioned by slaveholders yet fully set into motion by slave ship sailors.

In addition to women without children, females and their progeny similarly held a place within coastal sales. In a letter to his financiers, ship captain John Duncan declared, "It's true I had nine but two of them were children and the mother of them died before the briggs departure."[12] While substantiating the place of children in the transatlantic slave trade, Duncan's correspondence reaffirms the inclusion of black mothers sometimes enslaved alongside their offspring. Ordinarily, inland capturers sought to capture females without younger members of their immediate family because of transport difficulties and the lower values they generated. Such views, however, did not grant these women immunity from enslavement, evidenced through another buyer's purchase of multiple children, "between thirty and forty, both boys and girls, some sucking at their mother's breast."[13]

Nursing women and their infants posed significant challenges with oceanic transport, yet some sea captains agreed to their inclusion. In November 1788, eight women "with Children at Breast" were bundled together and forced to cross the Atlantic waters aboard the ship *Madampookata*.[14] Children represented long-term investments within the system of slavery, although this financial view varied between the world of plantations and slave ships. Historian Wilma King offers the salient point that "enslaved infants were economically worthless to owners at their birth because they were not productive laborers."[15] In much the same way of devaluation, ship captains viewed enslaved babies as not only far less lucrative but also more burdensome given the extensive and rather demanding responsibilities associated with their care at sea.

Precisely because of these maternal needs, separations regularly enforced between mothers and their children during sales required ship crews to rely on the nurturing abilities existent among other purchased females. After negotiating the purchase of an infant child, slave trader William Snelgrave instructed a crewman to "pitch on some motherly Woman, to take care of this poor Child." The sailor casually responded to the order: "He had already one in his Eye."[16] Much like other traders, Snelgrave sought to reduce the duties expected of his crew during the passage. Forcing boarded females to serve as temporary mothers and caregivers of enslaved children, whether related by blood or not, reduced the burden on their buyers while foreshadowing the importance of fictive kin within plantation communities. The mixture of bondwomen across lines of age and circumstance of motherhood debunks previously held ideas that females on slave ships solely comprised adult women, suggesting the critical need to both problematize and expand invocation of the term *women* in the context of the Middle Passage. If not, generalizations predicated upon the notion that every female placed in the slave trade—ranging from unborn female children, little girls, and elderly female slaves—equated to an adult woman. Delving deeper into the lexicon of gender used within the slave trade prohibits further exclusion of young and teenage girls, nursing mothers, and elderly women also tragically altered through the human manufacturing process.

With reproductive futures always in mind, seafaring men viewed all captives as potentially lucrative sexual beings. Demands that overseas buyers made relative to regional, local, crop, and individual needs held significant bearing on the types of slaves many merchants commanded slave ship sailors to secure from Africa. In relying upon distant and many times unseen cadres of desirable African laborers, investors were only able to superficially define preferential ages. Influenced by requests of distant consumers, merchants broadly conceptualized age into two groups—adults and children—representative of the most common binaries used to measure black human commodities. As such, infant, prepubescent, teenage, and elderly captives fell outside of prevailing socioeconomic desires and are therefore rarely accounted for in contemporary slave trade discussions.

Younger-age captives were not always preferred; nevertheless, they sometimes appeared aboard slave ships. One scholar contends, "Children were easier to capture and confine than adults."[17] Within the interior regions of Africa they were probably easier to kidnap because of their smaller size. Inland transport would only have been made worse by vocal expressions of fear through shrieks and cries that children exerted during their fateful march to the coast. Surgeon Ecroyde Claxton recounted the story surrounding the purchase of nine captives who appeared "dejected" once brought aboard ship from the island of Bimbe. Among those sold, a young girl, "a child of about ten or twelve years of age," learned she had been sold to an awaiting ship captain and "clung fast about the neck of her disposer, and eagerly embraced him" in hopes of reversing her ill-fated enslavement.[18] What may seem a tender moment for any observer shows the calculus of slavery and the human expressions of desire and desperation for freedom, which included children. Perhaps because of the challenges of care young captives routinely posed, one merchant demanded their exclusion, requesting "none under 14 if Possible, such being unfit to Travell y'e long journey."[19]

On the other end of the age spectrum, slaves believed to be beyond their prime years also held a precarious place in the slaving process. With heightened focus on securing young viable slaves, this created broad and often unclear definitions of age. Distinct terms referring to young adults, middle-aged, and the elderly became blurred and conflated into a binary between the young and old.[20] Penning the qualities understood as the most rewarding in overseas markets, many merchants attempted to offer the most basic means of assistance in helping mariners determine how these categories financially functioned within the industry. These idealistic desires filtered into coastal negotiations; however, a bondperson's body became the most key component on which their skin, face, hair, and health were assessed to make calculative predictions of age and labor for exploit by future slaveholders. Every slave was viewed and valued for possessing a healthy, young-like, and reproductively capable disposition. Conversely, any person perceived as unhealthy, old, or presumably barren in nature represented risky investments and thus extreme impediments in the process of securing future sales and satisfying customers.

Serving as central conduits of wisdom bridging the past with future generations, elderly men and women held a vital purpose throughout African communities. Emerging from varied ethnicities, many bondpeople carried common ideals of reverence for those advanced in age. However, the mistreatment that older slaves endured within the slave trade stood in stark contrast to the value and respect they formerly enjoyed in freedom. We therefore know far less about how blackness and age was conceived or how buyers read these understandings into the final selection of enslaved people. Judged against their younger counterparts, older captives were routinely overlooked by those believed to generate little or no tangible value for future buyers. Such sentiments enforced the regularity of orders forbidding their inclusion among a ship's cargo. Captain Smyth of the *Corsican Hero* received a dire warning from his financiers on this very matter to "be Carefull in your Choise as old ones sell for little and often die" once in a trader's possession.[21]

Age represented a critical factor prompting often bold demands within shoreline purchases. As Captain Peter Reme prepared to lead a voyage in 1787 to Africa aboard the ship *Tommy* on July 2, merchant Robert Bostock outlined his commercial expectations and specifically "the Quality of your Slaves," to which he warned, "don't take any old ones as they will fetch little or nothing in the West indies" slave markets.[22] These types of instructions were far from uncommon in the eighteenth century. Knowing the incredible difficulties attended with selling elderly captives, owners for sea captain Stephen Bower's vessel declared on June 19, 1788, that he was "not to purchase any old Slaves on any account" during his Atlantic travels. Going further they insisted that he "take care to examine them well as they are not Idiots nor Ruptur'd," because in their estimation "they will fetch nothing in the West indies."[23] While foregrounding the heightened restrictions held against aged captives during the legal era of the slave trade, these conversations reaffirm that value was not always about monies but also the social and political capital that bondpeople generated on the West African coast, aboard slave ships, within the marketplace, and, most of all, the terrain of plantations.

Many African coastal brokers considered that the exchange of goods and monies for purchased slaves solidified that they became the sole property of their new purchasers, thus freeing them from any further responsibilities required for their extensive shoreline captivity. Records rarely indicate how many older slaves came into bondage on the African side of the Atlantic, nor the motivations behind their purchase. The inclusion of older slaves on ships as viable prospects for future sales leaves open several key questions: How long were they held in coastal confinement before securing an interested buyer? What were the gendered differences of treatment elderly slaves confronted? Were they offered at a reduced price—perhaps to rid the area of unwanted slaves? Did their weakened state influence traders' perception of their bodies, and in what ways?

The Barometer of Enslaved Health

Operating as the primary link in the human manufacturing process through the Middle Passage, ship commanders were expected to take specific precautions with West African selections and sales. The motivating force for negotiations hinged on obtaining those physically and psychologically capable of enduring the hardships of bondage. "You will be remarkably choice in the Quality of your Negroes," Captain Charles Wilson's employers warned. "Buy none but those that are in the full Bloom of Youth, & health full chested, well Limbed, [and] without defect."[24] In 1752 South Carolina merchant John Guerard wrote to Captain Watts, similarly advising, "What I apprehend of Negroes if you Could get Negroes Suitable for this Place" should include adult male slaves. His correspondence insisted that Watts "take none with Crooked Limbs or other Blemishes" displayed on their bodies.[25] Merchants expressed a wide range of preferences in directing traveling seamen to obtain the most desirable captives. Some of these orders proved useful in assisting the complicated selection process; however, the regularity with which these specifics were obliged is unknown to contemporary scholars.

For the sake of reputation and profit, neither ship captains nor surgeons could afford to neglect matters of health; therefore, warnings were regularly issued to guard against fraudulent sales. Extensive processes were used to discern how fit a slave would be as a laborer imported to expand planters' profit margins. Poor health proliferated throughout slaving stations and coastal dungeons across Africa. To ensure captives' tenability, employed physicians were urged, "You must not be contented that they seem to be in Health" when moving toward an immediate purchase. Instead, they should guard against certain symptoms and diseases, especially in determining if "the Men [slaves] have *Gonorrhoeas,* or *Ulcers* in the *Rectum,* or *Fistulas,* and the Women [slaves] *Ulcers* in the[ir] Neck[s]" during examination. Because captives were often well aware of personal ailments manifesting within their bodies, medical practitioners learned that "they will hide [them] from you, (if you be not very careful)" while performing presale examinations. In one physician's estimation, many slaves drew upon such tactics due to the prevailing "fear of those who bring them on Board, because if they don't sell them, they will surely starve them to Death" once taken back ashore.[26]

Beyond preferences of skill, gender, or age, medical examinations proved critically necessary in assessing a captives' well-being. Slave ship surgeons were expected to offer expert knowledge diagnosing and restoring a person's health, although not every vessel sailed with a physician aboard. Legislation regimenting their inclusion varied widely across different nations depending on a merchant's needs and available finances. Offering written guidance for physicians traveling to West Africa, eighteenth-century medical practitioner T. Aubrey admonished, "I hold it absolutely necessary that you visit All the Slaves, before you suffer them to be bought, because in this Affair your own Reputation as well as the Owner's Interest lies at Stake."[27] As professionals, shipboard doctors held a rather tenuous place throughout the trade: being heavily relied upon for medical decisions despite a demonstrated lack of sustained familiarity with ailments indigenous to the tropics of Africa. Once docked inland, their duties began by helping ship commanders filter through captives to prevent the inclusion of those diseased or disabled and thus ensure the procurement of robust and healthy bodies.[28]

Whether sea captains relied on medical practitioners or designated crewmen, collectively these foreign men judged the soundness of bondpeople according to what their flesh overtly displayed. Diverse factors affected captives' present states of health, including the initial process of capture, treatment during the coastal march, duration of time in holding, and any methods of preservation extended during their shoreline captivity. Often forced outside in pairs, they were stripped naked with general queries made first about height, weight, and age. Venturing further, inspectors routinely scanned a person's bare skin for any disorders, twisting limbs and squeezing joints, muscles, and bones, endeavoring to secure the most vigorous bodies able to withstand ship confinement and arduous plantation labor. Setting out "to see that they were sound in wind and limb, making them jump, stretch out their arms swiftly," interested buyers followed by "looking in their mouths to judge of their age" through their oral health, probing a bondperson's teeth and gums. On many occasions, displayed slaves were also forced "to cry out, lie down, and hold their breath for a long time."[29]

Fondling a captive's genitalia was the most significant aspect of slave sales used to assess any dormant reproductive concerns.[30] Value that merchants and mariners attached to future laborers on the African side of the Atlantic relied not merely on agricultural capabilities but also on how and if these varied bodies could successfully reproduce. With young girls and adult women this invasive procedure meant strangers' frantic groping about their breasts, hips, buttocks, and vaginal areas. Male captives underwent similar public molestation to make certain "they have no Mark in the Groins, or Ficus's about the *Anus,* or Marks of Scabs having been about the *Scrotum*" or other orifices.[31] Foreign traders surveyed slave men according to the strength their muscles conveyed, often reinforcing stereotypical assumptions of black male sexual prowess. Knowing the vital assets both groups represented in the sexual economy of slavery, interested buyers scrutinized the lucrative potential that their captives' bodies could generate for future reproductive and breeding purposes.

Regardless of age, violation of bonded females and males under the auspices of medical treatment subjected them to degrading bodily scrutiny in which they were often handled in a cattle-like fashion.[32] One trader recalled examining "a Negro's eyes, to see whether he was blind," describing the procedure akin to that of "a horse in this country, if I was about to purchase him" for later use.[33] These coastal examinations constituted the first dimension of the auction block system captives regularly underwent. Considerable scholarly attention is given to Caribbean and Southern slave markets where, following a ship's arrival, imported black bodies were poked, prodded, and scrutinized by open crowds of potential buyers. This same system of preparatory assessment operated through far less public means much earlier in the slaving process as bondpeople passed through the countless hands of inland capturers, shoreline brokers, surgeons, sea captains, and assisting crewmen tasked with determining a slaves' economic and social value within the Middle Passage.

The Contentious Fate of the Refuse

Histories of the slave trade are many times based on slaves appraised, bought, and transported into different parts of the Atlantic world. Those physically landed and displaced into plantation communities comprise the primary framework for understanding the wholesale enterprise of human sales through the transatlantic slave trade. The multitude of captives known on the edges of history as "refuse slaves," about whom foreign traders expressed considerably limited interest and often rejected as purchasable goods, represent another aspect of the slaving story commonly silenced.[34] Buyers' avoidance of certain captives more often than not was related to unhealthy dispositions due to diseases, irregular body structures, inferior mental capacities, and advanced age, all of which had the greatest influence on final negotiations. With speculations always based on the physical aspect of black human merchandise, every offered slave was susceptible to inclusion within this complicated group. Keeping in mind the projections of value continuously invoked in slave sales, what did devaluation look like outside of the specter of reducing the price for someone's body?

Merchants employed sailors to manually appease and fulfill the overwhelming demand for a black labor force, yet they were critically dependent on the choices these seafaring men made for the future growth of slaving profits. Once docked and personally engaged in final negotiations, selections of bondpeople operated at the full discretion of sea captains and their attending crewmen. An enslaved person's age, gender, and the range of laboring skills they conceivably possessed were emphasized as commanders sought to make the right decision in accordance with the desires of overseas investors, brokers, and, most especially, buyers. Stephanie Smallwood reminds us that a "ship captain's most pressing concern was not his captives' qualifications for plantation labor; rather, what mattered most to the ship captain was whether captives would survive their passage aboard the slave ship."[35] Faced with the task of securing an ideal range of bondpeople to fulfill previously allocated instructions, sailors were never able to focus solely on the survivability of the passage for those enslaved. Instead they were expected to effectively manage distant orders alongside transport feasibility, both being financially critical to gain compensation and even future employment upon completion of an overseas journey.

Given the circulation of differing tastes, perspectives, and economic motives, a clearly defined rubric that coastal Africans and foreign traders used to determine who fell into this category of undesirables was nonexistent. Despite these uncertainties, seamen understood the viability of black bodies and those who exhibited far less value within distant market sales. Excluding captives conceivably deemed unable to command market interest, one captain confessed to refusing slaves "either lame, old, or blind."[36] Superficially, refused slaves displayed conditions arising from a range of physical and emotional challenges. The primary basis of these shoreline assessments rested firmly upon factors that "would make a Slave objectionable, as a prime Slave" to interested buyers. The smallest perceived defect, including "the loss of a tooth" or the appearance of "a blemish in his eye, tho' he might not be blind," could prohibit interest. On the other hand, "if they are afflicted with any infirmity, or are deformed, or have bad eyes or teeth," or if a bondperson was "lame, or weak in the joints, or distorted in the back, or of a slender make, or are narrow in the chest," ship commanders immediately rescinded all previous offers for their sale. Others were less concerned with the origin of certain perceived defects causing changes in a person's body. Those slaves most vulnerable to blatant refusal possessed what many considered an incurable condition, such as "loss of an hand . . . the total loss of an eye," or in many instances "old age," all of which could not be reversed and signified an extensive burden and uselessness in the slave economy.[37]

Price similarly played a critical factor, propelling bondpeoples' lives into an even greater fate of uncertainty. Coastal men were "not ignorant of these Marks" capable of reducing interest in slaves' bodies. Perhaps for this very reasoning, one trade participant pointed out that when coastal merchants "find you know them as well as they, you will have them at half the Price," due to the fact "they will rather sell them at any Price, than keep them" on their hands.[38] Offering captives at a lower cost shielded African sellers from any additional responsibilities for their upkeep. Intimately familiar with the process of business exchanges, many sea captains were well attuned to the looming possibilities of delaying negotiations to board slaves deemed worthy of purchase. Some withheld financial decisions, especially in the event of a disease or physical abnormality, "unless something is taken off from their prices, so as not to make them as high in price as prime Slaves."[39]

Financial incentives occasionally lured sailors to purchase captives who ordinarily may have been declined. On January 7, 1750, while docked at Rio Junque, John Newton sent a steward ashore to purchase a female captive, referred to as No. 46. "She cost 63 bars," he logged, despite that "she had a very bad mouth," implying that the bondwoman suffered from some type of facial contortion or pronounced bruise on her lips. Unclear is if her physical condition emerged from an ailment or perhaps a wound she incurred during her capture, coastal transport, or subsequent holding. Although agreeing to the negotiated sale, Newton recognized that he "could have bought her cheaper" than the asking price, because, as he explained, "the trade is in such a pass that they will very seldom bring a slave to a ship to sell" to any interested buyers.[40] Prevailing events, such as local wars and especially heavy market demands placed upon a particular region, influenced the feasibility of acquiring prime slaves. Such circumstances not only led to the tightening of human supplies but also enforced greater financial cost upon interested sea captains to secure value off a bondperson unable to command high prices.

Knowing the leverage foreign traders sought to utilize in obtaining black bodies, occasionally attempts were made to shield discovery of medical ailments among offered slaves. In one case a bondman was "brought in for sale, on a very wet day" from the interior hinterlands. Unaware of his circumstances, local buyers assumed that he had traveled a considerable distance, because "part of his legs and feet [were] covered with mud." This subversive tactic "was done to hide the leprosy, which had made the bottoms of his legs and feet perfectly white." As a result of the creative strategies employed, "the Slave was accordingly purchased"; however, his skin ailment became obvious shortly thereafter. The following morning his captors ordered him washed in preparation to "appear before the Chief," and as a consequence "this great defect which rendered him unsaleable" became visible. Discovery of the skin affliction would have proven too late to request, although unrecorded is whether inland capturers or even the bondman personally sought to hide his condition. Equally difficult to discern is if this male's purchasers attempted to employ similar deceptive methods to sell him as a prime slave or instead offered him at an arranged clearance price.

Reductions in cost did not always guarantee a slave's sale. "When the Owners of slaves from the country are satisfied that the Europeans will not buy them," it was not uncommon for coastal brokers to "sometimes sell a few of them to the people on the sea coast, for very low prices, and carry the rest back."[41] Speculating on the nature of slave dealing, captured slaves never returned to their homelands and were often showcased aboard other ships or carried to nearby regional fairs. In some instances of refusal, "the old or unsaleable" were sent back in canoes along with "the goods that have been paid for the slave" originally carried in hopes of enticing additional interest.[42] Bartering took place with local West African families to lodge rejected slaves, although age profoundly determined the contours of their future lives. Taking younger captives into nearby coastal homes proved tactically advantageous to improve their condition for future transactions. Whereas, knowing the limited possibility of securing successful sales for the elderly and diseased, their mere presence created burdensome responsibilities of observation, patience, and extra preservation undesired by slave trade workers. The continued displacement of undesirable captives enforced greater damages tied to their enforcement into bondage, but also their fate beyond exclusion.

Within the broad category of those refused, a person's youthfulness represented the most necessary factor in coastal market sales. "When the negroes, whom the black traders have to dispose of, are shewn to the European purchasers," on many occasions "they first examine them relative to their age."[43] Adult slaves underwent considerable scrutiny, whereas sailors configured children's viability directly within the vortex of trade and investments. Slave trader George Baille told a story about "a beautiful infant boy" displayed for purchase. Surviving records obscure the number of ships that the child was marketed aboard for purchase; however, the presiding broker in charge of his sale failed to gain foreign interest. In their last attempt they brought the young boy on the *Phoenix* and "threatened to toss it overboard if no one purchased it." Amid the conclusion of negotiations, several crewmen learned that the child had entered slavery when an undisclosed number of inland traders kidnapped him "with many other people the night before" and transported the coffle to the coast. Once placed for sale, his capturers soon found "they could not sell him, though they had sold the others." Ship stowage and consistent care of a baby within an oceanic passage posed extreme difficulty, yet perhaps softened by his uncertain fate, Baille "purchased the infant for a quarter cask of Vidonia wine."[44]

Inclusion of children in coastal sales and buyers' subsequent disregard for them was far from infrequent in the human manufacturing process. Seaman

James Fraser described an instance when he accompanied Captain Lawson of Liverpool at the River Ambris, where once ashore they purchased several captives, including a young bondwoman. During the transaction Fraser ventured along the coast "for the benefit of the air," taking the opportunity to tour the local coastal community, after which he came upon a linguist who felt obliged and showed him "where some countrywomen were going to put a suckling child to death." He queried the women's actions with the infant, to which they responded, "it was of no value." Unwilling to see the child's life taken, he determined, "In that case I should be obliged to them to make it a present to me." Relentless in their efforts, the gathered women reportedly negotiated for monetary compensation, intimating to Fraser that if he "had any use for the child it was worth money." With bartering widespread during this period, he "first offered them some knives," which they refused, yet later they agreed to sell the infant to him "for a jug of brandy." After climbing aboard ship with the young boy, he discovered "it proved to be the child of a woman purchased by captain Lawson" earlier that day. Excited by the prospect of reuniting with her child, according to Fraser, "the woman went upon her knees and kissed my feet."[45]

There are no additional details corroborating either of these stories or deeper explanations into whether many younger captives were kidnapped with parents, siblings, or any other family members. Seamen routinely bartered various goods in exchange for bondpeople, indicating that the view of human life was held in mere cash terms. The inclusion of children among coastal-bound coffles exposes the harsh reality of slave dealing while pointing to the very real possibility that other bondpeople, related or unrelated, were tasked with their upkeep during the inland transport. Unable to care for themselves, endure the physically and psychologically extensive process of captivity and transport, nor offer any significant laboring incentive in much the same way as adults, within the human manufacturing process children became expendable property, operating most times as mere supplements or bonuses to the conclusion of slave sales. Soliciting genuine foreign interest for younger captives proved invariably challenging, resulting in continued refusal and extended confinement within coastal West Africa, leaving them to the devices and decisions of local traders and residents.

Beyond mere exclusion, the disregard of slaves sometimes came at the cost of physical abuse against their flesh. "I have seen them sometimes beat [and] heard them threatened," one slave trade participant disclosed, noting the tendency among slaves to be "generally anxious to be sold with the rest of the Slaves" already purchased.[46] From a West African trader's standpoint, a buyer's disapproval of their human merchandise placed them in a precarious position as entrepreneurs by not only tarnishing a trader's personal reputation of supplying demands with quality slaves but also countering any clearance efforts to effectively reduce the number of captives held on hand. "Traders frequently beat those negroes which are objected to by captains," although "it matter[ed] not whether they were refused on account of age, illness, deformity, or for any other reason."[47] The accuracy of cruelty inflicted on refused slaves is far from deeply studied, yet the imposed aggression many experienced took on a variety of forms—sometimes even deadly. "Common practice [was] to kill all," one trader relayed, especially those deemed "unsaleable slaves[,]" by tying a stone to their necks and drowning them in the river during the night."[48] In other locales "it was a well known fact, that if the slaves which the Africans bring to market are so old and blemished, that they cannot get what they think a sufficient price for them, they will cut their throats before the faces of the Europeans."[49] Taking into account the susceptibility to create racialized exaggerations of alleged hostile occasions, these actions publicly solidified the perceived lack of social and financial worth refuse slaves were believed to hold. Even more is the heightened value placed particularly upon foreigners' interest and willingness to buy offered slaves, showing the greater effect white slave traders had on the fate of African captives, whether sold or unsold.

The inability of some captives to garner shoreline market interest invited physical violence into their market performance. While docked at River Ambris, north of Angola, slave trader James Fraser learned the deadly fate of "a Slave, who I would not purchase" during conducted sales. As a result of his rejection, the man's owner called a meeting of "traders and fishermen together under a tree," explaining that the bondman represented "the Slave, whom the white man would not buy" incessant tendency to run away. Because the African broker "derived no benefit from his labour" through continued negotiations, he felt obligated "to put him to death," seeing that this man's inability to attract a buyer could serve "as an example to the rest of his Slaves." Disciplinary tactics used enforced horrific pain upon the enslaved man's body. While under the tree, the owner allegedly began the tortuous spectacle by "cutting off his wrists, then at the elbows, and then stumps from his shoulders." He followed by lacerating the man's "ankles, the rest of his joints, and finished with cutting his head off" in view of the gathered crowd. Recollecting on the seller's tactics, Fraser intimated, "I did not suppose [him] to be very criminal" in nature. Forced to cooperate with local practices, he acknowledged, "They have a right to put their own Slaves to death," frequently including "any useless criminal or old Slave" who was deemed futile in the economy of slave dealing.[50]

Sailors' indifference toward a bondperson became the primary motivator for imposing violence. Fraser never physically witnessed the sequence of events, instead relying on transmission of the account through a local young boy employed as a servant. Central to the bondman's story is the testimony of torture, pain, and forcible death directly tied to his failure to solicit foreign interest. "A damaged head, a torn off arm, [and] an open belly will stare out at the observer," Elaine Scarry reminds, "and flood him with nausea of awe and terror" upon close inspection.[51] The effect that dismemberment of this male's body had on those still unsold is muted in surviving sources. As temporary visitors, sailors were unable to alter the local laws of coastal communities.[52] The bondman's death provides a visual image, albeit bloodied, to speculate more deeply on the violence routinely exercised against rejected bondpeople as a consequence of the slave trade and thus external forces.

Damages committed against repudiated slaves were not confined to the West African shoreline. Seaman Henry Ellison explained that one afternoon "a native black called Captain Lemma Lemma" climbed on ship to receive customs for captives previously bought during the vessel's stay. While awaiting payment he observed "a canoe paddling in shore with three people in (an old man, a young man, and a woman)" and beckoned it to sail over to Ellison's ship. Obliging his request, several men led the small boat across the waters, after which three captives were placed for sale. The chief mate expressed interest in buying the young male and female, yet because "the other was too old," he immediately "refused to buy him." Upon exclusion, Lemma forced the aged man back into the canoe, where "his head was laid upon one of the thwarts of the boat, and chopped off, and immediately thrown overboard."[53] Decapitation reinforced the extent of relentless power and command that some West African traders sought to create through psychological terror enacted on those in captivity. This power, publicly in view of sailors and slaves and far from indigenous to Africa and Africans, became replicated through equally gruesome ways in slavery at sea.

Considering the menial view that many white slave traders held of African culture, the practice of deadly aggression of business ventures further cast them as unjust and immoral. Looked at from the side of supply, coastal brokers sought to expedite a rapid process of exchange to fulfill overseas demand along with garnering compensation for their services. Any hindrances to this complicated cycle proved extremely consequential, both personally and professionally, within the entrepreneurial world of slave sales. Without any regard for personhood, all suppliers and buyers—foreign white traders, mixed race, and African brokers—assessed bondpeople's lives merely through the prospect of future profits. Knowing the inability to salvage significant value from refused slaves, the most cost-effective solution some coastal traders envisioned most economical in contrast to repeated rejections was murder.

Gender, however, did not prevent the misuse of other offered slaves. During his stay at Cape Coast Castle during the eighteenth century, John Fountain gained insight into local slaving customs related to the unsold, indicating, "If they are not saleable they are put to death." His clarity hastened most prominently through one African female described as "being very old and very infirm," brought to the castle for sale after being rejected by several captains and local residents. Once on display, she was once again unable to secure interest. "Because the Black trader would not be at the expence of her maintenance," Fountain learned that her captor "carried her into the Bush." Realizing the woman's inability to secure local or foreign interest, as well as expenses on his own time, the unnamed captor transported her to "a field or kind of meadow which is overrun with weeds and bushes." Concealed from public view, this grassland served as the last site and open space where this bondwoman considered her uncertain fate before she "was murthered, and afterwards found." Sources leave silent how this woman became enslaved and how she was killed, along with the duration of time her lifeless body lay discarded within the field of grass.[54]

Captives deemed useless within the specter of slave sales were executed, perhaps more often than the history reveals. Jerome Barnard Weuves related a case during his command at the fort of Annamaboe involving "a woman who was accused of witchcraft, or the wife of a man accused of witchcraft," historically marked as "very old" and brought in for purchase consideration. Observing the professed age of her displayed body, Weuves declined the proposed offer. During negotiations he learned "if I refused to purchase her that she would be put to death," yet, still unmoved, several locals charged with her sale took the woman away. Once carried from the fort, an employed servant reported, "It was the intent of the people in town to cut her head off," partly because of her accused crime and inability to attract a buyer. Weuves immediately sent a person after the traveling band to express that he "would take the woman, and give something for her," as he intimated, "rather than she should lose her life." Despite his effort, the messenger arrived "five minutes too late," finding once there "her head was off her shoulders."[55]

The violent deaths of these two women and the shattered lives of many others points to the evolution of several societal practices during the era of the slave trade. These circumstances likely did not play out in such simple terms as recorded, yet the immediacy of their murders underscores how the evolving disruption of social mores fueled by constant demand for black laborers and the lure of capital created a deep detachment from the social value of human life. With the primary objective always to maximize profits, slave ship sailors attended to the differences among bondpeople wherein which divergent factors of physical and mental health, size, disability, and, as already intimately revealed, age marked and defined their bodies. These bonded females were cast as worthless on either side of the Atlantic, and the perceived insignificance of their livess run counter to the way we understand value among captive black bodies. Their murders, moreover, expose the need to deepen our examinations into the externalities and hidden costs of slavery mitigated against bondpeople forcing them to confront rejections and at times the fatal consequences of market refusal.

Conclusion

The kidnap, transport, and confinement of captives in shoreline holdings made possible the trade of humans as viable goods. Establishing ties and brokering deals gave way to a pendulum of interactions as foreign sailors sorted through scores of men, women, children, and the elderly to secure those deemed most profitable. Setting out to determine a captive's feasibility of surviving shipboard captivity and appeasing plantation needs, sea captains were unable to be impartial in the selection process. Held to rigid accountability measures set forth by distant merchants, disaggregating captives according to age, body structure, gender, aesthetics, and particularly health, far outweighed the mere availability of black bodies. Surgeons and commanders sought to ensure fiscal responsibility by predicting the maximum value a bondperson could generate within distant slave societies. Their decisions functioned as the vital pretext for the making of enslaved laborers as they dictated where, how, and if any captive would fit into the vast landscape of Atlantic slavery.

Recounting the diverse stories involving the movement of African people into the Americas, we privilege those purchased, transported, and successfully imported into scattered slave societies. However, in turning attention to the range of captives displaced aboard foreign ships, the view also fully considers the cadre of those enslaved and devalued as potential commercial market goods. Uncovering the varied meanings of value that all slaves held on the African side of the Atlantic can then better explain how the financial decisions of foreign buyers led to reconfiguring the incalculable lives of those both sold and unsold. Some slaves, Stephanie Smallwood astutely reminds, understood their own commodification in the specter of coastal sales as they "learned that when they reach the littoral, their exchangeability on the Atlantic market outweighed any social value they might have."[56] With their bodies marked and possessed by their new owners following coastal negotiations, once pushed out at sea slaves more intimately understood the permanence, severity, and meaning of their movement off land and containment in an isolating world of suffering, violence, toxins, and, most of all, contagion.

3 Healthy Desires, Toxic Realities

Ship captain John Newton departed Liverpool on August 11, 1750, aboard his snow, *Duke of Argyle,* setting sail for the Windward Coast of Africa. Docking almost a month later, he immediately entered into business negotiations with local slave merchants to acquire available captives. With agreements finalized and the captives loaded and securely stowed within the vessel, Newton confronted several instances of declining health among them. Conditions worsened following his arrival at Rio Junque, prompting him to declare, "Having so many sick, am afraid [we] shall not be able to keep our boats going" further on the route. As illness filtered through the ship's hold, he sought coastal resources to preserve the lives of his human property, discharging several seamen during trade at Grand Basse to "put a boy on shoar, No. 27, being very bad with a flux." Three weeks after the captive's removal, the boy's designated caretaker, Andrew Ross, shared with Newton that, treatment notwithstanding, his health had deteriorated and he died. Despite the financial loss incurred by the boy's death, Newton indicated it was "indeed what I expected."[1]

Three months later, while preparing for his coastal departure, Newton faced yet another medical episode, this time with an enslaved girl referred to as "No. 92" similarly devastated by the flux. Much like her former shipmate, Newton sent the young female onshore to an unknown man named Peter Freeman—likely a broker, resident physician, or perhaps a member of his crew charged with her care. Recollecting the girl's transfer, Newton reasoned it was "not so much in hopes of recovery (for I fear she is past it)," but instead, as he professed, "to free the ship of a nuisance."[2] Both his perspective and actions convey a sense of indifference toward the young girl perceived as a medical threat; however, ship commanders were continuously faced with devising the best ways to minimize external threats to their slaving endeavors. On Wednesday morning, the next day, following her relocation and directly in line with Newton's prediction, "No. 92" died. Sources do not reveal when or even how this young girl's distemper manifested, yet the rapidness of her decline and death reinforce the difficulty and rather vulnerable position that sea captains faced in the buying and boarding slaves due to the ever potent threat of sickness. Ship commanders sorted through a broad range of human merchandise, actively in pursuit of slaves possessing a healthy disposition. However, with bacteria, germs, and viruses undetectable and contagion widely pervasive, the fate of the two boarded children, No. 27 and No. 92, centers the permanence of death while pointing to the fact that attempts were extended to restore a bondperson, health comprised the most critically unpredictable aspect of the slaving industry. Tracing the movement of captives on ships following coastal market transactions, this chapter interrogates the second and most crucial phase of slavery at sea. Doing so reveals the labor and profit risks involved in the movement and subsequent displacing of captives while turning attention towards the dangerous convergence of toxicity and power that engendered the deterioration of slaves' bodies.

Funneled from and through the hands of different slave traders until the final point of sale, bondpeople regularly confronted severe hunger, thirst, abuse, exhaustion, and poor sanitation. The terror of captivity, solidified through slaves' enforcement and temporary holdings within dungeons, barracoons, and pens, led to the initial decline and by far the inception of isolating psychological torment many captives underwent, being unsure of their fate in the near or far future. Environmental factors, as this chapter traces, including poor cleanliness, the meager allocation of non-nutritious foods, cramped conditions, and inclement weather imparted far greater damage to slaves' health, resulting in the further erosion and unmaking of their bodies. Even more central to the outplay of power, deprivation, and exploit facilitated through the Middle Passage was the remote landscape of ships and the Atlantic Ocean. The spatial freedom mariners gained in the secreted world of slavery at sea granted complete autonomy to impose the most intense dismantling of their human goods, which in turn exposed and more clearly defined the meanings and boundaries of "unfreedom" for transported slaves. Taken together, this phase of the human manufacturing process was merely a staging ground for the circulation of violence, terrorizing abuses, and the medical decline of slaves.

Bodies of Contention

African merchants set out to sell prime slaves to foreign buyers, but this did not always translate to providing the most humane conditions for those held on hand awaiting purchase. During the loading process, "some of them were very meager . . . when I received them on board," one slave trader observed, which in some cases was "owing to the great scarcity of provisions in the country from which they came."[3] Unable to keep up with the growing demand for black laborers, the supply of coastal rations occasionally ran low. Despite the potential value bondmen and bondwomen generated within the slaving industry, deprivation and unending violent mistreatment jeopardized the maintenance of slaves' health at sea. For this reason, Joseph Fayrer of the ship *Harlequin* was directed to "be very cautious of the Slaves you buy" given that on many occasions "they are often sickly."[4]

Sailors were advised on what to watch out for in slave selections and sales, yet local merchants and inland raiding parties did not always exert careful handling to avoid inflicting any exterior damages on captured slaves. "The skin of the wrist and arms" was commonly "excoriated from the friction of the country ropes with which they were tied."[5] Ropes, manacles, and neck collars marked their flesh, restricting their movements to prevent any attempts at fleeing. Traders were especially sensitive to the physical abuses bondpeople underwent onshore, knowing the expectations of long-term management they were tasked with in preserving and supplying blemish-free laborers. With goods and monies exchanged and sales complete, from the perspective of coastal men any bodily damages that surfaced during the vessel transfer of slaves became the primary responsibility of their new foreign owners.

Despite efforts exerted to procure healthy bodies, no captain or seamen could fully anticipate the medical horrors capable of decimating their financial dreams through newly bought slaves. To counter any possibility of infectious transmissions, "the cloth that they had round their middle was thrown overboard."[6] Such preventive measures appeased any initial fears of contamination, yet the intermingling of bondpeople into cramped ship holds facilitated the exchange of contagious diseases. Once disembarked from the West African coast, James Penny, captain of the vessel *Oisean,* encountered a high rate of African mortality when measles surfaced among approximately three hundred stowed slaves. The vessel's crew consisted of several sailors and "an experienced Surgeon, with Three other Assistant Surgeons." Prior to his departure from England, Penny placed "every Thing necessary for the Restoration" of slaves' health on board, including a variety of food provisions and medicines.[7] The diverse precautions of laborers and medical tools may have created a unified sense of preparedness, but his efforts proved useless in the cycle of illness and contagion as measles claimed the lives of many of the vessel's captives.

The end of coastal negotiations marked the beginning of widespread movement of diseases among sailors and slaves. Serving as temporary captives on loan during coastal sales, unexpected illnesses occurred in some cases through traders' use of "pawns." "The owner or friend of such pawns commonly borrow[s] Slaves from a ship which is not so forward in completing her cargo, and takes the pawn of the ship that is ready to depart, and puts it on board the other" until a vessel is completely filled. Such measures ensured awaiting traders their requested captives were en route. However, "epidemical disorders [were] conveyed from one ship to another by this practice," enforcing temporary yet sustained close contact that on occasion "destroyed a great number of Slaves."[8] Through the process some bondpeople functioned as bargaining chips, down payments, and physical loaners used to help finalize negotiations between coastal traders and white seamen. Their displacement on different vessels consequentially exposed them to unhealthy environments detrimental to sailors and especially those forced to lie in close proximity with boarded ailing captives.

Shipmasters preferred slaves whose bodies displayed optimal health, yet the transmission of virtually undetectable ailments among boarded captives affected future market sales as well as the labor commanded of them. A male slave purchased to relieve a pawn aboard the eighteenth-century vessel *Briton* and serviced by the ship's surgeon, Henry Ellison, demonstrated this dangerous reality.[9] Ellison detected the onset of smallpox in an offered bondman during a preliminary examination, after which he warned the presiding commander. Disregarding the physician's observations, the captain indicated "he did not believe it, and if it was [smallpox], he would keep him as he was a fine man." Once crewmen lodged the male slave within a corner hold aboard, smallpox broke out among "almost all the Slaves on the ship," leading to the death of ten captives discovered the next morning. Moving their diseased bodies onto the top deck for disposal, Ellison observed, "the flesh and skin ha[d] peeled off their wrists when we ha[d] taken hold of them," which in his professional estimation represented merely one devastation of the deadly medical disorder.[10] The confined spaces of slave ships facilitated the mobility and transmission of illness and decline that exacerbated slaves' vulnerability to disease, and in turn left sea captains and surgeons powerless in combating the physical decline of their purchased cargo.

Confined Dangers

Bondpeople boarded ships enfeebled from their landed experiences; however, unsanitary conditions pervasive within slave vessels added to the vulnerability of their future laboring lives. Debates persisted widely on the necessity of loose versus tight packing in the confinement of slaves, although with private trade dominating the eighteenth century, seafarers operated at the discretion of vessel owners and their own personal calculations. Managing trade risks, supplying live bodies, and enhancing profit outcomes, captains purchased slaves knowing full well the possibility of losses through shipboard mortality. The interior spaces of slave ships represented sites for the forcible gathering of bodies as decisions were made to counter sickness, trauma, and death. Whereas, the physical construction of ships determined the stowage and spatial arrangements of boarded slaves. Acting on preconceived security concerns, bondmen were most times immediately moved belowdecks. Surviving records vaguely hint at the stowage of female captives, leaving contemporary understanding to rest on the idea that all slaves were moved into the lower decks of vessels. Traditional narratives likewise emphasize gendered separations, whereas in some instances the "Whole of that Deck under the Gangway is covered with Negroes."[11] With accounts of the stowage of slaves based primarily on adult black men, particularities and evolving nuances of how sailors packed women and children on slave ships during the legal slave trade are many times less clear.

The greatest demands for slaves in the eighteenth century were largely predicated on the importation of male slaves to appease foreign interest. Precise boarding of slaves may not always be as easy to discern; however, the displacement of bondpeople within the interior of ships held significant bearing on their bodies. Holding rooms reserved for captives' oceanic passage were far from extensive, with length accommodations estimated at "about Five Feet Ten." Variations among slaves' height and weight affected their shipboard placement, and the transport experience resulted in repeatedly cramped bodies and flesh damages. "The Negro was laid on his Back," one source revealed, to ensure they "have sufficient Room for their Accommodation if they chose to turn on their Side."[12] In other ships, male slaves were "locked spoonways," or even in a head-to-foot spatial arrangement, forcing them to lie in close proximity to their fellow shipmates.[13] More problematic than the resulting skin injuries were the toxic consequences from bodily excrement that flowed easily between, from, and to the bodies of slaves within their constricted environments. Traders differed in their evaluation of the massive grouping of slaves relative to their stowage and transport, evidenced by one slave trader's contention that bondpeople "had always plenty of room to lay down in," to which he concluded, "had they had three times as much room they would lay all jammed close up together." These behaviors, he reported, "they always do . . . before the room is half full."[14] Instead of gaining ample space to maneuver themselves within the hollowed interior of ships, surgeon Alexander Falconbridge conversely emphasized, captives "had not so much room as a man in his coffin, neither in length or breadth, and it was impossible for them to turn or shift with any degree or ease."[15]

Equally devastating to slaves' transport was the lack of proper circulation of air. "Every ship has gratings, and most have air ports, but there are some ships, whose constructions do not admit of air ports in the usual manner."[16] Regulations specifying the construction of slave vessels were nonexistent, conforming instead with merchants' orders and a ship commander's needs. Knowing the dangers inherent with extended confinement of slaves without daily movement, Captain Spoor of the vessel *Ranger* received the warning, "You must allways be mindfull to give them as much fresh Air as you possibly can" while at sea.[17] Whether many vessel owners and sailors gave substantial thought to these necessary practices remains inconclusive. "They seldom complain of heat while the air is sweet," one trader declared, justifying the congested stowage of slaves because from his determination, "they are accustomed to heat, and find very few inconveniences from it." Arising often from locales with tropical climates, he surmised quite simply, "they can bear heat better than White People."[18]

Tremendous variance persisted among enslavers with the intensity of ship heat and captives' preference; however, the poor conditions into which slaves were forced greatly jeopardized their health. "Too close Confinement in the damp and foul Air of large Ships" created a higher probability of suffocation and disease transmission.[19] A vessel's size as well as sustained physical contact through the constraint of bodies proved equally critical in the management of boarded captives. Captain John Ashley Hall described these consequences, pointing out, "I have frequently heard them crying out when below for the want of air."[20] Some ships included ventilators, yet these devices were often unable to filter sufficient air among lodged slaves, forcing many to routinely confront extended hours and sometimes consecutive days of detention bound within heat-intensified rooms. Improper circulation caused stagnation and a heavy dampness, making breathing extremely difficult. Therefore, it was not uncommon that when "brought upon deck, some [were] fainting" while other slaves "die[d] within a few minutes after they have been brought upon deck, which proceeded from the corrupted state of the air and heat jointly."[21] Such observations directly counter the circulation of racialized ideas that African people were naturally capable of withstanding extreme temperatures without medical consequences while showing more forcefully the seaborne operation of unregulated methods of deprivation and torment.

The inability to breathe worsened slaves' conditions as they crossed the Atlantic. "I have seen their breasts heaving, and observed them draw their breath with all those laborious and anxious efforts for life," one surgeon detailed, arguing that respiratory problems frequently emerged through immersion in and the ingestion of toxic air from bodily fluids and excrement. "When the tarpaulins were, through ignorance or inadvertently thrown over the [air] gratings," covering the portholes and making their confinement even more burdensome, some slaves were seen "attempting to heave them up, and crying out 'Kickeraboo, Kickeraboo,'" linguistically signifying their unending awareness of the coming of death. "On removing the tarpaulins and gratings," another physician recalled, "I have seen them fly to the hatchway with all the signs of terror and dread of suffocation."[22] Language barriers persisted, yet the sense of terror and desperation that slaves vocalized proved unable to be disregarded by sound, sight, or affect within the isolated Atlantic waterways.

A multiplicity of cleaning procedures were employed to sterilize the often hazardous environments of ships, knowing the unhealthy risks anchored in the oceanic transport of bondpeople. "The practice of cleaning the ship," one captain explained, "is prejudicial to the health of the Slaves."[23] Sterile environments were necessary to the preservation of all aboard; therefore, any neglect of sanitation created fertile ground for bacterial transmission. Crewmen were sometimes ordered to scrub a ship's deck with bricks and sand followed by a full wash and rinse in which canvases were used to filter water from the head (toilet) pumps located between the various decks. These sanitizing measures assisted with removing any undetectable toxins lingering within the porous surface. Sweltering temperatures and damp conditions rampant at sea, the wooden boards of decks required sufficient drying to prevent the emergence of colds and flu, the rotting of wood, and constant movement of vermin able to thrive in damp conditions. Some commanders ordered pans placed in Africans' rooms, where fires were lit and burned for close to two hours to ensure proper drying.[24] Others used "Fires made of dried Wood sprinkled with any refinous Substance, such as Pitch [and] boiled Turpentine," to help purify the planks and reduce any toxic aromas.[25]

With the largest numbers of purchased captives belowdecks, the cleanliness of bottom holdings of ships were vital to the health of boarded slaves. Throughout a vessel's passage they were forced to lie naked within hollowed spaces that both submerged and exposed their cramped bodies to contaminated mixtures of bacteria, blood, and mucus shed from their shipmates. Often these largely neglected darkened spaces were cleaned at the discretion of sea captains. The surgeon of the ship *Swift* remarked in 1792 on the inattention the presiding commander gave to ship cleanliness, reporting that "another thing to be taken care of is keeping y'e ship clean which he neglected" in his duties. In hopes of providing greater credibility, he added, "Capt Laroe he knows that when he came on board he found the ship most tolerably dirty."[26] Sanitation duties on other vessels took place two to three times a week, depending on the weather and a ship's governance. During feeding and exercise periods, crewmen "and generally some of the boys, [we]re sent down below to scrape and swab the room" where captives were regularly locked.[27] These holding areas were frequently cleaned with "the Fumes of Tar or frankincense, and sprinkle[d] with Vinegar" to quell the stench of encased naked captives' bodies for long periods of time.[28] For this, crewmen occasionally burned tobacco and brimstone, filtering smoke to freshen these closed-off rooms.[29]

Regardless of the methods used to prevent unsanitary conditions, slave ships were well known for the smells they emitted. Captain Thomas Wilson shared that his officers and crew regularly "complained of the noxious smell . . . insomuch that they dreaded some infection."[30] Platforms, decks, and defecation tubs containing the blood, urine, fecal matter, and vomit of slaves were the primary catalysts for the offensive stench. Working and traveling aboard vessels, often for weeks and months at a time, fueled a sense of familiarity and tolerance among some seamen to the odors of slave ships. "As far as the Smell," one trader recounted, "that must depend on every Person's own Feelings."[31] Yet not every mariner shared these tolerable sentiments. "The stench to me," another sailor explained, "and I believe to every European unaccustomed to them, is intolerably offensive."[32] No matter a ship's point of origin in traveling from Africa, a stigma of filth became associated with a ship's sail and Atlantic arrival within different ports. Knowing the prospect of wealth represented by the bodies of transported slaves, brokers and potential buyers willingly risked their own health and prevailing fears of contamination by temporarily interacting within these foul spaces once docked into port.

With desires of profit outweighing the allocation of mistreatment, slave cleanliness was the most critically economical solution necessary to their health and future market sales. Bondpeople were never given the chance to regularly cleanse on their own terms. Instead they were "kept clean shaved," with excess hair being trimmed and shaved off male slaves' faces and heads.[33] Such measures reduced the accumulation of bacteria while helping to make bonded males appear younger to potential buyers. Female captives experienced hair growth in different parts of their body; therefore, we can reason that shaving practices were similarly forced to counter unforeseen bacteria. For all captives, "every Attention [was] paid to their Heads, that there be no Vermin lodged there."[34] Exorbitant ship temperatures contributed to the proliferation of flies, termites, lice, cockroaches, and mice, all of which, coupled with the closeness of bodies through tight packing, enabled faster routes of transmission. The heightened apprehension of disease and, most of all, the potential loss of capital therefore motivated many commanders to ensure that African slaves were cleansed, albeit through basic means, during a ship's passage.[35]

Several methods were used to keep bondpeople's bodies relatively clean. On some ships the morning ritual involved the use of "Tubs of Water" distributed for slaves to gather around and "wash their Hands and Face," followed by a surgeon's examination to ascertain any sores or complaints that may have emerged during the evening hours.[36] Recognizing the sporadic nature of captives' opportunities to clean themselves, it is reasonable to assume that these water basins were not regularly drained, resulting in an offensive smell. To extend the use of recycled ship water, a British Royal Navy surgeon suggested, "When your water is stinking, mix lemon juice or vinegar with it, and it will render it much less unwholesome."[37] Collective use of still water permitted the direct and dangerous exchange of bodily fluids in and through the different orifices of bondpeople's bodies. Even more, stagnant water often attracts flying vermin, which for slaves meant increased prospects of bacterial ingestion through the process of cleansing one's face.

Forced to wash on the open decks of slave ships, favorable weather conditions dictated the frequency of such practices for bondpeople. In some cases this occurred during "the Middle of the Day, if the Weather is fine, they are bathed all over."[38] On May 23, 1753, the captain of the *African* logged that his crew "washed the slaves which the weather has not allowed us to do this fortnight nearly."[39] Unable to clean the ship's human cargo, these instances fostered the greatest probability of sickness and transmission. To prevent captives from catching colds "when the Decks are Wet," one shipmaster received instructions urging, "let them be wash'd allways in the Evenings but Never in the Mornings."[40] The patterns of captives' bathing are far less clear in surviving sources; however, these measures depended on a ship commander's preference and trade expertise but especially the prevalence of sickness within a vessel's hold.

To counter the transmission of microorganisms, different cleaning strategies were employed to offset further damages in a bondperson's health. During periods of favorable weather, sailors permitted slaves "to wash themselves under the head pump." Physician T. Aubrey warned about the dangers of cleaning bondpeople by "forcing them into a Tub of cold Water every Day, and pouring the Water on their Heads by Bucketsfull." Although they were accustomed to bathing in their homelands, he explained, "Sometimes they may be little indisposed, and then they fear the Bath." Reinforcing the lines of power held over slaves denied privacy, "when some refuse the Bath," he encouraged the casual use of violence by any means deemed necessary, including with "Blows, and Kicks, and Cats" to counter any posture of insubordination.[41] Following a brief rinse, captives on some ships received palm oil to rub on their bodies to draw out any toxins and prevent the growth of skin conditions common with changing weather patterns.[42] These measures fundamentally helped to prevent contamination, stench, and any dryness of the skin while granting slaves temporary feelings of dignity regarding their personal hygiene. The greatest illusion, however, lay in the false sense of power it produced, if merely because bondpeople's lives were always determined and predicated on their captors' discretion and the ever constant threat of violence. Communal cleansing permitted control over one's body while increasing opportunities of contamination among other lodged captives. As a precautionary measure of cleanliness, owners of one vessel urged that the ship's crew "make the Slave[s] rub each other with a piece of Cloth every Morning," which they learned could "promote Circulation & prevent Swellings" from arising on a captive's flesh.[43] How and if these methods were regularly used, as well as their effectiveness, is contemporarily unknown. Use of the cloth raises particularly difficult questions about the number of people using these rags as well as details on if any sterilization and disposal were part of the cleaning process. Any disregard for the cleanliness of both vessels and slaves invited the filtration of illness and death, thereby hampering the availability and import of healthy bodies and viable future laborers.

The Constraint of Nutrition and Exercise

Along with sickness-related conditions, food was equally critical to maintaining the health of captured Africans. Many of the edible items bondpeople received came from different parts of the Atlantic. While preparing for their overseas ventures in England, seamen loaded various foodstuffs, including beans and in some cases "stockfish, flour, bread, and beef," along with an assortment of liquors.[44] Knowing the entanglement of dietary practices with the health and preservation of future laborers, merchants occasionally directed sailors' attention to these culinary matters. Captain Caleb Godfrey of the sloop *Hare* received instructions on November 8, 1755, regarding food distribution among boarded slaves ordering that he "let them have a Sufficiency of good Diet," to which was added, "As you are sensible in your Voyage depends upon their Health."[45]

Seafarers traveling the coastal waterways often bartered for a diversity of foods that comprised the basic items consumed during an oceanic passage. To accommodate any decrease in supplies, once docked at West Africa ship commanders sought goods such as seafood, corn, and cassava to supplement feeding captives.[46] Docked in Old Calabar in 1788, the commander of the slaver *Juba* negotiated for the purchase of several items, including "1 Gang Cask Brandy, Palm Oil, Pepper, Lime Juice, Goat, Dried Fish, &c for his slaves."[47] During coastal stays traders typically "got several articles, such as plantains, bananas, and several other refreshments," despite knowing these items "are not fit to keep at sea."[48] Storing these provisions within intensely hot environments of ships drastically deteriorated their form, in some cases causing food-borne illnesses if consumed. Unable to rely solely on vendibles carried from Europe, seafarers were dependent on shoreline foods to sustain captives not only during African market sales, but also during the transatlantic voyage.

Food dispersal took on different forms at sea. Under orders of some ships, captives received breakfast in the morning "soon after day-light," and evening meals were given during the four or five o'clock hour.[49] A vessel's size determined how slaves received their food: on smaller vessels they were brought up from the bottom holding for meals, whereas on larger vessels they were spread throughout the interior of the ship. Some were fed on the main deck as the chief mate, surgeon, and boatswain oversaw their congregation. When confined to the quarterdeck, the same location as the ship's captain, the second mate and surgeon's mate were stationed to watch over them.[50] Crewmen organized slaves across lines of sex during feeding times and into groups of ten to "mess by themselves, by which means no one can be overlooked, as they fit in a circle."[51] Gendered separation reinforced constant divisions between men and women; however, smaller groups empowered greater opportunities to enforce and maintain social order and surveillance by reducing the number of gathered slaves and guarding against any further insurgency.

Preservation of food on ships largely shaped the range of provisions included within most slaves' meals. The challenge of adequate storage created dependencies and imposed incredibly strict standards for food distribution.[52] Edible items typically consisted "mostly of Beef, Pork, Biscuit, Flour, Oatmeal, Pease, Butter, [and] Cheese."[53] Seafarers also carried salted meats, dried beans, rice, and yams because of their resistance to spoilage during lengthy voyages and to create larger meals accommodating with larger groups.[54] One surgeon recalled that bondpeople "are fed with Two Meals of comfortable wholesome Victuals."[55] The dynamics of shipboard captivity never permitted comfort nor were their meals vital to a bondperson's nutritional needs. Beyond sustenance, crewmen viewed these foodstuffs as necessary to preserve the basic health of boarded slaves. High temperatures and intermittent open sea weather patterns prohibited the allocation of fresh fruits and vegetables. Moreover, the restrictive nature of feeding on ships and cheap investment of black laborers hindered the extensive provision or even an abundance of meals due not only to large numbers of slaves but the fundamental nature of slavery at sea entangled by threads of power, exploit, and deprivation.

Shipboard food provisions fell primarily into three categories: starches, carbohydrates, and proteins. Starchy items were the most regular aspect of bondpeople's meals, including cassava, grains, Indian corn, barley, and shelled peas, boiled down and incorporated into different meals.[56] Carbohydrates were another staple on vessels, exemplified by the constant inclusion of bread, rice, and yams in captives' diets. In some cases they "have commonly one meal or more of yams a day given to them on the coast and on the Middle Passage."[57] Yams were also cheap and widely available across much of West Africa, leading in some cases to overreliance. This staple not only reflected customary dietary practices familiar to many slaves, but looked at from the perspective of their captors, yams also fed numerous captives, generated a feeling of fullness, and, most of all, served economic needs by making slaves appear less emaciated.

Bondpeople also received a diversity of proteins. These nutritional supplements were typically procured on the African coast and at other times following a ship's port arrival. Proteins ranged from beef, pork, chicken, and salt fish, but in the absence of preferred meats, sailors relied on locally available foods. The captain of the *Ranger* logged in 1790 that his crew, while docked at West Africa, "served the People with fresh Fish in lieu of Pork and Pease."[58] The pork and peas were likely carried from England, but to diversify the meals served on board, sailors bartered for fish in shoreline communities. Crewmen also drew from the sea to provide meals. On November 2, 1783, the commander of the vessel *Count du Nord* wrote, "This morning hook'd a Shark but the line being too small he broke it and made his escape" into the waters. Although unsuccessful, several weeks later their persistence proved fruitful when "at 10 a poor unfortunate Dolphin took the hook, Was Discover'd and Immediately hall'd In" the ship. The next day several crewmen "hook'd a Shark of a 11 feet long [and] hall'd it" on the ship and "he was Immediately Cut up & Devour'd."[59] Atlantic port communities supplied food rations that seamen used during slaving voyages, yet the oceanic highway granted access to an array of dietary items sometimes difficult to procure on land in mass quantities.

Different techniques were used in the storage and distribution of animal protein. To counter the intensity of heat and provide proper means of preservation, many meats were cured by adding salt and allowing them to sit in the open air.[60] These measures permitted sailors to preserve fleshy food items far longer, which, by increasing captives' salt intake, fostered a greater susceptibility to severe dehydration.[61] Bondpeople were "forced to eat too much Salt," which as one physician observed, "is a thing they little care for, unless it be in a very small Quantity."[62] Salt preferences varied according to personal taste and previous exposure, although economic needs trumped dietary desires. The preservation of meats ensured a sufficient amount of provisions made available; however, this practice came at heavy cost to slaves' health, as the overconsumption of high-sodium foods aggravated and even produced various complications they later confronted.[63]

Beans, along with meats, comprised another source of protein captives regularly consumed on slave ships. As a result of the routine use of dry goods in ship meals, some ships received explicit directions—"On their first coming on board feed them sparingly"—because previous experience revealed that "sudden change from a green Vegetable diet to dry food is apt to make them Costive, which the surgeon must guard against."[64] The range of attention seamen gave to this abrupt dietary shift, if they paid attention at all, is difficult to closely trace. However, slaves boarded ships hungry and malnourished, compounded by intense desperation for survival. To offer variation on the monotony of foodstuff, on some ships sailors mixed beans into various sauces to diversify offered meals. A dish regularly offered commonly known as "slauber-sauce" combined rice, beans, "palm oil, mixed with flour, water, and pepper."[65] Some slaves preferred this concoction, prompting one commander to suggest future English vessels traveling to Africa place "Dryed Flour on board for her slaves" in order to permit "the Capt to have doe Boy's made & well Boiled with the Slauber Sauce as is Customary."[66] Shipboard cooks also blended foods to create meals, including "Horse-beans boiled all to a Paste, and then stuff[ed] with rotten Herrings." Occasionally this mixture was served "with Palm Oil enough, a small Matter of Salt, and good Quantity of Pepper" and distributed among lodged captives.[67] The employment of creative culinary tactics depended on a ship's orders and available supplies; however, foods given within slavery at sea were far from extensive.

Several types of beverages were also distributed among bondpeople during their oceanic passages. Water was the most critical requirement; however, these barreled supplies were usually carried from England and stowed on ship for later use. Extended periods of time spent at sea led to dehydration only worsened by crewmen's enforcement of water restrictions. "Length of Voyage may run them short," surgeon Robert Norris explained, "but Ships in general have the Precaution to lay in Three Months of Water, or thereabouts, for a Passage of Six, Seven, or Eight Weeks."[68] A vessel's size, the number of bondpeople stowed aboard, and the duration of time spent in West Africa all affected the regularity and amount of water able to be distributed prior to and during the oceanic passage. Lengthy coastal stays therefore meant seamen had to gather additional water once docked at Africa, as evidenced by Captain James Fraser, who noted, "In some places I paid for wood and water, which is the general practice of the country." Confronted with unending challenges during his stay on the Angolan coast, he confessed, "It is very difficult to get the water on board from some places, on account of the difficulty of landing, where the water was to be procured."[69] Replenishing water supplies required planning and considerable labor, although necessary precautions for the preservation of both slaves and sailors.

Water restrictions depended on the number of people on a ship as well as heat. "When the weather is uncommonly warm," some traders felt it most advantageous to "serve them the same quantity of water in the middle of the day." Ship captain John Knox typically gave tin cups containing a half-pint of water allowance reserved for slaves during their morning rise and once again in the afternoon.[70] Considering the variety of body sizes and differences among slaves across gender, age, and health, equal distribution of water would have been insufficient for supplying necessary fluids according to personal bodily needs. "I usually laid in from 60 to 80 gallons a man," one vessel master recollected, "but I generally had a quarter of my stock left, when I arrived in the West Indies or America."[71] Set adrift beyond public view, ship commanders had complete control over the daily distribution of water, allowing them to determine the regularity of distribution but also to designate those slaves most worthy of preservation or deprivation. Their decisions of access affected the lives and physiological makeup of bondpeople, forcing some to suffer dehydration, become weak, endure swelling, and confront difficulties in dispelling toxins from their bodies.

Along with water, bondpeople received other liquids during shipboard mealtimes. American and English sailors carried various liquors to exchange for the coastal sale of bondpeople, but prior to departure, any unsold supplies were reserved for later use during the voyage. One commander explained, "I always had sufficient quantity of wine and spirituous liquors for the use of the negroes and the ship's company."[72] Relying on a system of gradual management, he dispersed diluted "inferior brandy and rum" among the enslaved. Ingesting such drinks within the confine of sweltering temperatures intensified feelings of intoxication and delirium as the temperature of captives' bodies began to rise and exhaustion soon followed.

Despite the intent to provide meal diversity with food and drink in the Middle Passage, tainted provisions surfaced within ship meals, placing captives' health under greater harm.[73] "One of the great Causes of losing the Slaves, comes from very bad Food," one surgeon wrote to his employers.[74] Physician O. P. Degraves offered a momentary glimpse into the consequences of serving toxic items, noting the loss of boarded slaves in Old Calabar "owing to a purchase of bad Yams." Fearful of other medical injuries arising that might affect his reputation, he added, "Our bread is all mouldy, and I am much afraid of the consequences."[75] Detailed information revealing the types of food or even how long these spoiled items were distributed among captives until their inferior quality was discovered is unnoted. Heavily dependent on various individuals and landed communities to supply necessary provisions placed sea travelers in a dangerous and rather vulnerable position with shipboard provisions. Working to extend future business relationships and most often faced with limited time, crewmen were unable to criticize coastal traders or vendors about storage time and climate in assessing the possibility of contaminated foods without jeopardy to future partnerships.

In addition to the purchase of putrefied items, various parasites often bred within ship provisions. Physician James Lind explained, "The dry provisions, oat-meal, peas, and flour, are apt to be corrupted and spoiled by weevils, maggots, and by growing damp and mouldy."[76] Perhaps because of these seaborne realities, commanders were encouraged to remove "your provisions out of the Rooms frequently" and permit them "to be Air'd" in hopes of facilitating longer use and preventing instances of spoilage. "You are to examine that your Cargoe not be Wet or Eat with Vermin as often as you can on the Outward Passage," warned one set of instructions.[77] Adapting to their host environment, many parasites were undetectable and thus easily hidden within boarded foods.[78] Sailors may have made concerted efforts to secure and carry noncontaminated items, yet the cramped and deplorable conditions of ships produced even greater complications with food storage and allocation.

Cost factors and the lack of exposure to certain provisions influenced the meager range of meals many bondpeople received. Shortly after his departure from Shebar, the captain of the *African* reported constraints he faced in providing sustenance to several boarded slaves. On March 21, 1753, he logged that they were forced to "give the slaves bread . . . for their breakfast" because they "cannot afford them 2 hot meals per day."[79] Monies were dispersed to cover various expenses for a ship's voyage; however, the bartering of goods became the typical method of acquiring different vessel needs, including food. Scarcity of coastal edibles significantly affected sea diets. Commander John Duncan wrote from Annamaboe in 1769 that with dull times widespread on the African coast, "it will take us some time to get corn and yams" because, as he found, "they are very scarce and not to be purchased without gould."[80] A ship captain lodged at the mouth of the Lawse River experienced similar food concerns, writing that "the boat is this day a Going to Serelion," as several were directed "to purchase Rice on the Bullarm Shoar." "I have bin forst to feed my slaves with flower," he reported, as "rice is very scarce."[81]

Contrary to dominant narratives of victimization within the trade, bondpeople occasionally demonstrated food preferences within the Middle Passage. Captain John Ashley Hall testified that in stowing provisions and water for the voyage, he found it was "not always the sort of provisions they liked best."[82] Seaman William Littleton offered similar observations, recounting, "We usually put a few pieces of ships beef, or salt fish amongst them—after eating them once or twice, they have become fond of them."[83] Language barriers hindered sailors from fully comprehending culinary practices and preferences, although sustained interaction within coastal communities and regularly traveling in close proximity with slaves created greater understanding, albeit generalized, of their dietary preferences and habits. "We can scarcely make them eat European provisions," Captain W. Woodville noted, "much less when they begin to complain & their appetite becomes weak."[84]

Unfamiliarity and the lack of acquired taste for certain provisions prompted slaves' rejection of offered foodstuffs. Horse beans were a main staple of the trade, but many bondpeople did not like them. Speaking further to this undesirable culinary item, surgeon Alexander Falconbridge described, some slaves "have such an aversion to the horse-beans, that unless they are narrowly watched, when fed upon deck, they will throw them overboard, or in each others faces when they quarrel."[85] Stripped of any personal control over their lives, bondpeople traveled at the mercy of their transporters, forcing a desperate willingness and acceptance of any and all offered shipboard foods. As evidenced, however, they also found ways, albeit minimally, to influence their shipboard experiences.

Agency that some bondpeople acted out helped to determine the amount of food they received. Many offered provisions were small portions, making survival even more paramount. Recognizing this depravity, some slaves took matters into their own hands through ulterior means. Physician Thomas Trotter recalled a case involving several bondmen who hid between the decks, "where the horse beans were kept," and secretly "had taken some, about two or three gallons, and hid them away in some of the cases that were between decks." How did these men burrow themselves from discovery? Sailors learned of the subversive tactics when they "heard them eating them in the night." Upon discovery of the slaves' actions, the attending commander "ordered four or five of the people that had done it upon deck, [and] gave them a severe horse-whipping first." Separating the two "supposed to be ringleaders," he forced "a thumbscrew on each [captive's] thumb" to punish them for their defiance. Such measures "tortured them very much," Trotter remembered, having witnessed "their groans and cries, the sweat running down their faces, and trembling as under a violent fit of the ague."[86] Therein, despite the ever looming possibility of violence, some bondpeople became agents in their own personal welfare.

Traveling in close proximity with slaves only fueled stereotypical associations crewmen held of their dietary habits. Sustained exposure gained through the trade yielded deeper insights, yet through shipboard surveillance this often led to generalized assumptions. Angolan captives were described as "eat[ing] whatever provisions were given them with cheerfulness."[87] While those from the Gold Coast gained reputations for "scarcely refus[ing] any food that is offered to them," enforcing the widely held belief that they "generally eat larger quantities of whatever is placed before them, than any other species of negroes."[88] Other assumptions prevailed during the era of the slave trade. "Yams are a favourite food of the Eboe, or Bight negroes," one surgeon offered, "and rice or corn, of those from the Gold and Windward Coasts; each preferring the produce of their own native soil."[89] The withholding of food forced all slaves, regardless of ethnic variation, to confront desperate struggles for survival during their Atlantic crossing. The oral culture of maritime workers centrally in operation, any of these seaborne observations could have influenced slaves' treatment on and off ships, leading to greater abuses of neglect, deprivation of food, and, most of all, the continued enforcement of violent disciplinary tool used against unruly black bodies.

As bondpeople were confined for long periods of time, forced exercise served as an equally critical measure in preserving human merchandise. Fitness represented a regular strategy some seamen incorporated to maintain physical health and counter any instances of psychological decline. Although widely pervasive, "it was not practised till their health made it absolute necessary that they should be allowed some exercise."[90] These necessities became most prominent when a captive appeared dispirited without any obvious signs of improvement. "In the afternoon after being fed," crewmen typically moved captives across the deck "to make them dance."[91] Gendered variations as well as daily patterns of physical abuse that sailors used to dance slaves in the Middle Passage is not always as clear in surviving records.[92] Unable to escape inclement weather conditions during periods of exercise, outside elements enforced even more preservation risks. "Exercise being deemed necessary for preservation of their health," slaves were typically "obliged to dance, when the weather will permit their coming on deck."[93] As such, a crewman ushered them on the top deck in the "morning between eight and nine o'clock," and returned them back into their holds "about four in the evening" for the remainder of the day.[94] Exercise and weather patterns had far greater meaning in slavery at sea than historically imagined. Bondpeople's lives were under constant attack not only from inclement weather but also from contamination and the lack of protections from the onslaught of daily environmental risks.

In compelling slaves to move their bodies, traders interpreted their movement through dance in a variety of ways. Africans were "accustomed to divert themselves at Home with Dancing, and Singing, and Drinking," which physicians strongly advocated during the Middle Passage. Some crewmen enforced these cultural practices, but most times through violent means. "They are always very ready" to dance, with the only exceptions being "a few sulky ones."[95] Bound in hollowed spaces for extended durations, some captives welcomed opportunities to stretch their limbs and gain fresh air, while for others dancing fostered a reconnection with the spirit world through sounds and prayers created through their feet. "They are made after each meal to jump up and down upon the beating of a drum." Fitness aided blood circulation while offering additional measures to induce proper digestion. "This is what I have heard called dancing, but not what I consider as dancing," because one slave trader attested, "it is not to music of their own."[96]

Sailors often contrasted African dances with European modes of style, yet their own biases hindered them from viewing black-derived moves as culturally acceptable. Being forced to dance to musical sounds many times unfamiliar to those from West Africa, bondpeople demonstrated a sense of awkwardness in their movements. Surgeon Thomas Trotter echoed these shipboard observations, explaining that slaves "dance[d] round the deck, with all those awkward gestures and motions which they call dancing."[97] These publicly enforced motions created an exposure of music between sailors and slaves. Regardless of the future economic and social roles bondpeople served in the economy of slavery, traders projected ongoing ideas of inferiority, casting slaves as less civilized and thus uncultured. The enforcement of dancing slaves, while implemented for health reasons, in many ways created new meanings on slave ships that took on a tone of coerced entertainment for a vessel's crew.

Bondpeople's health was particularly crucial to their overseas importation; however, refusal to exercise prompted immediate retaliation through aggressive means. Functioning similarly to plantation overseers, slave ship sailors violently left marks on unruly captives by whipping them, and thus commanding social order amid efforts of preservation. "The men, who were confined in irons, were ordered to stand up, and make what motion they could."[98] Regardless of gendered displays of disobedience, any unwillingness to oblige shipboard rules led to the use of punitive measures, a fact made strikingly clear through Captain John Ashley's recollection that bondpeople routinely "received a few strokes when they refused to perform . . . exercise, or to eat their victuals."[99] When others went about their exercises "reluctantly, or do not move with agility," terror intensified through flogging and use of other torturous tactics and devices,[100] further underscoring that the maintenance of optimal health often came at a violent cost to bondpeople's flesh.

Environmental Hazards of Catastrophe

Diet and fitness enabled greater preservation of transported slaves, yet environmental conditions countered the personal control crewmen sought to maintain on ships, and weather patterns posed perhaps the greatest obstacle to slaves' health within the Middle Passage. Rainy seasons in West Africa began in late May or early June and typically ended in October. Some believed the coming of rain depended on "the change of the Moon in the latter part of May."[101] To circumvent bad weather, many commanders sailed at night to ride with the land wind.[102] Despite these precautionary measures, the unpredictability of weather patterns contributed to a range of unforeseen problems with purchased slaves. Once docked at the River Gambia, ship captain Edward Taylor confronted the devastation of weather concerns, declaring, "The prescant Season of the Year, the Rains Coming on is Very unhealthy."[103] Crewmen tried to avoid sailing during unfavorable months, but persistent demands for black laborers meant facing risks of traveling at unseasonable times and jeopardizing the health of boarded slaves. While docked at the African coast aboard the *Jupiter*, Captain John Smith remarked, "Rainey season have been & still is Varey severe here." Inclement weather imposed difficulties with sailing; however, Smith's fears stemmed from acquiring several Africans still owed to him in holding on the coast.[104]

Unfavorable weather hampered slave dealings and a ship's speedy departure. On March 7, 1790, while docked at Annamaboe Road on the coast of Africa, Commander John Corran logged that the day "Begins with strong Breezes" culminating from the southwestern direction, producing what he described as "dark cloudy Weather." It is unclear if any damages ensued; however, he employed immediate protective measures for the ship and boarded captives. Weather patterns worsened later that evening and a northeastern wind came upon them, "attended with heavy claps of Thunder, dismal Flashes of Lightening and great rain till 10 PM."[105] Hurricane seasons greatly affected slaving voyages. Ship captain James Fraser attested to these devastations after his Caribbean arrival: "The Negroes were very much distressed during the bad weather—[and] there was a scarcity of water, and a total want of country provisions."[106] Whether on the African coast or following their Atlantic port arrival, sea captains were never free from the threat of perilous weather conditions. Even worse, atmospheric conditions affected the procurement and allocation of food and water, adding greater stress to the rise of adverse medical conditions. Cramped in the ship's hold, bondpeople were shielded from the open dangers of storms, many times forcing immersion within dark, damp, and toxic spaces that not only echoed loud weather patterns but revealed the fragility of their future lives in a more intensified way.

Poor weather conditions tied directly to the unhealthy state of those enslaved. A vessel commander faced the loss of sixty captives because "weather was very bad comeing down here & the slaves were unwell fitted," leading him to conclude, "the season is entirely against this voyage."[107] Most captains avoided transporting slaves during unfavorable seasons; however, such precautions were not always taken. Ship master John Hark remarked on the debilitating condition of his cargo stemming from their "being under water the whole way from the Coast."[108] Adrift in the open sea, his ship came under a constant downpour of rain leading to a leaky voyage, and held captive in different holding rooms—whether chained or not—bondpeople were unable to escape the influx of water, worsening the passage and their physical health. After leaving the coast fully slaved in an undisclosed year, Captain W. Woodville Jr. detailed how the health of slaves boarded on his ship suffered as "the incessant rains on the Coast & the cold weather afterwards brought on the flux."[109] The inability to move about the ship increased the prospects of colds and flu while further fueling the probability of adverse medical conditions. Perhaps more than other sites in the landscape of bondage, environmental factors had significant bearing on slave trading practices, ship departures, bondpeople's health, and the range of captives that crewmen successfully transported across and into the Americas.

Inclement weather affected the preservation of commercial human goods. Slaves' exposure to the climatic changes varied "from wet to dry, or from dry to wet" and gave impetus for further sicknesses at the onset of storms, rain, or fog, as bondpeople had to remain belowdecks, thus increasing their susceptibility to illness. Emerging from tropical environments, many slaves preferred moderate to warm temperatures, leading one sea captain to explain that they "are commonly so sensible of the cold, that restraint is not necessary to keep them below."[110] During instances of bad weather, "Water is carried down to them, and in that rough Weather Two or Three Chaffing Dishes, with Coals, are sent down into each Room, which corrects the Air."[111] These practices, along with burning fires and distributing flannel shirts to maintain heat in some ailing captives' bodies, conveyed a sense of concern if merely for the potentially lucrative value able to be gained off these foreign imports.[112] The fundamental nature of slavery at sea, however, did not set out to provide comfort for its victims, but instead to preserve the basic health of lodged slaves for future means of laboring profit.

The inability to predict natural disasters reduced sailors' control while exacerbating seaborne experiences many bondpeople fought to survive. On August 12, 1773, John Duncan, commander of the brigantine *Othello*, and Edward Fare, a mate aboard the vessel, submitted a public act in Middlesex, Virginia, detailing circumstances of unfavorable weather leading to the loss of several slaves. Bound for Charles Town, on May 24 they sailed from "Annamaboe on the coast of africa with Eighty three slaves." Three months into their passage, "there came on a violent gale of wind from the south west," which they declared "occasioned the ship to labour much" in traveling across the ocean. A second force of strong winds blew through the next day, which "sprung their foretopmast, split the mainsail and maintopsail" on the vessel. Much to their already growing alarm, another gale arose, causing them "to spring a leak" and forcing them to dock the ship in Virginia. Dangerous weather patterns caused significant ship damages, and they also "lost by sickness six slaves" lodged in the vessel's hold. Sources leave silent how these captives died, how their bodies were discovered after the sequence of storms, and, most of all, how the losses of shipmates affected the living. To shield themselves from legal ramifications connected with their shipboard losses, Duncan and Fare took an oath testifying that destruction on the ship's passage resulted from "the said hard gales of wind and bad weather."[113] This case and the two slave traders' immediate legal response make more vivid the unending challenges with manning vessels, maintaining business ventures, and protecting human cargoes that crewmen faced in struggling with the dangerous wind patterns, oceanic currents, and open environmental dangers inherent at sea. Sold and trapped within the wooden world of ships, the lines of power became enshrined through slaves' inability to protect themselves against their transporters and the hazards of the Atlantic crossing.

Conclusion

Sailors lined the western coast of Africa in pursuit of ideal slaves. The constant movement of bondpeople in and out of changing hands—inland capturers, coastal merchants, brokers, and different interested buyers—made slaves available across the Atlantic. Once slaves were boarded, the unhealthy conditions on ships played a significant role in their health, as toxicity became a relentless thread of power, deprivation, and social control. Seafarers sought to sustain captives' health through a diversity of preventive measures, yet a variety of factors, as previously revealed, made survival challenging, including diet, cleanliness, exercise, stowage, and weather amid the violent cycles of slavery at sea. Over time, an integral relationship of inadequate nutrition, trauma, violence, and contamination engendered slaves' susceptibility to illnesses and death. Meager diets, violent management, and oceanic isolation introduced slaves to the drastic meanings of bondage imposed upon them. Trapped within wooden confines and set adrift toward foreign locales, bondpeople navigated their seaborne surroundings devising innumerable ways not only to survive but also to physically resist and secure their permanent freedom.

4 Blood Memories

On December 23, 1773, the *Virginia Gazette* contained a letter extract from West Africa reporting the state of slave trading affairs at Fort James. Readers learned the fate of the snow *Britannia* as Captain Deane engaged in slave sales along the River Gambia. With negotiations complete and 230 captives stowed aboard, crewmen made preparations for the ship's departure, during which several slaves "got Possession of the Guns, &c, rose up and fought the white People for upwards of one Hour" in the vessel's hold. Amid the embroiling conflict, "many were killed on both Sides." Circulating stories reported, "Finding they were likely to be overpowered, the Blacks set Fire to the Magazine and blew up the Ship, whereby 300 Souls perished." One sailor escaped the revolt "by being on Shore"; however, severe casualties claimed the lives of others, as "most of the Officers were killed, among which were the two Doctors." Final reports indicated the captain "was wounded" during the outbreak, but he "soon recovered" from his injuries.[1]

Newspapers served a vital resource providing the literate world and oral culture of seaports in the eighteenth century a mere glimpse into the incalculable risks common with the traffic and production of African slaves. Imagery comprising the violent clash of bruised, bloodied, and dismembered bodies produced by and anchored within these editorials fueled fears of white sailors traveling into distant yet seemingly dangerous foreign African spaces. As the central backbone to wealth accrued through plantation labor, losses of slaves through shipboard insurrections represented incredible financial challenges to investors and awaiting planters reliant on the steady supply and import of a black labor force. Chaotic scenes of rebellion similar to the *Britannia* foregrounded the loss of heroic white seamen who, in dying at the hands of Africans, willingly placed their lives in jeopardy for the financial good of distant societies. Readers therefore never gained insight into the variation of black insurgents involved, the effect of captivity on their personal lives, nor the full intent of their resistive efforts.

As principal sources of new wealth, captives displaced on merchant vessels propelled a constellation of motives, desires, and expectations, entrapping them within a world of uncertainty. The highly toxic and tightly cramped spaces of cargo ships placed their basic means of survival in jeopardy, forging greater dependence and control on the part of their transporters. Capitalizing on these social realities, seamen extended the reliance on terror through their demands as they sought to enact an immediate and direct affect of fear and compliance among transported slaves. Delving deeper into the violent interiority of slavery at sea exposes the human costs and human damages that can never be counted and measured: the manifestations of psychological torment, spillage of blood, and multitude of deaths instigated between crewmen and captives. Ship revolts and the physical and psychological means that sailors used to manage disobedient slaves make up the most recognized modes of resistance and counterculture of resistance examined and largely expected within slaving voyages. Although fueled and constantly reinforced by one another, these slaving encounters were merely two manifestations of a much larger performance of terror widespread in the Middle Passage.

Building upon the violent history of human interface frequently common within the bowels of cargo ships, this chapter interrogates the calamitous interactions and, more concretely, the power that erupted as sailors forcibly transported bondpeople out of coastal West Africa into distant corners of the Atlantic. Always vulnerable to the possibility of a violent outbreak, whether docked on the coastal line or sailing within the open sea, the constant threat of warfare and bloodshed internal within slave ships made the Middle Passage akin to a war zone with "mobile battlefields."[2] Battle lines produced through these open bloody confrontations became inscribed amid revolts and the implementation of aggressively punitive measures used to discipline slaves. Crewmen may have served the economic needs of securing human goods for overseas imports, yet through their violent management these lines extended further onto the terrain of contained black bodies through sexual violence, poisoning, abortion, and the inability of enslaved mothers to protect their infant children from murder. Sailors' efforts to establish social order through rigidly terrorizing means proved necessary for the successful transport of demanded human goods and their own lives. Violence operated as a shared language through which bondpeople were routinely victimized, but one they repeatedly used against their transporters by disrupting the slaving process through the pursuit of freedom. Diverse tools were implemented to mold behaviors, quell fears, and manipulate many others; however, the body—regardless of race, gender, or age—became the vehicle, central site, and means through which power was affected and constantly reproduced aboard slave ships. Therein, the regularity of violence in the Middle Passage, as this chapter uncovers, served as the most tangible expression in the making and unmaking of slaves.

Dangerous Whispers

Editorials chronicling the state of overseas trade were a common feature of eighteenth-century newspapers. As competing slave trading nations became better familiarized with entrepreneurial pursuits within western Africa, journalistic updates became one of the most valued aspects of oceanic endeavors. Stories highlighted social unrest within the trade, filling the pages of periodicals in many places, including London, Liverpool, Bristol, Jamaica, Barbados, New England, and throughout the Southern colonies. Recounting the constant movement of employed ships, these news sources centralized the various individuals active within and connected to orchestrating the movement and sale of people as goods. Although concentrated on and largely shaping literate populations, these narratives held a similarly critical function among other populations of people across much of the Atlantic.

A diversity of readers scoured headlines to gain closer insight into slave trading affairs. Separated from husbands, brothers, fathers, and sons for months and sometimes years at a time, families of traveling crewmen anxiously read these reports with great interest. Letters penned at sea provided some level of comfort to those awaiting sailors' safe return; however, weekly papers proved far more useful through consistent reporting of ships' departures and arrivals. Merchants, much like sailors' families, were equally vested in receiving voyage updates given their integral necessity in operationalizing distant business ventures. Owing to the unpredictable nature of shipping, periodic lapses in communication forced entrepreneurs to rely on correspondences from fellow investors, brokers, and, most especially, newspapers in gaining information. The British paper *Country Journal* offered its readership regular updates of sailing vessels. On November 2, 1754, they reported, "The Admiral Blake, Talbot, from the Bite with 225 slaves, the Alice and Robert, Jackson from the windward coast, with 225; the Spencer, Roberts, from ditto, with 209, and the Bridget, Hastings, from ditto, with 180 are arrived at Barbados."[3] Similar entries proved viable for financiers, colonial factors, and planters looking to maintain and further fuel trade through the purchase of imported slaves.

Readers also routinely learned of the deadly fate that befell some sailors. In April 1731, on the American side of the Atlantic, the *Boston Weekly Newsletter* reported startling news to its audience: "We hear from Rhode Island, that Capt. George Scot of that place, who some time since went from thence to Guinea, and was returning with a Cargo of Negros," faced perilous circumstances in the ship's oceanic crossing. During the voyage an undisclosed number of captives "rose upon the said Commander & Company, and barbarously murder'd three of his Men" employed on the ship. "The said Captain and the rest of his company made their escape, tho' tis said they are all since dead" due to wounds incurred during the uprising. In closing, the newspaper article intimated, "The Negro's we are inform'd were afterwards taken and made Slaves of by those of another Nation."[4] Such graphic iterations impressed ideals of violent African societies, creating even greater racial justification for the necessity of the slave trade.

Reports of revolts activated by slaves frequently dominated trade news. Sailors were responsible for transporting a variety of valuable commodities, including different household items, cloth, and other luxuries desired by consumers and merchants. As living and breathing goods offered on the commercial market, bondpeople, unlike inanimate material items, posed the greatest obstacle to the successful sail of different vessels. The *British Gazetteer* briefly reported on September 18, 1756, "The Fortune and two other vessels are cut off by the negroes in the Gambia river."[5] Close to a decade later the *Boston Evening Post* received news from Newport, Rhode Island, identifying "Capt. Hopkins in a Brig belonging to Providence arrived at Antigua from the Coast of Africa." Following his coastal departure, "the Slaves rose upon the people," creating a grim outcome for investors as "80 of them were kill'd wounded and forced overboard by the captain and crew before the rest could be bro't to submit."[6] Insurgency waged aboard ships reaffirmed the often dangerous sphere of violence central within circuits of trade while foregrounding the confluence of forces many seamen confronted in the pursuit of profit.[7]

Illiteracy was common among seaborne laborers, yet this did not prevent them from gaining access to vital information concerning worldly events, including those in coastal West Africa. Once immersed within the cycle of travel and trade, consistent interactions in and out of different ports for extended periods helped sailors to foster a greater sense of familiarity as they forged connections and friendships, and engaged in a collective exchange of stories emanating from different people, traders, and societies. Well aware of the dangerous environment indigenous to a livelihood based upon the sea, many mariners understood the duties and subsequent risks attached to employment in slave trading. Moving within and beyond the boundaries of the literate world granted exposure to current news while permitting them to actively contribute to these slaving realities by transmitting personal interactions and those overheard within foreign locales.[8] Inflammatory accounts of violence produced in various newspapers forged incredible influence among the reading public, shaping a perception of Africa and Africans as unruly. The influence such stories bore, specifically upon seafarers as they traveled to the West African shoreline to solicit business, is not always as easily discernible. Most significant amid the transmission of violently tumultuous stories, however, was the need it created for an aggressive posture with Africans, both traders and boarded slaves.[9] These journalistic narratives therefore not only perpetuated racialized perceptions held of purchased captives, but they also held bearing on the day-to-day violence relied upon in the Middle Passage.

Perhaps in line with these lingering sentiments of precaution, guns were used as a means of exerting terror and creating some semblance of protection aboard slave ships.[10] Sailors traveled in far lower numbers than the scores of captives lodged within a vessel's hold, yet managing their lives fostered abstract feelings of power and privacy in crafting strategies and solutions to constrain unpredictable black behaviors. Captain John Newton remained constantly fearful of the threat captives could instigate aboard his vessel, *Duke of Argyle*. To counter any unforeseen opportunities, on December 7, 1750, he logged, "This day fixed 4 swivel blunderbusses in the barricado, which with the 2 carriage guns" they intended to "make a formidable appearance upon the main deck" by professing various types of arms. Preparing themselves for an outbreak, some crew members hoped this tactical motive would "be sufficient to intimidate the slaves from any thoughts of insurrection" arising within the vessel.[11] Ever mindful of the looming risk of death, the display of an array of artillery both visually and psychologically reinforced a symbolism of unrestrained authority sailors sought to invoke over their black cargo. Other ship commanders employed similar manipulative strategies; however, the nature of slave trade sources buries the long-term effectiveness of these strategies in successfully deterring such threats.

Alongside weaponry, upon boarding slaves, sailors immediately moved them into designated holdings confining them throughout much of the journey. Physical separation and the movement of captives into differing spaces varied according to commanders' preferences and a ship's size. As custodians within the human manufacturing process, their primary duty rested on employing precautionary measures to reduce any immediate prospects for future rebellion. Prevailing fears of unrest took on explicitly gendered overtones, routinely centering black men as the primary targets of uprisings, forcing them into the bottom holds of ships separate from the stowage of females and children. Dispersal throughout the ship and enforcement into these exclusive spaces marked the culmination of slavery, imposing black inferiority and making it more amenable for crewmen to control slaves' movements through constant surveillance. Spatial relocation as such therefore served as yet another weapon of power seafarers used to carry out their seaborne duties of protecting against internal dangers and transporting demanded human and material goods.

Ideas of violence—whether manufactured or actualized—could sufficiently prepare sailors for their confined interaction with bondpeople. Moving slaves into separate spaces often came with asserting control for even the slightest infraction. Seaman Henry Ellison explained that a ship commander referred to as Mr. Wilson ordered "eight or ten" captives up from the bottom holding "for making a little noise in the rooms at night." Once on the top deck, he directed several mariners to "tie them up to the booms, flog them very severely with a wire cat, and afterwards clap the thumb-screws upon them, and leave them in that situation till morning." The violence inflicted gave way to scars and severe pain upon the bondmen's bodies. Still historically unclear are the noises or how loud or even subtle the captives may have been in the bottom hold of the ship, yet this method of depersonalizing bondpeople and turning them into passive objects was far from uncommon. Ellison recalled, "I have seen the ends of their thumbs mortify from having been thumb-screwed so violently," which his experiences found often forced "them into fevers, and they have died."[12] For slave ship sailors the primary responsibility involved not only preserving live bodies but also maintaining complete control over all lodged slaves.

The enforcement of ship security was based in many ways on the belief of hyperaggressive bondpeople. Race, gender, and, most especially, a bondperson's physical stature increased the permanence of these concerns. Where and how these racialized fears of people of African descent originally emerged remains untold. Even more than the mass congregation of all slaves, crewmen were most fearful of adult black men. The presence of another group of males created a heightened sense of paranoia reflective of masculine notions of aggression, the reason being as one scholar reminds, "Black men, as men, constituted a potential challenge to the established order."[13] While securing sales and boarding captives, a captain underscored these concerns, evidenced by his recording, "Having now 12 men slaves on board began this day with chains and sentrys."[14] Taking into account the social environment of ships in the open arena of the Atlantic Ocean, sailors were never able to maintain distance from captives, fueling even deeper anxieties that caused them to travel in constant fear.

Angst surrounding the boarding of slaves transformed into domination for some commanders while others merely upheld racialized fears. Torment became an expression of power and personal amusement routinely used against lodged captives. Surgeon Thomas Trotter explained that while working aboard a docked ship, the commander "went on board to pay his respects" to the master of the Liverpool vessel *Myrtle*. After considerable time he returned "in the evening somewhat intoxicated." Boarding the ship in a drunken state, "he began to find fault with the officers," prompting him to grab hold of "a rope's end and beat several of the white people that were on the quarter deck" manning the vessel. Taking his erratic behaviors further, he ordered "the boatswain to knock a stout fellow, a Negro, out of irons." Several sailors brought a selected bondman into the fold and directed him "to stand on one side of the rope whilst" the captain "stood on the other, and put his foot to the black man's foot." According to Trotter, the shipmaster "then squared as if to box the man, saying, 'That he would learn him how to fight.'"

During the standoff, the inebriated captain taunted the designated slave. He "signified to the black fellow to make a blow at him" with his hands. Despite any enacted gestures, "the black fellow did not know how to do it" and stood in his place unmoved. Whether the captain used verbal and physical assaults to encourage the slave's participation is unknown. Affected by the prevailing circumstances, the bondman "gave the captain a terrible blow" upon his body. Consequentially, "the captain turned about, and went down into the cabin, brought up a horsewhip and beat him," as Trotter described, "most unmercifully." To enforce greater punishment against the captive for obliging the forcible request, the commander commenced "turning it and twisting the lash about his hand, with a full sweep with the butt end." His violent mistreatment continued until the bondman "evacuated both urine and excrement," reducing the captive's strength "insomuch that most of the ship's company thought he could not survive it."[15]

The slave trade was a hazardous enterprise within which sailors, slaves, and surgeons were contained. As custodians of goods—human and material—mariners and ship commanders were expected to manage and preserve order. These expectations often came at a great risk of violence, regardless of status, to assert unlimited power. Faced with constant mistreatment within a seafaring life, sailors were never protected from aggression, although, as historian Emma Christopher contends, yet and still their whiteness shielded them from the clutch of bondage.[16] With racial and cultural markers of inferiority cast particularly upon bondpeople, they suffered the cumulative blows—both physical and psychological—of captivity. Merchants etched particular orders; however, slaving voyages were predicated upon the secreted and isolated world that ship commanders constructed and ruled by directly affecting the lives, interactions, and tensions at sea. Amid that world, variations of management played out as the wooden decks of slave ships became the spatial battlefield where captives and sailors positioned themselves in defense of their respective interests. For some seamen these battle lines extended even further—onto the bodies of enslaved women.

The Enigma of Sexual Conquest

Violent trepidations harbored about black men often became transplanted into the lives of enslaved females. Much like ethnic separations, seafarers sought to prevent gendered intermingling "to disable normal social relations among the human cargo."[17] Designated holdings that captives were forced into maintained their segregation. Despite the varied spatial arrangements, male and female slaves were never fully separated during the process of transport. Some vessels had a high barricade constructed "as strongly put together as wood and iron can make it," so that "the women cannot see the men, nor the men the women."[18] Crewmen sought to create an appropriate security balance, yet more than mere division, perceived threats that male captives allegedly posed were not always about sailors' safety but were used instead to implicitly promote an idea of disastrous consequences for boarded females. To be sure, one sea captain intimated that women were "carefully kept from the men," to which he added, "I mean from the black men."[19] Fundamentally these tactics prohibited cross-gendered alliances of insurgency. With fears of black masculinity widely pronounced across the Atlantic, crewmen projected these anxieties onto bondwomen, placating the need for protection against black males who from their racial estimation might violate or threaten to violate their female shipmates. Given the gendered vulnerabilities pervasive throughout the Middle Passage, how could enslaved females guard themselves against the sexual intrusion of their captors?

Stereotypical ideas concerning the sexual prowess of black men abounded; black females, viewed through a prism of promiscuity on both sides of the Atlantic, were held within a permanent cycle of sexual expectations. While stationed at Annamaboe Fort in 1764, slave trader and former surgeon Archibald Dalzel wrote to a friend regarding his shoreline observations. Detailing the acquisition of trade profits, he confessed, "Still there is something a wanting to compleat my wishes which is not to be had here. I have been able as yet . . . to abstain from Amours with the black fair sex, tho' most of the Gentlemen here, have got wives."[20] Sexual arrangements with African women emerged from the constant influx of foreigners traveling into shoreline communities. "The usual custom was to discard such women at the end of a period of coastal residence, and indeed to change them quite frequently at other times."[21] For Dalzel, how long he withheld his own impulses belies the archive; however, his correspondence points to a much larger network of interracial liaisons within which black females were sexually central. The frequency of these "relationships" is difficult to discern, although the implications of these casual interactions reached much wider, putting the lives of even more global women—sailor's wives, lovers, and scores of black women within and beyond Africa—at great personal risk.

Moving across the Atlantic traveling from port to port, life on the waterways granted mariners access to highly sexual behaviors and opportunities. Familiarity and duration of time bore on their participation in an economy fueled by negotiations for and allocation of sexual services. No matter their personal

84 CHAPTER 4

interest, the dominance of brothels and establishment of personal businesses for the hiring of prostitutes—enslaved, free, white, and black—sailors were exposed to an intimate world created in port communities deeply entrenched in the buying and selling of sex.[22] Immersed in an industry of constant movement and demands, they lived a dual life where within their homes they strove to adhere to proper local manners and customs. Once employed as seafarers, they became different people driven by a different set of objectives, social rules, and entirely new identities anchored on notions of power and a greater sense of global promiscuous freedom unavailable within their families or local communities.

Engagement in the maritime world offered substantial contact with an assortment of women, including African females. In 1772 a Liverpool ship captain "obtained a girl as a mistress for the time being from king Tom of Sierra Leone." According to a nearby witness, "instead of returning her on shore when he went away, as is usually done," going against customary practices, "he took her away with him."[23] Details of the woman's fate are unknown; much more critical is the social phenomenon of loaning black females to white sailors for sexual purposes during the era of the slave trade. A relationship very well may have ensued between the ship commander and the loaned female. However, her removal stemmed from a range of reasons: she may have desired to leave the king; the captain may have requested her companionship during his coastal ventures; or in recognizing the lucrative value she generated within the current sexual enterprise, he may have stolen her, keeping the woman as part of the enslaved cargo for future exploit.[24] The existence of negotiations forged between African rulers and traveling sailors for the fulfillment of intimate needs by black women reinforces and further expands what legal scholar Adrienne Davis refers to as the "sexual economy of slavery," knowing how slave traders—across racial lines—used the transactional nature of sex to appease business relationships needed to purchase people for slaving purposes.[25] These coastal encounters extended a continuum of stereotypical assumptions held about black women's hypersexuality, thereby establishing the specter of sexual mistreatment routinely endured within slavery at sea.

The limited space of slave vessels exacerbated the double oppression many female captives confronted. Deborah Gray White argues that being both black and female, enslaved women were the most vulnerable group within antebellum slave communities.[26] Subjected to violating scrutiny, sold, and permanently made a part of the global enterprise of captivity, their lives were in a constant state of exploit and danger not merely within plantations but beginning on the African side of the Atlantic. "When the women and girls are taken on board a ship, naked, trembling, terrified . . . they are often exposed to the wanton rudeness of white savages." Thereafter, "the prey is divided upon the spot, and only reserved till opportunity offers."[27] Far from public view and legal interference, sexual taunting and physical humiliation that mariners enacted on slaving voyages created a hazardous environment within which all captives were sexually vulnerable, yet females were particularly unshielded. Crew members commonly referred to the women's quarters on one ship as "the whore hole."[28] With their bodies routinely sexualized throughout the trade, this labeling both literally and figuratively symbolized the function that bondwomen served in the minds of their transporters. Looking beyond language barriers, consistent use of such descriptors vocalized the sexual roles expected of boarded females while actualizing—through continued mistreatment—a consciousness of powerlessness and defeat that sailors sought to evoke over black females.

Occasionally crewmen distributed material items in hopes of enforcing bondwomen's obedience. "The women & girls divert themselves" on some ships by "amus[ing] themselves with arranging fanciful ornaments for their persons with beads," which, according to one slave trader, "they are plentifully supplied with."[29] The cultural origin of beads used aboard slave vessels varied between Europe and Africa. While the use of them allowed captives to reclaim a small measure of normalcy and cultural familiarity through bodily adornment and creative expression, these gestures of momentary kindness were enshrouded many times with sexual intentions. In one instance several seamen held a purchased female "prey of the ship's officers," explaining she would be "in danger of being flogged to death if she resisted." Acquiescing to the sailor's demands entitled her to "a handful of beads or a sailor's kerchief to tie around her waist."[30] Stripped of their personal possessions and any control over their immediate and future lives, crewmen anticipated receipt of such tokens temporarily distracted slaves from the hardships of their captivity. Much more significant is how the allocation of these objects played upon gendered ideas of female docility and the perceived ease of manipulation through sex and materialism. The most pressing danger anchored beneath these gifts was the sexualized symbolism reinforced through display on a captive's body—their hair, ear, or waist—thereby translating an impression of total possession by one or some crewmen with the intention of deterring any other interested parties.

Along with different trinkets, specialized roles were similarly used to maintain black women's allegiance to their captors. Ties of loyalty were presumed much easier to forge among females, demonstrated through the assertion that "the happy discovery and prevention of conspiracies that would have destroyed all their oppressors by the hands of their slaves, hath been owing to the faithful attachment of these negro women."[31] Advocating belief of a contradictory and rather vindictive role some bondwomen willingly upheld against their enslaved cohorts, these understandings reinforced what historian Ken Marshall explains as "the chauvinistic belief that the physically weaker females represented little if any real threat to the armed crew's safety."[32] Sailor Henry Ellison offered a description of the use of a bondwoman aboard the vessel *Nightingale* "whom we called the boatswain of the rest" of the lodged slaves "to keep them quiet when in the rooms, and when they were on deck likewise." Although useful to the ship crew in her leadership abilities, the woman's duties were short lived when "one day [she] disobliged the second mate," and as a result "he gave her a cut or two with a cat he had in his hand." Angered by the mistreatment, "she flew at him with great rage, but he pushed her away from him" and "struck her three or four times with the cat very smartly." The reasons for the violent interaction are unrecounted, yet recognizing "she could not have her revenge of him, she sprung two or three feet on deck, and dropped down dead. She was thrown overboard in about half an hour after, and tore to pieces by the sharks."[33] Whether the woman's death was accidental or perhaps intentional, her entrusted task, albeit temporary, did not shield her from the enforcement of punishment nor violent oceanic disposal. Displaying behaviors counter to crewmen's expectations, such shipboard experiences reiterate the limits of these "special" roles where as slaves they remained deeply trapped within the established boundaries of racialized power.

Nowhere was the desire for sexual conquest more apparent than through rape. A 1753 ship log detailed that while employed aboard the vessel *African,* sailor William Cooney felt liberated to violate a captive referred to as "number 83," described as "big with child." Taking considerable interest in the female, he forced her "into the room and lay with her brute like in view of the whole quarter deck."[34] The ship captain put him "in irons"; however, silent in surviving sources is if Cooney faced additional punishment for this misconduct. Unashamed in the violation of this bondwoman's body, his actions reveal that even pregnant females were not free from the aggressively blatant sense of sexual entitlement some mariners acted out.[35] The means through which he attacked the woman and her unborn child reinforce the open nature of these slave trade practices while likewise pointing to the possibility that impregnated females may have been targeted because of the lack of repercussions with insemination. No matter a captive's gender or physical state, as human chattel they were never free from the lash of violence—sexual or otherwise.

Regardless of age, females were regularly exposed to violence as seafarers sought to hold complete dominance over their personal lives. Deemed docile and thereby voiceless, black women had few if any methods to escape sexual violation. Instead, crewmen were "permitted to indulge their passions among them at pleasure" throughout the passage.[36] In one report a ship captain "mistreated a very pretty Negress, broke two of her teeth, and put her in such a state of languish that she could only be sold for a very low price at Saint Domingue, where she died two weeks later." Still unsatisfied, he "pushed his brutality to the point of violating a little girl of eight to ten years, whose mouth he closed to prevent her from screaming. This he did on three nights and put her in a deathly state."[37] Far from simply isolated encounters, females, both young and old, were frequent targets of molestation, during which sailors imprinted legacies of physical and psychological pain in and on their flesh. According to one belief, "Those of Africa," particularly the women, "have the superiority over those of Europe, in the real passions they have for the men who purchase them."[38] This remark, although suggestive of inherent powers black women forged over their captors, held damaging implications given the rationalization it provided for the continued practice of sexual aggression. With brute force a staple feature of slavery at sea, bondpeople, especially females, traveled the Atlantic, as Darlene Clark Hine aptly describes, as "sexual hostages" often to more than one crew member.[39]

For many seafarers, raping black women provided temporary and more personalized claims of power over females' bodies. Slave ship sailors were rarely held accountable for the resulting implications—pregnancy, venereal diseases, physical battery, or psychological torment—enacted through such violent encounters.[40] The mobility of their lives and work as well as their whiteness shielded them from any legal or financial backlash. Degrees of autonomy indigenous to seafaring labor equally permitted crewmen the freedom to sail home without consequence or to take employed advantage of other opportunities to travel back to Africa within the same ship or on a different voyage. Continued engagement within the trade allowed patterns of reckless sexual behaviors among sailors to persist without the threat of political, economic, legal, or social liability. At the same time, for crewmen already accustomed to openly sexual liaisons authorized on different sides of the Atlantic, managing human cargoes not only granted unparalleled access but also fostered opportunities for sex without the requirement of compensation.

Interracial sexual encounters during slavery were based entirely on relations of unequal power. Surgeon Alexander Falconbridge explained that on slave vessels he formerly serviced, "the common sailors are allowed to have intercourse with such of the black women whose consent they can procure."[41] Enslaved, sold, and displaced into a traffic driven by financial orders directing their lives, bodies, and future labor, slaves' consent or refusal held no bearing on the decisions or behaviors of their transporters. We may never come to fully know what consent looked like to females trapped within an isolated world where violence and the threat of sexual assault featured prominently in their daily lives. What is clear is that once boarded, all captives were "deprived of the right to keep their bodies private."[42] Visible and fully exposed with their naked bodies, continued interaction fueled certain conventions and curiosities that sailors acted upon by using sex as a tool of demanded obedience and a means of reinforcing complete power. These realities underscore the implicit dual "rite" in place aboard slave ships where, often deprived of sex for long periods of time out at sea, white seamen perceived the bonded status of black females and employed access as a "right" to violate their bodies. The circumstances of slavery prompted some women to use sexual relationships with their captors for personal gain; however, the rape of female captives within the Middle Passage became akin to a violent "rite of passage."[43] As such, the range of introductions created within the space of the Atlantic Ocean—including the cycle of varied sexual partners, sexual abuse, and the bodily and psychological suffering many bondpeople endured, bore witness to, and fought to survive—fell within a continuum of pain, trauma, and exploit that magnified within the landscape of New World plantations.

During times of warfare, sexually aggressive motives are often seen as by-products of war. Elaine Scarry offers a salient point: "The language of 'by-product' denotes 'accidental,' 'unwanted,' 'unsought,' 'unanticipated,' and 'useless.'"[44] Oceanic transport of bondpeople through the Middle Passage represented the epicenter of incredibly intense physical and psychological battles. Sailors manned vessels deeply insecure about the possibility of insurrections; however, the black female body became the intentional locus of pain and violent aggression, where instead of guns and knives, mariners used their hands, strength, genitals, and thus their entire bodies to enforce fear and compliance. Bondwomen and girls therefore may have been temporarily liberated from the weighted hold of shackles and irons, but they traveled the Atlantic under extreme duress knowing the constant threat of sexual terror to their bodies and personal lives, as evidenced through a ship log stating, "This morning found our women Slave apartments had been opened before by some of the ship's crew, the locks being spoiled and sundered."[45] These dangerous conditions, common across many vessels, produced an environment in which captive females were tormented by seamen's invasion of their quarters and their bodies without prior warning or the possibility of external concern or protection.

Serving as middlemen in supplying imported slaves, sailors exerted immense power through the violation of female captives that extended well beyond the confine of ships. The nature of slave trade sources and a lack of personal testimonies from captives and seafarers create enormous gaps within the history of bondage never to be recovered, permanently burying the full dimensions of rape within the world of slavery at sea. Merchants etched correspondences detailing expectations of shipboard unity and careful handling of transported captives, yet left unto themselves amid an isolating sea culture, slave ship sailors created societies governed by their own constructed rules and evolving laws of order. To be sure, building upon fraternal ties of loyalty in protecting their own reputation, it would not seem unusual for some slaving captains to with-

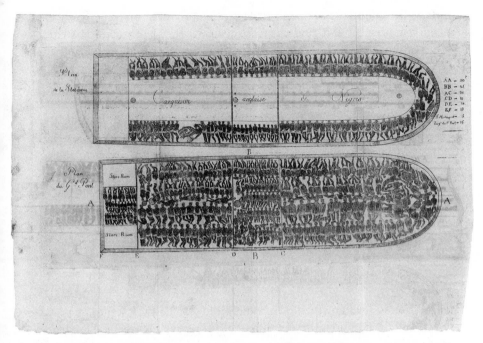

"Diagram of a Slave Ship." If you look closely, you will see a woman giving birth below the word "Cargaison" in the diagram. Résumé du témoignage donné devant un comité de la chamber des communes de la Grande Bretange et de l'Irlande, touchant la traite des négres, Geneva, 1814. Courtesy of the John Carter Brown Library at Brown University.

hold instances of damages—physical, sexual, or deadly—committed against lodged captives, knowing that if uncovered, reports of such behavior could convey a commander's inability to maintain order, manage risks, and thus fulfill their employed duties. Looking outside these archival silences, it is both the invisibility of wounds inflicted on bonded females and the clandestine world of shipping and trade that enabled mariners to act out tormenting possessive interactions without discovery or enforced legal means of accountability. The range, regularity, and personal affect these sexual attacks created in the lives of those enslaved goes unrecorded. Despite the rarity of documented cases available to contemporary scholars, these intrusive seaborne behaviors extended the cycle of power through the sexual exploitation that bondpeople were forced to bear and ultimately survive.

Anchored prominently at the core of these hostile motives was the assertion of racialized and gendered power. In reflecting on his oceanic captivity, Quobna Ottobah Cugoano shared, "It was common for the dirty filthy sailors to take the African women and lie upon their bodies."[46] These scenarios of sexual trauma are far more important not merely for the immediate traumatic experience but instead the long-term cumulative effects they produced off ship. It is rather limiting in perspective to presume these women ever became accustomed to assaults of any kind. While "rape asserted white dominance," repeated violations laid bare feelings of psychological grief, shock, extreme isolation, and perhaps even a healthy distrust of men that in turn made difficult any future sexual relationships bonded females engaged in or were consequentially forced into within plantations.[47] Therein, whether their partners were white or black, their previous maritime captivity inflicted far-reaching and rather permanent scars of fear, anxiety, anger, vulnerability, and altered views of their captive bodies.[48] Knowing the prevalence of forced coupling, breeding, and sadomasochistic practices pervasive throughout the Atlantic plantation complex across centuries, rape in the Middle Passage established the formative precursor of sexual expectations that sailors not only set into motion but brokers, auctioneers, and slaveholders further manipulated through market sales.[49]

The Violent Limits of Black Motherhood

In addition to shielding their own bodies from sexual terror, some female captives faced the additional responsibility of protecting their babies. Pregnancy among many West African women traditionally served as a rite of passage.[50] Taking great pride in motherhood, feelings of joy and accomplishment often permeated the birth of their newborns. As the maternal link continued to strengthen, "the African mother became the watchdog for her children."[51] The explosion of wealth and opportunities predicated on the traffic and sale of black people fostered an environment jeopardizing not only to one's personal safety but also in maintaining any control over the fate of loved ones.

Separations of African families persisted throughout the trade, undermining the essence of human and emotional connections. Although buyers were typically insensitive to familial connections among offered slaves on the African side of the Atlantic, on some occasions they made exceptions for "sucking children, who went with their mothers."[52] Children, particularly infants, held far lower representation aboard slave ships than adults; however, some sailors permitted the purchase of women and newborns rather than splitting them into preselected preferences. In many instances black females entered captivity alone, yet given the predominance of rape and coerced sexual couplings both on and off ship, resulting pregnancies created an increase of infants on slavers. Attesting to this reality, one slave ship surgeon explained that he bore witness to "four or five born on board" on a vessel he formerly worked.[53] Another physician echoed a similar prevalence of pregnancies within slaving voyages, intimating, "Out of four or five deliveries on shipboard two of the women had twins."[54]

Sailors considered the benefit of keeping bondwomen and their infants together; however, biased ideals scrutinizing black women and their skills of mothering circulated during the era of the slave trade. In one participant's estimation African females did not possess feelings for their children, because, as he asserted, "if they had, they would not treat them in the manner they do." Going further, he pointed out that given the absences of any nurturing capabilities, "a Black woman would think very little of pouring a spoonful of brandy into a child's mouth of two or three months old, at the breast." Whether cultural differences played a role or not, he reasoned that these maternal deficiencies originated from practices of polygamy widespread throughout Africa.[55] Biased conclusions about the parental abilities of African women were far from uncommon. Writing in 1763 concerning his coastal interactions among the Fante people, surgeon Archibald Dalzel explained how normal it seemed to see "a Boy of 5 years of age, smoke a pipe" or to witness "a Child in its mothers arms, drink a Dram."[56] His observations highlight prevailing local patterns while reinforcing that in lacking fundamental understandings of child care, black females acted out a sense of indifference to any life-threatening behaviors in which their children might engage.

While preconceived ideas held about black women as ill-equipped mothers prevailed, once these women were exiled within slavery at sea, the emotional behaviors they displayed in concern for their offspring countered many of these stereotypes. Some scholars contend that slavery did not permit bondwomen much room to express compassion regarding their children for fear of a perception of weakness.[57] Knowing the immediate and permanent displacement of captives into different ships bound for distant locales through the slave trade, bonded females continually expressed care for their children and the ability to stay with them. For this reason, slave trader James Towne pointed out, "It is a very rare matter for any captains of Guineaman that they ever buy women with children" due to the belief that when "their infants died, they grieved after them, and died themselves."[58] The nature of captivity and loss of control over their lives made protection and attempts to provide for their children extremely difficult for enslaved mothers. Slavery may have been unable to disrupt the emotional bond females forged with their newborns, yet death permanently severed the physical ties, creating greater potential for the emergence of psychological imbalances similar to symptoms of posttraumatic stress disorder and postpartum depression.

Under the violent tutelage of enslavement, female captives faced significant challenges in shielding their offspring from mistreatment. John Newton described an account involving a "mate of a ship in a long boat" who, during negotiations, "purchased a young woman, with a fine child, of about a year old, in her arms." Forced to stay ashore longer than anticipated to complete business, he stowed the bondwoman and her son with him on the "long boat." During the evening, "the child cried much and disturbed his sleep." The seaman immediately "rose up in great anger, and swore, that if the child did not cease making such a noise, he would presently silence it." Fearful of any harm that could ensue, the toddler's mother likely extended the only means of meager care bondage could permit in order to quiet the young boy. These efforts, however, went to no avail; her son continued to cry and the sailor "rose up a second time, tore the child from the mother, and threw [it] into the sea." Subjected to the callous realities of slavery anchored by a disregard for human suffering or personal loss, "it was not so easy to pacify the woman" as she continued to weep for her murdered child. Her cries posed a similar annoyance to the mariner; however, knowing "she was too valuable to be thrown overboard," he was "obliged to bear the sound of her lamentations, till he could put her on board his ship."[59]

Although largely unregulated, violence committed against enslaved children in front of their mothers represented a rare yet pronounced feature of the Middle Passage. In 1789 abolitionists Moses Brown and William Rotch Jr. exchanged correspondence regarding the state of international slave trading affairs as Rotch sought "to find what instances of barbarity could be substantiated" concerning a sailor who had "thrown a child overboard" off a New England slave ship.[60] During the passage a member of the crew "succeeded to the Command . . . by the death of the Cap'n & Mate." Using the new position to his advantage, according to Rotch, he "was so inhuman as to take a child by the feet whose crying afflicted him & repeatedly whipd it before its mother & once made an attempt to burn it by thrusting it into the Caboose."[61] With the transport of slaves focused exclusively on social order, all captives—including young children—were expected to oblige these demands, regardless of their maternal needs. Use of aggressive and deadly tactics against a distressed child demonstrated a blatant rejection of any notion of parental rights, forcing bondwomen to confront the extreme limits of motherhood.

While black women sought to protect their offspring as much as possible, the terror central to slavery at sea exposed personal inabilities further enshrining the powers of their captors. Former trade participant Isaac Parker told of a case involving a female captive purchased with her nine-month-old son by a man known as Captain Marshall. After transferring the pair aboard his vessel, the *Black Joke*, Marshall took particular interest in the bondwoman's son, due to the fact "the child took sulk, and would not eat." Despite exhibiting fits common to a young baby, the captain "took the child up in his hands" and flogged him with a cat-o'-nine-tails. Several bondpeople witnessed the child's beating, as "they saw it through a barricade, looking through the crevices," to which "they made a great murmuring, and did not seem to like it."

Punishment of the young boy temporarily altered Marshall's approach. Discovering "the child had swelled feet," he directed the ship's cook "to put on some water to heat to see if he could abate the swelling." Once the water boiled, he "ordered the child's feet to be put into the water, and the cook putting his finger in the water, said, 'Sir, it is too hot.'" Marshall responded, "'Damn it, never mind it, put the feet in,' and in so doing, the skin and nails came off" the baby's feet. Perhaps intending to appease the child's wounds, Marshall "got some sweet oil and cloths and wrapped round the [child's] feet in order to take the fire out of them." He offered him "rice mixed with palm oil," yet the young boy continued to refuse. Further enraged, Marshall "took the child up again, and flogged it, and said, 'Damn you, I will make you eat.'" The enforcement of darkened bruises and scars upon the baby's flesh continued for "four or five days at mess time, when the child would not eat" any offered foods. Enraged by his continued disobedience, Marshall one day "tied a log of mango, eighteen or twenty inches long, and about twelve or thirteen pound weight, to the child by a string round its neck." According to Parker, "The last time he took the child up and flogged it, and let it drop out of his hand, 'Damn you (says he) I will make you eat, or I will be the death of you;' and in three quarters of an hour after that the child died."

Instead of designating a member of the ship crew to dispose of the baby's lifeless body, Marshall "called the mother of the child to heave it overboard." Emotionally distraught by the death of her son, she "was not willing to do so," prompting an immediate flogging until she agreed to obey the commander's demands. Forced to bury her son in a makeshift watery grave beneath, "she took it in her hand, and went to the ship's side, holding her head on one side because she would not see the child go out of her hand, and she dropped the child overboard." Bearing witness to consecutive days of relentless aggression imposed upon her son with little or no recourse for prevention created a heavy psychological toll upon this bondwoman. Unable to provide a proper burial and violently forced instead to have to pick her son off the dampened floorboards, carry him, and ultimately throw his small yet battered corpse off ship and into the sea exacerbated the trauma, where afterward she "seemed very sorry, and cried for several hours."[62] Beyond the death of her son this woman grows dim within the written record, making it difficult to know if she physically survived the passage carrying the pain of profound loss into her enslaved life on land, or if the emotional wounds from her son's murder became too much for her to continue living.

Deaths of children during slavery are often attributed to the behaviors of bondwomen. Ideas of infanticide may have filtered through their minds during the passage, yet once placed at sea, preservation for enslaved mothers became less about themselves but instead the constant protection of their young children, unable to shield themselves from the brutalities of isolated captivity. Far more difficult in the transport and confine of newborns were not only challenges of proper care, but in many respects the unpredictability of needs they acted out through varied noises and childish behaviors. Sailors demanded and sought to enforce rigid rules of order and control over lodged slaves; however, unfamiliar with and thus unrestrained by adult expectations, children behaved in ways natural to their young understandings, even if it came at a cost to their lives. The limited social and financial value that younger captives were estimated to possess in the human manufacturing process proved equally detrimental to enslaved babies, marking them as expendable and thus permitting the free use of physical and even deadly battery. Once murdered, enslaved infants became sacrificial tokens, symbolically reinforcing the restrictive nature of captivity while physically and mentally reminding black women of the limits of their parental control. By revoking bondwomen's motherly duties to take matters into their own hands and manage seemingly disobedient children, seafarers forced females to confront hierarchies of gendered power within a masculine maritime world. This entrapment deepened the sense of alienation, laying bare extreme feelings of pain, suffering, and devastating losses most slaves were unable to prohibit.

Eruptions of Chaos

Tasked with transport and maintaining complete control over their human cargo, mariners traveled the Atlantic plagued with incredible uncertainty. Regulation of captives was a prominent fixture of slaving voyages, yet the direct and rather confrontational tactics that bondpeople drew upon extended fears of black hyperaggression, posing perhaps the greatest source of anxiety.[63] Traditional narratives foreground the role of black men engaged in physical battles, many times excluding black female captives. For this, David Richardson acknowledges, "the role of women in supporting and encouraging revolts has perhaps not been fully appreciated" within slave trade scholarship.[64] These insurgent practices, while expected at sea, found beginning expression across the Atlantic and were perpetuated by various shipboard actors.

Desires for freedom took on many different forms on slave vessels, yet insurrections created the most hostile environment. In 1776 a ship revolt broke out aboard the *Thames,* prompting the ship's physician, John Bell, to report, "The Voyage has been attended with nothing but losses & disappointments." Prior to the vessel's coastal departure, according to Bell, "36 of the best slaves we had" rose up against the crew "when there was only the Boatswain, Carpenter, and 3 White People & myself on board." Despite having "160 Slaves" lodged on board, directions were given to release an undisclosed number of captives "out of the Deck Chains in order to wash, [where] advantaged by this

They began by rising" for an almost hour-long battle. Immediate suppression revealed "34 Men & Men boys w't 2 women a rising," to which several seamen "fired 2 magnets amongst them" in hopes that firing bullets would quell their insubordinate behaviors.

The involvement of black males created concern, yet Bell emphasized a particular threat several females posed in the uprising. "Had the woman assisted them," he estimated, "in all probability your property here at this time would have been but small" given the likelihood of greater damage with a larger army. "Their having no time to consult about it," he reasoned, curtailed the involvement of more insurgents. Going further, Bell recollected, "They said themselves" while confined in isolation "they had 2 or 3 times before been going to attempt it." Although the women were perceived as a viable threat, Bell downplayed their possible desires for rising against the crew, saying, "The only reason we can give for their attempting any thing of the kind is, their being wearied at staying so long on board the ship" during the passage. Crammed and locked within deplorable conditions, their resistance was never solely about confinement but more the enforcement of bondage coupled with extreme vulnerability that they faced while in the hands of their buyers and tormentors. Unable to solicit intimate details connected to the origins of the outbreak, Bell explained, "Those left will give no reason for their riseing, but lay the blame entirely on those thats lost" from the ensuing rebellion.[65]

Bondwomen contemplated and actively participated in open resistance aboard slave ships, but motivating factors as well as any schematic plans they devised are not revealed in surviving records. Central to the incident on the *Thames* is not only the range of potential and actual participants crossing gendered lines but also the existence of a network and code of secrecy that, despite diverse language barriers, filtered among boarded captives. Equally paramount is the attribution of these defiantly rebellious threats to fatigue and anxiousness, thus denying the varied traumas inherent within forced captivity. Slave traders, regardless of their social status, may have tried to predict bondpeople's behaviors both on and off ship; however, being free and unaffected by the personal effects of enslavement, they were unable and unwilling to fully comprehend the reasons prompting these defiant behaviors. Therein, the mere threat of these women's violent alignment countered and directly challenged the prevailing gendered misconceptions of docility and obedience among black females.

Much like plantation owners, sailors were never "in control as fully as they would have liked."[66] In 1721 the slaver *Robert* disembarked from Sierra Leone with thirty purchased slaves. Amid the passage, five captives, including a female, planned to overthrow the crew. Unknown is how or at what point within the voyage they found means to strategize on their rebellious intentions. The unending quest for autonomy slaves acted out became an unspoken signal often difficult for mariners to detect although commonly embodied through violent expression. In serving as a spy, after determining the sailors were asleep, a bondwoman allegedly brought "a Hammer at the same time (all the Weapons that she could find) to execute the Treachery."[67] Knowing that females' quarters were in many cases stowed near the storage room, this enabled the woman to secure an array of arms for herself and her fellow insurgents. Traveling unbound by the physical restraints of shackles and irons in contrast to their male conspirators, some black women manipulated sailors' views of them as submissive and far less threatening, using it according to their own needs, even amid battle. Female captives, therefore, played much more vital roles in the implementation of slave ship rebellions, through which they affirmed their humanity, defied gendered stereotypes held about them, and took their fate out of their captors' hands and back into their own.

Although physically armed, by the time of the surprise attack only the woman and two of the men made up the band of insurgent captives on the *Robert*, making it easier for sailors to quickly thwart their rebellious efforts. Counter-resistance the ship's crewmen waged against the detected insurgents proved damaging not only against the attempted outbreak but also to its subsequent perpetrators. The ship captain, referred to as Harding, began by enforcing punishment against two bondmen actively involved, ordering several seamen to "whip and scarify them only." Three other captives accused of serving as "Abettors, but not Actors" were sentenced to death. Before their execution, to enforce greater dehumanization for their insubordinate actions, they were made to "first eat the Heart and Liver of one of them [sailors] killed." The sentence imposed upon the bondwoman was equally as unforgiving as that of her male counterparts. Employing the frequent use of public displays of brutality, she was "hoisted up by the Thumbs, whipp'd, [and] slashed . . . with Knives, before the other Slaves till she died."[68] Flogged, cut, and murdered in view of the entire ship, the triple punishment enacted on this woman's flesh served as a mechanism of reform and deterrence for others. The appearance of wounds and permanent scars on her body reinforced how "torture usually mimes the killing of people by inflicting pain, the sensory equivalent of death, substituting prolonged mock execution for execution."[69]

The bondwoman's conspiring role was unanticipated by the ship's sailors. On the African coastal line she professed economic value to buyers interested in the laboring capacities she could generate overseas. Stepping outside the boundaries of social control and social order by engaging in such a seditious act on ship, her value diminished in the eyes of her captors, and, as such, they mapped these frustrations onto her flesh through an even more severe punishment, using her as a sacrificial example for the entire ship. Bloody public exhibitions reserved for this woman and many others functioned as both warnings and celebrations.[70] Sailors' use of unrestrained violence against recalcitrant slaves operated as techniques to discipline future insurrectionists. While these ritualized punishments served to dismantle any perceived sentiment of African unity, they brought seamen together, creating a sense of strength, communal identity, and a symbolic notion of protection in hopes of dismantling any and all future ideas of black resistance.

Violent eruptions acted out by bondmen and bondwomen were far from uncommon on the oceanic highway of the Atlantic. In 1769, after sales were finalized and 425 slaves were boarded in hollowed corners of the Liverpool vessel *Unity,* the commander Richard Norris directed his crew to make preparations to expedite sail toward Jamaica. Prior to their departure, Norris reported, "The Slaves made an Insurrection," pointing out "[it] was soon quelled with y'e loss of two women." Archival records leave silent the number of people who rose in rebellion, the efforts used in their suppression, and any details intimating if these women participated in the fight for their freedom or if they were unfortunate casualties in the outbreak. With stories of black aggression crisscrossing the Atlantic and exposing audiences to the dangers sailors regularly confronted in the transport and management of slaves, Norris likely became familiar with these same maritime realities, preparing himself and his crew for a similar prospect of danger. Once personally compounded by the shoreline insurrection and loss of purchased captives aboard his own vessel, violence was no longer imaginary, forcing him to monitor more closely the remainder of an already troubling passage.

Much to his dismay, within days of the vessel's departure another revolt occurred. Details concerning the rebellious clash of bodies are unknown, yet what is clear is that a bondman referred to as "No. 1" perished. Instead of dying from physical battle, taking advantage of the chaotic circumstances at hand, he "jumped overboard & was drown'd" out at sea. Feeling powerless in combating the retaliatory behaviors capable of still embroiling among other captives, Norris and his crew "gave y'e women concerned 24 Lashes each" for their alleged roles. How many women did the crew reprimand for the uprising? Was the rebellion comprised solely of females? Did they orchestrate the rebellion, or were they perhaps accused while attempting to assist other insurrectionists? Marking their bodies through open means, they sought to intentionally quell the actions of any other undiscovered rebels; however, these measures seemed ineffective. Two days later the commander remarked, "The slaves this day proposed making an Insurrection" during the evening hours. While locked and stowed in the darkness of the vessel, several "[got] off their Handcuffs";

however, they reportedly "were detected in Time." With crewmen on constant guard, immediate suppression of the captives made all too clear the fears of violence any unchained slaves posed within the oceanic voyage.

Attuned to their every movement, sailors cautiously deployed maximum security against any resistive behaviors displayed on ship. With transporting an incredibly large number of slaves, surveillance became the tool relied upon to detect and help prohibit any outward signs of rebellion. On June 27 Norris chronicled, "The Slaves attempted to force up y'e Gratings in y'e Night," as he perceived, "with a design to murder y'e Whites and drown themselves" following a proposed plot. Faced with three plotted outbreaks, it is challenging to know if this was the original plan the captives outlined or perhaps racialized apprehensions Norris projected onto the insubordinate captives. Despite these unknowns, the slaves' efforts "were prev'ted by y'e watch" held in place to prevent another calamity. Charges of conspiracy were not dealt with until the next morning. Once confronted, several bondpeople "Confessed their Intentions, and that t'e women as well as the men were determn'd" that if they were unsuccessful in "Cutting off y'e whites," they would jump overboard. Language barriers made the extrapolation of details indecipherable; however, according to Norris, several captives expressed that they "resolved as their last resource to burn the Ship" in order to protect themselves against continued captivity. Enraged by their intended desires, Norris stated, "Their obstinacy put me under y'e Necissty of shooting y'e Ringleader." Far from conclusive, this tactic proved effectual in deterring other potential insurrectionists. Two weeks after the ordered death of the designated leader, "A Man No 3 [and] Woman N'o 4 . . . Died Mad." Norris recounted that in their final days aboard, the pair "had frequently attempted to drown themselves since their views were disappointed with y'e Insurrection." The next day following their deaths, much to Norris's satisfaction and that of the entire crew, on July 12 the *Unity* landed in Antigua and negotiations were made with local brokers to place the remaining lodged slaves for sale.[71]

Moving beyond lines of both gender and ethnicity, ship revolts encapsulated a collective language of resistance. Sailors continually sought to prevent "chaining those together who speak the same language."[72] Yet these divisive mechanisms often proved futile in thwarting collectivism among boarded captives. Forced to live altered lives as someone else's property, they formulated beginning ideals of a community grounded upon a shared struggle of oppression. Unfamiliar with their geographical locations far from land out at sea, bondpeople adapted to their forced surroundings, routinely drawing upon the terrain of ships to reclaim their own versions of power and freedom. Those held captive were many times, in one scholar's estimation, "unorganized, undisciplined, and united only in their insatiable desire for liberty."[73] Any behaviors slaves acted out that appeared abnormal cast them as deranged, prompting sailors to come together in constraining and penalizing any African instigators. Both groups boarded slave vessels as strangers; however, amid instances of violence they coalesced as temporary units to defend and protect their collective interests, albeit for means of profit or liberation.

Violence aboard slave ships created an expression understood primarily by its temporary inhabitants. "The voices of those who were its victims are rarely heard when one looks for evidence or explanations of shipboard slave revolts."[74] If resistance includes the nonverbal modes of communication carried out through illicit behavior, then the active voices and conversations of slaves' disdain can be interpreted through the incessant rumblings of rebellions widespread throughout the Middle Passage. Sacrificing their bodies and lives through violent eruptions, behavioral languages they acted out extended beyond racial lines, permitting seamen the ability to interpret the cultural meanings of insurrections. While some whites believed "civilized or not, Negroes . . . [were] cowards all their life-time and heroes for an instant," slave ship sailors sought to reconfigure bondpeople's freedom dreams by handling them through a language of counter-resistance.[75] Through this process, the bodies of captives, always under intense violation and scrutiny, became important sites of terrorizing power and pain.

The Art of Sedition

Ship revolts are typically associated as the primary route that slaves used to gain their freedom. These tenuous moments laid bare deep-seated fears, resentment, and a constant quest for control of the black body on the part of sailors and slaves. Physical combat was a tactic routinely activated that created a volatile environment throughout slaving voyages. Other insubordinate behaviors, similarly motivated by aggressive and rather deadly desires, also emerged in the transport phase of the human manufacturing process. Placing these alternate forms of enslaved insurgency—namely, poisoning and abortion—within a broader discourse of violence facilitates greater insight into the privately public means of resistance. Slaves conceived ideas of defiance in secrecy, yet the body became the terrain and public space where and how violence was performed. By viewing these shipboard interactions as simply psychological battles, scholars dismiss the violent intentions and outcomes that show even more how these motives sought to inflict maximum damage within a person's body.

Poisoning, although typically difficult to trace, represented a deeply covert strategy bondpeople used at sea. On June 16, 1751, John Newton, captain of the *Duke of Argyle,* recorded, "We were alarmed with a report that some of the Men Slaves had found means to poison the water in the scuttle casks upon deck." After attempting to investigate the attempted plot, Newton surmised, "they had only conveyed some of their Country fetishes, as they call them, or talismans," which in downplaying as harmless, he concluded, "they had the credulity to suppose must inevitably kill all who drank of it."[76] This conspiracy revealed the carryover of Africans' cultural knowledge of herbs, albeit for deadly repercussions. Newton's dismissal of their medicinal tools as mere "country fetishes" validates the "competing cultural meanings of poisoning" that historian John Savage contends continually existed between bondpeople and white populations.[77] While Newton's reflection dispels the importance of these insurgent efforts as non-life-threatening, for Africans, the philosophical beliefs they carried relative to the integral relationship of herbs, ritual, and the supernatural empowered them through their use of such methods.

This resistive technique ignited considerable panic across different plantation communities; however, these same fears circulated among slave ship sailors. An American seaman traveling in 1796 aboard the sloop *Dolphin* etched in his diary that an enslaved female and male were able to "fetch some poison" in order "to put into some rice that was on the fire" being prepared for the ship. The ingredients used for the duo's plot as well as details explaining how they circumvented the gender segregation required of purchased slaves is unknown. Particularly revealing within the incident is that, enraged by the captives' efforts, several sailors "whipt them severely."[78] Drawing upon herbal tools of resistance, both captives relied on premeditated and coercive measures, yet these intentions did not rest solely upon obtaining their liberation but also imposing health problems and even the death of their captors. The crew's response through physical violence points to the extreme terror that poisoning generated, largely because of the challenge of detecting these invisible toxins and moreover the personalized attack they felt on their own lives. Poisoning fostered a threatening environment that, while far-reaching on land, was perhaps even more potent within the tight confine of ships given the unpredictability of retaliatory behaviors.

Knowing that bondpeople boarded ships naked and stripped of all personal possessions, how these slaves gained access to their ulterior culinary needs and successfully implemented them remains a mystery. Sources leave muted how the captives found ways to hide roots, leaves, or spiritual totems within their bodies; if they used excrement from various vermin scattered about the ship to mix into available foods; or if perhaps these fears were merely racialized ideas sailors projected onto slaves due to their close proximity. Instead of targeting the complete overthrow of slavery, poisoning created an equal if not greater threat to the lives of sailors. To some scholars these methods represented "one of the most logical and lethal methods of resistance."[79] Difficulties persist in tracing the origins of this creative practice; however, use of poison underscores the vast knowledge base of botanical understandings some African captives carried to the New World.[80] Without detection, poisoning could appear as a natural cause of death, signaling the very real possibility that other occurrences of herbal interference lie buried and thereby silenced within slave trade documents. "Slaves struck frequently at the opposing white world" in ways difficult to recognize by sight or taste.[81] Malicious intentions were anchored throughout captives' plots to cause injury, illness, and even death among their transporters; most central to these motives, however, was not getting caught.

Largely outnumbered, mariners governed slaves with confinement, physical intimidation, and constant degradation. These measures fostered feelings of personal authority, yet their control was more symbolic and never without anxieties. To be sure, stories of black rebellion circulating on the Atlantic prompted the implementation of tactical security measures to protect against uprisings. Poisoning created a sense of instability particularly instructive to sailors in that they could never precisely dictate slaves' behaviors and, moreover, there really was no way of defending themselves against such invisible battles. Seamen anticipated and in many ways relied upon slaves' use of physical arms—knives, guns, and cutlasses—yet the cultural intellect some bondpeople possessed with manipulating herbs became an even greater impediment to the livelihood and personal safety of seafarers. For this, one scholar underscores "the impact the use of poison had" on the psyche, "at times producing collective panic and hysteria among the white populations."[82] Equally paramount is the vulnerability slaves were able to exploit through contamination of common sources of white exposure—food and drink—giving greater validity to how even the mere threat of poisoning triggered a constant source of unrest.

These tactics fostered fearful uncertainties, yet they communicated a level of violence fueling a greater sense of isolation, being unable to predict or protect oneself. Contrary to bloodshed, bruised limbs, and scars etched across the body amid physical battles, the secretive use of herbs became a weapon capable of producing wounds that, although unseen, could prove significantly damaging to the interior human cavity. The range of herbal cocktails bondpeople used as tools for murder within slaving voyages is by no means clear to contemporary audiences. Knowing the irreparable damage that administered toxins could inflict on a victim with regard to nausea, headaches, skin discoloration, violent episodes of vomiting, seizures, difficulty of breathing, and even heart attacks, reinforces that while the outplay of poisoning may be difficult to ascertain, the long-term implications are evidently clear. Sailors' fears were therefore well warranted owing not only to the lurking danger to a person's health and the prospect of death but, most of all, the lack of physical confrontation or violent use of hands.

Much like poisoning, gynecological resistance represented yet another method of subversive insurgency equally difficult for sailors to guard against.[83] Commonly recognized as a plantation phenomenon and rare within many slave ship records, some black women asserted reproductive control over their offspring through abortion. In April 1793, after finalizing sales, the ship *Sane* set sail. Several weeks into the passage, psychologically affected by the circumstances of bondage, a pregnant female chose to take the life of her unborn child through abortive means; however, complications arose from her efforts and on April 18 she died.[84] "Pregnancy left women vulnerable to various illnesses, disability, and death," which, combined with a lack of proper nutrition and prenatal care, could have collectively played a role in this woman's decline.[85] A similar encounter took place three years later aboard the ship *Mary* as another bonded female willingly used her body as a site of resistance by prematurely terminating a fetus growing within her womb. The dangerous and rather drastic measures this woman employed put her health at risk, and she died two months later.[86]

Inclusion of these pregnant slaves and the deaths they suffered as a result of their defiant actions leaves open several questions: Did both women enter the trade impregnated? Or were their children perhaps conceived during their coastal confinement? How far along were they in their pregnancies? What methods did any attending surgeon or crewmen use to determine abortion as the principal cause of their death? The reasons for aborting a child during slavery are diverse and far more complex than surviving sources can reveal. Behaviors these women displayed blatantly demonstrated their unwillingness to permit their unborn children to bear the pain of captivity while reinforcing that some females boldly engaged in reproductive politics against their enslavers, even at the risk of their own mortality. With their menses ended and their bodies changing as they felt a life beginning to grow, these females were compounded by intensely personal decisions extending far beyond the control of sailors. Reclaiming agency and full control over their bodies, untold is whether any of these women intentionally sought to sever their own ties to captivity through death. Their sufferings are unknown, but their actions make intimately vivid how they sought to permanently ensure that their children never bore witness to nor endured the traumas of bondage.

African women were well known for possessing herbal knowledge and serving in various roles of spirituality on different sides of the Atlantic. This realm of expertise granted some females familiarity with terminating unwanted pregnancies and even assisting other bondwomen with similar motives, although it remains incredibly challenging to uncover how they acted this out within the isolated confine of ships.[87] With the prevalence of sexual abuse of black females at sea, upon impregnation some women may have responded by attempting to destroy the offspring and thus the tangible reminder of sexual terror directly linked to their aggressors. Darlene Clark Hine astutely explains, "Slave children were sometimes pawns in a power struggle between plantation owners and their slaves."[88] In much the same way, females exiled aboard slave ships used the forcible deaths of their unborn children to prove to their tormentors the powers they also possessed and could wield most times without interference, further revealing that "the political lives of dead bodies," which on slave ships similarly included black boys and girls within the womb whose lives were terminated by mothers unwilling to bring them into a life of bondage.[89]

Crewmen remained focused on preventing the outbreak of revolts while bondwomen demonstrated how their personal bodies became unforeseeable weapons. Tasked with the movement and preservation of large numbers of slaves, sailors fully understood "there was no limit to the range of items aboard an oceangoing ship that could become weapons."[90] Viewed as far less threatening than their male counterparts, black females were rarely factored into these insurgent anxieties, most especially outside of insurrections. Abortions, however, produced a nuanced posture of gendered and equally violent realities sailors were forced to manage. The act of taking the life of one's child not only challenged the nature of power between sailors and slaves, but it ruptured the fixed social order sailors enforced and continually demanded at sea. Damaging defiance that black females ignited through aborting a fetus operated beyond the boundaries of social control that seafarers routinely inscribed on the lives of lodged slaves. Regardless of any punishment imposed, discovery of a child's murder and resulting corpse—whether within or external to a black female's body—conveyed a much larger message of crewmen's mismanagement and a lack of control.

Fully attuned to their value as laboring bodies within the web of slave sales, by injuring parts of their flesh through abortion, black females took control and greatly impacted the very reproductive capabilities that sailors scrutinized, bought, and transported them for overseas import. Whether they somehow ingested an herbal remedy or creatively gained access to a piece of wood or rusted tool on board and firmly forced it into their bodies, both means exacted violence upon themselves and their babies, causing them to expel large amounts of blood, weaken, and die. The bodies of bondwomen thus served as critically active sites of power, while their wombs became tombs wherein their children were buried. To their captors these defiant mothers ruined lives and destroyed valuable property. Feeling consigned to a life of constant degradation and exploit, these women asserted power through the only means available—their bodies and unborn children. Looking outside the moment, their abortive actions and, consequentially, their own deaths had a direct and palpable impact for the future that invariably became interlinked.

Given the regular loss of shipmates out at sea, death seemed the most effective and only logical solution for bondwomen in reflecting on the fate of their unborn children. With their futures uncertain and their lives drastically reshaped through bondage, prevailing circumstances made it difficult to see themselves as mothers able to provide the care, nurturing, and protection necessary for their children. "Slave mothers had a duty to preserve life"; however, as evidenced, these duties ceased within the physical realm, extending much further as their abortive actions prevented the spirit of their children from taking a human existence.[91] Slaving voyages were fraught with fatalities, yet bearing personal responsibility to the murder of one's child and subsequent separation created profound stress and suffering for these women. The violence inflicted upon their growing fetus, no matter the means, engendered immense psychological scarring these captives endured as they harbored the burden of grief and loss amid entrapment in bondage. Carrying unseen wounds proved challenging for crewmen or buyers to detect and, most especially, to manage the aftermath of sorrows capable of manifesting through a mother's physical decline or suicidal attempts at sea or on land.

Conclusion

The slave trade relied upon the unmitigated use of violence in obtaining human commodities, yet this took on a rather unique tone once contained within the social space of slave ships and the Atlantic Ocean. Disasters, both physical and environmental, regularly affected marine life as well as the preservation and transport of bonded Africans.[92] Sailors imposed stringent measures, domination, and sometimes revenge, whereas slaves conveyed their dissatisfaction with captivity by attempting to reclaim ownership of their personal lives through violence, all of which reveals the openly contentious struggle exerted for control of the black body. Far from mere isolated events contained in the secretive world of slave ships, these interactions comprised a series of trauma-inducing introductions to captivity that extended beyond the confine of ships.

Violence—perceived, imagined, and/or acted out—regularly manifested within the social space of slave ships, on the top deck and bowels beneath. "Every stage in the Negro traffic was marked by slave behavior which was uncooperative and belligerent," frequently hampering all intentions of trade.[93] The story of seaborne violence rests almost entirely upon ship revolts, yet sailors were tasked with guarding and transporting slaves while being forced to face physical combat. These violent measures operated not merely in the containment of captives but served in their own proprietary measures. Bondwomen "did not participate in the trade as fully as men"; however, in looking beyond statistical understandings, the vulnerable bodies of black females served as the human landscape where crewmen sought to assert control by forcing these captives to confront rape, with the attendant prospect of disease and pregnancy, and to bear witness without recourse to the death of their infants.[94]

These gendered discussions facilitate a beginning interrogation into the range of terrorizing conditions bondpeople faced in the process of slavery at sea. Doing so better focuses on interrelated themes of gender, sexuality, power, and resistance used to constrain and thereby dehumanize bondpeople in and through the manufacturing process.[95] Violence enacted on the Atlantic waterways went beyond physical wounds, laying bare the culmination of bondage that led to psychological consequences as the enslaved relied on more fatally self-directed motives to gain their freedom. In doing so, slave ships became the waterlogged coffins within which both seamen and bondpeople fought and in many cases drew their last breath championing their respective causes on the meanings of freedom.

5 Battered Bodies, Enfeebled Minds

During the summer of 1790, the brig *Ranger* set sail from Annamaboe bound for the island of Jamaica. On July 7, less than two weeks following departure, the presiding commander, John Corran, faced an unforeseeable series of events. At approximately five in the morning, "a Man slave that slept in the Boys room" for medical attention "endeavoured to cut his Throat" in hopes of ending his life. Secretly locating "a Knife or some other Instrument," he lacerated his body, reducing the value and potential interest able to be solicited from future buyers. Unsuccessful in taking his life, "at day light when the Hatch was taken off" to empty fecal tubs stowed within the bottom hold, he "came upon Deck and jumped overboard." His efforts once again proved futile, as several sailors went after him. Once secured back on ship and under strict surveillance, Corran remarked that the bondman operated "in a fair way of recovery."[1] Numerous attempts he waged for freedom during the morning hours alarmed the vessel's crew, although still unresolved is what led to the outbreak of these seemingly erratic behaviors and whether the male slave tried again to escape or chose to endure the passage into port.

Bondpeople underwent tremendous sorrow from initial capture to their displacement into distant slave societies. The various modes of self-sabotage the male captive employed on and off the *Ranger* can be cast as haphazard and rather openly desperate attempts some slaves acted out to escape bondage. These actions were not always about resistance, nor were they devoid of conscious intent; instead they comprised behavioral manifestations of the terror pervasive in the world of slavery at sea. Turning a knife upon one's self and jumping overboard reinforces the dangerous boundaries some slaves sacrificially probed while exposing the innumerable stakes crewmen faced in not only managing captives but in keeping them alive. Violence indigenous to slaving voyages—physical, sexual, and psychological—inscribed and largely reaffirmed notions of power that, as already seen, both sailors and slaves exerted in the contentious battle for control of the black body. Whereas for mariners, suicide represented something in their view catastrophic—the inability to maintain complete control over their transported human cargo—for slaves, as they lay crowded among the wounded, dead, and traumatized, it was a reminder of their own personal sense of loss and the disruption they endured over and over. This chapter centers how bondpeople coped with the shock of enslavement as agonizing personal choices were made on life or death. Doing so deemphasizes the assumption that all captives engaged in bloodied battles against their captors, while deepening the view of the unbearable psychological effects of slavery at sea.

Suicide, much like ship revolts, represented the undesirable yet largely anticipated consequences related to sale and transport of bondpeople into the New World. Viewing these behaviors external to collective physical combat, this chapter directly engages with slaves' psychological disposition within the oceanic slaving process. Such behaviors were magnified most when a bondperson attempted to kill or succeeded in killing him- or herself. Locating these behaviors amid the oceanic highway of the Atlantic, what follows is framed by three critical factors—the psyche, the body, and space—to reveal that while meaning is pertinent to understanding enslaved suicide, so too are the tools and, more importantly, the spatial arenas through which bondpeople asserted power amid attempts to escape slavery.[2] Forced exile did not always hinder captives from devising and treading upon a myriad of routes to freedom. Manipulating the geographical environment of their immediate surroundings, the terrain of ships and the vast waterways of the Atlantic Ocean became the active landscapes bondpeople repeatedly used to escape slavery. Space being central, this chapter widens the conversation of humans and the sea by introducing slave ship runaways, those who escaped the clutches of slavery by jumping overboard and thus running away. Fully aware of and intentional about their impending death, bondpeople willingly sought to sever the ties of slavery, end their physical existence in bondage, and gain permanent freedom.

The central core of the slave trade brought together enslaved people carrying a host of different occupations, spiritual systems, languages, ethnicities, customs, and rituals emanating from various African societies. Scholars regularly reference Igbo, women, and newly arrived Africans as the primary groups most likely to engage in suicidal behaviors during bondage.[3] Self-sabotaging practices did not extend to one particular ethnicity, gender, or age of captives within the Middle Passage. Instead, a diversity of bondpeople utilized this ultimate act of personal sacrifice, further exposing the calamitous interactions and thus the risks of business that sailors were forced to contend. Many slaves also carried diverse religious worldviews from their former communities. Taking Africans' cosmological orientation into consideration, the supernatural—the dual existence of spiritual and material worlds—is critically central to this chapter's discussion. Looking beyond belief of a beginning and a finite end to life, enslaved females and males never took their lives without regard to the broader implications of punishment or death. Not only did these motives operate as individual and equally significant forms of resistance consciously implemented to gain freedom, but in many respects their actions tapped into and further bridged the coexistence of two worlds: both seen and unseen. Tracing the psychological weakening of captives on ships, we see more intimately how the torment of sale and bondage became superimposed by Africans through bodily expression. Going further, this chapter examines how mental decline was perceived and managed, the cultural modes of expression bondpeople exerted, and how the diagnosis of psychological instability was loosely applied to bondpeople's shipboard behaviors.

Trapped within a degrading and contentiously violent world of uncertainty, slaves measured the costs of freedom, no matter how dangerous. With their bodies no longer their own, it leaves open questions on the deeper meaning of self-sabotage within slavery at sea. Suicide represented the intimate and rather private narratives of struggle that many captives publicly acted out. Although typically prohibited in their former communities, the deadly space of the Atlantic created an altered consciousness where some slaves found meaning and utility in self-murder. Through their life-ending actions they conveyed a duality of surrender and sacrifices boldly waged to reclaim power over their personal lives. Social order demanded through the terrorizing behaviors crewmen used to counter future instances of suicidal outbreaks extended the reins of power within the manufacturing process. To be sure, exiled in a fractured and disorienting world, the violent management of slaves deepened their sorrow and psychological wounds, thereby exacerbating the unmaking of captives' lives and bodies.

Elements of Contentious Precaution

Foreign traders privileged slaves potentially able to withstand and survive the hardships of oceanic transport. Many investors based their expectations on the external display of bondpeople's flesh; however, British merchant Humphrey Morice requested seamen give additional attention to captives' mental health during the inspection process. Within his 1722 orders, he directed the refusal of those considered "Lunaticks," "Idiots," or "Lithargicks."[4] Bondpeople regularly generated a subdued state throughout slavery; therefore, any barometer that slave traders used to assess the physical disposition and any characteristics emblematic of psychological deficiencies exhibited during coastal selections could never fully discern the future lifespan of a captive. Yet merchants and investors tried to manage these slave trading realities. On March 6, 1754, shipmaster Captain Watts received similar orders of caution from financiers for his voyage urging, "Let me beg of you to take none but what is Likely & young," especially slaves "free from any Disorders in mind body or any Defects whatsoever" that could be easily discerned.[5] Considering the immediacy of transactions often involved in slave sales, how were psychological disorders discovered? Were the strenuous demonstrations of laboring potential required of offered captives? Did traders and buyers rely on violence or the threat of death to test a captive's mental aptitude? Historians most often focus on the primary points of coastal evaluations—skin, bones, and muscles—to understand the financial and social value foreign traders used to acquire ideal slaves. The varied methods of psychological scrutiny sailors employed are difficult to uncover; however, the minds of available slaves were critical to these shoreline speculations and germane to understanding where and how the body and psyche fit into the final decisions buyers made in purchasing people. Not only would the emotional well-being of a psychologically weakened captive prove dangerously fragile and hazardous to shipboard conditions, but their absorption within a plantation community could create difficulties related to management, control, and unpredictable behaviors.

In order to guarantee the procurement of healthy slaves, instructions were routinely distributed to assist sailors with negotiations. Moving in and out of seaports and bidding on varied black bodies, ship commanders and surgeons became familiar with traits commonly associated with different captives. Physicians traveling to western Africa received warning: "It is highly necessary for you to endeavour to be acquainted with the Nature and Constitution" of black people. Such an expertise could "better qualify you for preserving their Health, and also restoring them when afflicted." To accommodate these necessities, seaborne travelers received an array of certain characteristics to ascertain those slaves requiring additional attention. Among those listed, one group was identified as "naturally sad, sluggish, sullen, peevish . . . self-conceited, proper at nothing," and was historically archived as "naturally Coward[s]."[6] In view of the traumatic circumstances indigenous to the trade normalizing grief within bondage, such broad descriptors could apply to virtually any available captive.

Contusions of Emotional Suffering

Merchants sought to prohibit the purchase of psychologically enfeebled slaves, yet these efforts did not always prevent their sale into the trade. Severed from familial and communal ties, Africans boarded slave ships in a weakened mental and physical state. "Most of them, at coming on board, shew signs of extreme distress, and some of them even looks of despair." Often kidnapped from their communities, grouped into coastal-bound coffles, and forced to survive weeks and many times months in crowded dungeons and slave pens, bondpeople experienced trauma that manifested in their minds and became outwardly expressed through their faces and body language. Due to largely insufficient lodging, starvation, and forced dehydration undergone within their coastal imprisonments, they "frequently come on Board the Ships in a diseased state."[7] The panorama of such experiences represented the beginning of the Middle Passage as captives increasingly became aware of their inability to return home. Weakness prevailed; however, an altered state took root not only in slaves' physical health but also in the psychological terror they confronted on shore by sight, sound, and, most especially, personal experiences. Emotionally wounded by the control they no longer had over their own lives, bondpeople carried psychological devastation that only intensified once placed into shoreline auctions.

Subjected to violating scrutiny over what their bodies could or could not generate within the economy of slavery, grief was an indelible part of bondpeople's lives that was exacerbated on board foreign ships. These realities manifested most prominently through the story of a man sold after being captured near the Galenas River. Once stowed in the vessel, several sailors noticed he "seemed so cast down." During continuation of business affairs, a native ruler referred to as King Battou came aboard and recognized the bondman "sitting in a very melancholy manner on deck." Going over to the man, the king queried the man on how he became enslaved. Records obscure knowing if the captive was a friend, relative, former business partner, or even if the local king tried to negotiate for the man's freedom, but given the ruler's familiarity with the male captive, it is probable the bondman emerged from or near by the surrounding coastal community. Doubtful at the prospect of being freed following his interaction with the king, the bondman's dejected state worsened as crewmen "could not make the man eat by any means," despite administering a "flogging, and then put[ting him] in irons." Sailors routinely drew upon violence to discipline insubordinate slaves; however, unable to restore the bondman's dismal disposition even by way of scars and bruises, "in a very little time he died."[8]

Unbearable sorrows captives lodged within their memories after being forced within the trade intensified further once they were locked within their holding rooms and permanently cut off from any landed sense of familiarity. During a ship's journey, the psyche of uncertainty in some cases intensified in the evening hours when bondpeople "were often heard making a howling melancholy kind of noise, something expressive of extreme anguish."[9] Confined in darkened hollowed corners of slave ships, powerlessness and anger took hold as they reflected on their shattered lives. Emotional outbursts of grief, one slave trader reasoned, were "occasioned by finding themselves in a slave room, after dreaming that they had been in their own country amongst their friends and relations." Surgeon Thomas Trotter surmised that their despair arose from "a feeling for their situation, and regret at being torn from their friends and connections." In his view, slaves were "capable of retaining those [depressed] impressions for a very long time."[10] The heightened sense of loss, isolation, and sufferings internalized was far from minute. Sailors may have speculated on the effects of bondage inflicted on their human goods, yet they could never fully understand the totality of damage personally undergone.

Lingering remorse also existed among enslaved females. While in command of the *Duke of Argyle*, John Newton confronted depression through a black woman purchased and stowed aboard. On January 9, 1750, he recorded, "This day buried a fine woman slave No. 11, having been ailing some time" while on ship. According to his recollection, they "never thought her in danger till within these 2 days." As she was grouped among other slaves equally somber from captivity, the daily behaviors she acted out may not have signaled distress to her captors and perhaps had gone unnoticed. The longer she remained on board, the more intense her despair became, creating a much more public recognition of her grief. "She was taken with a lethargick disorder," which, according to Newton, "they seldom recover from."[11] In spite of the efforts crewmen employed to liven slaves' spirits and manage the risks associated with sadness, bondage drastically altered bondpeople's lives, making recovery far more difficult. The final moments of this woman's life and the wide range of thoughts and emotions she felt prior to her death are murky, yet the pain felt manifested through action.

Regardless of gender, the extremes of captivity placed a heavy toll on bond-people that frequently led to unpreventable fatalities. In the early part of the eighteenth century, lethargy was considered one of several dangerous conditions stemming from melancholic circumstances. Once afflicted, patients became "continually sluggish, and sleepy, scarcely answering if often spoke to" and on occasion "only opening their Eyes and shutting them again" in a rapid fashion. Most characteristic was the unending "desire to sleep," which victims were believed to be "never satisfy'd without it, or indeed with it." A person in many cases also endured "a gentle Fever, a high Pulse, and Breath [that became] weak" as their condition declined. Some physicians also believed these symptoms arose from excessive "Flegm, cooling the Brain in its Windings and hindmost Cells."[12] Newton never disclosed any bodily changes the bonded female underwent upon discovery of her condition. However, being stowed within an intensely hot and unsanitary environment and crammed beside the naked bodies of her shipmates worsened her psychological and physical health, making her even more susceptible to death.

The Specter of Familial Separations

The nature of slavery inflicted permanent scars as traders moved purchased captives off land, separating married couples, parents and children, siblings, and other relatives. A surgeon offered testimony on this prevalent practice, testifying that while embarked trading at Cape Coast Castle, the captain he worked with ordered that he "choose eighteen Slaves out of the yard." The number of bondpeople congregated and evaluated for purchase is unclear, yet the physician "objected to one that was meager, and put him aside" to focus on procuring those more potentially valuable. Taking note of the young man originally declined, the surgeon, according to sources, "observed a tear to steal down his cheek," which he believed the boy "endeavoured to conceal." After the conclusion of sales, the physician's curiosity about the young child persisted, and he inquired about the cause of the boy's grief, relying on a coastal interpreter to learn the source of his pronounced sadness. He learned that the bonded boy's somber feelings emerged because "he was going to be parted from his brother," already selected for transport. Perhaps softened by the pain of the boy's loss, the surgeon purchased him to provide an opportunity, even if temporary, to remain with his brother during the transatlantic crossing. Once sold offshore and under the control of their new captors, the fate of these siblings fades within the historical record; however, their case reveals the existence of familial connections within slaving voyages. Their lives were further ruptured once sold into different hands and exiled into distant locales; however, bearing the brutalities of captivity alongside their kin helped to lessen the blow for some bondpeople.[13] Familial ties served as the most critical mechanism of survival, underscoring personal connections already in place prior to slaves' displacement into plantation societies.

The trauma of familial separations emerged during inland capture and coastal sales; however, it operated far differently once at sea. Married captives occasionally comprised disparate groups captured, auctioned, and sold to interested buyers. One trader recollected witnessing "two or three husbands and wives, and many other relations of different degrees of kindred" enslaved together on the same vessel.[14] "When a Man and Wife are on Board they are permitted to speak to each other" only with the help of interpreters and fellow shipmates.[15] Gendered separations were a primary facet of ship life, owing not only to fears of violent uprisings but also the prospect of suicide. "Any intercourse betwixt the husbands and wives," physician Thomas Trotter explained, "was carried betwixt them by the boys which ran about the decks."[16] Appeasing boarded family members, even if on a temporary basis, some traders hoped these meager opportunities for communication reduced lingering thoughts of self-sabotage capable of manifesting.

The fundamental core of slavery disjoined African families; however, on rare occasions some relatives were fortunate to board the same vessel. A bondman understood by traders to originate among the "Breeches" and described as "styled of the higher class" was offered and sold to a European slave trader. Once boarded, the male captive "seemed to take his situation a great deal to heart, and go ill." Displaced off land and permanently severed from his homeland, making any reconnection with his family impossible, collectively contributed to this decline. Observing his saddened disposition, several "indulgences [were] granted to him" with the intention of aiding in his improvement. Amid the man's restoration, the vessel commander continued negotiating for other slaves in preparation for the ship's departure. One of the captives purchased and transferred aboard was a young female. In closely observing the bonded girl, several sailors discovered similarities of "countenance and colour" that suggested she and the ailing male were related. They later learned their speculations were true, as the female "proved to be his sister." Upon seeing each other, the two captives "stood with silence and amazement, and looked at each other apparently with the greatest affection. They rushed into each others arms—embraced—separated themselves again—and again embraced." Taking note of the pair's interaction, the ship's surgeon observed "tears run down the female's cheek."

The siblings' reconnection, however, was short lived. During the passage the bondman "had a return of his former complaint," an unknown condition weakening his body. Fully aware of her brother's poor health, the man's sister offered to assist in his recovery and "attended him with the greatest care imaginable." The duration of his suffering and details on the medical and emotional support his sister gave him are unrecorded. One morning after helping her enfeebled brother, the bonded girl beckoned the ship surgeon to "enquire how her brother did." Although hopeful of his improvement, she learned "he at length died." It is simply impossible to know if the bondman died from a lingering sickness or if he perhaps gave up on living a life in captivity. Receipt of the news greatly affected the young girl in a drastic manner. According to the attending physician, she "wept bitterly, tore her hair," and allegedly "shewed other signs of distraction."[17] Deeply internalizing the loss of her brother after a set of mere brief encounters, and unable to aid in his full recovery, she very well may have blamed herself for his death.

Traveling with her weakened brother permitted the girl to manage the stress of slavery at sea, albeit through temporary means. Once deprived of his presence and displaced far from the reach of any of her family, emotional turmoil ensued, making it more than reasonable that she traveled the remaining part of the voyage compounded by unbearable sorrow. Slave trade records do not intimate how crewmen managed her sadness or if in feeling completely alone and vulnerable among strangers she tried to take her own life. Sailors bore witness to and perhaps even showed meager sympathy for the emotions she acted out aboard ship, but her grief did not dissuade them from attempting to profit from her inclusion by placing her for sale to interested buyers once imported into South America. Undergoing tremendous pain after being forcibly separated from her homeland and forced to watch her brother decline with no sense of recourse, she carried a deep sense of hurt on shore. The culmination of traumatic experiences this girl endured prior to her overseas displacement collectively created a foundation of trepidation she could have harbored against establishing close ties with other plantation slaves to protect herself from undergoing a similar episode of physical, emotional, and psychological loss through separation or death.

The Gendering of Psychological Instability

Slave ship sailors traveled well informed of the frequent violence captives used to secure their freedom during slaving voyages. The expectation of battles prompted many vessels to set sail secured with arms onboard while crewmen attempted to remain attuned to potential outbreaks. Damages slaves personally inflicted to kill themselves created risks oftentimes challenging for sailors to manage.[18] With private trade the dominant force of the slaving industry throughout the eighteenth century, slave ships were devoid of standards outlining methods of controlling captives compounded by psychological conditions. Relying instead on personal experience and their immediate needs, crewmen responded through the only means possible: punishing recalcitrant slaves in order to terrorize and prohibit self-destructive behaviors among others.

Mental instability was exceptionally challenging to predict among bondpeople. Surgeon Clement Noble described an account involving an enslaved black man offered to foreign buyers. Although the male slave was cleared as physical and mentally fit and boarded on the ship, his behaviors created a troubling presence, forcing the physician to confess, "I should not have bought him." Focusing on several imbalances exemplified through his shipboard interactions, Noble observed that the bondman "stormed and made a great noise" about the ship and at other times "threw himself about in an extraordinary manner and shewed every sign of being mad."[19] The daily realities of captivity exacerbated feelings of emotional stress, anger, and frustration, although there is no indication the bondman's behaviors resulted in any form of self-injury. He, much like other captives, could have feigned madness with the hope of thwarting his transport or even securing his freedom. Noble's observation underscores the prescribed pattern of obedience under which all boarded slaves were held, regardless of the traumatic circumstances of captivity. Anything contrary to these desires invited not only a critique of captives' mental health but also the never-ending reliance on violence.

Many slaves sailed across the Atlantic disheartened by their forced migration. With depressed conditions a regularity on slave ships, the term "fixed melancholy" became a common descriptor used to characterize what many sailors believed represented an irreversible condition exemplified by "lowness of spirits and despondency."[20] Immersed in an enterprise hinged on tragedy and turmoil through the buying and selling of slaves, many crewmen became intimately familiar with the suffering and pain that captives acted out on ship. Visible damages of trauma were not always as easy to locate within bondpeople's bodies; however, inattention could come at a cost to their lives. "If they are not kept in heart and good spirits," one surgeon explained, "it is odd but they sicken and die." To assist with keeping them upbeat, sailors were occasionally encouraged to "order them now and then a Glass of Brandy" when a bondperson appeared "a little dull and melancholy."[21] The effectiveness and regularity of such remedies is challenging to recover; however, it could have been countered among bondpeople by poor nutrition and dehydration widespread on slave ships. Moreover, the distribution of wine and other spirits filtered quickly to a bondperson's brain, reducing some of their anxiety, even if temporarily placing them in an inebriated state and a vulnerable point of control.

The calculation of emotional wounds on slaving voyages forced crewmen to employ diverse tactics and precautionary methods in hopes of countering the outplay of enslaved suicides. Ship alterations and sailing at night were techniques routinely used. Rails were also occasionally constructed on the top deck, while on other ships thickened ropes were draped "by nettings" and placed "round the quarter deck, main deck, and poop, to a considerable height."[22] The primary intent was "to prevent the Slaves, from any accident, [or] falling overboard."[23] Another strategy employed was disembarking from the coast "when all the slaves were secured below," which some commanders believed helped to prevent slaves "from murmuring, and shewing any signs of discontent at leaving the coast."[24] Coming out from their holds unaware of a ship's departure and thus confined far from the sight of land engendered even greater torment. Sailing during the evening hours hindered slaves' visibility of their forced departure, yet the peril of captivity could never destroy the collective memories of their families, homelands, nor constant desire for freedom.[25]

In maintaining a semblance of order in slavery at sea, sailors implemented a code of conduct expected and regularly enforced. Medical practitioner Isaac Wilson recounted the transfer of a male captive who "came on board apparently well" in his overall health. "Shortly after" being stowed on the ship, he began "to look pensive and melancholy" in his disposition. His grievous state allegedly created "a certain degree of wildness" that, according to the attending physician, "appeared in his countenance." Instead of posing a particular violent threat, the bondman's "wildness," Wilson attributed it to an instance when he "began to eat his food voraciously" while at other times "he refused it entirely." "On several occasions he used the expression 'Armourer,'" referring to a sailor "called upon to take the Slaves out of irons when necessary." Forced to oversee and attend to the management of other captives, crewmen disregarded this man's requests except during periodic episodes when he "disturb[ed] the ship's company" during the journey. His behaviors proved an annoyance to his captors; however, prior to the vessel's port arrival, the surgeon determined that the bondman "died insane."[26] With the trauma of exile in full operation, sailors did not always know how to fully interpret the range of emotional and often erratic behaviors that emerged from boarded slaves.

In transporting slaves into and between different continents, rigidly structured order became crucial to mariners' duties and their own sense of safety. The heightened need for precaution stemmed from not only having to manage large groups of potentially violent slaves but also having to treat and preserve those mentally disturbed by slavery. Forceful methods of constraint and violence were often relied upon to maintain captives' psychological health in demanding certain behaviors. Captured and forced into bondage for varied reasons and entrepreneurial desires, bondpeople never responded to slavery in a uniform way. "We now and then met with sulky ones," one seaman explained, "that would not eat without force, and we then endeavoured to persuade them."[27] With aggression and physical abuse core tenets of the Middle Passage, encouragement primarily came through violent enticement. "The general method was flogging, or taking them out of [shared] irons, and putting them into irons by themselves," enabling greater surveillance and isolating them as deviants. During the process, "both hands [were] handcuffed, and both legs shackled, with a collar about their neck with a chain," thus inflicting bodily pain and imposing an individualized measure of social control to enforce shame by publicly denying their humanity even more. Bondpeople's sadness was directly tied to isolation, separation, and tremendous loss, yet for mariners it translated to defiance. Therefore, it was not uncommon that a sailor was "apt to give them a blow with his hand" to maintain some sense of ship order, although another trader learned the hard way that "the more you beat them, the more sulky they are."[28]

Regardless of the intent to program slaves' behaviors, physical abuse many times proved insufficient for quelling their deadly desires. Captain John Ashley Hall recounted his slaving experiences, noting the regularity with which sailors "heard them say in their language, that they wished to die."[29] In cutting off slaves from their former lives, starved, overcrowded in unsanitary conditions, and subjected to a constant threat of intrusive violence, the Middle Passage made the meanings of slavery much more vivid, deepening bondpeople's desires to escape the long-term prospect of degradation and brutal hardship. Amid "the act of chastisement or flagellation," one surgeon recalled, "I have seen the Slaves look up at me with a smile on their countenance, and in their own language say, 'Presently we shall be no more.'"[30] Recognizing that freedom existed within another cosmic space, many captives held firmly to a belief in the continuation of life beyond the human world.[31] Equipped with spiritual understandings hinged upon a dual existence of worlds, they believed that the physical death of their bodies—whether through external causes or self-inflicted—enabled their spirits to transcend into a different realm, thus freeing them from captivity.

Always under constant surveillance, the morose behaviors of bondpeople never went unnoticed. Slave trader George Millar shared the case of a female captive brought aboard ship who "refused any sustenance, [and] neither would she speak." As a result of her insolence, "she was at last ordered to have thumb-screws put upon her" to reinforce the control held over her. Primary intent with this particular device for any captive was "to take the stubbornness out of them."[32] Twisting her digits and crushing them within the metal object made the bondwoman yell out in agony. Going further, several sailors suspended her body "in the mizzen rigging" and used a cat-o'-nine-tails to lash and scar her once-valuable flesh, although in Millar's view these strategies operated "all to no purpose." She suffered from a range of violence and became a public spectacle for the ship, yet "died three or four days" after carrying out her own designated sentence. Questions circulated on the methods she used to end her life. Following her death and the subsequent discovery of her body, Millar reported, "I was told by some of the women Slaves that she spoke to some of them the night before she died," intimating to her shipmates that "she was going to her friends."[33] Any violent persuasions used to extract information from the remaining bondwomen are unrecounted in surviving sources, yet operation of the "female network" while crowded together in the darkened hold facilitated a code of secrecy that shielded discovery of the bondwoman's efforts, thus permitting the defiant female to follow through with her liberating design.[34]

Gendered displays of trauma erupted as boarded females and males dealt with their sorrow in ways specific to their own personal realities.[35] "It frequently happens that the negroes, on being purchased by the Europeans, become raving mad. Many of them die in that state," one enslaver noted, "particularly the women."[36] Sailors viewed most female captives as docile and more fragile than bondmen, yet their behaviors—on and off ship—were scrutinized according to any potential security threats that they may pose. Alexander Falconbridge explained that a young girl procured in the Bonny River "had lost her senses, soon after she was purchased and taken on board."[37] The circumstances landing this female into slavery, what she endured and bore witness to on the coast, and even how long she was offered for sale remain unclear. How did she act out that prompted Falconbridge's final diagnosis? Did she emit strange sounds? Did she convey a sense of anger or perhaps a melancholic and detached manner viewed as dangerous to herself and those aboard?

The extent of damage bondpeople suffered under captivity is not always visible. Physician Thomas Trotter relayed, "This exquisite degree of insensibility was particularly pervasive among the women" in ships he serviced, where it was not uncommon to find them "in violent hysteric fits."[38] What did hysteria look like especially for bonded female on slave ships? Did they cry out, pull at their hair, or were some bondwomen known for exhibiting retaliatory violent behaviors against crewmen? Visiting the vessel *Emilia* while on the coast, a surgeon recounted seeing "a woman chained on deck," and when he queried her circumstances, an attending sailor responded, "She was mad."[39] The extent to which she became unmanageable along with the barometer used to base these psychological conclusions belie contemporary understandings if merely due to the nature of these behaviors and the sources. What we can determine is that although she underwent lucid intervals throughout the transatlantic passage, once she was landed and displayed for sale, buyers disregarded her mental state, focusing instead on the reproductive and physical value they predicted she could generate within the cycle of slavery and breeding. Perceived for the business opportunity her life conveyed for future productive and reproductive profit gain, "she was sold to a planter in Jamaica."[40] Psychotic episodes of irrational behavior positioned enslaved females as threats equal to men in the domain of shipboard security; otherwise their docility went widely assumed and routinely exploited by seamen and interested planters.[41]

Although crewmen regularly dealt with tormented and anguished slaves, there was a limit to how much they would tolerate from the captives. A bonded female was reprimanded for "refusing to take food" on a merchant ship. Although "repeatedly flogged" for her insubordinate behaviors, the torture endured as she was subjected to "victuals forced into her mouth" by the ship's crew. The sequences of abusive strategies marked her body with scars and caused pain within her mouth, yet they proved useless, as "no force could make her swallow" any of the offered food. Refusing all efforts to sustain her health, the surgeon concluded, "She lived for the four last days in a state of torpid insensibility."[42] Undergoing a sequential and traumatic loss of control over her life, her appetite may have become suppressed, or she very well could have been skeptical about the sailors' intentions with her. Interpreting her food refusal as insolence only further fueled the violent mistreatment and mishandling she consequently underwent.

Gendered forms of madness filtered through the Atlantic, yet slaving voyages produced and contained a collection of psychological distresses unfound on land. The close proximity of seafarers and slaves permitted greater surveillance while perpetuating a panorama of anxieties related to safety and preservation.

With slaves regularly sustained in a closed and isolated manner for extended periods of time, ideas of madness and psychological instability were casually projected on different moments of black resistance believed to operate outside the boundaries of ship order. Outnumbered by their human cargo, many mariners felt themselves to be vulnerable targets. In the absence of a policing public and any legal means of accountability at sea, slave ship sailors held enormous freedom to cast and treat slaves they perceived as "mad" through means they saw best fit. Use of such terms as "mad" and "wild" were likewise rooted in racialized understandings and fear. These descriptors and diagnoses in turn created long-term ramifications relative to how different captives were perceived and thus treated as wild, insane, unstable, less manageable, and far less valuable to the economy of slave societies.

Cultural Expressions of Sorrow

The constrained environments of slave vessels worsened the depressive state many captives displayed. They were "generally of a cheerful disposition," one shipmaster recalled, given that "they had frequent amusements peculiar to their own country," as well as "some little games with stones or shells, dancing, and jumping and wrestling."[43] These activities were encouraged to distract captives from their sorrows, quell any thoughts of resistance, and attempt to foster a temporary sense of normalcy in their lives. Anchored within this observation is the idea that bondpeople were properly treated by their captors. Available evidence suggests the contrary: that boarded captives experienced extreme anxiety owing to restrictive confinement, repeated abuses, and most of all the terror of slavery at sea. To reduce bondpeople's decline, mariners were advised to "divert them often with Drum, [and] Dancing" in an effort to "dissipate the sorrowful Thoughts of quitting their own native Country, Friends, and Relations."[44] Crewmen employed a range of schemes to keep captives in lively spirits, which some slaves engaged in if only to keep themselves free from physical abuse.

From various rituals, celebrations, and processes of mourning, music held a significantly central function within African culture.[45] Drums represented a critical component of these occasions. Within the context of bondage, drumming served as a collective art form in which bondpeople engaged with their fellow shipmates.[46] Once played, this hollowed instrument provided a polyrhythmic foundation encouraging participants to dance. Drums typically called forth spirits through the creation of syncopated rhythms drummers had to be well versed in understanding and producing.[47] These musical tools helped to momentarily bridge the material and spiritual world for its observers, providing a portal of entry for pervading spirits. Sailors were often unaware of these spiritual inclusions. For bondpeople, given the diversity of occupations, skill sets, and supernatural beliefs pervasive on slavers, many carried knowledge of divination, ritual, and other shamanistic practices secretly incorporated during permitted periods of song and dance.

The availability of instruments differed according to resources provided on voyages. Occasionally bondpeople were given "a drum which they beat, and others dance" to formulate a variety of rhythmic beats toward fostering the participatory nature of these communal activities.[48] Recounting the use of shipboard drums, surgeon Alexander Falconbridge explained, "Their musick . . . consist[ed] of a drum, sometimes within only one head," and at other times "when that is worn out, they do not scruple to make use of the bottom of one of the tubs" stowed aboard.[49] Sailors influenced the regularity of music and tools used to produce musical rhythms within the Middle Passage; however, bondpeople adapted their cultural practices amid the forced environment of neglect, abuse, and death. By asserting their own preferences on the formulation of different patterns of sounds, some slaves exploited the degrees of freedom granted to produce music on the Atlantic waterways.

Along with the drum, songs also served as a vehicle of expression for those held in bondage. "The poor wretches are frequently compelled to sing," one trade participant recalled.[50] Outside of aggression, what were the methods crewmen used to enforce these behaviors? Many captives often relied on the power of collective composition. "At the time of their dancing," one observer noted, "they always sing to some tune or other in their own way."[51] Language diversity on slave ships created cultural barriers for white sailors, yet close confinement permitted a sensitivity and gradual understanding of spoken dialects assistive in the creation of song variations and nuanced interpretations of music.[52] Women were known for engaging in song, although it was not uncommon to hear reports that "the Men sing their Country Songs, and the Boys dance" during an Atlantic crossing.[53] Far from age or gender specific, these cultural moments were communally shared through song and dance. Through the process they became the collaborative mode of communication bondpeople actively drew upon to open the veils and draw the connections greater between themselves and prevailing spirits. Songs they produced and sang comprised a language of pain and sorrow reflective of their captivity. This seaborne cultural exchange formulated the beginning version of creolized languages that slaves temporarily devised and adapted among themselves. At the same time, these musical testimonies of hardship and strife in the human world directed their echoed intentions and prayers toward the spirit realm in hopes of gaining otherworldly assistance.[54]

Musical forms converging on slave ships regularly took on a sorrowful tone. Recollecting enslaved songs, a crewman pointed out that he "never found it anything joyous, but [instead] lamentations."[55] Sailors may have expected or perhaps preferred more upbeat songs to reduce feelings of captive dejection and appease their own musical desires, but melancholic songs were far from extraordinary in the Middle Passage. "I have very often heard them sing mournful tunes when in their rooms in the night time," a slave trader remarked.[56] Scattered and confined across different parts of a ship, both sailors and slaves heard the chorus of melodic voices of which deeper lyrical meanings may not have been widely understood by all.

Captives produced sounds often cast as depressing, yet the content varied. The primary composition of many of these songs centered slaves' separation from family members and friends. Relaying deep-seated "fears of being beat, [and] of their want of victuals," they vocalized the pain, suffering, neglect, and relentless abuses. On other occasions, captives demonstrated an awareness "of their never returning to their own country." Stripped of everything, sold against their will, and faced with incredible psychological trauma, they were never oblivious to their present circumstances. Considerably rare in describing bondpeople within slave trade records, surgeon Ecroyde Claxton recollected hearing slaves on a ship he serviced sing out: "Madda! Madda! Yeira! Bemini! Madda! Aufera!" According to his linguistic familiarity, this meant "they were all sick, and by and by they should be no more."[57] The close confinement of sailors and physicians with transported slaves heightened some cultural understandings, yet surviving sources obscure whether interpreters were used to translate the captives' songs. Taking into account cosmological understandings of the coexistence of two worlds believed among many slaves, neither language barriers nor sickness hindered slaves from collectively constructing music. As lyrically conveyed, regardless of their current state of exile and mistreatment, freedom from slavery would come once transferred into the spirit world through death.

Integrally connected, drumming, song, and dance represented varied methods of communication actively shared among bondpeople. With the binding factor for its practitioners as well as pervading spiritual forces anchored at its core, these cultural practices held intrinsic meaning for slaves, allowing them to bridge connections between worlds. Bondage facilitated a shared language of sorrow that many exhibited through cultural expression. Serving as the oral text transmitting folkloric and often grim details of their displacement, songs that captives sang and danced to encapsulated their tears in portable form while emulating a wide range of human emotions deeply felt and regularly experienced at sea. Many of these lyrics served as canonical stories sung on ship, yet they filtered the diaspora through the memories of violence undergone and routinely witness by lodged slaves who carried the pain of knowing and remembering onward into plantation communities.

The Disruption of Tortured Souls

Cultural outlets of drum, song, and dance permitted a means for slaves to publicly express their discontent. Bondpeople also relied on more inner-directed extremes through self-sabotage within slavery at sea. Some of these efforts were desperate and unplanned opportunities exploited to pursue their own objectives of obtaining freedom. Beyond accidents or unconscious behaviors, suicide meant much more to slaves as they sought to make meaning of their reoriented lives.[58] It comprised a highly personalized decision embedded within physical expression that became a theatrical outlet through which they engaged in active psychological battles with their captors in pursuit of a permanent escape from bondage.[59] Through these motives they protested and fundamentally sought to reshape their forced exile by means of self-murder, most often through hangings, hunger/medical strikes, or jumping overboard.[60]

Hangings represented the rarest form of privatized self-destruction that slaves acted out at sea.[61] Secretly locating and manipulating ropes and other tools viewed as futile by their transporters, they voluntarily tied these instruments around their necks, allowing their bodies to become the most potent weapons to inflict death. These tactics, although irregular, proved extremely troublesome to traders, as demonstrated explicitly through the case of a bondwoman who "found means to convey below, the night proceeding, rope yarn" to end her life. Grabbing the cord and hiding it from the vessel's crew, she waited until the evening hour and tied it "to the head of the armourer's vice," which had been "placed in the women's room." "She fastened it round her neck," tightened the grip of the tangled fibers on her flesh, and consequentially choked the life out of her body. "On the morning she was found dead," the attending physician described seeing "her head laying on her shoulder." Observing her contorted and lifeless body, several crewmen concluded, "She must have made use of very great exertions to have accomplished her design" of gaining freedom.[62] Many captives, much like this woman, fully understood that self-sabotage countered the cyclical order of life; however, as historian Michael Gomez astutely reminds us, hardships converging within the Middle Passage forced reconsideration of slaves' priorities and means of daily survival.[63]

Bondpeople regularly drew upon calculated measures to vocalize their resentment of captivity through tangible action. Unconcerned and many times unable to understand the varied layers of trauma that slaves were forced to endure, some sailors saw these resistive actions as unintentional. "It is customary," physician Isaac Wilson explained, "when any accident of that kind happens," a surgeon is normally summoned to examine the deceased slave's body and determine the cause of death. Unwilling to endure the relentless cycle of terrorizing and bloodied chaos within the human manufacturing process, another female captive similarly took her life during a ship's eighteenth-century passage. Securing some "rope yarn" into her possession, unbeknownst to her captors, she tied the thickened thread "to that part of the platform where she usually lay." After ensuring its security, she "made a noose, and put her neck in" the self-made contraption. What happened within the passage that made her follow through on such fatal means? How long did she devise the proposed plan? Relying on the constant swaying of the ship as it journeyed forward, she purposely maneuvered her body and "slipt off the platform," which, according to a crewman's estimation, "put a period to her existence." The next morning, "she was found warm," indicating that she had activated her intentions shortly before daybreak. Discovery of her warm body may have conveyed a chance to save her; however, upon close scrutiny the physician determined that "every symptom of life was gone."[64]

Personal experiences both of these females endured, as well as any "psychological hurt" they bore witness to leading up to their last days aboard ship are unknown.[65] Their final fates reveal that suicidal murder by hanging represented a strategy some slaves actively used, leaving seamen to bear the responsibility of mismanagement and financial repercussions. Walter Johnson contends that losses incurred through captives' disobedient behaviors served as explicit threats to slavery.[66] The premeditated sentences these bondwomen imposed upon themselves suggest a similar meaning of intentionality and rather open defiance of their captors most evident in the energy both spent to locate, place in their possession, and use the available rope to permanently sever the hold of bondage. The motives of these women were unpredictable, yet the disdain of captivity—harbored through their deaths—became publicly enshrined in the symbolic representation of their corpses. Their lifeless bodies became expressive mediums signaling incurred losses and differences between the living and the dead while underscoring the limitations of control sailors were really ever able to maintain over bondpeople, including insubordinate women.[67]

Instead of hangings, other captives welcomed death by refusing food and medicine. Some slaves overtly expressed their torment while others became more reclusive. "I once knew a negro woman," surgeon Alexander Falconbridge recounted, "too sensible of her woes, who pined for a considerable time, and was taken ill of a fever and dysentery." Preservation of the female traumatized by grief and psychological distress proved far more for crewmen to manage. Confined among other captives, albeit marginal strangers, shock and a damaging sense of isolation became insurmountable, and, "declaring it to be her determination to die, she refused all food and medical aid, and, in about a fortnight after, expired." Bondpeople, despite the onslaught of mental despair, were well attuned to the consequences of suicide. Unable to keep the female's decomposing corpse aboard after her death, sailors threw her into the Atlantic, where "her body was instantly torn to pieces by the sharks."[68]

Much like females, bondmen also regularly displayed despondent behaviors in the Middle Passage. Commander James Fraser relayed the story of a male transported to the Caribbean who suffered from an unlisted ailment. As the man's physical condition deteriorated, "the chief mate and surgeon" informed the captain "there was a man upon the main deck that would neither eat, drink, or speak." Fraser immediately ordered the crew to "use every means in their power to persuade him to speak"; however, the man "still remained obstinate" in his refusal to oblige the crew's orders. "Not knowing whether it was sulkiness or insanity," the captain gave instructions "to present him with a piece of fire in one hand and a piece of yam in the other" and determine "what effect that had upon him." Perhaps fearful of further reliance on brutally aggressive tactics, "he took the yam and eat it, and threw the fire overboard." This abrupt change in his overall shipboard disposition led sailors later to entrust him by giving the bondman "a frock and pair of trousers" to carry out "washing and mending their cloaths." Mentally restored and deemed capable of useful labor, at least by his captors, once landed he "was sold afterwards for upwards of 40£ at Grenada."[69]

The emotional wounds of sale and displacement created a stressful experience for many bondpeople. The case of a male captive who "had been a trader" and one day "quarreled with the chief" within his former community is best illustrative of these slaving realities. Angered by the verbal altercation, the local administrator "revenged upon him, accused him of witchcraft," and as a consequence sold the man, "his mother, wife, and two daughters" into slavery. Once unfree, the bondman's relatives "exhibited every sign of affliction," while he displayed "every symptom of sullen melancholy." The process by which the various family members were gathered, the distances they marched to the coast, as well as the amount of time they were held in shoreline holdings is inconclusive.

Economically the future of this family became interlinked within the global network of slave sales, yet the bondman traveled the Atlantic overcome by the damaging circumstances of captivity that rendered him unable to shield his loved ones from the very enterprise he once benefited. Plunged into intense feelings of shame due to the protections he thought in place to prevent his own captivity, "he refused all sustenance" offered to him. Affected even further, he "made an attempt to cut his throat," resulting in the loss of "little more than a pint of blood." To prevent any infection, the bondman's wounds "were immediately secured by sutures." Later that evening he "not only tore out the sutures" but went further by attempting to cut the other side of his neck. Unsuccessful and restrained from causing further damage, he allegedly declared, "he would never go with white men" and thereafter "looked wistfully at the skies, and uttered incoherent sentences" in his native tongue.

Deep and bloodied scars the bondman inflicted upon his flesh prompted an investigation into the tools used to assist his deadly desires. A "diligent search was made throughout all the rooms," yet much to the sailors' dismay, "no instrument could be found" to confirm their speculation. "The ragged edges of the wound, and blood upon his finger ends" led the presiding physician to contend that the bondman "had torn the part" of his neck "with his nails" instead of relying on any outside instrument. To be sure, his hands were immediately "secured to prevent any further attempt." These restrictive constraints went to no avail, as the bondman resorted to a hunger strike and "died in about a week or ten days" later. According to the attending physician, he perished from the "mere want of food."[70] Many of the bondman's family traveled the Atlantic on the same vessel, yet his death imposed a separation that spanned three generations. Not knowing his fate nor ever laying eyes on their son, husband, and father again extended their own sense of trauma, grief, and concern.

In contrast to the more private means of agency activated within the holds of slave ships, jumping overboard operated as one of the most predictable yet public means bondpeople used to escape slavery.[71] During the trading process on the coastal shoreline, many of them sought to flee in hopes of returning to the families and communities from which they had been separated. Once aboard ship and displaced far from the sight or reach of land, hurling themselves into the Atlantic Ocean took on an entirely new meaning in the quest for freedom. The terrain of vessels and varied tools scattered about became the same viable weapons that slaves utilized within their wooden confine. Dangerous seaborne highways that crewmen navigated in carrying captives to distant locales represented far more than watery graves for decomposing black bodies or sites for feeding sharks and other sea creatures. Instead the ocean became the primary portal slaves used to escape by jumping overboard and thus running away from slavery.

No matter the geographical origin of their protest, eluding captivity by diving into the oceanic waters slaves conveyed a relentless desire for freedom. Many fought to survive the manufacturing process, while others probed the rather limited possibilities available for their escape. In 1753 a sea captain logged that crewmen began transporting captives purchased from Mana in western Africa. Moving on and off the vessel, securing slaves into designated corners of the ship, "one [of the captives] that was sick jumped overboard." Enfeebled by an undisclosed ailment, he propelled his body into the dense waters, wading forward; however, several sailors reacted quickly, pulling him back aboard. His escape and recovery created a sense of panic that was short lived. He "dyed immediately between his weakness and the salt water he had swallowed" during his escape attempt.[72]

Transporting and managing crowds of transported human cargoes, mariners relied on aggression, rigid structures of order, and fear tactics to maintain absolute control. Because of the violence routinely leveled against bondpeople, some, according to surviving sources, "attempted to jump overboard, and at other times have gone mad, and died in that situation."[73] The precarious environment of slavery at sea proved weakening and rather disorienting for many captives, yet they continued to calculate the means necessary to obtain their permanent freedom. An episodic outbreak on a vessel a surgeon serviced occurred when "the captain and officers were at dinner in the cabin" and they "heard the alarm of a Slave being overboard" who successfully fled the ship. Running to the top deck they saw the bondman "making every exertion he could to drown himself" as he continued "putting his head under water, and lifting his hands up," moving within the waves beneath. Shortly thereafter, the physician recalled, he "went down as if exulting that he got away."[74] In a similar instance, "a sickly Slave got through the necessary [nets], and in swimming bore herself higher upon the water" as she maneuvered her body through a pendulum of waves. But what prompted this woman's decision to flee? Seeing this once valuable female swim away, rendering it impossible for her return, the shipmaster allegedly declared, "'Damn her, let her go, she is not worth picking up.'"[75]

Some slaves escaped by chance, while others devised intricate plans to remove themselves from the imposition of captivity. Seafarers implemented a diversity of tactics to counter attempts at self-sabotage, yet despite such strategies, some slaves "were so artful as to elude all our precautions," one surgeon described in reference to an escape plan devised by a small band of captives on the slave ship. Netting had been previously draped around the top deck to prohibit suicidal incidents, and defecation tubs sat "in the corner next to where the netting was lashed" for sailors to throw over any bodily waste. Taking note of the crewmen's negligence in leaving the netting unsecured, "Some of the Slaves had premeditated their escape," the attending surgeon surmised. The duration of time that passed after their discovery is difficult to ascertain; however, while hunched in a stooped position over the makeshift toilet, several captives "were secretly unloosing the lashings" unbeknownst to their transporters. Using the undiscovered design to their advantage, "two actually did throw themselves overboard," hurling their bodies backward off the ship and into the water, while the third captive "was caught when he was three parts overboard."[76]

Safeguards were routinely employed to prevent slaves from escaping; however, fear of substantial losses prompted some mariners to rely on more violent responses to terrorize and control the behaviors of others. The oral culture of the maritime world fostered the commingling of sailors from varying nations to converse and regularly exchange information on the process of trade and its inherent dangers, including the traffic and management of slaves. Surgeon Ecroyde Claxton explained that a captain under whom he formerly served had learned—conceivably through common seaport connections—about a measure deemed effective in thwarting future suicidal attempts by "cutting off the first and all succeeding Slaves heads who died" through means of self-murder. This would be followed by throwing a captive's dismembered "body overboard" to intimate to others, "if they were determined to go back to their own country, they should go back without their heads." An unexpected onboard suicide of a male captive prompted the commander to implement the prescribed penal measures, and he "ordered all the Slaves . . . to be brought upon deck to be witness to this operation." They were relocated and gathered, "excepting one man" who allegedly "was very unwilling to come up," frustrated by the panorama of violent mistreatment endured on the ship's passage.

Refusing to permit the man to stay below, several crewmen grabbed hold and transported him up toward the gathered spectacle. Although he tried to remain belowdecks, they dragged him up the stairs to where "the carpenter was standing with his hatchet up, waiting for the command to cut off the dead Slave's head." Seeing the corpse and the ritualized fashion in which the sailors gathered around the dead slave's body with the sharpened device, the bondman "perceived the situation of affairs" and immediately "made a violent exertion to disentangle himself from the sailors," being fearful of his own fate. Aware of the nettings formerly loosened "for the purpose of emptying the tubs," he ran in that direction and "darted himself through the hole overboard." Crewmen scurried to recapture the terrified man; however, "perceiving that he was going to be caught," he propelled his entire body underwater and swam "some few yards from the vessel." According to Claxton, the bondman "made signs which it is impossible for me to describe" except as emotions fully "expressive of the happiness he had in escaping from us." Assured he was freed from capture, he "again went down," forcing his body deeper into the ocean, after which the crowd of sailors gathered in view of the escape "saw him no more." The bondman's flee signaled an unexpected loss for his captors; however, his emotional response to the planned theater of violence, at least in this instance, spared his fellow shipmates from being forced to witness the decapitation and mishandling of a dead shipmate's body. Fearful of yet another outbreak, the commander was forced to "desist from our intended scheme" and instead "keep a strict watch over them."[77]

Fleeing ships and creating a spectacle of escape within the open waters, slaves forced crewmen to bear witness to and grapple with the gravity of their cargo losses. As they jumped out of their wooden confine and into the sea, runaway slaves obstructed the parameters of a ship's social order, magnifying crewmen's lack of power to completely control and reclaim their commodified slave bodies. Their escape made more visible what many sailors usually ignored: the ocean as an ever present accessible route to freedom. The Atlantic served as the central pathway mariners charted in the transport of purchased captives, yet with the sea unable to be manipulated, it produced several challenges unfound during plantation escapes: limited manpower and the permanence of losses due to geographical constraints of water depths and dangerous sea creatures including sharks. Uncertainties and dangers common to a maritime life may have hardened crewmen to the deaths of slaves. Whether they were left to dispose of suicidal bodies, forced to watch captives be eaten by sharks or drown in the ocean, inscriptions of numbers assigned to slaves bought and boarded on the West African coastline left permanent records that made sailors vulnerable to scrutiny, where casual indifference was never an option.

Merchant vessels provided the structural means of not only handling imports and exports but also containing desired human commercial goods. Within the domain of ships, crewmen were able to evoke power, restrict insurgents, condone torture, and demand authority and compliance. The constraints of slavery, however, went beyond the physical holds of shackles and chains and extended further into the psychological control sailors continually sought to enforce. Moreover, the social reign of terror that sailors consistently relied on both produced and invariably reactivated traumas through the interpersonal dynamics of slavery at sea. The scars may not have always been visible, yet the devastation was staggering; therein, suicide became a viable option for captives. Its unpredictability struck directly at the core of any confident feelings of management sailors harbored with their black cargoes, underscoring the clear and present danger slaves posed not only to themselves but most of all to the institution of slavery. Without protections in place to counter the abuses routinely suffered, in running away from slavery by jumping overboard, bondpeople asserted control over their lives regardless of the hazards lurking beneath. Compounded by agony and the constant stresses of captivity, they used the oceanic landscape in navigating toward freedom, becoming more than outlaws existing on the margins of recapture. Their actions fully embody and thus broaden the interpretation of the term "maritime fugitives" and slave ship runaways.[78]

The ocean represented varied meanings and needs for sailors and captives. On the one hand, it served as a repository of bodies, death, pain, and suffering. Yet on the other hand, it comprised a multifaceted arena where desires, hopes, and dreams were enacted as bodies were set into motion moving across, within, and through these watery spaces. Symbolically, water has held a long and delicate relationship with people of African descent, characterized by mobility, exploitation of skills, displacement, and disasters.[79] For slave ship runaways, the sea encompassed an underwater railroad and passage to freedom they pursued in jumping overboard to their deaths. Devoid of geographical options available to rebels on land, within the Middle Passage boarded slaves were faced with two critical choices: endure captivity or escape through death.

For fugitives, the ocean served as a portal to flee from slavery and enter into other cosmic spaces. Boarded captives held a diversity of religious and spiritual understandings, yet the underlying basis for many involved a shared understanding of a supreme power, a hierarchy of spiritual forces, and, more importantly, the coexistence of the material and spiritual worlds. Some believed inanimate entities inhabited aspects of nature, including earth, air, trees, fire, rivers, and oceans.[80] Variance of philosophies, spiritual knowledge, and scarcity of sources make it difficult to know whether Christian ideals of a heaven and hell were part of many slaves' worldview.[81] However, they carried understandings of an active spirit realm comprised by deities, ancestors, and the spirits of loved ones already passed and collectively central in the lives of the living. Oftentimes socialized within their former communities that death represented the end of existence for their mere physical bodies, many bondpeople believed their souls moved onto a cosmic space populated by spiritual entities. Others believed water encompassed the primary pathway toward reincarnation.[82] Taken together, in seeking to escape slavery by oceanic means, bondpeople fled ships not merely bound for death. Much like bands of fugitives known throughout the Caribbean and the Americas, they ran toward a natural sanctuary akin to a maroon community inhabited by spiritual forces existing beyond the grasp and control of their enslavers. The transitional process of death and multidimensionality most times defies contemporary human understandings. Within the abode of the sea, what is for certain is that by jumping overboard and out of the reach of their designated guards, slave ship runaways were able to reclaim their former lives and identities and in turn establish permanent independence from a life of human bondage remotely envisioned for them.

Conclusion

The Middle Passage played a crucially prominent role in the world of Atlantic slavery that not only encompassed the transport of future laborers into distant lands but also ushered in the transformation and dramatic reorientation of bondpeople's lives. Sailors relied on surveillance, vulnerability, and violent power in the management of boarded slaves. The physical effects of these interactions produced bloodied wounds and dismembered limbs; however, the psychological scars persisted beyond such momentary scenes of intense violence. Envisioning freedom outside the constraint of whips, chains, and unending abuse, some slaves bore blemished and rather visible remnants of slavery resulting from the battles they waged against their captors. Resistance activated within the transatlantic crossing took many forms, including ship revolts, but also, as revealed through the suicidal behaviors of bonded females and males, they contemplated the meaning of a future in life and death in the clutch of bondage. Whether through public or covert means, bondpeople manipulated the social spaces of ships and the sea, creating financial losses for crewmen while enabling opportunities to regain control over their own bodies and lives.

Crewmen paid little regard to the consequences of torment and psychological suffering, relying heavily on terror as a tool to inflict maximum control over slaves. The integral relationship of power, constant monitoring, and brute force manifested through agency and many other factors that were incredibly difficult for sailors to predict. By taking one's life on ship or within the ocean beneath, bondpeople activated the layered sites of slavery at sea. The greatest irony was that the same watery routes and paths mariners used to navigate toward the New World proved to be the same oceanic highways that posed a fundamental threat to slaving profits as captives ran away by fleeing into the sea. These formative patterns of resistance—practiced and witnessed—were magnified more deeply once slaves were exiled into foreign spaces and sold into plantation communities. With the physical and psychological pain of slaving voyages unique, human, and real, the combined effect of the Atlantic human manufacturing process made slaves' more vulnerable to more frequent eruptions of illness and diseases that began in the mind and wreaked consequential havoc on the physical body. Self-murder may have proven significantly difficult to thwart, whereas to awaiting merchants it demonstrated property losses and the inability of employed workers to manage and deliver previously contracted goods.

6 The Anatomy of Suffering

On July 21, 1792, surgeon Christopher Bowes of the slave ship *Lord Stanley* recorded the medical complaint of an enslaved male, "No. 24," compounded by "pains in the bowels with diarrhea." Observing the man's gradual stabilization over the course of three days, Bowes documented that the captive fluctuated between "rather easier," "the same," and "pretty easy." As the vessel journeyed forward, the slave grew increasingly sleepy, his pulse quickened, and in the physician's estimation he began to exhibit symptoms commonly associated with delirium. It likewise became increasingly difficult for the captive to stand due to "continual tremors particularly about his heart, [and] his skin [was] extremely hot." The crowding of bodies and intensified heat worsened bondpeople's health without end. For the declining male captive, the desolate nature of the maritime world forced the physician to confront severe limits in medically restoring his health, and as a consequence, five days later at approximately one o'clock in the afternoon the bondman died.[1]

Sailors emphasized soundness in assessing slaves' social and financial value on the African side of the Atlantic; however, the confine of ships exposed the fragility of bondpeople's lives and the risks of preservation. The intimate process of oceanic transport forced the confluence of violence and psychological sufferings that imposed perilous burdens on captives' bodies. More than the ruthless tactics mariners relied upon to prohibit and therefore disrupt instances of black agency, the interior holds of slave ships became dangerous havens of disease and death. Regardless of race or gender, individuals traveling across the Atlantic were never granted immunity from the inundation of medical ailments or bodily decline. This chapter does not compare or contrast the seaborne medical experiences of bondpeople and crewmen; instead it uncovers the monitoring and management of slaves' illnesses, while going further to interrogate the extent of medical treatment offered to them by physicians. Recasting surgeons' intricate role within the human manufacturing process shows more closely how their participation generated both economic and professional benefits often unattainable in their homelands while placing them in the vortex of frequently fractured shipboard relationships.

The agony of crippling symptoms and pain that slaves endured from sickness can never be quantified into a singular narrative of suffering. Infusing medical understandings of the various seaborne diseases long familiar on land during the eighteenth century, this chapter interrogates the range of bodily symptoms and curative methods that emerged on slave ships, all of which enables mapping the deterioration of bondpeople's health amid transatlantic voyages.[2] Cargo vessels functioned as dual spaces of patient recovery and sometimes death, transforming slavers into what became akin to "floating hospitals" owing to the multitude of medical calamities that emerged unnoticed and yet claimed the lives of multitudes of boarded slaves. Centering epidemiology and the varied responses exerted to combat poor health among bondpeople opens untapped forays into the medical world of slavery at sea. A multitude of afflictions manifested on the flesh of slaves' bodies; therefore, the crux of the discussion that follows centers on the most common ailments, respiratory illnesses, fevers, and reproductive disorders that emerged among captives shipped for commercial means during the height of the slave trade. An untold number of men, women, and children died from the onslaught of various debilitating and infectious diseases within the Middle Passage. Their experiences of illness and decline were as much about the violent control that sailors perpetuated as about the contaminating environment of ships. Immersion of slaves into deplorable and inhumane conditions became a performance of dependence and vulnerability that worsened the collective tolls of slavery at sea crewmen regularly exploited in the production of these future black laborers. No matter the safeguards implemented to constrain and preserve, the totality of the oceanic slaving process manifested most prominently through the continuum of toxicity, trauma, and illness that took hold of captives during their transport. This chapter establishes an even larger possibility that the unintended and cumulative effects of violent power, malnutrition, bacteria, terror, and extreme deprivation manifested on and through the bodies of slaves where through the journey, slaves became—and were thus made into—products of their environment.

The Panorama of Sickness

As medicine evolved during the eighteenth century, physicians sought to classify the range of diseases common in the Western world.[3] Characterized as an age of rationalism and experimentation, this period saw several shifts as medical knowledge moved from concentration on theories about body structure toward the use of empirical data to comprehend the proliferation of diseases within the human body.[4] The medical profession therefore depended on autopsies and the use of unclaimed cadavers to enhance practitioners' training and develop a better understanding of recovery.[5] Many medical devastations familiar to land-based communities appeared on ships as sustained contact between sailors and slaves fostered what one scholar describes as the "geographical movement of diseases" enacted through the slave trade.[6] With necessary resources restricted and many times unavailable, treatment drastically differed at sea. Despite the diversity of measures implemented to maintain slaves' health, a wide range of illnesses took hold, claiming the lives of those trapped within these floating hospitals. Therein, beyond the quest for ideal black bodies, the seaborne manifestation of disease became a great equalizer, underscoring that even the most prime slaves were susceptible to mortality.

Prevalence Abounds

Scurvy was one of the most recognized conditions resulting from the regular digestion of foods deficient in water-soluble vitamins B and C.[7] This disease commonly resulted from "frequent voyages [taken] to the most distant parts of the world." Symptoms that victims underwent were, in one physician's estimation, "regular and constant" features of ship life as, he pointed out, "the most ignorant sailor, in the first long voyage, becomes well acquainted with it."[8] The heightened growth of overseas trade generated an increase in medical information offered to seamen for prevention and treatment of various illnesses, including scurvy. With scores of mariners devastated by this ailment, health practitioners suggested a variety of causes, knowing the commonality of nutrient-depleted diets and unhealthy environments at sea.

Food was considered the primary catalyst involved with scurvy. Often consisting of "hard dry food," one writer declared, "the sea-diet is extremely wholesome." Foods allocated on ships, being limited by inadequate storage and preservation, were comprised of items often described as "extremely gross, viscid, and hard of digestion."[9] Conscious of the regular inclusion of salty foods, sailors were advised to "eat very little flesh, particularly salt meat," which coupled with heat could worsen any person's ailments.[10] Unable to transport nor consume different types of fruits and vegetables, sailors found that this suggestion proved a difficult feat. "Eating much of salt beef or pork in hot climates brings on the scurvy." If consumed, "neither should be eat[en] above once a week each, and even then with plenty of vinegar, onions, and mustard."[11] To counter the possibility of scurvy among sea travelers, the most common meals suggested were "of light and easy digestion," making sure to include "more greens and vegetables of all kinds."[12] Along with green leafy vegetables, physician James Lind explained, "ripe fruits, are the best remedies" in protecting a person's body.[13] During the latter part of the century, seamen were encouraged to carry and consume citrus fruits for the vitamins and ascorbic acid they offered scurvy patients.[14] Perhaps aware of the dietary suggestion, surgeon Robert Norris served "a Mixture of Lime Juice, Melasses, and Water [that] was formed into a Beverage" to prevent any sort of outbreak.[15]

Despite the range of preventive measures suggested, scurvy continued to impose a devastating affect on bondpeople. In 1796 John Spencer, commander of the vessel *Thomas*, purchased and boarded slaves to transport across the Atlantic. During the passage, the ship's physician, William Francis, discovered scurvy developing on the bodies of a bondman and bondwoman. At the onset of this medical condition it was believed "the person eats and drinks heartily and seem in a perfect health."[16] With food regularly withheld from slaves, these particular observations would belie a crowded ship. However, understanding that "rottenness of the gums is always a sign of this disease," these symptoms easily could have served as the initial indicator for Francis or any doctor familiar with scurvy to discern the ailment.[17]

Throughout the eighteenth century scurvy victims were also known to exhibit "a great weariness and heaviness of the limbs, not caring to move or stir" in any capacity. Lethargic behaviors exhibited on ships only welcomed the use of physical violence. Respiratory concerns for some also posed a problem due to the "difficulty of breathing on the least motion."[18] Bodily scars routinely emerged in "different colour'd spots dispersed over the whole Body, especially the Legs and Arms."[19] These blemishes proliferated "on the skin of various colors" ranging from "yellow, red, purple, dark-coloured, blue or black; at first small, but when the disease is advanced, more large."[20] Because slaves typically traveled naked and fully exposed, eruptions of these physical demarcations exacerbated not only the vulnerability they endured but also the shame inflicted through the uncontrollable and ongoing changes in their bodies. Even more psychologically scarring would have been the customary hemorrhages known to arise "without the least Appearance of any Wound on it," forcing some patients to emit blood from their "Lips, Gums, Throat, Nose, Lungs, Stomach, Intestines, Liver, Pancreas, Kidneys, and Bladder."[21]

The symptoms of scurvy shaped the gendered experiences of slave sickness within the Middle Passage. Patients were long known to endure "swelled legs."[22] The onset of the disease was usually "first observed on their ancles" and over time "gradually advance[d] up the leg" of its victims.[23] Because of heightened security concerns, male captives traveled the Atlantic bound in irons, yet scurvy manifested in the bondman's body through means unknown. In lieu of typical concerns with swelling, the clutch of chains, cramped confinement in tightened spaces, and the constant swaying of the ship inflicted intermittent pain on him. Because unchained, the bondwoman's experience may have differed from that of her ailing male shipmate. However, both women and men were known to endure "violent Effusions of Blood," often flowing "from every internal and External Part of the Body."[24] Surviving records leave unclear any details intimating the outplay of sickness and agonizing pain that both captives individually endured. Their fates became permanently entwined on May 13, 1796, when they both died from scurvy.[25]

Scurvy caused significant concern, yet the flux was perhaps the leading cause of death among bondpeople forced to survive slavery at sea. Descriptive terms for this ailment included the "Bloody flux," "Obstinate flux," and the "Violent flux." Diversity of labeling aside, due to its regular appearance, seamen and captives were aware of the fatal dangers. "You must observe, that when this Flux comes upon them [slaves]," one physician warned, "they know they shall surely dye, and that is the Reason they will neither eat or drink" any offered foods.[26] The deadly consequences of the flux were recognized far and wide among traders and merchants, who feared potential losses of boarded slaves. William Roper departed Africa on September 28, 1791, with "177 Slaves of My own Purchase" aboard the *Crescent*. Eight bondpeople died from the flux during the ship's passage, and as the medical threat loomed following their arrival in Barbados, Roper lamented, "I have 3 more Slaves I expect to Die."[27] Slave trader John Newton encountered similar deaths of valuable slaves afflicted with the flux. On February 23, 1751, he recorded in his log that a male slave died while aboard the *Duke of Argyle,* "having been a fortnight ill of a flux." The bondman underwent tormenting pain for close to two weeks, and, according to Newton, the captive's debilitated state "baffled all our medicines."[28] Ship captains employed varied methods to counter the effects of this condition, yet the greatest threat was not merely the difficulty of tracing its symptoms, but controlling its outbreak in the first place.

Indiscriminate in its victims, the flux materialized through the deaths of many boarded slaves. In 1792 the ship *Shelbourne Castle* set sail across the Atlantic with a human cargo among which were two boys that commander John Fouks had purchased during coastal sales. William Dickinson, the ship's surgeon, observed that both young men began to decline once afflicted with what many viewed as "an incurable *Diarrhoea*." Some believed it developed "moderately for twenty-four Hours and then augment[ed]" in other variations.[29] Many patients, however, underwent "frequent discharge of blood from the bowels," underscoring the bloody connotation commonly associated with slave ships. Equally devastating, the fecal matter of flux victims was sometimes "mixed with flimsy sharp matter" that created in some victims "severe grip[p]ing pains, and a perpetual desire of going to stool."[30] The duration of a patient's condition extended "perhaps fifteen or sixteen Days till the *humor radicalis* be totally desiccated, and the Spirits dissipated, and the sanguinary Mass converted into a venomous virulent Matter" inside his or her body. Symptoms often took full control of a person's body during later stages of this disease, which reportedly "stagnates and deprives them of Life."[31]

Treatment recommendations for the flux varied considerably. Caretakers were told, "The patient must be extremely cautious to guard against cold" and remain "comfortably warm and dry."[32] Held as captives, the two young boys on the *Shelbourne Castle* found themselves confined in a dark, hot, and dampened stowage room for weeks at a time. With incessant vomiting routinely rampant among patients, many were warned, "The patient should never ease himself in the head or over the side of the ship, but always use a bucket." These assistive items were to "be kept constantly clean and empty" and to contain "warm water in it (if possible) for the patient to sit over." Practitioners emphasized the role of a light diet including "sago, rice, weak broth, very slight portable soup or gruel" to use as mobile restoratives. Suggested drinks ranged from "barley or rice water" to "rum or brandy and water," which patients were encouraged to take in doses of "(a spoonful or two to a point) but not malt liquor."[33]

Diverse medicinal remedies were used to combat flux outbreaks. Forced bleeding was widely practiced in the eighteenth century, where some medical practitioners bled a patient "six or eight ounces" to dispel toxins from a person's body.[34] In detoxifying slaves infected with the flux, surgeon Isaac Wilson often relied on "clearing the stomach or bowels from any putrid matter that might be lodged therein" through the use of mild astringents or a purging.[35] Herbal remedies included a concoction of "a half a dram of rhubarb and 5 grams of calomel, mixed up thick with a little Syrup." Some medical practitioners also recommended "two grains of ipecacoanha, and half a dram of diascordium" served to ailing victims "every third day till the disorder is better."[36] Intimately familiar with medical care during the slave trade, one physician suggested, "The Surgeon commonly take this Flux for a simple *Diarrhoea,* and so vomit them with *Ipecacoanha,*" relying heavily upon administering various astringents, which in his estimation was "only throwing away their Medicines and torturing the poor Slave."[37] Advice occasionally offered to sea travelers in combating the flux varied and often proved contradictory. In the case of the two boys on the *Shelbourne Castle*, despite any techniques the ship's surgeon used to restore their health, on July 27 one young boy died several days before the ship's arrival into the Port of Kingston, and on August 3, 1792, the other similarly perished.[38]

Smallpox represented another major disorder claiming the lives of captives trapped in the Middle Passage. In the early part of the century physicians considered this disease "an *Inflammatory Fever* . . . with a peculiar Malignancy or Poison."[39] Among many medical professionals smallpox was widely perceived to have two variations—distinct and confluent—which produced four unique phases of the infection. Stages of this dangerous disease were detailed for those traveling at sea: "(1) Feverish State—when the patient is seized until Smallpox appears; (2) Eruptive State—the period that smallpox formulates and pustules are dispersed across the entire body; (3) The State of Maturation or Ripening—the point that spots of the smallpox are all out until they turn or begin to scab; and (4) The State of Declination or Scabbing—the stage when the pimple-like wounds begin to turn until they are scaled off."[40]

The symptomatic processes of smallpox took on different varieties among those affected. Some physicians noted that at the onset, patients underwent feelings of "drowsiness . . . sleepiness, [and] sometimes delirium and fits" accompanied by "a great propensity to sweat." Others were "commonly seized with a great Heaviness and Pain in the Head and Back, a gentle Fever, and Vomiting or Nauseas."[41] Sufferers' "eyelids are puffed up" and their hands often swelled. "Violent Symptoms, such as Bleeding at the Nose or Mouth," were far from uncommon along with "excruciating Pains" that further weakened slaves' bodies.[42] The proliferation of "spots or pimples" on a patient's flesh were the most characteristic features of smallpox. As the ailment took control, "the whole surface of the skin is covered with a rash."[43] Body blemishes described as "the bigness of little pinheads," appeared among some victims "first in the head and face; then in the neck and breast, hands and arms, and then afterwards all over the body." Pustules, "rough and whitish," appeared on some people's flesh "not unlike a white skin glued to the face." The more severe a person's condition, "the more black the pustules [would] turn." Over time these scabs began to "throw out a yellowish matter, in colour like a honey-comb."[44] Smallpox affected scores of bondpeople in different ways that engendered great vulnerability, personal suffering, embarrassment, and in all likelihood incredible frustration with being rendered powerless to thwart the disease or hinder the ongoing alterations to their bodies.

Treatments offered for this disease targeted physical conditions and dietary combinations. Once affected, it was recommended, "Great care must be taken to supply . . . [patients] with pure cool air." Many in the medical world believed that "hot air in this disease is of the most fatal consequence."[45] Intensified heat pervasive on ships, boarded slaves were never able to enjoy the luxury of cooler temperatures. "The Patient [must] be cover'd," one physician explained, "with as many Cloaths as may reasonably be suppos'd" to provide needed warmth.[46] Another countered this advice, declaring, "The patient ought not to be stifled by heat and cloaths."[47] Due to prevailing fears about the transmission of illness through clothing, food restrictions, and, most of all, slave bodies, those suffering were deprived of any attention to their personal comfort. Dietary suggestions offered to counter the effects, including oatmeal and barley gruel, were highly recommended along with encouraging patients to "drink plentifully of diluting Liquors" given the prevailing belief that "there is something Caustick and acrimonious in the Infection." Favorable drinks similarly included, "Herb Teas, Barley Water, Water Gruel or Sack Whey."[48] Other sea travelers relied on "good small beer, sharpened with orange or lemon juice" to promote increased relief and recovery.[49]

In 1742 ship captain Joseph Drape confronted the devastation of this ailment. He traveled to Guinea and purchased 216 Africans; however, prior to his coastal departure, smallpox broke out among several captives. "In a very Short time there were no less than 170 ill of that Distemper all at once." As the symptoms persisted, Drape feared losing more slaves afflicted by the outbreak. Hoping to appease the circumstances at hand, a ship officer suggested that he "infuse a Quantity of Tar in Water, and give it [to] the Slaves to drink, saying it was practised in the Same Case with good Success."[50] Adhering to the advice, Drape ordered the treatment prepared and offered it to a male captive, who "obstinately refused it, and so did many more." Within three days the bondman died, yet according to surviving sources, the slaves who witnessed the man's death "were more easily brought to compliance; so that partly by persuasion, partly by force, the rest were all brought to drink" the water mixture.

The success of the cure enforced a curious response among the vessel's slaves. They "came upon Deck, and crowding about a Tub of Tar Water, that was Set therefore for them," according to Drape, and "drank plentifully of it, from Time to Time, of their own accord." No other captive perished among the remaining 169 captives, described as "grown persons." Having witnessed the fatal consequences of their shipmate's unwillingness, "the Negroes continued drinking Tar-Water after their Recovery," Drape recorded, "which they found so much Relief from, that they could hardly be brought to drink any other."[51] Sailors experimented with methods to quell sickness; however, this case offers a rare glimpse into the collectivity of uncertain and rather vulnerable moments jeopardizing to a slave's health and, most of all, to the successful delivery of commanded commercial goods.

Much like smallpox, apoplexy devastated the lives of transported slaves. The descriptive diagnosis frequently listed for this malaise varied from "Apoplexy," "Fits," and "Appolitick Fit." Although it claimed lives and continually affected the seafaring world of slavery, this condition receives far less attention as a cause of death in the histories of the Middle Passage. Ship commander Robert Elliot confronted these unintended consequences while sailing from Fort James in West Africa with "24 Prime Slaves on Board" bound for the Island Des Loss. Four days into the passage, Elliot reported, he and his crew "had the Misfortune to lose a fine Man slave, [who] was taken in a fit and before we could get his Irons off he died."[52] Victims often endured "foaming or froth about the mouth." While at other times it took hold and "deprive[d] the whole body of sense and motion," causing a person to breathe heavily, snore, or sleep deeply.[53] The final moments of this man's medical condition are muted, yet his captors became joined through decisions centered on not only treatment but most of all how best to preserve his life and body from decline throughout the remainder of the passage.

Apoplexy affected many sea travelers, prompting an increase of warnings to combat the symptomatic process. Medical practitioners surmised that apoplexy was either "sanguineous or pituitous." Seeing patterns most often among the "young, or middle aged people of a hot constitution, who are full of blood," some practitioners focused on their treatment, while others specifically targeted patients of a "cold phlegmatic constitution."[54] "If the fit is very severe, it carries off the patient in a few days, and sometimes much sooner." Medical providers were aware of the condition's debilitating effects, yet for Elliot these outbreaks became an up-close reality. With apoplexy deemed sanguineous, physicians emphasized "plentiful and frequent bleeding" of a patient. Others relied on a recipe composed of a purging pill along with an "ounce of tincture of fenna, and three drams of syrup of buckthorn."[55] Contrary to common practices of eighteenth-century medicine, slave ship physicians were warned, "You must not bleed so freely," but instead rely on forced vomiting followed with "a strong glyster or purge" administered as needed. Blistering agents, known best as another treatment, were most effective when applied to a patient's "back, thighs, legs, or feet, and last of all to the head."[56]

Though the management and manifestation of trauma among bondpeople, crewmen also confronted a condition known as dropsy. Capable of manifesting in a patient's head, breast, scrotum, or abdomen, many medical practitioners believed it resulted from "a super-abundant collection of watery fluid in some cavity of the body."[57] In other instances, dropsy became "induced either by excessive hemorrhages and losses of blood, or by acute diseases of great length."[58] A range of victims perished from this condition, of which women were considered the primary group of people likely to suffer from its symptoms. Seeing white women as the primary victims, physician Richard Wilkes wrote in 1787 that most female patients "after the time of their menses, are much more frequent sufferers," which occasionally led to barrenness.[59]

This illness moved beyond one ship, claiming several slaves' lives lodged on the *Iris* in 1792. Amid the oceanic journey, two females and one bondman fell victim to what the doctor determined was dropsy.[60] The barometer he used to discern the diagnosis as well as any need for conducting an autopsy on the ailing slaves' bodies is unknown in surviving sources. For some patients "their veins on the backs of their hands, and upon their bellies, are swelled, and of a blackish colour" visible to the eye.[61] Others confronted "great heat, thirst, pain in the legs, feet," accompanied by "a swelling, difficulty of motion, breathing, and sleeping." The salted open air, common to the maritime world, made them even more susceptible to "dry coughs, shortness of breath," that routinely emerged "especially upon motion." Thirst was another characteristic of dropsy, often described as "one of the most constant and troublesome complaints that attend." Severe dehydration coupled with the circulation of intense heat and receipt of limited amounts of water made it difficult for captives to expel toxins from their bodies. These collective conditions forced patients to suffer from a range of bodily responses, including "hard stools, with a mucose matter, and bad urine."[62]

Medical advice circulated among practitioners; however, this condition posed a considerable challenge to restorative efforts: "The Dropsy is a sore disease, of which few recover." Some physicians found that afflicted women proved far more difficult to cure than men.[63] "Vomits are often of great service," and sea travelers were advised to carry emetic substances to induce such tactics.[64] Sweating likewise promoted proper circulation accompanied with "rubbing the skin with a fresh brush or coarse woolen cloth, and exercise."[65] We can never know the range of options the attending surgeon aboard the *Iris* considered and administered in restoration of the ailing slaves. However, the death of the three captives proved that dropsy was "not only unpleasant to behold, but very difficult to cure."[66]

Vermin and parasites similarly took hold of slaves' bodies, forcing crewmen to face the possibility of financial losses and the inability to shield their human investments. While aboard the *Duke of Argyle* slaving on the West African coast, John Newton ordered several crewmen to begin mending the ship's sails. Damages caused by several rats hindered the conclusion of repairs, as Newton reported, "We have so many on board that they are ready to devour every thing." While walking about the ship, he found they "actually bite the people when they catch asleep, and have even begun to nibble at the cables."[67] Unsanitary conditions customary aboard slave ships created fertile ground for bacteria to inundate and contaminate a ship's hold, thereby endangering the slaves' health and lives longterm. Irregular cleaning of ships, dampness, and crowding of bodies similarily created ideal conditions for rodents and larvae developing on slavers. Echoing the commonality of these occurrence, a ship officer explained that the crewmen he sailed with were forced to "shift every foot of plank in her bottom, being quite destroyed by the worms."[68] The chain of consequences anchored in the human manufacturing process bore layered structural problems with current ship technology that both merchants and consumers relied on to fulfill global human product demands.

The presence of vermin permitted the ease of pathogens nurtured through the process of maritime life. Ship captain M. Dineley encountered parasites through a young male slave boarded following shoreline purchase. A tiny specimen grew in strength within the bonded boy's body, requiring the crew to maintain a careful eye on his delicate condition until they were able to draw upon immediate local resources. Locally used medicines or herbal combinations that were administered to remove toxins from the boy's body are unrecorded. However, Dineley reported the successful restoration of his well-being to his employers, noting that a nearby doctor placed in charge of his health once landed "quiled a tape Worm 18 feet in length." Physicians understood the variations between worms in different ways. Tapeworms were more generally known as "the *Solitary Worm*," due to their solitary nature. A medical reference explained, "No species of intestinal worms is more destructive to human nature, or more difficult to be totally destroyed." Difficulties of treatment persisted significantly once inside the host's body, rendering treatment even more strenuous because "it sometimes equals in length the whole intestinal canal."[69] Much to the satisfaction of the young boy, his transporters, and financiers, despite the worm's microbial invasion he did not die. His recovery created an immediate increase in his potential value: where once cast as sick and unstable, agents priced him at £5. Once freed from his former medical complaint, however, his market price jumped almost eight times to £40.[70] Bondpeople represented the lifeblood of money, wealth, and power within the Atlantic human manufacturing process. The unnamed boy's confrontation with a life-depleting worm shows more intimately how the decline in a slave's health, above all else, proved the pinnacle threat to any slaving desires.

For others not so fortunate, worms growing within their bodies led to losses of life and property. A young male slave confined on the ship *George* suffered from worms, although the type of worm is unclear. Among tapeworms in particular, some practitioners believed there were two classes: the *ascaridies*, often characterized as "being small worms," and the *lumbrici teres*, described as round and long.[71] Fragmentary sources do not reveal how the ship's surgeon, David Stephen, forced the live toxic specimen from the boy's body, yet despite the bacterial extraction, his health became further aggravated and he died on May 12. Reinforcing the specter of dismantled lives, one week after the boy's death, a female captive also fell prey to a deadly microbial parasite manifesting within the interior cavity of her body. She, much like all other slaves, traveled exposed to deplorable conditions and harmful diseases rampant on board; however, the vessel's doctor, Stephen, recorded that she perished from worms. These specimens were long known to "draw nourishment from the substance of the stomach and bowels." Yet we are still left to speculate into how the woman became infected in such a way that became a breeding ground for worm growth. "The poor, far more often than others," according to one medical guide, "labour under this complaint on account of the want of proper food." Seafarers were therefore advised to include certain foods in seaborne meals. "Many crude indigestible vegetables, immature fruits, legumina, sweets, cheese and fresh fish proved useful in restoring a person's health suffering worm invasion."[72] However, these were never found in abundance nor regularly given to transported slaves. The conditions and diet differed drastically from those medically suggested on land, making even more clear the consequences of life and death that slaves were forced to battle and survive. As property, they had to depend on their buyers and subsequent transporters for their well-being, which in turn refined and thus transformed slaves' behaviors toward the needs and demands of a ship captain, crew, and a commercial industry based on the powerless. To be sure, the routine operation of malnutrition, violent abuses, and full immersion in toxic and stressful spaces worsened slaves' already failing health.

The cheap investment in maintaining the health of boarded slaves forced them to travel in a constant state of jeopardy, making the scale of losses not only widespread but immeasurable. Several other captives also perished from the attending condition of worms, showing that these specimens crossed gendered bodies. Over a two-week period, prior to the *George*'s arrival at Jamaica, three bondmen and another woman consecutively suffered from symptoms associated with worms. "The abdomen becomes hard and distended with air," and on some occasions "rumbling noise takes place frequently in it," along with "fetid breath, nausea and vomiting." These maggots were long known to feed within a person's body, causing a patient's appetite to regularly fluctuate, being "at times impaired" and at other times "ravenous and insatiable." Patients' pupils dilated, and many victims also experienced "involuntary discharge of saliva" along with suffering "pain in the head, and sometimes delirium." A person's urine could also appear "frothy and of a whitish appearance." Equally devastating, the "vehement itching of the anus . . . and frequent inclination to stool" worsened a slave's suffering.

The multiplicity of methods that slave ship surgeons used to attempt to discern the presence of worms within a slaves health from their anatomical queries are unrecorded; however, medical ramifications ensued. As the worms maneuvered, curving around and in between internal organs throughout a victim's body, they caused significant internal discomfort. Intestinal irritation often led to "nausea, vomiting . . . itching of the nose, and various convulsive affections, [such] as epilepsy convulsions." Upon exhuming a worm-infested body, one physician noted that he and others "very frequently discover them in the cavity of the abdomen, and a perforation [is] made into the intestines."[73] The slave-related duties expected of seamen extended far beyond brutal management to imposing critical and often immediate choices in preserving the living or the dying. For bondpeople, the proliferation of worms amplified and made fully undeniable the power of slavery. The unending cycles of mistreatment, neglect, deplorable immersion, filth, and the limited and occasional offering of expired foods waged collective devastation. The sequential terror, deprivation, and toxicity led to the dismantling of those slaves transported and delivered into the Americas, giving greater meaning to the importation of a cheap labor force.

Threads of Respiratory Decline

Respiratory illnesses also affected slavery at sea. Some physicians believed the lungs were "apt to be corrupted, because their structure is so delicate and tender," creating fertile ground for medical adversities. Slave ships were routinely exposed to hazards of the sea, placing travelers' lives, including pneumonia victims, in a vulnerable position. For some this condition emerged with "a violent Inflammation of the Lungs" as blood became trapped, "obstructing very many of the pulmonic and bronchial Arteries." Dissections on land revealed that a patient's "Lungs have been found quite stuffed up with concreted Blood, red, hard, and as it were fleshy," and often darkened in color. Medical practitioner John Huxam described the illness as "a Disease so common, either as an original Malady, or consequent to some other," that in his estimation, "its Nature should be diligently studied by every Physician."[74]

Sailing from Angola in 1792, Captain George Maxwell confronted the crippling effect of pneumonia aboard the ship *Torn*. Two bondmen exhibited symptoms of the condition and died on the passage. Soon after, the vessel's surgeon, Richard Kirkum, discovered the failing health of a nursing slave woman. Bearing greater responsibility of medical survival for themselves and their children, black females with infant children faced significant hardships amid the trade and traffic of slaves. Victims frequently confronted "a Load at the Breast, a short difficulty Breathing, a Cough," and fevers that signaled a bondwoman's growing weakness. In other cases, patients "begin to spit a *thin, gleety, bloody, or very dark-coloured Matter,* frequently of a very *offensive Smell.*" Their urine was also "a blackish dull Hue, . . . *as if a small Portion of Blood was dissolved in it.*" The enslaved woman went through various stages of the debilitating symptoms of pneumonia, igniting pain and decimating her health in ways muted in the historical record. On the eighteenth of October, Kirkum logged that this bondwoman died. The medical consequences connected with this woman extended even further four days later when her infant son died, succumbing to the same fatal condition as his mother.[75]

Quite similar to pneumonia, consumption also proved a respiratory danger to the health of many boarded slaves. Some doctors believed two versions often arose through this condition: "acute Consumption, or a chronical one." The disease appeared in four primary stages, the first of which was the lodging of matter within the lungs, whereas the second included "Stuffing of the Lungs, when Matter is actually deposited and lodg'd upon the Lungs, so as to cause a Shortness of Breath." Swelling of the glands in the lungs was common to the third stage, while the fourth phase frequently resulted in "an Inflammation, and at last an Ulcer, of the Lungs." Confined far from public view and additional medical help, bondpeople's shipboard conditions were exacerbated by the toxicity of ship conditions, unhealthy meals, and, most of all, the terrorizing cycle of brutalities they suffered, further unmaking all slaves in the process.

In 1793, sailors on the *Brothers of Liverpool* faced head-on the potent threat that consumption posed to lodged captives. While docked on the Windward Coast of Africa, the ship's captain, Thomas Payne, moved several captives onto his vessel. As the ship's crew prepared to sail to the Island Des Loss, a boarded bondman underwent severe complications associated with consumption, which frequently included, "Spitting of Blood, or internal Ulcers corroding the Lungs." Some physicians believed "the Stomach is often loaden with Phlegm of a saltish Nature, which gives Pain where it is, and Swellings" further weaken patients. The ship's surgeon, John Thirtle, attempted to restore the man's health and salvage any minimal value able to be collected through his impossible recovery. Despite the measures Thirtle used, symptoms persisted in the erosion of the bondman's body and on April 4 he died.

Power Unseen

Although rarely addressed in many studies of the Middle Passage, a wide range of gender-specific reproductive illnesses proliferated across slave ships. The physical makeup of male and female slaves' bodies made them privy to certain conditions incapable of arising among their gendered counterparts. Several males traveling aboard the slaver *Venus* died from "Part of the Scrotum torn off w'th their Irons."[76] Their sufferings are unrecorded, yet the constant swaying of the ship intensified the agony these black men confronted. Any lack of proper medicines, tools, and even delayed discovery or neglect of their wounds would have likewise proven perilous to their recovery, causing them to weaken even more if toxins entered and poisoned their bodies. The crowding of slaves and the inability of physicians and seamen to offer extensive medical treatment countered any immediate prospect of captives' recovery. However, the undetectability of bacteria within slave ships produced injuries and deadly infections that enabled the closeness of death. How did the attending crewmen discover the cause of death for these men? Was an autopsy performed? Probing more deeply, the interconnectedness reveals the dual symptoms of torment facilitated through the movement of the ship or perhaps one another, thereby making more easy the simultaneous pulling of skin on their genitals.

While traveling aboard the vessel *Mary* in 1788, a male captive was diagnosed with anasarca, known to create an accumulation of fluid throughout the body. This condition inflicted immeasurable pain, yet he also suffered from "Hydrocale of the Scrotum," which surviving sources reveal caused intense swelling in the genitalia. The deplorable conditions and restricted environment of slavery at sea induced greater medical torture. Permanent stowage below decks meant continual friction while the bondman lay on the floor boards and also when violently forced from the bottom hold to the top deck for feeding and exercise. Any accidental hitting or physical violence inflicted by his captors only worsened his condition, making the passage even more unbearable. The suffering persisted, bringing death much closer, and on March 13 he died.

Female captives also faced reproductive complications that jeopardized their survival. From the moment of capture, bidding, and sale, slaves' lives were assessed according to their reproductive value.[77] Venereal complaints comprised a regular source of death for females during the eighteenth century.[78] Patients who were "poxed, injured, or affected with the venereal disease, pox, or bad distemper" faced calamitous circumstances "when the venereal poison has been received into the system" of their body.[79] Typically understood and studied as pervasive among white women, venereal diseases also emerged among black females transplanted aboard slave ships. A 1792 bill receipt for "Medicines &c, &a for venereal complaint" showed a physician received £1 and 10 shillings for the medical attention he provided several women traveling aboard the schooner *James*.[80] This exchange confirming the presence of gynecological examinations aboard slave ships underscores the commercial intricacies of the slave trading networks through the monetary valuation of human goods and the treatment of the sickly bondwomen.

Reproductive disorders arose at other points during the transatlantic passage. In 1793 a black woman was offered for sale on the coast of Gaboon, after which Captain Daniel Collins purchased and ordered her transported aboard the ship *Apollo*. The vessel, carrying 287 captives, departed the African coast on March 7 bound for the Port of Speights in Barbados. Three weeks into the passage, surgeon Robert Scow recorded that the unnamed bondwoman died of a disease listed as "venereal."[81] In the same year, traders placed another female into bondage and sold her onto the ship *Sane*. She survived close to four months at sea; however, her health became compromised by the end of the passage, making future market sale uncertain. The techniques and herbal elixirs Joseph Cankore used for her treatment are unrecorded. Unable to restore the woman's health, after attending to her corpse he recorded that on April 23 she died of a "venerial" related issue found in her body.[82] Still perplexed about her condition, Cankore conducted an autopsy on the woman's body, acting upon the privilege, right, and power granted to him as both a professional and slave trade worker over an ailing and dead slave. Violating her body through

"The abolition of the slave trade; or, The inhumanity of dealers in human flesh
exemplified in Captain Kimber's treatment of a young Negro girl of 15 for her
virjen modesty." Illustration by abolitionist, attributed to Isaac Cruikshank.
(Cartoon Prints, British Library of Congress, Prints and Photographs Division,
LC-USZC4-254.)

the medical violence inflicted within the interior cavity of her body for knowledge expansion undeniably useful for his career, he discovered the presence of
a venereal virus.

Archival sources shield fully understanding the pain and trauma these two
women experienced at sea. Those affected by venereal complications were forced
to combat "swellings in the groin" that sometimes "form matter and admit a
discharge." "Warts or excrescences" were also regular occurrences, forcing physicians to conclude that these acne-like eruptions were "sometimes unnecessarily
made the objects of terror to the patient."[83] Viewing such symptoms as a concern within the reproductive organs, doctors during this period believed that
for women and men, "It is possible for many other parts beside the genitals to
receive this disease," evidenced by the ability of this toxic virus to emerge "in the
anus, mouth, nose, eyes, ears" and even "in the nipples of women."[84] Venereal
disorders surfaced in diverse and rather interesting ways in the female body. "A
woman may have this species of the venereal disease without knowing it herself,"

one physician surmised, which would render it far more difficult to discern "even on inspection."[85] Some practitioners reasoned that if a woman was affected in her genitalia, this induced damages within "the vagina, urethra, labia, clitoris, or nymphae."[86] At the onset, symptoms began with "an itching of the orifice of the urethra." Over time, "the itching changes into pain, more particularly at the time of voiding the urine."[87] As the disease continued to progress, "the natural flimsy discharges from the glands of the urethra is first changed," evolving occasionally from a "fine transparent ropy secretion to a watery, whitish fluid."[88] Venereal complaints frequently resulted from sexual encounters, further expanding the long-term implication of rape and sexual assaults beyond psychological damage to include internal and external bodily damages that slave traders imposed on bonded females. Also left open was the possibility of repeated attacks that left some bondwomen held as human goods on ships scarred, traumatized, feeling unclean, and rendered powerless and unable to rid themselves of their tormentors—physically, emotionally, and psychologically.

Pregnant captives also faced debilitating medical conditions on slaving voyages. The captain of the vessel *Eliza* set sail for the Caribbean in January 1792. One month following the ship's departure, an enslaved mother stowed among the vessel's cargo suffered a miscarriage and died.[89] African women possessed extensive herbal knowledge of terminating unwanted pregnancies; however, still indeterminable is if this woman abruptly lost her child or forcibly took its life. Miscarriages some women experienced during this period involved "pains of the uterus [that] are situated low in the pelvis, between the bladder and rectum." Aggravation and soreness within the woman's womb strengthened concern for the health of the unborn child. Labor-like cramps extended agonizing pains in her "stomach, occasioning nausea, vomiting."[90] Receipt of any nutrient-deprived meals hampered successful development of her unborn child, depleting her already weakening body.[91] No matter the efforts the sailors extended to preserve this female captive as an investment, the personal and violent abuses she witnessed by sight and sound inscribed the terror-making process. Traveling in close quarters privy to the constant cycle of public whippings, the stress of slavery at sea intensified, widening the culmination of tragedy that imposed a massive toll on this woman's health and claimed her life.[92]

Burdens of Hostile Treatment

With toxic environments ever present and damaging to the health of boarded slaves, sailors were regularly tasked with medical attention toward commercial preservation. Some merchants employed physicians to work on board while others relied on crew members to manage outbreaks of sickness and provide medical services amid other shipboard duties.[93] With monopolies waning in the early decades of the 1700s, the private trade of African people was largely micromanaged by merchants, without external requirements of surgeons for much of the century. Legislation stipulating the inclusion of medical professionals on slaving voyages arose in 1788 through the British Parliament's Slave Trade Act, infamously known as Sir Dolbien's Act; however, views on such personnel varied widely across the Atlantic.

Following the conclusion of shoreline slave sales in West Africa, surgeons' duties shifted off coast and toward maintaining the health of the boarded human cargo. Although employed as physicians, they took on a multiplicity of roles, often serving as overseers, birth attendants, nurses, and morticians. Much like sailors, the work of surgeons began in the morning and continued the same each day as they attended to immediate medical concerns and kept close watch on the overall health of all boarded slaves.[94] Larger vessels employed surgeons along with several mates to assist in distributing medical treatment, yet "it is the duty of the surgeon to examine through the whole of the slaves on board."[95]

Medicines carried on ships depended heavily on the resources acquired prior to a vessel's initial departure. Merchants provided money for the purchase of necessary herbs, medicines, and other preventive tonics. "The surgeon, if a man of experience in the trade, takes the assortment which he judges best." On the other hand, "if he never was on the [African] coast before, he commonly takes such an assortment as he has been advised to do by a man of experience"; other investigated items "the apothecary or druggist has sent in other vessels in the same trade."[96] A physician's chest typically contained a variety of medicines, including gum camphor, pulverized rhubarb, cinnamon water, and mustard. These supplies were primarily reserved for the passage to and from Africa, yet they were also available while the ship lay on the coast as cargo was brought aboard.[97] "When any complaining Slaves declare their complaints to the Surgeon, he generally gives them what medicine his judgment and practice declare him" necessary for the restoration of their health.[98] Surgeons managed the depletion of medical resources at sea through varying methods. Seasoned physicians drew upon familiarity with previous oceanic passages while newcomers were forced to rely on personal knowledge, available books, and a trial-by-trial basis. Boarding medicines demonstrated at least basic considerations of health on ships while creating a sense of preparedness for distant merchants. The isolation of the waterways demanded that surgeons and sailors invoke and adapt their medical expertise in a world of slaving characterized by extreme scarcity and lack of extensive medical assistance.

Once in close proximity and fully responsible for captives' health, some physicians faced challenges with providing medical services. Ethnic and linguistic diversity prevailed among boarded slaves, with language barriers posing challenges in preserving bondpeople for market sales and subsequent purchase.[99] While fear and anxiety characterized many slaves' experiences, some devised simple and creative ways to call attention to any emerging ailments or pain, making more real their humanity as transported goods. Some "will endeavour to make the Commander and his Crew sensible of their Illness," one physician found, and on occasions they did so "by pointing to their Stomach, or Belly, and saying *Yarry, Yarry*."[100] Bodily gestures translated pain, while at other times medical distresses became learned by "the complaints of the Negroes, through the mouths of three, four, or five interpreters."[101] Such methods temporarily addressed emerging medical problems; however, the inability of patients to fully communicate the variance of their agony and symptoms posed a severe threat not only for discerning necessary treatment but also for predicting the value able to be generated from an ailing slave body.

The constrained spaces of slave ships proved far more detrimental than language in managing captives' suffering. When sickness arose, sailors enforced separate accommodations in attending to a bondperson's failing health. Isolation took on different forms given a vessel's size and the number of slaves boarded to ensure that "they would be most out of the way of the other Slaves" and to counter any unforeseen toxic transmissions, but also to garner space in managing the needs of the suffering and the dying.[102] These reserved locations, known in parts of the trade as "apartments," were semi-quarantined rooms akin to infirmaries, where once separated from the bottom holdings, bondpeople received hands-on medical attention and were "less likely to be molested or disturbed."[103] A letter sent on January 4 from an undisclosed author requested "an account of the Surgeon's stores with his orders at the bottom of it, and also a copy of the orders given to the Captain, so far as it relates to the Surgeon" regarding the ship *Pearl*. Particular to the query was the interest in written instructions stipulating that the commander "leave the care of the Slaves to the Surgeon's, as soon and as long as they are on board, and to Direct the Master to leave the arrangement of the Decks below under the direction of the Surgeon, with as much assistence from the crew as will be consistent."[104] Available corners were occasionally provided, but in most cases surgeons had no choice but to attend to enslaved patients wherever their bodies lay during the passage. Massive outbreaks of epidemics made the quarantine of individuals close to impossible through the enforced commingling of the living, dead, and ailing, transforming slave ships into floating hospitals.

Tightened spaces of ships, the closeness of bodies, and lack of proper cleanliness imposed staggering effects on transported captives. Every person traveling the Atlantic through the Middle Passage—sailors, captives, and surgeons—confronted dire threats to their health through infectious diseases and the omnipresence of decomposing bodies. "Among the men, sometimes a dead and living negroe [are] fastened by their irons together. When this is the case, they are brought upon the deck, and being laid on the grating, the living negroe is disengaged; and the dead one thrown overboard."[105] Lying next to and most often chained alongside sickly or dead shipmates produced traumatic tolls among boarded captives. For sailors and physicians, the handling of corroding bodies imposed similar health risks due to the regularity of physical contact involved with moving dead and diseased slave bodies on deck or discarding them off ship. Seafarers could rarely wash their hands prior to the distribution or consumption of collective sources of water or food, placing all those aboard in harm's way. Moving from body to body, daily exchanges between physicians and slaves engendered the doctor-patient relationship, conveying a semblance of hope for their restoration through the offering of medical attendance while unknowingly compromising chances of improvement. Without the opportunity to sterilize their hands or medical instruments, the constant interaction of surgeons and sailors tasked with attending to boarded slaves created bacterial transfers and a range of fatal consequences to an already contaminated environment where bondpeople lay unprotected.

As medical practitioners, slave ship sailors were granted unabated access to Africans' ailing bodies. They helped to determine the viability of slaves' health and vitality and to counter the purchase of any deemed inferior on the African coastline. Their open accessibility aboard slave vessels, while hazardous and incredibly difficult to carry out, permitted incredible opportunities unfound on either landed sides of the Atlantic to understand the black body through interrogation of the various techniques and medicines necessary for treatment without public view, scrutiny, or interruption. Once transplanted within the slave trade, surgeons became a part of what is argued here as migratory medical apprenticeships that proved complementary to their medical training and knowledge base that extended beyond locally familiar arenas throughout Europe and the Americas. Far from stationary in their slave trade employment, traveling to and between landed sites of slavery granted these medical men substantial understanding of both the effectiveness and limits of certain medicines, surgical procedures necessary at sea, the filtration of toxicity, and how best to manage unending sickness and death. Prior to their shipboard employment, physicians had observed primarily white patients; however, moving across geographical boundaries through the operation of slavery at sea permitted physicians to act upon any looming racialized curiosities through the study of captive African bodies. As unending students of the world, these slaving interactions—anchored undeniably on power—facilitated within the waterways and foreign locales assisted in sharpening the medical understandings that many surgeons carried back to their homelands and professional careers. The bodies of boarded slaves, much like landed practices, functioned as what one scholar aptly labels "repositories of mystery" operative within the medical world of bondage, including for slave ship surgeons.[106]

Close interaction with black cadavers enabled physicians to both study and practice the seaborne process of health management. One physician described the situation of a "stout man" deemed healthy during a conducted coastal examination; once transferred aboard, however, his health took a dramatic turn for the worse. The next morning crew members found him dead. Baffled by the bondman's death, "I had the curiosity to open him," the attending surgeon explained, and he queried the ship captain for approval to conduct an autopsy. The commander agreed, "providing it was done with decency." Decency was rarely found in the slave trade, once left under the transport and violent preservation of slave ship workers. Fully permitted, the surgeon "opened the thorax and abdomen, and found the respective contents in a healthy state," leading him to conclude that the man had suffocated while stowed in the ship's bowels.[107] During the surgeon's 1790 testimony before the British House of Commons, interviewers questioned him on whether a deadly affliction might have been present in the male slave's brain. "Every man that knows any thing of anatomy," the physician responded, "knows that opening the head in a dextrous manner, so as to expose the brain, is often no easy thing, and I had neither time nor conveniences in that instance to do it," given the extensive duties required of him. He therefore had performed an examination of the man's body "at candlelight, upon the deck, after all the Slaves were below."[108] Since the crew were expected to manage the concerns of other captives throughout much of the day, unexplained is how they preserved the bondman for later use, where they stored his body, the amount of time the surgeon spent cutting open or observing the bondman's interior cavity, and what was done with the body and internal organs at the conclusion of the postmortem examination.

Use of the enslaved man's body for medical study reinforces the professional power that physicians were granted and fully able to enact at sea. Sailing as part of the ship's crew, they served a medical need while gaining sole authority over the lives of bondpeople.[109] For many of these medical men, far from home and an easily accessible professional world, the slave trade represented opportunities for an increase of both social and economic status. The greatest payoff rested beyond money; instead, slaves served as clinical material on ships, routinely exploited by the medical profession to gain empirical data, whether for experimental purposes or malignant intent. Deaths of slaves within the cycle of slavery—on and off ship—permitted greater understanding of black mortality in attempting to distinguish and purport medical theories of racial superiority. Acting upon the successes and failures of their seaborne medical residencies, physicians created substantial benefit through publications, lectures, and expansion of their professional status and careers, making more necessary the interrogation of their role in the history of slavery at sea.

Medical treatment in the Middle Passage represented massive undertakings with both benefits and challenges. Physical inspections conducted within the open sea were far more difficult than those performed on land. Spatial constraints created a recurring problem without sophisticated instruments and a

wider profession to draw upon for medical advice, forcing slave ship surgeons
to rely on previous training and exploratory means to manage and restore
the health of slaves. In protecting against future medical outbreaks as well
as enhancing their own practical knowledge, some physicians therefore drew
upon the corpses of slaves ravaged by diseases. Vulnerabilities of sickness and
death widespread on slaving voyages provided a cadre of exploitable bodies
available for dissection. Once under the surgeon's knife, bondpeople served as
voiceless specimens whose stiffened bodies endured medical violence without
the prospect of intervention. With their flesh cut and opened in the postmortem
state to satisfy looming medical curiosities, the dead bodies of boarded slaves
became the vehicles many physicians used to enhance their medical intellect
and professional lives.[110]

Working aboard slave ships greatly expanded surgeons' medical understanding of black bodies, yet the incompetency of treatment some offered placed the
lives and future value of bondpeople in great danger. While making preparations for his England departure in 1791, ship captain Thomas King received a
letter from Thomas Addison explaining that efforts were being made to secure a
surgeon for the vessel *Trelawney*. "He has never been in Africa," King learned,
"but from his appearance I address we doubt not but you will find him a clever
active young man." Addison offered him a job for twelve guineas in agreement
to serve as the ship's surgeon for the ship's voyage.[111] Whether the commander
perceived this man as "clever" is unclear; however, approval for his employment
was likely based not only on the necessity of a medical professional but also
the physician's youth and willingness to serve within the trade. These casual
decisions fulfilled labor needs while imposing perilous risks to the preservation
of captives observed and treated by practitioners sometimes devoid of experience in shipboard care or restoring lives across racial lines. Captain William
Blake confronted such devastations while trading on the coast of West Africa
in the eighteenth century. He recounted, "The Doctor is not fit for this trade,"
owing to the crew "burying so many in the River."[112] Qualities necessary for
medical assistance on ships varied widely; however, skill deficiencies among
employed physicians came at a deadly cost to building a viable black labor force.
Eruptions of diseases and death altered financial views of their bodies, casting
them as not only financially worthless but disposable in the waters beneath.

The limits of surgeons' medical abilities were far from extraordinary. Being
tasked with managing a ship's crew to secure and transport a predetermined
cargo overseas, captains were regularly able to observe a physician's performance of work. Many surgeons professed capabilities of managing slaves'
health; however, once placed within the trade, their limited knowledge became
alarmingly clear. Forced to shorten his coastal stay on the Old Calabar coast
in August 1790, the commander of the *Pearl* explained, "We have been very
Sickly for Six weeks past [and] have Buried 13 Woman & Girls & 56 Men &

boys," after an unforeseen medical outbreak. Deaths of a significantly high number of slaves led him to conclude, "Our Doctor is not Acquainted with this Country's Disorders." Calamitous circumstances during the passage affected the reputations of surgeons and commanders, prompting the shipmaster to warn his financiers, "Hope you will never be Deceived by another."[113]

Preservation of transported slaves relied not only on maintenance and violent security but, most especially, adequate medical treatment. The close environment of ships affected slaves and sailors, but also a surgeon's work. On February 20, 1792, a physician complained that a young boy "George Crompton & the Slaves playing together in the Cabbin, broke the thermometer" carried aboard for ship use.[114] The enterprise of shared duties on slaving voyages often solidified tensions at sea. Surgeon Thomas Trotter recollected an instance when the presiding commander he served with "very frequently accused me of ignorance of my profession." According to Trotter, throughout the passage he was subjected without end to continuous "abusive language," which he said the captain "very frequently bestowed upon me as the Slaves were dying, which he was pleased to call 'the machinations of the doctor and devil.'"[115] Physicians's shipboard employment did not equate to nor guarantee friendships. The differing classes and statuses in the former homelands of those on board reveal how tension, power, and discord affected the preservation of bondpeople. Commander Samuel Stribling endured a gradual increase of slave mortality making it even more clear that "the Doctor has Not Made a Care of Any One of them." Archival silences make it impossible to determine how the surgeon became medically negligent or if the commander perhaps became physically disruptive in his medical attempts. What we can discern is that the boarded slaves were "in A Dangerous State," and Stribling declared, "I hope I Shall Not Burry but a few More without Some Great Alteration In thirre Health."[116] Bearing direct responsibility for the health of purchased slaves created significant and oftentimes overwhelming pressures on surgeons. Due to the high financial stakes for merchants, sailors, brokers, buyers, and their own futures, these expectations intensified most prominently amid the deaths of captives and verbal confrontations.

Slave ship surgeons endured significant pressures; however, recognizing the opportunities for lucrative gain, some falsified the extent of their medical abilities. In one instance a physician "Advertised In all the News Papers to Care [for] the Deaf & blind." Once hired through means undisclosed, the commander who hired the dishonest physician suffered from the doctor's misleading intention, writing to his investors, "He has Not made a Cure of 20 Slaves Sence the first of the Passage."[117] Any inabilities the physician acted out may have stemmed from a genuine unfamiliarity with treating the particular outbreak or perhaps an unwillingness to work. Although claiming the ability to work with those most vulnerable and deemed incurable, much like many others, he sought to act upon promises, the lure of money, and medical knowledge believed existent for professionals on slaving voyages.

Physicians played a major role in the arrival of healthy slaves, yet in some cases they faced hostile work environments. Surgeon Thomas Loma experienced such disrespect in his shipboard employment when the attending captain he worked with "would not let me continue y'e same medicines for one day," nor would he permit the use of astringents. Instead, in Loma's perspective, the shipmaster focused more on "filling them with raw plantains which every man in his sences will contradict." Lamenting further, he complained, "When I was sick he debarred me of everything necessary for a person in my low state of health."[118]

With personal reputations and the financial stakes of commanders and physicians differing within the trade network of slaves, stories transmitted to distant merchants varied in the blame placed on other ship employees and the preservation of transported human goods. While wading on the coast of Old Calabar in 1790, surgeon O. P. Degraves of the ship *Pearl* observed several captives "perishing for want of knowing what to do" in restoring their health. Over a hundred captives died, for which he blamed the commander: "Many were bought against my opinion & others without my advice."[119] Offering closer insight into his shipboard employment, he declared, "My Situation is most deplorable; at 5 o'clock I rise & go to bed at 8 at night." As a consequence, "I am on my leggs, and my greatest employment is worse than that of a waiter at the Bush inn." Feeling his professional expertise was being cast aside, he reasoned, "I am only a mere Surgeon and am never consulted in one thing conserning this trade, I make no doubt that your Captain will give you other informations concerning Such things as do not belong to me." Tensions only continued to intensify, and when the physician suggested the "purchase [of] a goat for the sick Slaves & white people," Degraves reported on the captain's denial, saying, "He knows what was good for them better than I did, and that I was continually talking nonsense."[120]

On December 14, 1790, ship captain Richard Martin interacted with the *Pearl,* reporting, "On my Arrival at old Calabar, I found C't Blake more forward in his Purchase then I could have expected, but the Slaves were in a most miserable condition through a mistaken notion of economy, in purchasing bad provisions, & the neglect and ignorance of M'r Degraves (as I was informed)," presumably through shoreline line conversations. As a consequence, the neighboring observing captain described, "The Slaves were in such a state with the Flux, yaws. & Cracaus that they had but little chance of mending much" toward a full recovery.[121] Dynamics between surgeons and ship captains played out in ways still unknown to contemporary scholars. Medical treatment allocated for their invested bodies became arenas for struggles of power based on the social and financial values projected for the preservation and overseas transport of black people.

Conclusion

The core operation in the sale and traffic of shipped Africans was the import of live bodies, most preferably healthy. Precautionary measures were employed to counter any medical outbreaks, but seaborne illnesses extended beyond racial and gendered lines, claiming the lives of scores of black and white populations. Movement of diseases across geographical boundaries, as this chapter revealed, owed to slaves' interactions with sailors and extended into toxic corners of ships that fueled the transport of contagious and deadly ailments. Seamen and physicians were often limited in the restorative care extended to bondpeople due to constrained resources and unfamiliarity with treating African bodies. The presence of slave ship surgeons was never based on humanitarianism, but served instead as a catalyst to obtain wealth and professional advancement toward furthering their understandings of medical treatment.[122] Sickness prevailed belowdecks on slave ships, taking lives and yielding important stories of struggle that shaped the final moments of many bondpeople's lives.

The varied testimonies of failing slave health provide greater texture to the human experiences of personal pain and medical terror bondpeople commonly faced while likewise enabling a viable opportunity to reconstruct the social landscape of medical management and treatment of the diseased, suffering, and dying. These deadly seaborne realities underscore the seminal point that "the Middle Passage was a crossroads and marketplace of diseases."[123] With health marked as the primary determinant of value for future market sales, preserving slaves' whole body was crucially fundamental to the journey and to the importation of an exploitable live black workforce.[124] Therein we see much more intimately how the ongoing infusion of sickness, diseases, malnourishment, starvation, and incredible grief activated the tolls of slavery at sea, making historically impossible the import of strong, healthy, prime, desirable, and disease and trauma-free captives.

7 A Tide of Bodies

On December 20, 1773, ship captain John Thornton remarked on the import of several slaves into Fredericksburg, Virginia. The sale of thirty-one slaves generated an estimated £1,373 and 6 shillings, while twenty-one others remained unsold. "Those left on hand," Thornton intimated, "you may believe must be of much less value than the others" previously bought. The unsold included "9 old women [and] 4 Men," three of the latter described as "old & blemished," along with "4 very small girls & 4 very small Boys" left under his direction. Foreseeing difficulty in the current climate of slave auctions, he warned, "There is little prospect of doing anything with them till the spring," Doing so ensured sufficient time to improve their physical appearance and solicit interest among future buyers.[1]

Scarcity of details makes it difficult to know if the additional time granted Thornton the opportunity to successfully secure sales or if he was forced later to travel to another port in hopes of gaining profit. The fate of these unsold and undesired captives remains a mystery. Thornton's report, however, provides a necessary glimpse into the types of slaves—young and old—carried inland and made a part of local Atlantic slave auctions. Their inclusion and differences in age revive the critical need to engage the human merchandise and more precisely the complexity of slave markets that ship captains confronted in the hopes of securing lucrative deals. Planters expressed decided preferences on a diversity of commercially imported goods, which sailors worked to satisfy by funneling various commodities, most especially slaves, into local seaports. Distant desires were projected for the purchase and delivery of ideal, robust, and largely healthy African captives to appease varying financial and laboring needs. This chapter investigates the landing of bondpeople carried through the Middle Passage and immediately forced into arranged auction sales. It looks outside the quantitative lens to take more seriously the need to delve deeper into the body as politic. It makes tangible meaning of imported black bodies—degraded and most times unable to be celebrated owing to the prevalence of toxicity and insatiable violence. Using the body as evidence, this chapter attempts quite simply to address slaves' sense of well-being both physically and psychologically following their import into distant Atlantic seaports. Typically we are devoid of concrete details explaining if any wounds or markings etched across a slave's body somehow occurred during their capture, while in their coastal holdings, or during the ship's oceanic passage. Despite these historical omissions, transported slaves arrived broken, weak, emaciated, vulnerable, and permanently displaced into foreign spaces. Regardless of the geographical sites to which captives were exiled, they carried with them the remnants of traumatic manifestations and memories of terrorizing violence, visible and invisible, endured on the ocean waterways, thereby problematizing the idea that captives were really ever able to move beyond the Middle Passage.

Slaveholders depended greatly on the commercial enterprise of African females and males for the replenishment of black laborers. Negotiations and sales forged between ship captains, merchants, and slaveholders marked the initial introduction of bondpeople into plantation communities across the Americas. Outside the fertile possibilities of wealth and future labor, the fundamental basis of these entrepreneurial exchanges rested firmly on the terrain of the black human body. Many slaves arrived with varied occupations, skills, laboring expertise, and cultural understandings. Using captives' bodies in lieu of their most times unattainable voices, their flesh serves here as a historic record to find unavoidable truth in the bruises, anxiety, wounds, and incurable and untreatable scars of the slaving process. As such, this chapter foregrounds the complicated terrain of age, sickness, physical disabilities, as well as psychological traumas that affected imported slaves as well as the prospect of final sales. The buying and bidding process in these economic ventures reveals important insights into the social determinations of value extended from its West African origins and similarly ascribed onto bondpeople within Atlantic ports.

Examining the various destinations to which bondpeople were transported is useful to understanding *where* they landed. Re-linking the slave ship experience to plantations as an interconnected extension of slavery at sea, this chapter's sole focus is with *how* slaves arrived in Atlantic slave societies. It investigates the cumulative effects that the Middle Passage bore within people's bodies to better humanize the suffering, the pain, and the ugly impermeable scars of slavery that numbers cannot always fully account. The interconnected financial hands of sea captains, merchants, and buyers enabled and thereby sanctioned the practice and continuation of violent mistreatment leading to intercontinental slaving transactions that crossed time and space. But, most of all, operation of such networks fueled by capital growth and capital gain justified the kidnap, purchase, and export of African people while serving as long-lasting reminders of the racial debasement defining the chattel status forced upon newly arriving captives.

Some slaves arrived contrary to Atlantic market desires, forcing some planters to forgo sale or to occasionally purchase those cast as undesirable both on cash terms or physical interest. Buyers traveled to local markets in pursuit of prime slaves, especially those perceived as most ideal and robust with long-term value. The discussion that follows widens the gaze to include the unfamiliar and often unrecorded slaves who did not always align with buyers' needs. Far from synonymous, giving attention to the altered, wounded, and traumatized offers a critical opportunity for expansion and reconsideration of the diversity of human cargoes and maritime experiences represented within Atlantic slave markets to better understand the collective narratives of pain, desperation, damage, survival, and loss. However, it is not just the movement of diverse and available workers into distant locales. In entering the third and final phase of the human manufacturing process—product delivery—this chapter unveils the importation of bruised, diseased, scarred, disabled, and, most of all, manufactured black bodies shaped and refined by their seaborne experiences. Offering such an exposure permits closer engagement with arriving slaves' sense of well-being following import. From this vantage point, we see not only the buying of disease and trauma through the arrival of imported slave bodies but also the totality exacted on them as they arrived broken and yet made by the violent world of slavery at sea.

The Gloved Hands of Control

Among the various goods transported across the oceanic waters as part of free market trade, the greatest emphasis was on black bodies as a source for labor and accumulated wealth. Regardless of tangible interactions with slaves or not, societies benefited most from the range of human goods transported, manufactured, and thus made through the Middle Passage. Within this enterprise, innumerable people were socially and financially invested in the extraction of captives out of Africa and distributed across the Americas. Slaveholders expressed initial demand, merchants allocated monies, and factors and agents of different slave trading firms served as intermediaries to locally facilitate these commercial ventures. Planters represented the primary consumers most reliant on slaves' incorporation into distant plantation communities, while sailors personally navigated foreign locales and relationships to transport, preserve, and provide the very human goods upon which global demands were made.

Once slave ships were docked, mariners were often expected to participate in presale preparations in assisting and expediting market sales. Much like on the African side of the Atlantic, crewmen forged shoreline relationships, this time with local white agents who gathered buyers and helped to ensure immediate sales of newly imported slaves. Owners of the vessel that Captain William Doyle led wrote, "Take care that you exert yourself in the Sale of the Slaves," suggesting that any accrued wealth rested on his personal involvement.[2] Merchants circulated instructions specifying orders on the process of trade. Traveling in close confinement with full management of boarded slaves for a significant period of time empowered sailors to expound on the qualities best represented among lodged slaves. Although many government-sanctioned monopolies began to dissolve in the early part of the eighteenth century, ship commanders served as representatives for private trade companies and came with many obligations to their employers beyond the transport of slaves. George McMinn of the *Ingram* received written instructions for his docked cargo, articulating, "Your average indeed will greatly depend upon Your own Conduct" in shoreline affairs. He was urged to assert control with local agents by "not allowing them to pick any Slaves before the Day of Sale," or as they outlined, "to sell too many in one Lott to close the Sales" in an expedited fashion.[3] Regardless of the various business procedures expected of sailors after crossing the Atlantic, distant merchants sought to instigate control over local sales in order to guarantee receipt of a fair amount of profits for themselves.[4]

Keenly aware of their central role in market sales, many investors tried to predict consumer interests and thus satisfy slaveholders. In 1775 slave trader Henry Laurens wrote to a merchant in St. Christopher emphasizing that "an entire parcel of fine Negroes must enable us to remit quicker than we can for a Cargo which consists of a mixture of all sorts & sizes" brought into port. Upon ending he declared, "Those which are prime enable us to pick our Customers."[5] Buyers' perceptions of captives had as much to do with the successes and failures of market sales as it did the public display of black bodies. On April 30, 1783, Leyland Penny & Co. wrote to sea captain Charles Wilson about his participation in market sales, intimating, "We take leave to recommend to you that you put the Negroes into small Lots," comprised of "15 or 20 Negroes in a Lot" during open sales. The diverse cadre of slaves unable to be sent back encouraged Wilson's "mixing the Indifferent Negroes with the best" of those brought to port.[6] Slave sales hinged directly upon strategic marketing and presentation. Looked at from the side of supply, assembling diverse captives not only drew larger crowds, but it could also potentially increase the value of those cast as inferior during open auctions.

Untangling the Violent Strains of Slave Sales

Preliminary guidelines of marketing and sales appeased investors, yet there were specific methods employed in selling slaves to the general public. With profit at stake, sailors and agents worked together in promoting auctions through handbills, posters, newspapers, and through word of mouth with the intent of sales occurring either the day a ship docked or, as one trader pointed out, "four or five days or a week after our arrival," to quickly move slaves off hand. Most times additional days were taken to prepare the captives and market as widely as possible for attracting larger crowds, especially since "some of the purchasers live at a remote distance from the place of Sale."[7] The average number of attendees present for sales of recently imported slaves remains uncertain, yet many traveled from various urban and rural spaces. These specialty markets for selling newly arriving captives coexisted with auctions centered on inland sales of seasoned and creolized slaves through the domestic slave trade and local plantation communities. Already owning different types of slaves, planters who gathered together for inspections and bidding of captives directly from Africa knew full well the intense management required with integrating new imports into plantation communities. Fueled by diverse needs and interests, the lure of available and exploitable black bodies "generally brought together a considerable number of buyers."[8]

Amid efforts to market forthcoming sales, bondpeople were made ready for public presentation. Speculations on demography, including gender, age, and ethnicity, factored into transactional decisions; however, the physical appearance of a captive's flesh affected final decisions of sales. Slave ships represented confined spaces of filth, regularly producing offensive smells. To counter any possibilities of contamination and jeopardizing future transactions, seamen were obligated to give attention to slaves' hygiene through tactics many times unknown to contemporary scholars. Once docked into the Caribbean in 1789, Captain Edward Williams received orders specifying, "You are to put the Cargo into there hands," presumably referring to local factors, "and take care to have them well Clean'd" to ensure "that there be no Complaints made" during conducted auctions.[9] Dousing their bodies at least with water helped to counter the intense odor typically emitted from slaves' bodies, having been cramped in holds with corpses, rodents, and unending exposure to urine, vomit, blood, and fecal matter.

Focusing on basic grooming, slave traders sought not only to display the highest quality but also to force slaves "to lose all trace of the 'fatigue' of the journey."[10] To prevent any drying and cracking of their skin once sufficiently cleansed, captives were rubbed with oil on their face, hair, torso, legs, and feet. This moisturized their skin, albeit temporarily, while creating a high-glossed look to counter discovery of any blemishes or other imperfections during inspections. Bondpeople's skin, teeth, muscles, limbs, and genitals were the primary points of scrutiny, similar to the coastal evaluations sea captains conducted in western Africa to assess a slave's superiority. Central in the minds of prospective Atlantic white purchasers was securing captives with a lifetime probability not only to attend to housework and agricultural needs but also to fulfill breeding purposes by producing children and extending a slaveholder's future with more slaves. Perhaps in building upon such desires, the commander of the *African* logged on May 24, 1753, that crewmen "Shaved the slaves' fore heads."[11] Such measures reduced the filtration of bacteria, but for bondmen especially, removing any gray strains and other remaining facial hairs on captives helped to convey a young and seemingly ageless look. Archival records do not offer substantial insight into specific preparations used at Atlantic ports with newly arriving black females, yet creativity was undeniably employed to convey even an illusion of exploitable perfection.

With the intended date of public auction secured and captives primed and ready for display, the process of trade unfolded. Two primary modes of sale were commonly conducted for imported slaves: scramble sales on board and off ship in sales conducted in an open yard. Trade varied according to agents, buyers, and the pervading culture within certain locales. In some instances the process took place within the confines of a ship, granting potential buyers privately authorized access. Once the *Emilia* docked at Port Maria during an undisclosed year, surgeon Alexander Falconbridge recorded that crewmen prepared the vessel for buyers, making sure "the ship was darkened with sails, and covered round."[12] Captives were moved to specified areas on the ship—"the men are on the main deck, and the women all on the quarter deck"—in order to facilitate greater ease of consumer selections.[13] The buying of newly imported slaves produced a unique culture predicated upon an interwoven network of international customers maintained by the regularity of participation, as well as the exclusion of certain types of individuals from engaging in this intimately personalized market.

Close to the predetermined hour on the day of sale, interested buyers gathered and mingled on the shoreline. "The purchasers on shore were informed a gun would be fired when they were ready to open the sale."[14] On other occasions they were permitted to pre-board ships in hopes of expediting the auction process and thus the movement of slaves into the domain of plantations. As such, "different people intending to be purchasers exert themselves to get as early as possible in among the Slaves, for the purpose of obtaining a good choice" in those made available.[15] Conceivably unbothered by entering and moving through these vile spaces, buyers boarded with the intent of claiming new ownership and leaving with an increase of property. "A great number of people came on board with tallies or cards in their hands," often inscribed "with their own name upon them" symbolically marking buyers' choice of slaves, while extending the permanent inclusion of a bondperson in the human manufacturing process.[16]

As shots were fired and other signals were made, buyers filtered throughout tightened corners onto ships. Some "rushed through the barricado door," one trader noted, "with the ferocity of brutes."[17] Others entered "at the gangway, betwixt those places," and with sales fully open to customers, "they rush in fore and aft, and suit themselves as well as they can, clapping their tallies on whatever they mean to take."[18] Many boarded with general ideas on their slaving needs, moving among the captives and making rather frantic choices to secure those believed most ideal. Competing with other buyers, they touched, fondled, and grabbed at slaves' bodies to assess their value and laboring potential. As consumers pondered final decisions of sale, they publicly claimed the lives of selected captives by clamping their tallies "about the necks of such Slaves as they make choice of."[19] Sales were driven by the quest for healthy captives as well as increasing numbers; therefore, it was not uncommon for buyers to have "three or four handkerchiefs tied together, to encircle as many as they thought fit for their purpose."[20]

The method of sales conducted on land differed, albeit marginally, from shipboard scrambles. Sea commanders often moved a cargo "in both ways"; however, primary sources reveal, "It is commonly on shore."[21] Sales off ship permitted the engagement of even more buyers while reducing opportunities for captives to jump overboard and flee. In preparation for market inspections, "the Slaves were then placed in a close yard, [and] ranged in order for sale." Conducted in public view, sales were performed in a restricted yet open space, most often requiring prior approval. To better protect their property from any external disruptions, surrounding gates were "shut immediately before the sale commenced," and thereafter "a great gun was fired," signaling the beginning of selections. Far from the ceremonious gathering of crowds casually gazing and making bids upon an individual slave, these sales erupted in a mob-like fashion as buyers moved from slave to slave rapidly seeking to obtain the most viable human goods. "Purchasers with their adherents and assistants, rushed into the yard with great violence, and laid hold of the most healthy and good looking Slaves, which parcels they afterwards picked and culled in their minds."[22] In hopes of countering losses to any competing customers, selected captives "were immediately purchased and hurried out of the yard."[23] Markets remained open until all of the highly preferred captives were sold; those remaining were forced into a different set of sales reserved for "refuse slaves."

Severely traumatized and weakened from the seaborne passage, bondpeople were far from unresponsive during post-voyage sales. Buyers aggressively converged on open arenas, creating mass hysteria among displayed slaves. A trader recounted witnessing an escalated scene in Grenada seaport where "the women were so terrified, that several of them got out of the yard, and ran about St. George's town, as if they were mad." Having personally endured or witnessed the sights and sounds of sexual and other brutal assaults at sea, such interactions reactivated already deep-seated fears for their own lives. As slaves aboard the snow *Tryall* saw crowds of white bodies frantically heading toward them, "forty or fifty of the Slaves leaped into the sea" to escape what they conceived as a dangerous unknown. Despite their efforts, several crewmen jumped into a boat and "took up some of them."[24] Unsure of their already devastated lives, some captives tried drowning themselves while others relied on the water to swim away from their boarded tormentors.

Viewing the import of Africans solely according to their economic desires, traders were far less concerned with the parceling of slaves and breaking apart lives. Forced into foreign lands comprised of unfamiliar languages and people, many captives contemplated their still uncertain fates. Reduced to commodities and profits of sale, the process "had an astonishing effect upon the Slaves," as buyers remained relentless in their market endeavors.[25] Displayed men, women, and children gazed upon aggressive spectacles of buying power prompting many of them to "cry and beg that such a man or woman (their friend or relation) might be bought and sent with them, wherever they were going."[26] With the acquisition of laboring bodies centrally in their minds, planters looked past such emotional pleas for sales, often to their own detriment. When a buyer "would not purchase a man's wife," one physician recalled, "the next day I was informed the man hanged himself."[27] Confined alongside family members and strangers from varying ethnicities and communities, slaves' oceanic transport created a shared sense of struggle enabling the formulation of kin-like ties with shipmates. As purchasers pushed back crowds to grab hold of preferred slaves, many bondpeople "were crying out for their friends with all the language of affliction at being separated."[28] Amid the roar of crowds and conversations, buyers paid little regard to pronounced displays of sadness or what a surviving document described as "a general cry, and a noise through the whole ship." Many captives shed tears and cried out not merely for themselves but for the ones they held dear to if they "think they are going to be parted from their husbands, wives, mothers, children, &c."[29]

Open auctions permitted buyers the chance to filter through and actualize their former demands, while for docked slaves the frenzy of market sales extended the sequential process of terror. Countless buyers laid hands on slaves' bodies, ritualizing their movement on land and into the domestic sphere of captivity. Navigating through preselected spaces in a synchronized fashion, they went beyond mere casual spectators to touch and tangibly assess the value of parcels of black human imports. Slave markets produced an economy of violence devoid of bloodshed, dismemberment, and wounded bodies. Instead, the touching of skin, grabbing of hair, pulling on limbs, prying of mouths, fondling of genitalia, and forced bending of bodies for economic reasoning inscribed new forms of power that gathered buyers mitigated against every slave imported into the Caribbean and across the Americas. The public nature of market sales sanctioned the violence, as they carried tallies marking private personal decisions of sale while what scholar Saadiyah Haartman labels "scenes of subjection" operated openly, reinforcing the status of black people as sellable goods; and thus slaves.[30] As such, "every person employed about the streets . . . had almost daily opportunities of observing" such humiliating scenes.[31] Psychologically scarred from their forcible exile, slaves were followed by distress not only as their lives were publicly determined and solidified by the needs and desires of strangers, agents, and buyers but also as they found themselves insulated within yet another violent world of disorienting trauma—this time off ship.

For those captives unsold and unable to gain market interest, agonizing uncertainty about their fate extended further once placed in separate second-tiered sales. "Those Slaves that do not average with the cargo are sold by auction" and moved immediately after into specialized markets known as "vendue" sales.[32] Arriving bondpeople came ashore as damaged and traumatized symbols and products of the refinement process. Scores came in extremely weak, diseased, disabled, and "sometimes in the agonies of death," after which they were relocated to alternative venues; infants, young children, and aged slaves unable to entice buyers were similarly grouped. "I have frequently seen the very refuse (as they are termed)," one trade participant recalled, "of the Slaves of Guinea ships landed and carried to the vendue masters in a very wretched state" of physical health.[33] Dismissed, passed over, discarded, and devalued as fragile and worthless bodies in contrast to other captives, this did not make them any less immune to invasive scrutiny or market torment. The categorical labeling upon them in many ways reflected base determinations made about virtually all slaves: cheap, exploitable black labor. Sources cannot always disentangle buyers' reasoning for sales nor the types of work reserved for less desirable slaves. However, in a profit-driven enterprise, consumers employed creative strategies to monetize lives and extract labor.

The lure of cheaper bodies fueled both interest and financial concerns. Unsellable slaves typically "remain longer on hand, until purchasers offer" to buy them. "A number of people, who speculated in the purchase of the Slaves," investigated the condition of those unsold "either for the purpose of carrying them to the country, and retailing them," or instead having them "shipped off the island to foreign parts."[34] No matter if gathered crowds comprised slave dealers, farmers, physicians, bankers, or curious local residents, the influx of an available workforce created a steady business environment in the eighteenth century with ready markets, consumers, and looming profits to be cultivated. For some buyers, refuse slaves represented a mere supplement to other slaves already bought, whereas other purchasers entered such markets specifically aimed at securing those cast aside and perceived as devoid of any real financial and social value in the economy of slavery. The extent to which slaves' reduced prices factored into abuses and neglect meted out within the space of plantations will remain buried in the archive of memory.

Pending vendue sales often came with expectations of lower-priced captives. Some bondpeople "sold at very small prices, even as low as a dollar."[35] Surgeon Alexander Falconbridge recounted sixteen slaves "sold in the Alexander by auction" and given depreciated values. The ship's physician professed, "one or two of them [sold] so low as five dollars—a piece" in final agreements. Despite finding buyers during the bidding process, "they all died before we sailed."[36] Other merchants confronted similar business opportunities riddled with disaster. James Baille & Co. wrote from Grenada to James Rogers & Co. in 1791 concerning the conclusion of sales with slaves carried from Old Calabar aboard the *Daniel*: "We are reproached every day with some of the different parcels we sold having Died in 24 hours" once removed into the hands of buyers. Minimal profits were gained; however, "Six of those sold at Vendue died emmediately," imposing even greater liability. The factors later intimated that "in a Word they were such a parcell, that we never desire, to See their like again" with future imports.[37]

Disaggregated Bodies

Demands for Africans resulted in the pouring of scores of bondpeople into the coastal waterways of port communities throughout the Americas. The constant influx of black bodies reinforced the need for more imports while imposing clear distinctions of those least preferred along lines of gender, age, and health. Capitalizing on the evolving intensity, merchants, buyers, and factors became further immersed within the entangled systems of slave commerce. Strict orders were disseminated to determine the movement of slaves in, around, and through market sales, yet who made up these imported black mixtures?

Bondmen commanded the highest interest among newly arriving Africans. Laboring needs varied; however, the predominance of black males boarded and shipped on slave vessels generally aligned with the desires for healthy, able-bodied slaves capable of carrying out agricultural and domestic needs envisioned within local plantation communities. Consumers vied for the influx of adult black men, yet how did such demands affect slave sales across the Atlantic? Liverpool merchant Thomas Leyland and the trading firm Eustace Barron & Co. exchanged correspondence on the state of slaving affairs in May 1786. As Leyland explained, "It is impossible to buy a Cargo of Negroes in Africa all Males."[38] John Guerard wrote to merchants Harmington & Stricts on June 10, 1752, regarding a similar matter of slave shipments that Captain Wells carried to Charleston, which comprised "too many little ones." Knowing the difficulty of future market sales, Guerard emphasized, "My request to our Friend was to the Contrary for Men chiefly" to satisfy orders. "I find it Cou'd not be avoided neither co'd they be Obtain'd cheaper," because "there was such a Demand for them" among foreign traders of other nations.[39] Sailors confronted the implications of unsatisfactory business, as certain captives—namely, black men—proved far more challenging at times to supply explosive demands. These difficult feats underscore trade challenges and the varying costs of demand while revealing that regardless of consumer interest, merchants and buyers had to adapt their slaving endeavors according to available and thus imported human supplies.

Adult male slaves were widely requested, yet agents of slave trading firms balanced the influx of other captives alongside recruiting planter interest. On July 30, 1780, colonial factor James Rollan referenced a "long Conversation" he shared with ship captain Walker regarding expectations for future slave importations. Much of his concern rested with "the size, Age, & Sex" of bondpeople that he "apprehended would meet with the most ready Sale" within Antiguan markets. The type of slaves Rollan felt most favorable to planter demands included "a Cargoe of about 2 to 300 well assorted, such as young Men & boys, young Women, & Girls from a good Country" within Africa.[40] Gender dominated many preferences and decisions of sale; however, age played a far greater role in sales of newly arrived slaves than contemporary scholars have considered. Two categories of imported Africans fostering the strongest dispositions upon port arrival were small children and slaves considered beyond their prime years. Reservations harbored against these groups dealt less with any laboring possibilities and more with the additional needs required with their upkeep, which ran counter to buyers' financial visions.

Explicit demands for the exclusion of young and aged captives emerged across different sectors of the Atlantic. In 1789 merchant Francis Grant articulated his hope of arriving ships carrying healthy slaves, although he did not want "too large a proportion of Old or Young among them."[41] From a commercial standpoint, consumers anticipated immediate production of labor to further bolster local economies. Merchants dictated how the process should unfold; therefore, knowing the business challenges at stake not only with satisfying distant orders but with securing successful market sales as well, some traders employed discriminatory practices within coastal Africa. One slave trader reported that while he was on the shore of Mana in West Africa, several local blacks sailed a canoe overloaded with four slaves and offered them for sale. The ship captain, however, "refused them all, 2 being too old, and 2 too young."[42] As middlemen, mariners were directly responsible for the numbers and types of slaves brought into the New World. Looking beyond simply filling a cargo hold, some commanders thought further into the dynamics of overseas slave markets, assessing and consequentially determining the value or lack thereof of certain captives before their displacement. Incalculable numbers of slaves may have been forced into the human manufacturing process, yet these exclusionary practices challenge the notion that every offered slave equated value in the eyes of white traders.

Considerable measures were implemented to prevent the coastal purchase and inclusion of children and elderly slaves, but many of them nevertheless landed on foreign shores and were placed for sale. In September 1753, the snow *Elizabeth* docked at South Carolina from Gambia carrying 145 slaves. Most of the ship's cargo fostered market satisfaction, yet the import of "24 Boys" and "15 Girls" generated wide concern. The attending merchant professed he had done "the Best I cou'd possibly do with Them" during vessel sales, despite "there being too many old & Small ones" among those brought to port.[43] Similar market anxieties were felt in 1792 as the ship *Fame* arrived with an inferior cargo of slaves transported into Grenada from Old Calabar. Concerned about the prospects for profit, the commander lamented, "I am Sorry to Say I Belive there was Never a Worse Cargo of Slave Ships from Africa," which in his view "will be greatly to your Disadvantage." Sources do not indicate that the inferiority of any of the imported slaves owed to diseases, wounds, or disabilities. Therein, we can reason that the commander's frustrations reflected more his disappointment with the arrival of "11 Girls under five" along with "13 Infants at [the] Breast."[44]

Basing the forced movement of bondpeople on slave ships solely through adult men and women, younger slaves, including toddlers and infants, are rarely accounted for in narratives of the Middle Passage. Several crew members may have found difficulty with securing prime slaves on the West African shoreline; however, still unclear is how a significantly high number of children were not only forced into slavery but also purchased, boarded on a ship, and transported through a slaving voyage. The sea captain could have received a price reduction for sales of the small girls or gained some of them as a complement to sales while bartering material goods on the African coastline. On the other hand, the existence of more than a dozen infants necessitates an examination of pregnancies and childbirth in the transatlantic slave trade. Fragmentary sources leave unspoken if these new mothers entered captivity with children already conceived or if they perhaps became impregnated during the slaving process. The pervasive culture of sexual abuse in slave pens, coastal dungeons, and inland raids conducted during the human manufacturing process suggests a higher probability that many of these children were products of rape. Their shipboard inclusion similarly leaves open several questions: Were they captured and forced into the trade or born during the ship's passage? Did higher numbers of children result from the birth of twins, triplets, or quadruplets? Were any children sold with their mothers or perhaps forced into the care of unknown boarded females? With violence, malnutrition, and deprivation a predominate feature of the manufacturing process, how did they endure and thus survive slavery at sea? Queries about children in the slave trade persist, yet the fragmentary nature of sources and complexities surrounding their enforcement into the slaving cycle seldom renders their oceanic experiences as well as receipt of them in port auctions permanently silent.

Children generally represented long-term investments within plantations; however, investors, buyers, and sailors viewed their placement into slave markets through a rather different lens. James Baille & Co. wrote in 1791 from Grenada reporting on the arrival of captives aboard the vessel *Daniel*. They explained, "Capt'n Laroche will without [a] doubt report to you, how very averse he was even at Old Calabar, to take charge" of what they characterized as "such a miserable Sett of people" carried into the Caribbean. Seventy-three of the ship's slaves sold at an average of £32; however, presiding factors directed "21 [of them] to Vendue," where they believed once there "they will sell for a Trifle" given the lower prices offered for each of them. With a slave's ability to perform labor the primary focal point even during clearance sales, many buyers maintained strict preferences on investments of imported slaves. Therein, auctioneers faced continued challenges in generating interest with the vessel's remaining captives, because those still on hand included "infants so small, that nobody will look at them."[45] Their young lives passed over and deemed useless to an economy of slavery with immediate productive needs, unclear in the sources is if these children remained in Grenada; were reboarded and offered for sale in other islands; or perhaps parceled out, gifted, or even absorbed into local families.

Many children endured the transatlantic crossing without familial ties, although it was not uncommon to find women and their progeny aboard different slavers. Merchant William Grumly reported the arrival of the ship *Fly* into Tortola. Surviving records indicate the sale of "1 Woman & Child at the Breast" to a buyer named William Gregory, who purchased the female for £66 and her child at £4.[46] Bearing in mind the maternal needs many newborns required that would have affected any labor this mother performed, we can never know the reasons prompting Gregory to keep these two captives together. Several slaves carried into Kingston, Jamaica, aboard the ship *Fanny* in January 1793, being unable to attract any interested buyers, were "sold at Vendue." Among those sent, "two were infants." Puzzled by the import of newborns, local agents reasoned they "must have been given with their Mothers" during coastal African sales.[47] The marginalizing of histories of children in the slave trade overlooks their presence on slave ships, treatment endured at sailors hands, and, most of all, how they survived the transatlantic passage. Captivity and exile into foreign spaces bore deep-seated traumas that drastically affected any bondperson, regardless of age. Undeniably devastating to the institution of slavery was not only separation from a loved one but the loss of a parent through death, and having to bear the pain of bondage feeling un-nurtured, unprotected, and thus alone. Account sales for an unnamed ship revealed that the "Sum Rec'd for a negroe Child whose mother Died on the passage" was £9.[48] Sources do not intimate how this mother perished, if her child witnessed her death, nor if any care was extended to this young captive during the remaining voyage. Heavily dependent on their parents for survival, socialization, and a sense of belonging, enslaved children, perhaps more than teenagers and their adult counterparts, faced tremendous vulnerability, grief, and isolation within the specter of slavery at sea unable to be measured or quantified.[49]

Aged slaves similarly fostered resentment in slave sales, yet they commonly came into the Americas through the Middle Passage. Within plantations slave-holders held clear understandings of the limits of exploitable bodies. Metrics conceptualizing the meaning of "old" were nonexistent in slave markets and thus left to the personal gaze and speculation of sailors, surgeons, factors, and buyers. As a consequence, broad descriptors, including "elderly," "old," and "very old," were routinely employed, economically castigating aged slaves as weak, fragile, and in many ways worthless to laboring needs.[50] A 1756 exchange shared between South Carolina merchant Henry Laurens and Rhode Island merchants Samuel and William Vernon offers beginning insight into the parameters of blackness and age. Delving into current slave markets, Laurens remarked, "The young people found purchasers pretty readily"; however, those "on the Wrong Side [of] 30 years of Age wont move at all."[51] Such observations provide a foundational basis and tangible age toward defining a bondperson, yet still unclear is how, amid language barriers and the trauma of slave auctions, buyers could discern the ages of displayed captives. The bodies of slaves encompassed the primary terrain of laboring scrutiny wherein which infirmities not only created an immediate reduction in the perceived value of aged slaves, but also raised critical queries about a bondperson's productive capacity.[52] Rejected through often brutal means on the African coast, elderly slaves faced a similar process of devaluation and exclusion that extended across the seas to Atlantic market sales.

Efforts were made to hinder the presence of older captives in slave sales; however, once imported, they fueled concerns among many merchants surrounding the prospect of a foreseeable customer base. Surgeon Thomas Lomas of the *Swift* explained the circumstances through which several less than desirable slaves were landed into port: "Perhaps you may think it something surprizing that our Mortality was so great" during the passage. "It is not surprizing at all," he professed, given that the vessel commander "bought Old Slaves I am certain none of your others Masters would of bought."[53] Orders circulated across the Atlantic with the goal of preventing the shipment of aged slaves, yet these demands—contingent on the state of West African markets and sailors' attentiveness to these matters—were never certain. Ahxaridne Quidoe, a Jamaican merchant, reported the arrival of the vessel *Pearl* commanded by Samuel Stribling and carrying 356 slaves into port. Much to Quidoe's disappointment, "The Slaves were of a very inferior quality," because as surviving sources reveal, "many of them [are] aged and infirm." Equally devastating to future business was "his having lost near 120—on the middle passage," leading therefore to far fewer supplies of docked slaves than originally anticipated.[54] We do not know the cause of any slaves' deaths nor variation among the victims lost at sea along lines of gender or age. Given the economic desire to move imported slaves off hand, a bondperson's advanced age became an impediment, and their purchase imposed a measure of burden that shifted from sailors and merchants and on to buyers.

The responsibility of markets and public sales fully in their charge, factors often expressed tremendous frustration concerning the arrival of aged slaves. In 1790 Captain Martin carried 189 slaves from Old Calabar aboard the brig *Daniel*. Many of those boarded were described as "thin" and "a number of old people amongst them," which fostered deep resentment. Despite auction concerns, local agents "exposed the slaves for sale," which generated considerable revenue with captives selling "at an average of £37.7.3 Sterling." At the conclusion of sales, 68 captives remained unsold. Because many were "so low in flesh," factors complained, with "so many old people among them . . . we cannot with precision ascertain their value" among future buyers.[55] Similar anxieties emerged after the landing of several slaves in Grenada aboard the ship *Fame* in 1792. The makeup of the entire cargo is unknown, yet particularly rare in slave trade records was the arrival of "128 Women all [with] fallen Breast & Grayhears."[56] The history of black women and slavery is often overshadowed by conversations centered on rape, breeding, and pregnancy, focusing exclusively on younger females. Such an emphasis overshadows and renders older black women invisible, while likewise casting them as sexually useless within the plantation regime and histories produced. There is no evidence pointing to the success or failures confronted in recruiting buyers for such a high number of imported female captives. Focusing especially on these women's bodies, hair, and varying conceptions of beauty during market inspections, they may have fulfilled duties of child care, field, domestic, and other personal servant needs within plantations. However, some consumers perceived many of these women as unattractive, barren, and thus less likely to contribute to the labor space of reproduction.

Buyers operated on a single principle of securing profitable laborers; therefore, age became the deciding factor of value placed on all imported slaves. Much to the dismay of local slaving interests, the 1787 ship *Ville d'Honfleux* transported several elderly captives across the Atlantic. The ship manifest listed "Number of Men 50 old maimed and sick 20 thin," although an inscribed note relayed that their "Youth gave great room to hope for their Reestablishment." In addition, "10 Women" similarly lodged in the vessel's hold were recorded as "old and sick, [and] decidedly bad."[57] The stressful environment of slave ships affected the health of slaves, yet the presence of physical impairments and advanced age compounded the already poor conditions some slaves faced on entering the trade. How were these slaves filtered into the manufacturing process? What type of medical care did crewmen employ to sustain them through to port arrival? Maimed, sick, and thin, many of these bondpeople represented failed investments. Given the gendered nature of captivity, we may never come to know what "decidedly bad" meant for several elderly black women carried ashore. More than the difficulty of capital able to be gleaned off their declining bodies, the psychological scars they carried on land reached much further, having lived most of their former lives in freedom, being sold into slavery later in their life, devalued for the limited profit they could generate, and being forced to adjust and survive in a foreign locale characterized by violent labor expectations.

Silences surrounding elderly slaves' presence in the slave trade make it impossible to know their regularity in the history or if they entered Atlantic slave markets alongside family members. The 1774 Rhode Island vessel *Othello* provides a unique opportunity to consider these slaving realities. On April 2, 1774, a buyer listed as David Baird purchased four captives, including one "Elderly" woman, a girl listed as "her Daugh'r," and two boys, for a collective sum of £125. Several weeks later a man referred to as William Dangerfield bought a "very old" woman and a bondman listed as "her son" during vendue sales. Both captives sold for an estimated £81.[58] Sources do not reveal how agents determined these familial connections, although it is probable crewmen communicated these previous shoreline observations or consumers perhaps took note of their behaviors toward one another during auction sales. Similarly unclear is why these buyers chose to maintain these connections as well as the types of labor they envisioned most demanding, particularly among the slaves of advanced age. The life these captives underwent once displaced into plantation life is unknown; their Atlantic arrival reveals more closely the continuation of trauma beyond import that may have permitted some families to remained structurally intact from West Africa at least through Atlantic market sales.

The Intrusion of Undesirable Flesh

Children and aged captives represented massive undertakings in slave sales, yet buyers were also forced to contend with the arrival of unhealthy bodies. Such imports generated an intense reaction, jeopardizing the varied calculations and commercial desires that merchants, factors, and consumers collectively based on the movement and exploit of African slaves. Deprivation and neglect filtered throughout the capture and coastal holding of slaves; however, these abuses extended further on ships, creating a devastating impact on their physical and psychological well-being. Studies of slave markets often focus on prices, credit, and the transactional nature of auctions, giving little attention to the social manifestation of illness, disability, and trauma among newly arrived captives. Looking beyond the exchange of monies toward the range of black human goods trafficked through the Middle Passage foregrounds how imported slaves bore every resemblance of terror-centered captivity within their flesh during Atlantic markets.

Moving between spaces, from vessels and onto land, forced bondpeople to undergo drastic shifts in climates and weather patterns. No matter the space of slave sales—on ship or in selected yards—the bidding and buying of bondpeople exposed them to open environments undeniably damaging to their health. In 1752 Captain Wells engaged in coastal negotiations for slaves in western Africa. Although "he bo't them all alive," once boarded, "a few Contracted Disorders by Colds," that emerged during the oceanic passage. The ship's crew conceivably employed measures to restore the slaves' health, yet according to an attending Charleston agent, "We Lost two during the Sales and have three now under doctors hands w'ch am in hopes will Recover."[59] Inclement weather, crammed bodies, and intense heat on ships forged a direct and palpable impact on slaves' health that only worsened once on land. During the summer of 1740, South Carolina merchant Robert Pringle offered details on the current state of slaving affairs: "The Season is now become exceeding Hott," creating exhaustive conditions, "which makes Business very fatigueing & prejudicial to [the] health" of not only captives but agents and prospective buyers as well. For slaves, however, the greatest danger came from "being obliged to be so much in the Scorching Sun" during market inspections.[60] Several months later, winter followed the December arrival of the vessel *Griffin* from Angola "with about 250 negros," and sales began one week after the ship's arrival. Much to Pringle's disagreement, he reported, "The Weather has been so extreamly Cold ever since & Continues with hard frosts & Snow," thus posing "a great Detriment to the Negroes."[61]

The enfeebled health of bondpeople is often attributed to the traumatic circumstances of bondage, often overlooking the integral effect of seasonal

changes. Constant touching of bodies by different buyers produced a contaminated environment for slaves and consumers during auction sales. Yet the
unpredictability of weather and constant staging of slaves for open display
created an even greater state of vulnerability. Minimal protective measures,
including food, clothing, meager medical attention, and movement indoors
out of inclement weather, were implemented to provide some small measure
of preservation against a slave's decline. With bondpeople a principal source
of capital, public sales were critically necessary in generating revenue for
future voyages. Therefore, all attention was focused on ridding agents and
sailors of the additional care required with selling and permanently moving
newly docked human imports into the hands of interested owners and local
communities.

Changing weather patterns led to minor colds, yet some captives arrived already affected by far greater health concerns. In 1752 South Carolina merchant
John Guerard penned a letter to Captain Watts regarding future imports from
West Africa. Expounding on various commercial needs specific to the region,
he referenced a young captive carried to port: "The boy you brought with [a]
Sore Arm is under the Doc's hands" on shore. Sources do not indicate details
surrounding the young man's import, the source of his medical complaint, nor
how his transporters discovered his complaints. As such, buried in the archive
of memory is if he plausibly fell during the ship's passage, a sailor violently
handled him, he engaged in a revolt, or a disease or bloodied gash emerged
that became infected. Conveying his growing concerns for the boy's restoration,
Guerard lamented, "I fear the Arm will be Lost at Last," due to the unknown
bodily complaint.[62] The origin of his medical concern is uncertain, but we can
surmise that both Guerard's and the boy's anxieties intensified—for drastically
different reasons—if his condition worsened, forcing the attending physician
to sever his arm, leaving the young captive with a pained and irregular body
structure.

Bodily distresses among imported slaves were far from isolated. On May 21,
1752, merchant William Toliff received a notice regarding the import of slaves
docked aboard the ship *Molly*. Immediately following the vessel's arrival, local
factors "disposed of 44 Men, 20 Women, 23 Boys, & 7 Girls of the Negroes,"
which collectively "amount[ed] to £19096." Despite previous successful sales,
"4 Men, 1 Girl and 1 Boy" lay in waiting, still unsold. Toliff learned that "two
[of] the Men are sick & lame in their thighs, [and] one almost blind," invariably reducing public interest in their purchases. Medical examinations likewise
revealed "the other Man & the Girl [were] very bad w'th the Yaws," keeping
them both in an unhealthy state.[63] One month later a local agent offered an
update, noting, "There is none of the Negroes sold Since my Last, but we
have had the ill Luck to loose two Men," through reasons undisclosed.[64] The

subsequent bidding of transported captives exposed human frailties and the damages slavery inflicted on slaves' bodies. Surviving sources obscure how each of these captives entered the trade on the African side of the Atlantic; however, as revealed, the continuum of deplorable toxic conditions extended the prevalence of sickness, vision problems, and crippled conditions that inscribed incalculable damages on bondpeople through the Middle Passage. The number of slaves driven aboard the *Molly* able to generate profits exceeded those unsold and cast as unusable; however, many of these rejected captives carried personal stresses and a profound sense of trauma, shock, and incredible uncertainty through their displacement into New World plantation communities.

Sickness and disabilities burrowed within captives' bodies, worsening the trauma of kidnap and displacement in a foreign land. Twelve unsold slaves affected by several health complications and transported into Virginia on the brig *Othello* offer incredible insight into these port realities. On April 21, 1775, agents with John Thornton & Co. facilitated vendue sales, among which included one man and two "Elderly" slaves, both female and male, described as "wanting an Eye." Several other slaves recorded as "Sickly" were attended with various diseases and health complications that, while lowering interest in other sales, secured buyer interest with offers of reduced prices. Particularly extraordinary among the auctioned slaves was the inclusion of one aged male slave who had "lost the use of his Right Hand" along with an older female captive deprived of sensation within the same hand, particularly her "fore fingers."[65] There really is no way to determine how paralysis ensued, making it difficult for either captive to coordinate movement. Whether envisioned to satisfy temporary or long term needs, unable to be sent back to Africa, buyers overlooked slaves' inability to control their hand movement, looking instead to how their increased ages would have bearing on a lifespan of exploit.

Debilitation was a common devastation of slavery at sea. In 1788 William Grumly remarked on the arrival of the sloop *Fly*, highlighting the enfeebled condition of a male captive contained in the ship's cargo. In his view the bondman was "picking up his flesh" or rather improving through the use of local land-based resources. Although his improvement continued, he "was loseing one of his eyes" due to a persistent inflammation.[66] Plantations regularly included blind slaves, yet scholars rarely connect the influx of blindness from slaving voyages with market sales. Merchant Henry Laurens wrote James Skinner on October 3, 1755, explaining that a sea captain by the name of Bennett endured "the loss of his Doctor," leaving the crew to endure "a great mortality" stemming from the deaths of thirty-four slaves during the transatlantic passage. With his problems compounded by the lack of medical assistance and an unnamed medical outbreak, the shipmaster "deliver'd about 30 [who] were loaden with infirmitys" of various kinds. We are left to speculate on the types of disorders surfacing among several docked slaves; however, surviving records reveal "10 of them almost blind," leading to a lower average sale price of "£33.14/Sterling."[67] The fate of these captives and even how their blindness ensued are inconclusive. Outside of their failing eyesight, slaveholders viewed blind slaves as valuable workers, making it more than probable that some buyers found financial usefulness with their purchase. However, being imported into a foreign land, sold into distant spaces far less familiar, and thus incapable of comprehending their future peril made bondage tremendously more difficult by enforcing greater dependencies and needs within the slave community.

Diseases among newly arrived slaves took on different forms and personal affect. In 1793 Allan White & Co. reported the carrying in of slaves into Jamaica on the brig *Fanny*. Among those transported were "eight diseased people" transferred on land. The cause of their medical complaints remains unknown, yet their potential inclusion in market sales produced considerable concern. Local agents decided that, given their attending ailments, these grouped slaves "could not possibly be brought forward in our Sales," and in looking less toward profit they "were therefore sold at Vendue" for much lower prices than originally anticipated.[68] Illnesses were far from extraordinary in the world of slave auctions. South Carolina merchant John Cross addressed a letter to Paul Cross on March 2, 1776, in the Gallinas River of West Africa, detailing business ventures ongoing within the local area. He referenced the sales of three captives—a boy, a young girl of 4 feet and 6 inches, and an adult male slave—totaling the combined price of £171 2s 6d. The process of their inspections and the recruited buyers exist only in the archive of memory; however, even more critical to the merchant's letter and the medical history of slavery was a brief marking that "her Nose [was] almost Eataway with the yaws."[69]

Several symptoms common to victims of the yaws emerged in the eighteenth century. One physician explained that it "proceeds from Coition with an unclean Person."[70] With the inability for proper cleanliness and the prevalence of shipboard interactions between black females and sailors through sexual abuse, such behaviors could very well have exposed the young girl to this ailment. "It makes its first appearance in little spots on the skin not bigger than a pin's point," which, at the onset of this condition, for some victims "increase daily, and rise like pimples."[71] Some patients endured the proliferation of "numerous superficial sores of no great size, in each of which are small spherical prominences, in appearance like a raspberry."[72] Without any sort of prevention, yaws could "appear in all parts of the body"; therefore, it was not uncommon to find "they are most plentiful and of the largest size about the groin, private parts, fundament, arm-pits, and face." Unclear is if the aforementioned young girl suffered from more than one yaw. According to a practitioner, "They are largest when fewest in number," and the sores "are not painful unless roughly handled" as the disease spreads throughout the body.[73] Set adrift amid unstable waters and a relentless world of violence, power deprivation, and exploit, bondpeople were denied any sort of comfort or gentle treatment during the oceanic passage. However, more critical to this disorder and the bonded girl's experience was belief that it arose "from want of care and proper management," often causing "the torments of the *yaws* to surpass all description, from the *bone ache*, and dreadful agonizing curvatures" transforming parts of a person's body.[74] Therein, negligence of medical attention or even unfamiliarity with proper treatment likely worsened the girl's ailment, leading to the prominent facial alteration.

Surviving records prevent any deeper analysis into the transmission and treatment of her condition, yet the severity of this girl's disfigurement foregrounds the need for greater curiosity into the specter of diseased and altered bodies in histories of slave sales and plantation communities. Yaws, perhaps lying undetected by her captors or coastal buyer, emerged in her capture, during the coastal holding, or even on ship. It is simply impossible to reconstruct the process and duration of time that passed as her nose became modified; however, knowing that female captives were routinely judged according to their bodies and physical attraction, this little girl's face comprised the primary point of speculation that buyers would have scrutinized first in assessing her long-term value. The frontal location of her disease and disfigured nose prevented the use of any commonly deceptive sale tactics, rendering any agent or prospective buyer unable to disregard her pronounced contusion. The outplay of her disease likewise required an additional and unexpected investment of restorative care to aid her physical improvement as well as any emotional and psychological scars that could detonate within a plantation household or community. Being sold and displaced into a land-based slave society engendered severe isolation for this young girl through the persistence of differences relative to language and cultural barriers as well as any extreme ridicule interlinked with any self-conscious image she maintained about herself into her adult years, thus underscoring how the many scars bondpeople carried through slavery at sea were not always invisible.

Slavery imposed tremendous burdens upon captives' potentially laboring bodies. On September 4, 1792, the commander of the ship *Fame* reported on the range of devastations attending the transport of slaves from Old Calabar into Grenada. "I have Bury'd 65," he wrote, along with enduring the sickly disposition of several others brought to shore. The unanticipated despair led him to declare, "God Knows I hope I Never Shall Experince the Uneaseness of Mine as I have this Pasedge." Despite the enfeebled state in which many captives arrived, he advertised their sale while also "Indivering to get them up" through the use of "as much as Meat & Drink will do" to improve their conditions. One imported slave was "Bline, [with] one Eye," while an unreported number of others were "Loasing fingers [and] some Toas," forcing the captain to conclude, "I am afraid it will be a Low Avrige" anticipated with future sales.[75]

The arrival of damaged slaves demonstrates the far-reaching effects that the transport phase of the human manufacturing process bore on bondpeople's health, their bodies, and future labor. Instead of being overlooked in market sales, the physical state of these slaves altered the types of work slaveholders envisioned many of them could perform, particularly tasks involving their hands. Where and how these bondpeople entered the trade, prices they sold for, as well as attention on the buyers interested in their purchases are among the many looming questions. The *Fame*'s captain conveyed an urgent and rather vague sense of frustration, specifically concerning the arrival and upkeep of these particular imported slaves. Their disfigured bodies reveal more about the seaborne circumstances than what the commander chose to reveal to his employers. To be sure, the fragmentary and depersonalized nature of slave trade records prohibits fully tracing the chain of terror bondpeople confronted from the point of capture through import into the Americas. Equally paramount is not merely the extraction of labor that planters anticipated exploiting, but also the personal feelings captives harbored about themselves as disabled foreigners.

Although marginalized in many histories of bondage, disabled slaves were represented in Atlantic slave societies.[76] How did some bondpeople enter the Americas with such physical alterations? What was the regularity with which ship captains used strict and discriminatory selections of slaves within coastal African markets to counter the inclusion of physically impaired people? What we do know is that immersion in violently inhumane environments of slave ships irrevocably defined and shaped the experiences of all boarded slaves. As a consequence, eye inflammations, including glaucoma and other ophthalmic conditions, proved widely pervasive in unhealthy spaces of slavers, leaving many captives to become sightless. Where and how this unnamed slave lost an eye during the manufacturing process is muted, yet the decomposing flesh of his shipmates underscores the risks of mistreatment in the world of slavery at sea. The loss of limbs and digits without the interference of violence is rare in many records of slavery. The locations of these bodily losses—hands and feet—suggest the even greater possibility of what is commonly known as gangrene, which went beyond the mere loss of feeling in one's body. With chains and shackles comprising prominent tools of control on slavers, they not only bound captives' bodies, but, once tightened, they restricted blood supply and in turn created the wounds and damages sailors were employed with managing. Poor circulation led to infections and created a higher susceptibility of dissolving tissue and torn ligaments, thereby causing slaves' fingers and toes to corrode and fall off. Advanced age, lingering injuries, and weakened immune systems only further fueled the devastation. More than the allocation of violence, forcing slaves to endure much of the passage confined by irons aided in the destruction of slaves' bodies, leading to the arrival of such an unfavorable group. Taken together, this case exposes the utility of the body as evidence in showing how imported slaves, despite the use of fraud marketing, bore the scars and vestiges of the Middle Passage within their bodies.

Wounds inflicted on bondpeople's flesh emerged from punitive measures that sailors implemented, yet the agency some slaves acted out enforced a toll. Merchant Munro Mcfarlane wrote James Rogers & Co. on November 18, 1792, concerning the arrival of the *Mermaid* into Grenada mastered by Captain Edward Taylor. The ship's 128 slaves carried into port "sold at an Average of £44 Stg [Sterling]" within auction sales. To counter any price discrepancies, Mcfarlane emphasized that the captives were "by no means ill chosen" and could have produced a higher return of profit "but for the disasterous circumstances which attended the Voyage." Prior to Taylor's departure from Gambia, "an insurrection happened" between the captives and crew through which "a good many of the Slaves lost their Lives" during the outbreak. Taylor wrote a letter to his employers several weeks earlier, lamenting, "I am sorry to inform you of my Looseing . . . 30 Slaves by Insurection & Death."[77] The circumstances surrounding the uprising or mention of any gendered variations among the insurgents are unrecorded. Rebellious interactions regularly emerged on the African side of the Atlantic, yet the implications of this insurgent moment extended further beyond the ship's passage. "Many of those who lived to be brought to Market had wounds in their bodies which gave an unfavorable impression" during presale inspections.[78] Sources do not indicate the employment of a surgeon or the allocation of shipboard medicine following the insurrection; however, outside the bloodied revolt and bearing witness to the clash of violence on both sides were the lingering effects of the slaves' scars. Battle wounds incurred through the revolt inflicted pain and tarnished their bodies, yet once slaves were landed into the Americas, any welts and blisters they publicly bore marked them as uncontrollable and thus potential threats to security. Regardless of gender, these war-induced blemishes reaffirmed and gave greater meaning to the projections of black aggression that merchants, buyers, and sailors racially read into their bodies and the need for captivity. For the slaves, surviving such a deadly design imposed physical and psychological trauma they carried not only into market sales but onward into the plantations on which they were displaced to labor.

The visibility of scars among imported captives was not always as prominently recognized. In 1755 Caleb Godfrey mastered the vessel *Hare* traveling from Africa to Barbados. On February 15 he wrote to his financiers describing two captives carried into port: "Theirs Two Girls that are so low that I had as Good knock them in y'e head as Protend to carry them away," to which he added, "they are some thing recruited," owing to their subdued dispositions.[79] How Godfrey sought to prepare them for market sales remains uncertain. Once sales of the remaining cargo were complete, he set sail for his next destination, after which the vessel's owners took financial responsibility by offering to pay for the girls' medical care. A physician received £37.18 "for Medicines & Attendance of two Girls."[80] What prompted the need for treatment? What was their fate beyond the received medical attention? The lives of these girls, although unrecorded, were constantly reshaped by their personal experiences and unknown scenes of violence on the *Hare*, rendering their trauma through port landing and into sales. We can therefore reason that once sold to interested buyers, these young captives carried the emotional wounds of the seaborne passage into the plantation environment and their future lives in captivity.

Setting sail from the Caribbean bound for Charlestown, South Carolina, Godfrey paid no mind to the fate of the two girls previously rid off the ship. Once landed in the Southern coastal region, he faced yet another episode of mental angst in the health of another "Negro girl" carried on the vessel. According to the local slaving firm Austin & Laurens, the young slave "was so manag'd" during the process of slave sales "that the Girl had not the least appearance of any disorder in the Yard." "The very next day," however, she became "unable to stir with the foul disease" taking hold. As crowds of consumers subjected her to invasive market scrutiny, she piqued the interest of Benjamin Yarnold, who purchased her for £180, out of which £30 was used "to cure her of a shocking disorder." Feeling cheated by the unexpected psychological ailment causing the bonded girl's downward spiral, a representative from Austin & Laurens wrote, "The purchaser sends her back to us," which they adamantly refused. Fearful of the financial jeopardy this decision could inflict upon future business, they "obliged to consent to refer the matter to two or three impartial judges" to ascertain whether "she should be cured at the Expence & Risque of the Owners."

Financial matters embroiled between the tradesmen while the enslaved girl's health waned. On July 24, 1756, the Austin & Laurens representative wrote, "The Negro Girl we mentioned to you in our last continues greatly out of order" as a result of the lingering affliction. "She is in the hands of one of our best Doc'rs," he added, upon whom they remained confident that "he will see her to rights by & by." An unnamed medical practitioner received monies "to Board, Nursing &c 1 Negro Girl"; however, while under his professional care, the young girl continued to weaken. Symptoms she physically and psychologically underwent along with any remedies offered for her restoration are unknown, yet she reportedly "lingered under the Doc'rs hands" for a year's time "and then dyed." Legal ramifications between Yarnold and Austin & Laurens immediately followed the victim's death, during which time £8 was allocated "To Coffin &c y'e Girl that Dy'd."[81]

Suffering for several months outside of the oceanic passage, whether the young girl lived or died, her life mattered most according to the financial benefit and laboring potential she could afford Yarnold and Austin & Laurens. With the fate of boarded slaves determined by their transporters and potential buyers, devastations they endured—on ship and within market sales—moved their experiences beyond momentary suffering as traders, crewmen, and interested purchasers confronted the varied and often unpredictable challenges of actively pursuing human laborers. Although extremely rare in exposing the cumulative tolls and effect the Middle Passage inscribed on bondpeople, details recovering what happened aboard the *Hare* causing the torment of the girl and her fellow shipmates are rendered mute if merely because of the secreted nature of slavery at sea. The consecutive manner of at least three recorded traumatic breakdowns once landed suggests a much more complex set of factors and crossfire of abuses inflicted on ship. Scars and deaths of slaves, overlooked and disregarded by many consumers amid the lure of profit, served as enduring reminders to many not only of the human costs of slavery but likewise the casualties of commerce as well. Details on the *Hare*'s passage remain forever lost within the Atlantic waterways, yet we can speculate upon several contributing factors to what Nell Painter aptly refers to as "soul murder and psychological hurt" that these and other captives endured in the domain of bondage. Having been sold into slavery, forced to overcome familial separations, exiled and immersed in a violent and hazardous oceanic passage, arriving in a foreign land, and, most of all, displaced as young girls into and between the hands of uncertain strangers.

Conclusion

Seamen, merchants, colonial factors, and, most importantly, slaveholders sought a range of desirable human merchandise. Different types of captives—females, children, elderly, the diseased and disabled—were forced into the Atlantic slave economy. Ship captains sought to appease consumptive patterns; however, the choices offered were not always amenable to a planter's preferences or needs. Chronicling the diversity of bondpeople carried and offered for sale provides viable opportunities to more closely speculate on their displacement and how they arrived as potentially valuable workers. We can no longer simply trace the history of the slave trade solely through the prism of black, male, perfect, and presumably healthy bodies. Previous chapters have revealed the extent of these precise impossibilities, due largely to the fundamental nature of the slave trade being hinged on cheap yet violently debilitating preservation. Giving sustained attention to the altered, wounded, disabled, and terrorized captives compels a direct engagement with a more complex web of individuals imported and made part of slave markets and Atlantic plantations.

Interactions aboard slave ships and within the market sales of newly docked African slaves reveal how inextricably linked the two processes were in the economy of violence and the brutality inflicted on bondpeople. Scholars often define the Middle Passage as the movement of slaves from western Africa to a singular predetermined destination, wherein which the journey physically ended once taken ashore, sold to interested buyers, and forced to toil and survive within a plantation community. The catalog of abuses, exploitative deprivation, and profound losses captives likewise carried into Atlantic seaports further extended the damages of slavery at sea. Moreover, in foregrounding the physical descriptors and the effects of slavery both physically and psychologically inscribed on the bodies of imported captives, this chapter raises as many questions as it does speculations on the process of sale and bondpeople's fate once fully immersed within and fully made a part of Atlantic plantation communities. We gain temporary access to the terror of slavery through the diversity of scars that manifested in and on slaves' flesh in rather unexpected ways. These alterations and physical disfigurements served as markers of imported and buyable merchandise. Moreover, the wounds of seaborne transport and traumatically aggressive market behaviors that soon followed import introductorily defined slaves' lives through these life-altering land-based moments as they became further disembodied filtering through the slaving cycle.

Epilogue

The Frankenstein of Slavery:
A Meditation on Memory

"Your first born has returned, Father. Did you think I wouldn't
find you? Did you imagine that I was dead? That I *could* die?
You know better, Frankenstein. I would seek you even until
the maelstrom of the blackest tempest of the darkest night.—
Stand and face me!"
—*Penny Dreadful*, Showtime, 2014

The dead are not remembered in the cycle of slavery's horrors. We look for
them in novels, graveyards, histories, plays, and films, searching for the closest version of heroes and sheroes who boldly fought for freedom during the
diaspora's most iconic fate of black struggle. Yet, we recoil at the bloodied,
naked, castrated, decapitated, starved bodies, burned flesh, mangled limbs,
half-bald slaves scarred in their souls by the pain of bondage. If the dead are
remembered, how are they remembered? And if the dead are indeed celebrated
among present and future generations, who are the dead that we remember? The
consequences of history loom ever present, forcing the more difficult question:
in remembering some of slavery's dead and long since gone, who do we in turn
permit to become, or perhaps to remain, historically forgotten?

   Absence of familiar stories of seaborne terror has less to do with the scarcity
of surviving historical materials and more reckoning with a deeper, darker,
haunting-like shadow of angst, horror, and shame in resurrecting awful memories of a racial time that exposes humanity at its absolute lowest in a multi-
centuried chapter in global history. "Everyone knows that physical abuse and
slavery go together, but historians rarely trace the descent of that conjunction."[1]
Slavery at Sea seeks to navigate these violent spaces, where the numerical queries cannot fully account nor really ever access the abyss of visible and invisible
sufferings within the human manufacturing process and, more directly, the
Middle Passage. In doing so, this book constructed layers intentionally stitched
together, although not always readily apparent, to enforce an up-close and

direct engagement with the dualities of slavery at sea: the dead and the living and, most of all, silences and memory that forge generational legacies still operative today. Reclaiming the history from literary imagining that has in ways blurred the memories of what really happened on slave ships, the view here is multifaceted, three-dimensional, historically inclusive, and more than just the theoretical sum of stories and gendered bodies. Rather it is a holistic treatment of an industry and terror-producing system that devastated the lives of an incalculable many through the normalized continuation of the transatlantic slave trade. As an integrated macro-micro study of the Middle Passage—the choices and consequences explored through the systematic institutionalizing of black bodies—requires innovative questions. The particular set of analytical tools used here help decode the persistence of slaving signs and symbols to better center the violence of human behavior.

Slavery's dead are merely part(s) of a gruesome whole. This book gives greater attention to the body than ever before in written histories of the Middle Passage. Each chapter represents one or some specific corroding limbs and body parts violently fragmented through the uproar of slavery and reattached, albeit in unfamiliar and disparate parts, through the human manufacturing process. The many testimonies of bondage told of women, men, and children forced into a massive slaving vortex comprise a body of many parts representative most of those snatched, raided, traumatized, bartered, drastically altered, sold, rejected, and sometimes even murdered as a consequence of finite choices and decisions made by distant strangers lured by the prospect of capital gain, who were thus unbothered by the use of explosive brutality deeply aligned with the specificities of war to appease their invested dreams. With personal finances entangled in and directly sponsoring a slaving industry, the theoretical body of slavery at sea here includes those on slave ships but also those who made the negotiations, agreements, investments, and hiring decisions to physically move toward manifesting a global slaving capital. Meditating much more deeply on the terror and incalculable injuries to the soul that slavery at sea produced, the body—perhaps more than any other remnant of time—serves as the most efficient access point for understanding the past and the exacting tolls of human life and death. To be sure, within this book the body is framed and understood as more than a mere individual; it represents a collectivity of behavior, motivations, and desires across racial lines that allow the body to serve as a vehicle for accessing lives filled with and seen as incredibly lucrative possibilities. The body also provides the physical point of fleshed entry in tracing the extraordinary agony and catastrophic dismantling of a targeted group of people's lives, reminding us that the historical bodies of slavery always have meaning. With the body being the primary portal to recount a global slaving past, water here takes on equal and even greater importance as an axis and looming bridge between worlds and a depository of dreams, planned routes, and most of all littered and dead bodies no longer deemed worthy of preservation. All of this shows the integral relationship of people and the sea that many easily miss through disparate and thus separate histories, historiographies, and ongoing discourses in studies of slave trade, shipping, and maritime culture.

When looked at from the side of memory, slavery at sea produced a violated and grossly fractured body with far deeper meaning than at least historically imagined. The coming of white foreigners and the subsequent clash of forces within chapter 1, "Waves of Calamity," is where the first limbs emerge through the outstretched hands and arms of this historically invisible but looming body of slavery that set into motion the bringing of gifts; the setting of terms, negotiations, contracts, and inland capture; and the welcoming of strangers and the violent supplying of vulnerable black bodies. Chapter 2, "Imagined Bodies," is best seen through the chest, torso, and genitalia—three key areas of slaves' bodies, both men and women, where productive and reproductive dreams were measured and financially projected. It unveils the assessments, demands, rejections, and sales of the vulnerable and unprotected, especially of enslaved children and elderly, commonly rejected and sometimes even murdered as a consequence of their immediate future lacking possibilities. Through discussion of the toxic environment of ships that slaves boarded, chapter 3, "Healthy Desires, Toxic Realities," reminds us of the integration of bacteria, vermin, infections, and environmental factors both internal and external to ships that contributed to slaves' medical decline. Here the body of slavery's dead takes further shape as the blemished skin, weakened skeletal bones, and blackened internal organs begin to emerge, moving across, under, and throughout the bodied landscape of slavery, showing the constant jeopardy to the lifeline of healthy black bodies. Blood being the centerpiece of the human manufacturing process, in chapter 4, "Blood Memories," the fragmented hips and muscle-torn thighs of the dead and living emerge through a panoramic view of the revolts, poisoning, and gynecological power that black women boldly took back in response to their bonded inclusion. Chapter 5, "Battered Bodies, Enfeebled Minds," calls unprecedented attention to how bondpeople psychologically coped with and sought to survive the shock of enslavement. In doing so, the head, neck, and face become likewise attached to this unique invisible body. Slavery at sea takes the most crucial shape through chapter 6, "The Anatomy of Suffering," by showing more forcefully the making and unmaking of bondpeople's bodies as the knees, shins, and calves—representative of another key set of body parts necessary to an institutional quest for robust and productive laborers—take greater form. Harmed, decimated, or fatally wounded through the devastation of sickness and disease, this chapter and the attaching of diseased and disabled body parts point to relentless medical threats to both the trade and import of viable slaves. The docking of slaves addressed in chapter 7, "A Tide of Bodies," offers a bodily summation of the refinement of slaves preconditioned for plantation life through the human manufacturing process. Through it, the body takes tangible shape with the ankles and feet stitched to permanently fuse the living and dead—fully constructed with the limbs, bones, and muscles fragmented from the lives of centuries many lost. The final and most vital aspect in awakening and thus electrifying slavery's constructed body relates to how the manufacturing system fueled many bodies through displacement and captivity. Yet the collective engine that proved most powerful came through intent, the movement of monies, and thus the endorsing of violence to maintain a global economic system. The amassed body of slavery's dead, as shown through historical evidence that offers top-down and bottom-up perspective throughout *Slavery at Sea,* reveals how the invention and financial desires of others electrified and thus sustained the violent disruption of faraway people, lands, economies, and modes of life that produced consequences and casualties that transcended mortality and memory.

Taken from this intellectual vantage point, the slave ship experience concretely parallels the abominable and manlike monster comprised of the stitched-together parts of the dead and the living embodied in the impermeable fusion of both the creator (Viktor) and his creation (the monster) known best to many through Mary Shelley's iconic work, *Frankenstein*.[2] Employing a much more bodied perspective on the past through symbolism enables a theoretical overlay to better decipher the construction of slavery's body, to which the concept of the "Frankenstein of slavery" takes on much greater meaning and use when decoding the past of the slave trade. If Viktor Frankenstein and the monster are seen and therefore historically imagined as perhaps one and the same, interconnected and separated through mere images of the mind, then the Middle Passage represents more than a moment, a ship, or one even voyage, but instead an ongoing duality made up of multitudes of people, ships, crowds, and destinations. If this integrated world of creator and monster are embodied as and through the human manufacturing process historically traced throughout this book, then the choices, decisions, and movement of money, people, goods, and ideas that sponsored an ugly and horrid history by consequently fueling a devastating war to forge a slaving empire becomes much clearer. To be sure, invocation of the very name or use of the term "Frankenstein" conjures iconic visuals far from pleasant in the public mind and perhaps best understood through descriptors such as *ugly, vile, demonic,* and *abominable.* So too is the Middle Passage understood best as war, bloodshed, carnage, diseased, comprised of uncertainty and drastically life-altering outcomes, marking it as the archetypal "Frankenstein of slavery." More aptly put, comprising the most abominable and shameful chapter of the history of bondage, least favored and intentionally unremembered even in the annals of slavery's history, the Middle Passage is most representative of the deeper meanings of Frankenstein.

Memory of the Middle Passage has long been overshadowed by the lure and visual imagination placing emphasis solely on plantations and slave run-aways—namely, within the long revered and imagined American South. However, the devastating terror uncovered in this book—nuanced by the questions and centering of unfamiliar categories of people and tangible experiences, the culmination of slave ship violence and why many lack deeper understanding of an active slaving past tied to the slave trade—points to an undercurrent that not only disconnects the historical memory of plantation bondage from the slave ship experience but also privileges slave societies. Far from challenged by any lack of archival materials; the persistence of silences on slavery at sea; and, more to the point, the rewriting of history to exclude, rename, and thus erase a nation's ties to a racially based financial system hinged on the violent trafficking of another group of people for laboring needs, it incites more than mere discomfort. The loom of racial anxieties that slavery and more precisely the Middle Passage frequently produce reaffirm Michel-Rolph Trouillot's poignant perspective on the power of production of history as he reminds that "silences crisscross or accumulate over time to produce a unique mixture."[3] To some the Atlantic slave trade represents an incredible stain in global history, while for others it embodies heroism, resiliency, survival, and uplift aboard the most iconic site of black struggle.

Left alone unspoken about, denied, and thus abandoned as a necessary aspect of human history worth remembering, the terrorizing moments of suffering become generationally forgotten. Growing tendencies of avoidance in educational curricular changes and the production of historical narratives without the very real, violent, painful, and lucrative process of slavery at sea erode the memory of the dead. The debasement and violently brutal making and marking of slaves on ships as expressed and produced through the Middle Passage for some offers, quite simply, nothing value-worthy to remember. To be sure, devoid of the loyal long-standing black house servant, cross-racial friendships forged between the children of slaves and masters, the faithful and ever cheerful slave musician, abolitionist involvement, or jubilant narratives of freedom, the Middle Passage instead offers a multi-centuried history of racial terror. Terror, however, does not produce kindness nor kind stories that many choose to acknowledge, celebrate, or memorialize.

The testimonies contained within this book show the continuity of war, if war is theoretically understood as waged not merely through the construction, dissection, and moving of body parts toward the making of immortality of slavery's body for economic gain, but also through the layers of war the human manufacturing process unleashed in the lives of bondpeople. Elaine Scarry astutely outlines that war "requires both the reciprocal infliction of massive injury and the eventual disowning of the injury so that its attributes can be transferred elsewhere, as they cannot if they are permitted to cling to the original site of the wound, the human body."[4] The war waged explosively amid the cycles of slavery at sea, was more than one way, going from, to, through, and across the Atlantic, anchored in the human toll and consequences of war that came at a great cost to humanity. The aftermath of human conflict lay bare many realities—discovery of the wounded and disfigured dead, the shattering of lives, loss of family and property, bloodshed, death, heartbreak, uncertainty, and, most of all, the vengeful anguished creation and half-dead unintended ghosts of slavery that linger.

When slavery at sea is viewed as a war of the soul, two components most operative in the aftermath of war that take even greater form rests with the profound sensory experiences that slavery at sea engendered, as well as the required removal, discarding, burial, or even the literal abandoning of bodies, people, and storied histories capable in the open waters of the Atlantic. A history of senses takes on deeper dimensions and understandings within the confines of slavery; however, with the Middle Passage as an often ungovernable landless space set adrift in the oceanic waterways, slaving voyages contained and produced particular smells, looks, sounds, touch, and feelings unfound most times in landed corners of captivity. Therefore throughout *Slavery at Sea*, the touching of bodies is central in and read much like ritualized violence because of the unseen and largely inseparable connections slavery profoundly forced between bondpeople and sailors. Enshrouded in deafening secrecy, slave ships serve as a classified archive, exposing what broke slaves while likewise altering sailors' view on the world and the reach of those around them. The outplay of violence in the seafaring world of slavery comes closest to what Nell Painter rightly defines as "soul murder" in the allocation of control, oppression, and production of disturbing agony forged among enslaved black lives in profound ways. Yet, within the isolated, secret, hidden, and thus publicly unseen space of the Atlantic Ocean, so too was the terror enacted, most times for financial needs, that enabled homicidal murders of bondpeople casually thrown off ship to remain unsolved and unaccounted for in the numbering of many slavery's dead.

Both the *Zong* massacre (1781) and the *Polly* incident (1791) directly gender the violent economy that the slave trade produced. More than mere episodic moments, these cases resulted in great tragedy hidden in plain sight. Close to 133 men, women, and ailing children were mistreated and cast among the selected dying and sick jettisoned off the *Zong* over a three-day period at the orders of British surgeon and trader Luke Collingwood in the pursuit of capital anchored within the ship's insurance policy.[5] The American slave ship *Polly* saw the same use of commerce to enact extreme isolation, surveillance, and unimaginable violence and death on a singular middle-age black woman riddled with smallpox and valued as worthless. Deemed as having high potential to inflict medical terror to the remaining cargo through her mere shipboard presence, the woman was quarantined, tied to a chair, bound, and left for dead in the Atlantic Ocean. The express orders to take such actions came from Rhode Island slave trader James "Captain Jim" D'Wolf, who was similarly driven in financial ways as he also sought to counter any obstacles—personal or material—to hinder the amassing of wealth for his family's three-generational American and Caribbean slaving pursuits.[6] Recently written about and visually documented on both sides of the Atlantic during the final decades of the legalized vortex of eighteenth-century slave trade—as both nations struggled with their institutional ties to a history of legalized and commercial slavery and slave trading—these two cases represent unexpected testimonies of the intentional and literal abandoning of a people, a history, and thus a bodied archive thrown into an ever present watery grave, most times to hide evidence of the reliance on fatal violence for economic gambles. How and, more aptly, can the dead be remembered if many of slavery's dead are never found?

In navigating the fluid worlds of the living and the dead through the imprisoning cycles of slavery at sea, the histories contained here provide a historical regression to a past curiously unfamiliar to a great many. The questions and exposure of the human manufacturing system for the first time serves to show the way through the historically shamanic approach employed to move between worlds, recover stories, moments, and secrets of the dead. To know is to awaken and acknowledge, repair, and restore meanings of the past, while silences maintain the unawakened and uninformed. This book exposes the normalized grueling and rather gut-wrenching aspects of a global slaving industry—before abolitionists, public outcry, or concern for legislative bans on the import of black people for laboring needs. What responsibility do we bear in acknowledging and remembering the Middle Passage—if at all? We observe and participate in these histories through active learning and acknowledgment of the past. However, what dead do we remember, and how do we best remember and memorialize their living? The fundamental nature of slavery at sea meant a lack of accountability with reporting on all enslaved lives, most times beyond mere cheap preservation within a commercial industry that offers momentary glimpses into the fragility of human life and human loss. More than the histories produced, the barometer of an active slaving past lies more with the meanings made of slavery's perilously scarred history and local and national consciousness as it wrestles with silences and memory.

* * *

Slaving voyages operated as the connective fiber integral to the growth and evolution of the eighteenth-century Atlantic world. Colonies depended greatly on this slave-based enterprise to gain imported slaves for the replenishment of laborers. Their negotiations and the conclusions of sales between traders, merchants, and planters marked the initial introduction of bondpeople. The preceding chapters sought to probe and make greater meaning of the isolated world of slavery at sea within which sailors, slaves, and surgeons coexisted. The landscape of the sea became the oceanic routes they traveled as the meanings of slavery were introduced, reinforced, and physically manifested in the lives of captives. As death became a permanent feature, ships became the only coffins for the decaying and dying, and those deemed worthless were cast overboard, littered into makeshift watery graves of the Atlantic Ocean. Much more than simply hollowed wooden structures, slave ships evolved to become physical and economic symbols of technology, power, and authority transcending geographical boundaries. Effectively bridging people, ports, and ideas, these merchant vessels were infamously characterized by unbridled violence and death. Closely tracing the sequential process bondpeople confronted through the three phased manufacturing process—warehousing, transport, and product delivery—this book diverges from the predominance of tracing disconnected merchants, rebellious adult black male slaves, and triangulated goods moving across the Atlantic. It centers the forcible movement of slaves across continents as more than a simple trip, event, cruise ship, or historical moment, but instead as a terrorizing process fueled through investments that served as financial deposits igniting the devastation of lives through the Middle Passage. Framing the slave trade as a central part of what is herein described as a human manufacturing system that produced a multi-centuried slaving process, this book expands the intellectual landscapes of slavery to better show the interconnectedness of power; the diversity of enslaved resistance; the socio-medical history of illness and death, diet, toxicity, and medical treatment; the treatment of the dead; and, most of all, the painful and enduring legacies of slavery's terror.

The fundamental nature of obtaining and transporting slaves across the Atlantic ushered in a world comprised of unimaginable terror and violence. Once they were trapped in the transport phase, kidnapping, physical abuse, and wars that landed bondpeople into sales on the African coast. However, within the space of ships and the sea, violence became an unequivocal and productive tool that crewmen relied upon in the making and unmaking of slaves. The aggressive management of slaves took different forms at sea, as seen through this book, which shows in very real terms how the slave ship experience served as the first historical iteration in the mass detention of black people—shackling, surveillance, disciplining of bodies, stripping of freedom, guarding of contained property, exploit of labor and laborers, dangled freesom, and the ever present threat of fatal aggression. As such, this history of racialized terror and confinement of black people with uninhibited economical potential and exploit in carceral spaces found its deepest roots in the bowels of slavery at sea.

Legacies of violent power directly interconnect the Middle Passage with slave societies as evidenced by the evolving rise of slave rebellions as well as the tightened enforcement of slave codes from the fifteenth through the nineteenth centuries. Terror produces the formation of new laws to protect security and local interests. As black bodies were imported, planters across the diaspora drew upon legal and terrorizing means of overseeing imported slaves; however, the power they inflicted was magnified on ships, leaving indelible imprints of trauma. To be sure, stories of rape during slavery rest almost entirely within plantations and thus separate from the continuum of damages that extend the history and legacy of sexual terror, psychological suffering, bearing the children of tormenters, as well as evidence of shipboard crimes against captives' bodies through the transmission of venereal diseases taking hold within their bonded flesh that extended off ship. The counting of slaves leaves silent the multitudes of suffering.

This book and its findings challenge the idea of plantations as the formative site in the production of bondpeople, thereby pushing greater expansion of the critical sites of slavery's devastation to make meaning of the slave ship experience and to take more seriously the long overlooked questions necessary to understanding gender, terror, the social value of black bodies, disease, trauma, disability, violence, and death in its many forms. Bridging the sea centrally back into the historical narratives of bondage, this book locates the Middle Passage within the long known traditions of struggle, claims for power, and varied iterations of slavery and freedom forged both on and off ship. Newly arriving slaves bore the physical and psychological remnants of the human manufacturing process, which permit and invariably demand the (re-)mapping of slaving voyages back into the gendered landscape of Atlantic slavery. *Slavery at Sea* reveals moreover that the slave ship experience is not about the final destination to which slaves were displaced, but instead how they were transformed through the refinement process. Taken together, the testimonies of a much larger scale of devastation, bloodshed, and heartbreak matter little when the meaning and the memory are inscribed into silences surrounding the alchemy of horrors that slavery at sea produced. Following ship arrival into Atlantic seaports, the operative needs that fueled the global cycle of a slaving industry and the violence of slave ships became merely adapted in the next phase and next force of commercial disruption and displacement of imported slaves, but this time on land.

Notes

Introduction

1. Eighteenth-century maps refer to a place called Jaqueen Road. See William Snelgrave, "A New Map of That Part of Africa Called the Coast of Guinea," in *A New Account of Some Parts of Guinea and the Slave Trade* (London: Frank Cass & Co., 1734), 19–26, 59–68.

2. The term "aged" is employed according to descriptors in primary source materials although recognizing slave traders' difficulty in ascertaining the actual ages of bondpeople.

3. Paul Lovejoy and David Richardson recount Snelgrave's history in Whydah and the Dahomey slave trade. See "The Business of Slaving: Pawnship in Western Africa, 1600–1810," *Journal of African History* 42, no. 19 (2001): 67–89. Both women were offered for sale in 1734, which fell under the rule of King Agaja, who ruled the Dahomeys until his death in 1740. See David Henige and Marion Johnson, "Agaja and the Slave Trade: Another Look at the Slave Trade," *History in Africa* 3 (1976): 57–67; Robin Law, "Slave-Raiders and Middle Men, Monopolists, and Free-Traders: The Supply of Slaves for the Atlantic Trade in Dahomey c. 1715–1850," *Journal of African History* 30 (1989): 45–68; J. Cameron Monroe, "Continuity, Revolution, or Evolution on the Slave Coast of West Africa? Royal Architecture and Political Order in Pre-Colonial Dahomey," *Journal of African History* 48 (2007): 349–73.

4. The entirety of this story arises from Snelgrave, *New Account*, 97–106.

5. W.E.B. Du Bois, *The Suppression of the African Slave Trade to the United States of America, 1638–1870* (New York: Longmans, Green, and Co., 1896).

6. Philip D. Curtin, *The Atlantic Slave Trade: A Census* (Madison: University of Wisconsin Press, 1969).

7. Outstanding work continues to enhance the public Trans-Atlantic Slave Trade Database in tracing the history of the slave trade. See www.slavingvoyages.org.

8. See Marcus Rediker, *The Slave Ship: A Human History* (New York: Viking Press, 2008); Emma Christopher, *Slave Ship Sailors and Their Captive Cargoes, 1730–1807*

(Cambridge: Cambridge University Press, 2006); Stephanie Smallwood, *Saltwater Slavery: A Middle Passage from Africa to American Diaspora* (Cambridge, MA: Harvard University Press, 2007); Eric Taylor, *If We Must Die: Shipboard Insurrections in the Era of the Atlantic Slave Trade* (Baton Rouge: Louisiana State University Press, 2006).

9. Smallwood, *Saltwater Slavery*, 56.

10. Christopher, *Slave Ship Sailors*.

11. Taylor, *If We Must Die*.

12. For the most in-depth and recent exploration of space as a manipulative site during slavery, see Stephanie M. H. Camp, *Closer to Freedom: Enslaved Women and Everyday Resistance in the Plantation South* (Chapel Hill: University of North Carolina Press, 2004).

13. For more on humans' relationship with the sea, see W. Jeffrey Bolster, *Black Jacks: African American Seamen in the Age of Sail* (Cambridge, MA: Harvard University Press, 1998); David Cecelski, *The Waterman's Song: Slavery and Freedom in Maritime North Carolina* (Chapel Hill: University of North Carolina Press, 2001); Alain Corbin and Jocelyn Phelps, *Lure of the Sea: Discovery of the Seaside in the Western World, 1750–1840* (New York: Penguin, 1995); Paul D'Arcy, *People of the Sea: Environment, Identity, and History in Oceania* (Honolulu: University of Hawaii Press, 2008); Thor Heyerdahl, *Early Man and the Ocean: A Search for the Beginnings of Navigation and Seaborne Civilizations* (New York: Doubleday, 1979); Marcus Rediker, *Between the Devil and the Deep Blue Sea: Merchant Seamen, Pirates, and the Anglo-American Maritime World, 1700–1750* (New York: Cambridge University Press, 1989); Marcus Rediker, "The Red Atlantic, or, 'a terrible blast swept over the heaving sea,'" in *Sea Changes: Historicizing the Ocean,* ed. Bernhard Klein and Gesa Mackenthun (New York: Routledge, 2003); Stanley Rogers, *Ships and Sailors: Tales of the Sea* (New York: George G. Harrap, 1928); David M. Williams, "Humankind and the Sea: The Changing Relationship since the Mid-Eighteenth Century," *International Journal of Maritime History* 22 (2010): 1–14.

14. On the Atlantic ocean as a zone of death during the transatlantic crossing, see Sowande' Mustakeem, "'She Must Go Overboard & Shall Go Overboard': Diseased Bodies and the Spectacle of Murder at Sea," *Atlantic Studies* 8, no. 3 (2011): 302.

15. For sharks and the slave trade, see Marcus Rediker, "History from Below the Waterline: Sharks and the Atlantic Slave Trade, *Atlantic Studies* 5, no.2 (2008): 285–97. For the most recent discussion of the jettisoning of slaves during the Middle Passage, see James Walvin, *The Zong: A Massacre, the Law, and End of Slavery* (New Haven, CT: Yale University Press, 2011); and Mustakeem, "'She Must Go Overboard.'"

16. "Seasoning" is a historic phenomenon understood primarily throughout the Caribbean. Hilary Beckles offers a useful definition explaining that newly arrived captives were "protected from the full rigours of plantation life. The objective of this policy was to allow slaves time to recover their physical and psychological strength, build up some immunity to the new disease environment and learn the routine of plantation labour organization." *Natural Rebels: A Social History of Enslaved Black Women in Barbadoes* (New Brunswick, NJ: Rutgers University Press, 1989), 30. Once boarded on ships, slaves were deprived of any time to acclimate their minds or bodies to the confine of their sur-

roundings, instead having to bear and thus survive constant assaults—violent, traumatic, and medical. For further discussion of "seasoning," see Richard Sheridan, "Africa and the Caribbean in the Atlantic Slave Trade," *American Historical Review* 88, no. 1 (1972): 28, 33; Hilary Beckles, *Centering Women: Gender Discourses in Caribbean Slave Society* (Kingston, Jamaica: Ian Randle Publishers, 1999); Verene Shepherd and Hilary Beckles, *Caribbean Slavery in the Atlantic World* (Kingston, Jamaica: Ian Randle Publishers, 1999); David Eltis, Frank D. Lewis, and David Richardson, "Caribbean Slave Prices, the Slave Trade, and Productivity," *Economic History Review* 58 (Nov. 2005): 677.

17. The concept of "unmaking of bodies" builds upon Simone Gigliotti in her discussion of Jewish deportation trains during the Holocaust. See *The Train Journey: Transit, Captivity, and Witnessing in the Holocaust* (New York: Berghahn Books, 2009), 3.

18. For first hand accounts of the trade, see Oladuah Equiano, *The Interesting Narrative of the Life of Oladuah Equiano or Gustavus Vassa, the African, Written by Himself* (London: Printed and sold for the author, 1789); James Walvin, *An African's Life, 1745–1797: The Life and Times of Oladuah Equiano* (New York: Continuum, 2000); Vincent Carretta, *Equiano the African: Biography of a Self Made Man* (Athens: University of Georgia Press, 2005); Paul E. Lovejoy, "Autobiography and Memory: Gustavus Vassa, alias Oladuah Equiano, the African," *Slavery & Abolition* 27 (2006): 317–47; Phillis Wheatley, *Complete Writings* (New York: Penguin Classics, 2001; Ann Rinaldi, *Hang a Thousand Trees with Ribbons: The Story of Phillis Wheatley* (Boston: Graphia, 2005); Henry Louis Gates Jr., *The Trials of Phillis Wheatley: America's First Poet and Her Encounters with the Founding Fathers* (New York: Basic Civitas, 2003); Afua Cooper, *My Name Is Phillis Wheatley: A Story of Slavery and Freedom* (Toronto: Kids Can Press, 2009).

19. See Deborah Gray White, "Mining the Forgotten: Manuscript Sources for Black Women's History," *Journal of American History* 74 (June 1987): 237–42.

20. See Rediker, *Between the Devil and the Deep Blue Sea*; Christopher, *Slave Ship Sailors*; and Bolster, *Black Jacks*.

21. Robin Blackburn, *The Making of New World Slavery: From the Baroque to the Modern*, 1492–1800 (New York: Verso, 2010), 377. On the idea of slave societies and societies with slaves, see Ira Berlin, *Many Thousands Gone: The First Two Centuries of Slavery in North America* (Cambridge, MA: Harvard University Press, 1998).

22. Blackburn, *Making of New World Slavery*, 383.

23. On the power of archives in reconstructing history, see Marisa Fuentes, "Power and Historical Figuring: Rachael Pringle's Polgreen's Troubled Archive," *Gender and History* 22 (Nov. 2010): 564–84.

24. Jamaica Kincaid, *A Small Place* (New York: Farrar, Straus and Giroux), 31–32.

Chapter One. Waves of Calamity

1. This area is located among the Santee River in Ghana. See Mary-Antoinette Smith, ed., *Thomas Clarkson and Ottobah Cugoano: Essays on the Slavery and Commerce of the Human Species* (New York: Broadview Press, 2010), 19.

2. On ideas of fears of white cannibalism during the period of slave trading, see William Piersen, "White Cannibals, Black Martyrs: Fear, Depression, and Religious Faith

as Causes of Suicide among New Slaves," *Journal of Negro History* 62 (1977): 147–59; Basil Davidson, *The African Slave Trade: Pre-Colonial History, 1450–1850* (Boston: Little, Brown, 1961), 96–101; E. J. Alagoa and C. C. Wrigley, "Cannibalism and the Slave Trade," *Journal of African History* 25 (1984): 463–64; and John Thornton, "Cannibals, Witches, and Slave Traders in the Atlantic World," *William and Mary Quarterly* 60 (April 2003): 273–94.

3. The summary of Cugoano's experiences was extracted from Quobna Ottobah Cugoano, *Thoughts and Sentiments on the Evil of Slavery*, edited and with an introduction and notes by Vincent Carretta (1787; New York: Penguin, 1999), 12–16.

4. Two groups were primarily active within the coastal slave trade in Africa. The first group represents those people located across the Atlantic who financed the voyages that ship captains led to Africa, and subsequently the Caribbean and the Americas, variously called "merchants," "entrepreneurs," "financiers," or "investors." The other group, involved in shoreline slave-sale negotiations, included Africans with different positions: local leaders, "African brokers," "factors," "coastal brokers," "African suppliers," and inland capturers.

5. R. Paul Thomas and R. Nelson Bean, "The Fishers of Men: The Profits of the Slave Trade," *Journal of Economic History* 34, no. 4 (1974): 894.

6. Ibid., 897.

7. Marcus Rediker offers a detailed discussion of lower-class workers—seamen and ship captains—operating as employees of trade orchestrated by distant merchants. See *Between the Devil and the Deep Blue Sea: Merchant Seamen, Pirates, and the Anglo-American Maritime World, 1700–1750* (Cambridge: Cambridge University Press, 1987).

8. David Tuohy Papers, Liverpool Record Office, Liverpool, England.

9. Slavery Collection, 1709–1864, New York Historical Society, New York City.

10. Ibid.

11. David Tuohy Papers.

12. James Dumbell Papers, University of Liverpool, Sydney Jones Library, Liverpool, England.

13. Letter Book of Robert Bostock (1779–1790), Liverpool Record Office, Liverpool, England.

14. Albert van Dantzig offers useful distinctions between the various trading posts that left a legacy of slave trading operations within Africa. He explains that castles represented the biggest of the historical sites of slavery, often located within gun range of each other, and included sites such as Elmina, Cape Coast, and Goree Island. Forts, however, were smaller versions of the fortified buildings many traders utilized. The small trade factories, which he refers to as *lodges*, were smaller trading venues that were not fortified. Instead of hardened cement, they were typically mud huts that individuals were tasked with protecting. See Van Dantzig, *Forts and Castles of Ghana* (Ghana: Sedco Publishing, 1980), i–ii.

15. This concept builds on discussions of "built environment" offered in Richard McKinley Mizelle Jr., "Backwater Blues: The 1927 Flood Disaster, Race, and the Remaking of Regional Identity, 1900–1930," PhD diss., Rutgers University, New Brunswick, New Jersey, 2006, 15; and Denise L. Lawrence and Setha M. Low, "The Built Environment and Spatial Form," *Annual Review of Anthropology* 19 (1990): 453–505.

16. See Van Dantzig, *Forts and Castles,* ix. For further discussion of the integral history of coastal occupation by Europeans during the slave trade, see Magbaily Fyle, *Introduction to the History of African Civilization*, vol. 1: *Pre-Colonial Africa* (Lanham, MD: University Press of America, 1999), 114–15; Darold J. Wax, "'A People of Beastly Living': Europe, Africa, and the Atlantic Slave Trade," *Phylon* 41, no. 1 (1980): 18; Winthrop Jordan, *White over Black: American Attitudes towards the Negro, 1550–1812* (Chapel Hill: University of North Carolina Press, 1968), 4; James Walvin, *Black Ivory: A History of British Slavery* (London: HarperCollins, 1993), 34; and Catherine Coquer-Vidrovitch, *The History of African Cities South of the Sahara: From the Origins to Colonization* (Princeton, NJ: Markus Wiener, 2005), 137–45.

17. For a discussion of the utility of coastal lagoons, rivers, and internal waterways in coastal West Africa, see David Eltis, "The Volume and Structure of the Atlantic Slave Trade: A Reassessment," *William and Mary Quarterly* 58, no. 1 (2001): 32. There were also health dangers believed to arise once slave ships were docked at Africa. According to one reference, "On the coast of Guinea and on all unhealthy costs," efforts should be made to keep a considerable distance in order to "have the benefit of the seabreezes," which in many cases fostered "perfect health." Anonymous (A Surgeon of the Royal Navy), *The Ship-Master's Medical Assistant; or, Physical Advice to All Masters of Ships Who Carry No Surgeons; Particularly Useful to Those Who Trade Abroad in Hot or Cold Climates Containing a Brief Description of Diseases, Especially Those Peculiar to Seamen in Long Voyages with a Concise Method of Cure, the Result of Many Years, Practice and Experience in All Climates* (London: J. Wilkie, 1777), ix (hereafter cited as *Ship-Master's Medical Assistant*).

18. William Snelgrave, *A New Account of Some Parts of Guinea and the Slave Trade* (London Frank Cass & Co., 1734), introduction.

19. The term used for these small boats was either *yawls* or *cannoes.* The latter was described as being made "of a single Tree" if carried and used by natives. The former were small dinghies attached to larger vessels traveling from Europe.

20. Testimony of Alexander Falconbridge, in Sheila Lambert, ed., *House of Commons Sessional Papers of the Eighteenth Century* (hereafter, *HCSP*) (Wilmington, DE: Scholarly Resources, 1975), 72:299. In addition to rulers, Falconbridge also mentioned the expectation of giving gifts to those within a king's entourage. According to him, "After the king has been entertained on board, his parliament gentlemen expect to be treated with a small quantity of bread and salt beef."

21. Testimony of James Fraser, *HCSP,* 71:20–21. The phrase *breaks trade* implied opening up the trade for active participation.

22. David Eltis writes that merchants commonly sent cargoes to preselected markets because "Africans had regionally distinct preferences for merchandise." See Eltis, "Volume and Structure," 31. On the cooperative venture maintained between Africans and Europeans, see Robin Law and Kristin Mann, "West Africa in the Atlantic Community: The Case of the Slave Coast," *William and Mary Quarterly* 56, no. 2 (1999): 313.

23. See Walvin, *Black Ivory*, 31; Christopher Fyfe, "West African Trade A.D. 1000–1800," in *A Thousand Years of West African History*, ed. J. F. Ade Ajayi and Ian Espie (London: Nelson, 1965), 237–52; and Joseph Harris, *Africans and Their History* (New York: Meridian Books, 1998), 83–85.

24. Walvin, *Black Ivory*, 35. Christopher Fyfe offers an interesting response to these cultural interactions evolving between Europeans and coastal Africans. He argues that during the exchange of goods, Africans received luxuries, necessities, and mostly consumer goods. "Once they had been worn out, smoked, drunk, etc., they were gone forever"; whereas Europeans "were given slaves who were employed to create wealth across the Atlantic," leading Fyfe to conclude that these barters were inherently unequal. Fyfe, "West African Trade," 249.

25. Some could argue that this exposure revealed certain tendencies and behaviors cast as weaknesses that traders exploited upon their return trips. For instance, William Smith in his travel narrative noted that "the Women also are addicted to Drinking." This belief could have provided the catalyst for offering excess amounts of alcohol when deemed necessary. Smith likewise declared that Africans "cannot read or write, by which Means as to the Knowledge of their Antiquity, History, &c little is to be learnt, every Thing here being uncertain and traditional." This declaration perpetuated the idea that Africans lacked any fundamental basis of history. Filtration of these ideas likely influenced the intentional miscalculation of monies some traders used, working with the idea of Africans' illiteracy. William Smith, *New Voyage to Guinea: Describing the Customs, Manners, Soil, Climate, Habits, Buildings, Education, Manual Arts, Agriculture, Trade, Employments, Languages, Ranks of Distinction, Habitations, Diversions, Marriages, and Whatever Else Is Memorable among the Inhabitants* (London: Frank Cass & Co. 1744), 212.

26. Walvin, *Black Ivory*, 30.

27. Christopher Fyfe further expands the mutual benefit of kings and other chiefs in this role by demanding customary due: commissions on each slave sold as well as traditional gifts. In exchange, many of these rulers willingly looked to offer sailors physical protection along with "supplying their everyday wants (housing, food, and wives)." Fyfe, "West African Trade," 250.

28. For an engaged discussion of this phenomenon, especially regarding travel literature, see Jennifer Morgan, *Laboring Women: Reproduction and Gender in New World Slavery* (Philadelphia: University of Pennsylvania Press: 2004); Anthony J. Barker, *The African Link: British Attitudes towards the Negro in the Era of the Atlantic Slave Trade* (London: Frank Cass & Co., 1978); and Wax, "'People of Beastly Living.'" Travel literature circulated among literate populations across England and the colonial societies of the New World, helping to create widespread influences. Critical to these discourses are the personal observations and conclusions sailors created and filtered that operated outside of the reading mainstream.

29. Barker, *African Link*, 107.

30. Testimony of James Fraser, *HCSP*, 71:9.

31. See Walter Rodney, "Upper Guinea Coast and the Significance of the Origins of Africans Enslaved in the New World," *Journal of Negro History* 54, no. 4 (1969): 327–45; Walter Rodney, "African Slavery and Other Forms of Social Oppression on the Upper Guinea Coast in the Context of the Atlantic Slave Trade," *Journal of African History* 7, no. 3 (1966): 431–43; Law and Mann, "West Africa in the Atlantic Community," 316–17; George E. Brooks, *Eurafricans in Western Africa: Commerce, Social*

Status, Gender, and Religious Observance from the Sixteenth to the Eighteenth Century (Athens: Ohio University Press, 2003).

32. Snelgrave, *New Account*, introduction.

33. Testimony of Jerome Barnard Weuves, *HCSP,* 68:208.

34. Ibid.

35. Testimony of Richard Miles *HCSP,* 68:52.

36. Trying to understand the African role in the trade is a rather difficult task. For further discussion, see George Metcalf, "A Microcosm of Why Africans Sold Slaves: Akan Consumption Patterns in the 1770s," *Journal of African History* 28, no. 3 (1987): 377–94; Herbert J. Foster, "Partners or Captives in Commerce? The Role of Africans in the Slave Trade," *Journal of Black Studies* 6, no. 4 (1976): 421–34; Sylviane A. Diouf, ed., *Fighting the Slave Trade: West African Strategies* (Athens: Ohio University Press, 2003); Anne C. Bailey, *African Voices of the Atlantic Slave Trade: Beyond the Silence and the Shame* (Boston: Beacon Press, 2005); J. D. Fage, "Slavery and Slave Trade in the Context of West African History, *Journal of African History* 10, no. 3 (1969): 393–404; Lansine' Kaba, "The Atlantic Slave Trade Was Not a Black-on-Black Holocaust," *African Studies Review* 44, no. 1 (2001): 1–20; Charles Piot, "Of Slaves and the Gift: Kabre Sale of Kin during the Era of the Slave Trade," *Journal of African History* 37, no. 1 (1996): 31–49; and J. D. Fage, "African Societies and the African Slave Trade," *Past and Present* 125 (Nov. 1989): 97–115.

37. Archibald Dalzel Papers.

38. Letter Book of Robert Bostock, 1779–1790.

39. Testimony of Richard Story, *HCSP*, 82:10.

40. Testimony of Charles Berns Wadstrom, *HCSP,* 73:134.

41. Testimony of James Towne, *HCSP,* 82:18. The same assertion is made in another testimony; see Testimony of Richard Story, *HCSP,* 82:10.

42. Testimony of Charles Berns Wadstrom, *HCSP,* 73:134.

43. See Fyfe, "West African Trade," 248. He points out that special types of arms were created especially for the trade, particularly long-barreled guns, dangerous to both users and their victims. See also Gavin White, "Firearms in Africa: An Introduction," *Journal of African History* 12, no. 2 (1971): 173–84; Joseph E. Inikori, "The Import of Firearms into West Africa, 1750–1807: A Quantitative Analysis," *Journal of African History* 18, no. 3 (1977): 339–68; W. A. Richards, "The Import of Firearms into West Africa in the Eighteenth Century," *Journal of African History* 21, no. 1 (1980): 43–59.

44. Walvin, *Black Ivory*, 30; see also Blackburn, *Making of New World Slavery*, 385–86.

45. Davidson, *African Slave Trade*, 153.

46. Testimony of Richard Story, *HCSP,* 82:10. For further discussion of the poor quality of guns, see Walvin, *Black Ivory*, 31; and J. D. Fage, "African Societies," 103.

47. Harris, *Africans and Their History*, 83.

48. Marcus Rediker, *The Slave Ship: A Human History* (New York: Viking Press, 2007), 77.

49. Testimony of James Fraser, *HCSP,* 71:19.

50. Testimony of Isaac Parker, *HCSP,* 73:125.

51. See Testimony of Captain John Ashley Hall, *HCSP*, 72:226. Winston McGowan posits that kidnapping and raiding persisted as long as the slave trade; see McGowan, "African Resistance to the Atlantic Slave Trade in West Africa," *Slavery and Abolition* 11 (May 1990): 10. Some people were sold and born into slavery and in other cases were exchanged by seamen without the threat of violence, yet that subject is beyond the scope of this work. For an expanded discussion of the background of enslavement among West Africans, see Richard Sheridan, "Resistance and Rebellion of African Captives in the Transatlantic Slave Trade before Becoming Seasoned Labourers in the British Caribbean, 1690–1807," in *Working Slavery, Pricing Freedom: Perspectives from the Caribbean, Africa, and the African Diaspora*, ed. Verene A. Shepherd (Kingston, Jamaica: Ian Randle Publishers, 2002), 183.

52. Testimony of Alexander Falconbridge, *HCSP*, 72:294–95.

53. Walvin, *Black Ivory*, 26.

54. Testimony of John Bowman, *HCSP*, 82:114.

55. Testimony of John Douglas, *HCSP*, 82:122.

56. Testimony of James Towne, *HCSP*, 82:16.

57. Testimony of John Douglas, *HCSP*, 82:122.

58. Testimony of Alexander Falconbridge, *HCSP*, 72:294–95.

59. Barker, *African Link*, 189. An endless debate persists about African "slavery" relative to the coming of Europeans during the era of the slave trade. Regarding the African side of bondage, historian Darold Wax contends it had grown out of local circumstances allowing it to adapt into a local condition. Therefore, in his estimation it "bore no more than a superficial resemblance to the institution that developed in the Americas." See Wax, "'People of Beastly Living,'" 23; Fyle, *Introduction to the History*, 121.

60. Testimony of John Bowman, *HCSP*, 82:113.

61. Testimony of James Towne, *HCSP*, 82:20. For another instance of using alcohol to procure slaves, see Testimony of Captain James Morley, *HCSP*, 73:155.

62. Davidson, *African Slave Trade*, 104.

63. Ibid. See also Douglas Chambers, "Ethnicity in the Diaspora: The Slave Trade and the Creation of African 'Nations' in the Americas," *Slavery and Abolition* 22, no. 3 (2001): 26.

64. Gwendolyn Midlo Hall, *Slavery and African Ethnicities in the Americas: Restoring the Links* (Chapel Hill: University of North Carolina Press, 2005), 37.

Chapter Two. Imagined Bodies

1. Letter Book of Robert Bostock, 1779–1790, Liverpool Record Office, Liverpool, England.

2. See G. Ugo Nwokeji, "African Conceptions of Gender and Slave Traffic," *William and Mary Quarterly* 58, no. 1 (2001): 47–68; David Eltis and Stanley Engerman, "Was the Slave Trade Dominated by Men?" *Journal of Interdisciplinary History* 23, no. 2 (1992): 237–57; David Eltis, "The Volume, Age/Sex Ratios, and the African Impact of the Slave Trade: Some Refinements of Paul Lovejoy's Review of the Literature," *Journal of African History* 31, no. 3 (1990): 485–92; David Eltis and Stanley Engerman,

"Fluctuation in Sex and Age Ratios in the Trans-Atlantic Slave Trade, 1663–1864," *Economic History Review* 46, no. 2 (1993): 308–323.

3. John Guerard Letter Book, South Carolina Historical Society, Charleston, South Carolina.

4. Slavery Collection, 1709–1864, New York Historical Society, New York City.

5. Account Books of Ships of Thomas Leyland and Co., Liverpool Record Office, Liverpool, England.

6. Phillip Hamer, ed., *The Papers of Henry Laurens, 1724–1792*, vol. 1. (Columbia: University of South Carolina Press, 1981).

7. Testimony of James Fraser, *HCSP*, 71:23.

8. Add. MSS 48590, British Library, London, England.

9. For a case contrary to these notions of beauty among female captives, see Bernard Martin and Mark Spurrell, eds., *The Journal of a Slave Trader (John Newton), 1750–1754, with Newton's Thoughts upon the African Slave Trade* (London: Epworth, 1962), 28–29.

10. Add. MSS 48590.

11. Certificate of Slaves Taken on Board Ships, House of Lords Record Office, London, England. For an example, see Martin and Spurrell, *Journal of a Slave Trader*, 32.

12. Slavery Collection, 1709–1864.

13. Testimony of William Dove, *HCSP,* 73:82–83.

14. Extracts of Such Journals of the Surgeons Employed in Ship Trading to the Coast of Africa, House of Lords Record Office, London, England.

15. Wilma King, "'Mad' Enough to Kill: Enslaved Women, Murder, and Southern Courts," *Journal of African American History* 92, no. 1 (2007): 47.

16. William Snelgrave, *A New Account of Some Parts of Guinea and the Slave Trade* (1734; London: Frank Cass & Co., 1971), 12–13.

17. Nwokeji, "African Conceptions," 11. Robin Blackburn points out that children (those under fifteen) were carried on ships less often than men during the eighteenth century; far fewer were transported younger than ten years old. See *The Making of New World Slavery: From the Baroque to the Modern, 1492–1800* (New York: Verso, 1997), 384.

18. Testimony of Ecroyde Claxton, *HCSP,* 82:34–35.

19. Add. MSS 48590.

20. This chapter employs terms such as *older, elderly, old,* and *advanced* based on primary sources. Recognizing the difficulty in ascertaining the actual ages of bondpeople, these subjective terms are used to mean a person perceived as "older" in age according to their bodily structure—hair, face, body parts, and skin. Stressors, especially captivity, could have increased the "aged" look of a person, thus making someone appear much more mature in age.

21. Slavery Collection, 1709–1864.

22. Letter Book of Robert Bostock, 1779–1790.

23. Ibid.

24. James Dumbell Papers, University of Liverpool, Sydney Jones Library, Liverpool, England.

25. John Guerard Letter Book, 1752–1754.

26. T. Aubrey, *The Sea Surgeon; or, the Guinea Mean's Vade Mecum In which is laid down, The method of curing such Diseases as usually happen Abroad, especially on the Coast of Guinea; with the best way of treating Negroes, both in Health and in Sickness* (London: John Clark, 1729), 118.

27. Ibid.

28. For another primary view of surgeons' coastal work of inspecting African potential slaves, see Testimony of James Morley, *HCSP,* 73:168. Several scholars have also discussed the role of physical inspections with the assistance of medical professionals. See Hugh Thomas, *The Slave Trade: The History of the Atlantic Slave Trade, 1440–1870* (New York: Simon and Schuster, 1997), 393; Richard B. Sheridan, "The Guinea Surgeons on the Middle Passage: The Provision of Medical Services in the British Slave Trade," *International Journal of African Historical Studies* 14, no. 4 (1981): 615; Richard H. Steckel and Richard A. Jensen, "New Evidence on the Causes of Slave and Crew Mortality in the Atlantic Slave Trade," *Journal of Economic History* 46 (March 1986): 73–74.

29. H. Thomas, *Slave Trade*, 393–94, 432.

30. Alexander Falconbridge, *An Account of the Slave Trade on the Coast of Africa* (London: Printed and sold by James Phillips, 1788), 17.

31. Aubrey, *Sea Surgeon,* 119.

32. Regarding the similarity of the use of black bodies to the manner in which cattle are handled, see Winthrop Jordan, *White over Black: American Attitudes towards the Negro, 1550–1812* (Chapel Hill: University of North Carolina Press, 1968), 29.

33. Testimony of John Fountain, vol. 68, 274.

34. See Stephanie Smallwood, *Saltwater Slavery: A Middle Passage from Africa to American Diaspora* (Cambridge, MA: Harvard University Press, 2007), 176–78; Wilma King, *Stolen Childhood: Slave Youth in Nineteenth-Century America* (Bloomington: Indiana University Press, 1995); Michael Tadman, *Speculators and Slaves: Masters, Traders, and Slaves in the Old South* (Madison: University of Wisconsin Press, 1989).

35. Smallwood, *Saltwater Slavery,* 81–82.

36. Martin and Spurrell, *Journal of a Slave Trader,* 67.

37. Testimony of John Fountain, *HCSP,* 68:272, 276–77.

38. Aubrey, *Sea Surgeon,* 120.

39. Testimony of John Fountain, *HCSP,* 68:276–77.

40. Martin and Spurrell, *Journal of a Slave Trader*, 28–29.

41. Testimony of James Fraser, *HCSP,* 71:13–14.

42. Ibid., 71:19.

43. Falconbridge, *Account of the Slave Trade*, 17.

44. Testimony of George Baille, *HCSP*, 73:208.

45. Testimony of James Fraser, *HCSP*, 71:52–53.

46. Ibid., 71:13–14.

47. Falconbridge, *Account of the Slave Trade*, 18.

48. Sierra Leone Company, *Substance of the report of the court of directors of the Sierra Leone Company, delivered to the general court of proprietors, on Thursday the 26th of February, 1795* (Philadelphia: Printed by Thomas Dobson, 1795), 97.

49. Anonymous, *A treatise upon the trade from Great-Britain to Africa: Humbly recommended to the attention of government by an African merchant* (Printed for R. Baldwin, 1772), 11.

50. Testimony of James Fraser, *HCSP*, 71:52–53; Falconbridge, *Account of the Slave Trade*, 18.

51. Elaine Scarry, *The Body in Pain: The Making and the Unmaking of the World* (New York: Oxford University Press, 1987), 77.

52. Testimony of John Fountain, *HCSP*, 68:246. See also this same testimony for a similar case of violence committed against a refused black woman.

53. Testimony of Henry Ellison, *HCSP*, 73:367–68.

54. Testimony of John Fountain, *HCSP*, 68:246.

55. Testimony of Jerome Bernard Weuves, *HCSP*, 68:224.

56. Smallwood, *Saltwater Slavery*, 52.

Chapter Three. Healthy Desires, Toxic Realities

1. Bernard Martin and Mark Spurrell, eds., *The Journal of a Slave Trader (John Newton), 1750–1754, with Newton's Thoughts upon the African Slave Trade* (London: Epworth, 1962), 30.

2. Ibid., 48. On the day "No. 92" died, Newton reported, "I have had 5 slaves taken with the same disorder [the flux] within these 2 days, but am unable either to account for it or to remedy it." Whether this young captive became the catalyst for contagion aboard his vessel or not, these testimonies demonstrate how flux was a common a source of sickness and death among bondpeople.

3. Testimony of William Littleton, 68:292.

4. James Dumbell Papers, University of Liverpool, Sydney Jones Library, Liverpool, England.

5. Testimony of Alexander Falconbridge, *HCSP*, 72:298.

6. Testimony of George Millar, *HCSP*, 73:394.

7. Testimony of James Penny, *HCSP*, 68:37.

8. Testimony of James Fraser, *HCSP*, 71:14–15.

9. Richard H. Steckel and Richard A. Jensen define *pawns* as "captives held as security before transactions were complete." See "New Evidence on the Causes of Slave and Crew Mortality in the Atlantic Slave Trade," *Journal of Economic History* 46 (March 1986): 58.

10. Testimony of Henry Ellison, *HCSP*, 73:373.

11. Testimony of Robert Norris, *HCSP*, 68:7.

12. Ibid., 68:6–7.

13. Testimony of Thomas Trotter, *HCSP*, 73:85. James Fraser justified close confinement of slaves, indicating, "It is a custom with the Africans to lay close together, in such a manner that one does not breathe into the other's face—this is also a very common custom amongst the Slaves on board the ships." See Testimony of James Fraser, *HCSP*, 71:85.

14. Testimony of Clement Noble, *HCSP*, 73:119.

15. Testimony of Alexander Falconbridge, *HCSP*, 72:301.

16. Testimony of James Fraser, *HCSP*, 71:31.

17. David Tuohy Papers, Liverpool Record Office, Liverpool, England.

18. Testimony of James Fraser, *HCSP,* 71:32.

19. James Lind, *An essay on the most effectual means of preserving the health of seamen, in the Royal Navy. Containing directions proper for all those who undertake long voyages at sea, or reside in unhealthy situations. With cautions necessary for the preservation of such persons as attend the sick in fevers* (London: D. Wilson, 1762), ix.

20. Testimony of Captain John Ashley Hall, *HCSP,* 72:231, 275–76.

21. Ibid.

22. Testimony of Thomas Trotter, *HCSP,* 73:85. Concerning the word *kickeraboo,* Ian Hancock provides a brief explanation of the etymology and employment of the different variations of this phrase. This word has different spellings, including *kekrebu, kickzeboo, kecrebu,* and *kickaraboo.* The original word appears to have West African origins stemming from the Ga language spoken in Sierra Leone. For further reference, see Hancock, "On the Anglophone Creole Item Kekrebu," *American Speech* 60, no. 3 (1985): 281–83.

23. Testimony of James Fraser, *HCSP,* 71:30–31.

24. See Testimony of Thomas Trotter, *HCSP,* 73:30–31.

25. Lind, *Essay on the most effectual means,* 105.

26. "Ship *Swift,*" James Rogers Papers, Duke University Special Collections, Durham, North Carolina.

27. Testimony of William Littleton, *HCSP,* 68:294.

28. Testimony of Robert Norris, *HCSP,* 68:5; Testimony of William Littleton, *HCSP,* 68:294. Some seamen also steeped "a red hot loggerhead" in vinegar for a deeper cleaning; physician James Lind offers discussion of ship cleanliness with vinegar. See Lind, *Essay on the most effectual means,* 115.

29. John Newton mentions the use of tobacco and brimstone to cleanse his vessel. See Martin and Spurrell, *Journal of a Slave Trader,* 28–29.

30. Testimony of Captain Thomas Wilson, *HCSP,* 73:11.

31. Testimony of Richard Norris, *HCSP,* 68:18.

32. Testimony of Captain Thomas Wilson, *HCSP,* 73:11.

33. Testimony of Robert Norris, *HCSP,* 68:4–5.

34. Ibid.

35. While aboard the *Duke of Argyle,* John Newton reported, "In the fore noon, being pretty warm, got up the men and washed all the slaves with fresh water." Continuing, he explained, "I am much afraid of another ravage from the flux, for we have had 8 taken within these few days." Martin and Spurrell, *Journal of a Slave Trader,* 56–57.

36. Testimony of John Matthews, *HCSP,* 71:134.

37. Anonymous (A Surgeon of the Royal Navy), *The Ship-Master's Medical Assistant; or, Physical Advice to All Masters of Ships Who Carry No Surgeons; Particularly Useful to Those Who Trade Abroad in Hot or Cold Climates Containing a Brief Description of Diseases, Especially Those Peculiar to Seamen in Long Voyages with a Concise Method of Cure, the Result of Many Years' Practice and Experience in All Climates* (London: J. Wilkie, 1777), vii.

38. Testimony of Robert Norris, *HCSP*, 68:4–5.

39. Martin and Spurrell, *Journal of a Slave Trader*, 80.

40. David Tuohy Papers.

41. T. Aubrey, *The Sea Surgeon, or the Guinea Man's Vade Mecum In which is laid down, The method of curing such Diseases as usually happen Abroad, especially on the Coast of Guinea; with the best way of treating Negroes, both in Health and in Sickness* (London: John Clark, 1729), 131.

42. Testimony of James Fraser, *HCSP,* 71:26–27. Eighteenth-century physician T. Aubrey discussed Africans' use of palm oil as a healing property. He related that if affected with any sort of ailment, "they bathe three or four times, and stand in the Sun, and rub themselves all over with the Palm-oil, and so they sweat prodigiously, insomuch that the Venom is partly carried off by Sweat." See *Sea Surgeon,* 113.

43. David Tuohy Papers.

44. Testimony of James Fraser, *HCSP*, 71:26–27.

45. Slavery Collection, 1709–1864, New York Historical Society, New York City.

46. Testimony of James Fraser, *HCSP,* 71:26. With regard to the latter item, a *Gentleman's Magazine* article in October 1764 alluded to the difference of spelling for this item in the eighteenth century. It indicated that the "Cassada, or Cassava, yields a poisonous juice, yet its meal, after that juice is expressed, makes a wholesome well-tasted bread." See *Gentlemen's Magazine* (Oct. 1764): 487–488.

47. "Ship *Pearl*," James Rogers Papers.

48. Testimony of James Fraser, *HCSP,* 71:27–28.

49. Testimony of William Littleton, *HCSP,* 68:294.

50. Testimony of James Fraser, *HCSP,* 71:29–30.

51. Testimony of John Knox, *HCSP,* 68:78.

52. For discussion of food preservation as a historical problem, see Anne C. Wilson, ed., *Waste Not, Want Not: Food Preservation in Britain from Early Times to the Present Day* (Edinburgh: Edinburgh University Press, 1991).

53. Anthony Addington, *An Essay on Sea-Scurvy Wherein Is Proposed an Easy Method of Curing That Distemper at Sea; and of Preserving Water Sweet for Any Cruize or Voyage* (London: Printed by C. Mickleright, 1753), 8.

54. Richard Sheridan contends that some slavers grew largely dependent on salted meats because of the ability for easier preservation. See "The Guinea Surgeons on the Middle Passage: The Provision of Medical Services in the British Slave Trade," *International Journal of African Historical Studies* 14, no. 4 (1981): 601–602. For further discussion, see also Kenneth and Virginia Kiple, "Nutritional Link with Slave Infant and Child Mortality in Brazil," *Hispanic American Historical Review* 69, no. 4 (1989): 681.

55. Testimony of Robert Norris, *HCSP,* 68:4–5.

56. The Kiples posit that individuals whose diets were primarily made up of rice over time became deficient in thiamine. See Kiple and Kiple, "Nutritional Link," 677.

57. Testimony of James Fraser, *HCSP,* 71:34. It is questionable if overdependence on bread could provide the necessary fiber for enslaved people to digest the nutrients in their meager ship diets. On the digestibility and absorption of nutrients, see George V. Vahouny and David Kritchevsky, eds., *Dietary Fiber in Health and Disease* (New York: Plenum, 1982), 46. Countering the idea of fecal stoppage due to carbohydrate

consumption, I. MacDonald and C. A. Williams point out that "if the concentration of the carbohydrate is high, this can lead to osmatic diarrhoea." This gives one possible explanation for the presence of diarrhea aboard ships. See "Dietary Carbs, Health, and Disease," in Michael Turner, ed., *Nutrition of Health, a Perspective: The Current Status of Research on Diet-Related Diseases* (New York: Alan R. Liss, 1982), 152.

58. Log of the Slave Brig *Ranger,* Liverpool Record Office, Liverpool, England.

59. Ship Log Entries for Ships *Count du Nord* and *Madampookata,* 1782–1790, Liverpool Record Office, Liverpool, England. Jeffrey Bolster discusses the ensuing relationship of people and the sea, revealing that during the Age of the Ocean, different people "relied on ocean products and services as never before." See Bolster, "Putting the Ocean in Atlantic History: Maritime Communities and Marine Ecology in the Northwest Atlantic, 1500–1800," *American Historical Review* 113, no. 1 (2008): 23.

60. Leslie Owens describes how preservation of food was a perpetual challenge to the ingenuity of men. See *This Species of Property: Slave Life and Culture in the Old South* (New York: Oxford University Press, 1976), 51.

61. See Kenneth Kiple and Brian T. Higgins, "Mortality Caused by Dehydration during the Middle Passage," *Social Science History* 13, no. 4 (1989): 421–37.

62. T. Aubrey, *Sea Surgeon,* 127.

63. There is an existing body of literature concerning the relationship of ineffective and unbalanced diets as the catalyst for disease. For further reference, see Charles H. Halsted and Robert B. Rucker, eds., *Nutrition and the Origins of Disease* (San Diego: Academic Press, 1989); Kenneth F. Kiple and Virginia H. King, *Another Dimension to the Black Diaspora: Diet, Racism, and Disease* (Cambridge: Cambridge University Press, 1981). Additionally, one book specifically addresses nutrition at sea; see J. Watt, E. J. Freeman, and W. F. Bynum, eds., *Starving Sailors: The Influence of Nutrition upon Naval and Maritime History* (Bristol, Eng.: National Maritime Museum, 1981).

64. James Dumbell Papers.

65. Alexander Falconbridge, *An Account of the Slave Trade on the Coast of Africa* (London: Printed and sold by James Phillips, 1788), 21. Sheridan makes reference to "slauber-sauce," which he points out included the use of scuttlefish over rice and beef bones in water. See "Guinea Surgeons," 617.

66. "Ship *Pearl,*" James Rogers Papers.

67. T. Aubrey, *Sea Surgeon,* 128. Robert Norris also offers discussion concerning the "dabadab," which he describes as a mixture of Indian corn "boiled to a thick Consistence, known by the Name of a Dabadab, to which they have Sauce composed of Fish and Meat, seasoned also with Palm Oil, Pepper, and Salt." See Testimony of Robert Norris, *HCSP,* 68:8.

68. Testimony of Robert Norris, *HCSP,* 68:10.

69. Testimony of James Fraser, *HCSP,* 71:23, 28–29.

70. Testimony of John Knox, *HCSP,* 68:178.

71. Testimony of James Fraser, *HCSP,* 71:50.

72. Ibid., 71:26–27.

73. Raymond Cohn makes the case that attempts were made to carry only noncontaminated foods and water. See Cohn, "Death of Slaves in the Middle Passage," *Journal of Economic History* 45 (1985): 692.

74. T. Aubrey, *Sea Surgeon,* 126.

75. "Ship *Pearl*," James Rogers Papers.

76. James Lind, *A Treatise of the Scurvy in Three Parts Containing an Inquiry into the Nature, Causes, and Cure, of That Disease Together with a Critical and Chronological View of What Has Been Published on the Subject* (London, 1753), 238. Physician Anthony Addington similarly disclosed that a "putrid diet" was common aboard ships. As such, it was not uncommon for sea travelers to receive foods "mouldy or eaten by worms and weevils." See *Essay on Sea-Scurvy*, 6.

77. David Tuohy Papers.

78. William McNeil in his classic study mentions the relationship of food, parasites, and bacteria, which he argues undergirded civilized history. See *Plagues and People* (Garden City, NY: Anchor, 1976).

79. Martin and Spurrell, *Journal of a Slave Trader,* 78.

80. Slavery Collection, 1709–1864.

81. Ibid.

82. Testimony of James Fraser, *HCSP* 71:38–39.

83. Testimony of William Littleton, *HCSP,* 68:292.

84. "Ship *Rodney*," James Rogers Papers.

85. Falconbridge, *Account of the Slave Trade*, 22.

86. Testimony of Thomas Trotter, *HCSP*, 73:103–104.

87. Testimony of James Fraser, *HCSP,* 71:28–29.

88. Falconbridge, *Account of the Slave Trade*, 22.

89. Ibid., 21. For more on slave preferences of food at sea, see Testimony of James Fraser, *HCSP,* 71:44.

90. Testimony of Thomas Trotter, *HCSP*, 73:87.

91. Testimony of James Towne, *HCSP*, 82:20.

92. For another discussion of the purpose of requiring dance within bondage, see Lynne Fauley Emery, *Black Dance from 1619 to Today* (Princeton, NJ: Princeton Book Company, 1972), 12.

93. Falconbridge, *Account of the Slave Trade*, 23.

94. Testimony of James Towne, *HCSP*, 82:20.

95. Testimony of Clement Noble, *HCSP*, 73:120.

96. Testimony of Captain John Ashley Hall, *HCSP,* 72:231.

97. Testimony of Thomas Trotter, *HCSP,* 73:87.

98. Ibid.

99. Testimony of Captain John Ashley Hall, *HCSP,* 72:271.

100. Falconbridge, *Account of the Slave Trade*, 23.

101. Testimony of William Littleton, *HCSP,* 68:296–97.

102. Testimony of John Fountain, *HCSP,* 68:248.

103. "Ship *Mermaid*," James Rogers Papers. For further reference regarding discussion of mortality following rainy seasons on the coast of Africa, see Testimony of John Barnes, *HCSP,* 68:86.

104. "Ship *Jupiter*," James Rogers Papers.

105. Log of the Slave Brig *Ranger,* Liverpool Record Office, Liverpool, England/

106. Testimony of James Fraser, *HCSP,* 71:38.

107. Ibid. Surgeon and notorious slave trader Archibald Dalzel offered additional discussion of mortality relating to inclement weather; see Testimony of Archibald Dalzel, *HCSP,* 68:34–35.

108. "Ship *Dragon,*" James Rogers Papers.

109. "Ship *Rodney,*" James Rogers Papers.

110. Testimony of James Fraser, *HCSP,* 71:31–32.

111. Testimony of Robert Norris, *HCSP,* 68:7.

112. "Ship *Rodney,*" James Rogers Papers.

113. Slavery Collection, 1709–1864.

Chapter Four. Blood Memories

1. *Virginia Gazette,* 23 December 1773.

2. Sowande' Mustakeem, "Make Haste & Let Me See You with a Good Cargo of Negroes: Gender, Power, and the Centrality of Violence in the Eighteenth-Century Atlantic Slave Trade," in *Gender, Race, Ethnicity, and Power in Maritime America,* ed. Glenn Gordinier (Mystic, CT: Mystic Seaport Museum, 2008), 3–21.

3. *Country Journal or the Craftsman,* 2 November 1754.

4. *Boston Weekly Newsletter,* 22 April to 29 April 1731.

5. *Read's Weekly Journal or British Gazetteer,* 18 September 1756.

6. *Boston Evening Post,* 25 November 1765.

7. See Harvey Wish, "American Slave Insurrections before 1861," *Journal of Negro History* 22, no. 3 (1937): 300.

8. For further discussion of the unique maritime culture cultivated among seafarers, see Jeffrey Bolster, *Black Jacks: African American Seamen in the Age of Sail* (Cambridge, MA: Harvard University Press, 1997); Marcus Rediker, *Between the Devil and the Deep Blue Sea: Merchant Seamen, Pirates, and the Anglo-American Maritime World, 1700–1750* (New York: Cambridge University Press, 1987); David Cecleski, The *Waterman's Song: Slavery and Freedom in Maritime North Carolina* (Chapel Hill: University of North Carolina Press, 2001); and Daniel Vickers and Vince Walsh, *Young Men and the Sea: Yankee Seafarers in the Age of Sail* (New Haven, CT: Yale University Press, 2007).

9. For more on the production of ideas of people and bodies through eighteenth-century media, see Gwen Morgan and Peter Rushton, "Visible Bodies: Power, Subordination, and Identity in the Eighteenth-Century Atlantic World," *Journal of Social History* 39, no. 1 (2005): 39–64.

10. For a glimpse into the stowage of guns transported on slave vessels out of Rhode Island, see Newport Intendant of Trade, 1785–1790, Newport Historical Society, Newport, Rhode Island.

11. Bernard Martin and Mark Spurrell, eds., *The Journal of a Slave Trader (John Newton), 1750–1754, with Newton's Thoughts upon the African Slave Trade* (London: Epworth, 1962), 22.

12. Testimony of Henry Ellison, *HCSP,* 73:374–75.

13. Jacqueline Dowd Hall, "'The Mind That Burns in Each Body': Women, Rape, and Racial Violence," in *Powers of Desire: The Politics of Sexuality,* ed. Ann Snitow,

Christine Stansell, and Sharon Thompson (New York: Monthly Review Press, 1983), 331.

14. Martin and Spurrell, *Journal of a Slave Trader*, 25.

15. Testimony of Henry Ellison, *HCSP*, 73:103–104.

16. See Emma Christopher, *Slave Ship Sailors and Their African Cargoes, 1730–1807* (Cambridge: Cambridge University Press, 2006).

17. Stephanie Smallwood, *Saltwater Slavery: A Middle Passage from Africa to American Diaspora* (Cambridge, MA: Harvard University Press, 2007), 76.

18. Testimony of James Towne, *HCSP*, 82:22.

19. Martin and Spurrell, *Journal of a Slave Trader*.

20. Letters of Archibald Dalzel, 1762–1807, University of Liverpool, Sydney Jones Library, Liverpool, England. Marcus Rediker also found that seamen took an African "wife" during the passage. See Rediker, *The Slave Ship: A Human History* (New York: Viking Press, 2007), 161.

21. Anthony J. Barker, *The African Link: British Attitudes towards the Negro in the Era of the Atlantic Slave Trade, 1550–1807* (London: Frank Cass & Co., 1978), 126.

22. See Hilary Beckles, *Natural Rebels: A Social History of Enslaved Black Women in Barbadoes* (New Brunswick, NJ: Rutgers University Press, 1989); Marisa Fuentes, *Dispossessed Lives: Enslaved Women, Violence, and the Archive* (Philadelphia: University of Pennsylvania Press, 2016).

23. Testimony of George Baillie, *HCSP*, 73:208.

24. See Rediker, *Slave Ship*, 241–43.

25. See Adrienne Davis, "Don't Let Nobody Bother Yo' Principle: The Sexual Economy of American Slavery," in *Sister Circle: Black Women and Work*, ed. Sharon Harley and the Black Women and Work Collective, 103–127 (New Brunswick, NJ: Rutgers University Press, 2002).

26. See Deborah Gray White, *Ar'n't I a Woman? Female Slaves in the Plantation South* (1985; New York: W. W. Norton, 1999).

27. Martin and Spurrell, *Journal of a Slave Trader*, 105.

28. Johannes Postma, *The Dutch in the Atlantic Slave Trade, 1600–1815* (Cambridge: Cambridge University Press, 1990), 243.

29. Add. 18272, Collections Relating to the Slave Trade, 1775–1788, British Library, London, England. For another example of the distribution of beads among black female captives, see Falconbridge, *Account of the Slave Trade*, 23.

30. Daniel Mannix and Malcolm Cowley, *Black Cargoes: A History of the Atlantic Slave Trade, 1518–1865* (New York: Viking, 1962), 113.

31. Abbe Raynal, *Slave Trade: A Full Account of This Species of Commerce; with Arguments Against It, Spirited and Philosophical* (Southwark: T. Cox, 1792), 35.

32. Kenneth E. Marshall, "Powerful and Righteous: The Transatlantic Survival and Cultural Resistance of an Enslaved African Family in Eighteenth-Century New Jersey," *Journal of American Ethnic History* 23 (Winter 2004): 32. In exchange for their presumed loyalty, on several occasions different roles were distributed to female captives once at sea. For an example, see Testimony of Thomas Trotter, *HCSP*, 73:86.

33. Testimony of Henry Ellison, *HCSP*, 73:375.

34. John Newton Manuscript Journal, 1750–1754, Log/M/46, National Maritime Museum, Greenwich, England.

35. For a discussion of pregnancy and slavery, see Wendy Anne Warren, "'The Cause of Her Grief': Rape of a Slave in Early New England Slavery," *Journal of American History* 93 (March 2007): 1047.

36. Falconbridge, *Account of the Slave Trade,* 23–24.

37. Robert Stein, *The French Slave Trade in the Eighteenth Century: An Old Regime Business.* (Madison: University of Wisconsin Press, 1979), 101.

38. Raynal, *Slave Trade*, 35.

39. Darlene Clark Hine employs the concept of 'sexual hostage.' See "Rape and The Inner Lives of Black Women in the Middle West," *Signs* 14 (Summer 1989): 915.

40. Hazel Carby analyzes this phenomenon through the context of master-slave relationship within the American plantation system. See *Reconstructing Womanhood: The Emergence of the Afro-American Woman Novelist* (New York: Oxford University Press, 1987), 27.

41. Falconbridge, *Account of the Slave Trade*, 23.

42. Morgan and Rushton, "Visible Bodies," 40.

43. Wilma King originates this concept of "rite" and its relation to the sexual exploitation of black females within plantation slavery. See "'Mad' Enough to Kill," 40.

44. Elaine Scarry, *The Body in Pain: The Making and Unmaking of the World* (New York: Oxford University Press, 1987), 73.

45. Jay Coughtry, *The Notorious Triangle: Rhode Island and the African Slave Trade, 1700–1800* (Philadelphia: Temple University Press, 1981), 11.

46. Quobna Ottobah Cugoano, *Thoughts and Sentiments on the Evil of Slavery* (1787; New York: Penguin, 1999), 15.

47. Dowd Hall, "'Mind That Burns,'" 333.

48. For discussion of the long-term affects regarding sexual exploitation, see Nell Irvin Painter, *Soul Murder and Slavery,* Charles Edmondson Historical Lecture Series, 15 (Waco, TX: Baylor University Press, 1995). Darlene Clark Hine offers details concerning gender relations based on sex common between black women and men during bondage. See "Lifting the Veil, Shattering the Silences: Black Women's History in Slavery and Freedom," in *The State of the Afro-American Past, Present, and Future,* ed. Darlene Clarke Hine (Baton Rouge: Louisiana State University Press, 1986), 226.

49. On rape, forced breeding, and sadomasochism, see James Sweet, *Recreating Africa: Culture, Kinship, and Religion in the African-Portuguese World, 1441–1770* (Chapel Hill: University of North Carolina Press, 2003); Jennifer Morgan, *Laboring Women: Reproduction and Gender in New World Slavery* (Philadelphia: University of Pennsylvania Press, 2004); Daina Ramey Berry, *Swing the Sickle for the Harvest Is Ripe: Gender and Slavery in Antebellum Georgia,* (Urbana: University of Illinois Press, 2007); Thomas Foster, "Sexual Abuse of Black Men under Slavery," *Journal of the History of Sexuality* 20 (Sept. 2011): 445–64; Trevor Burnard, *Master, Tyranny, and Desire: Thomas Thistlewood and His Slaves in the Anglo-Jamaican World* (Chapel Hill: University of North Carolina Press, 2003).

50. John Mbiti offers a useful analysis of the interplay of communalism and the spiritual linkages connected with pregnancy and motherhood within traditional West

African societies. See Mbiti, *African Religions and Philosophy* (New York: Praeger, 1969).

51. D. White, *Ar'n't I a Woman?* 107.

52. Testimony of Isaac Parker, *HCSP,* 73:125.

53. Testimony of William Dove, *HCSP*, 73:82–83.

54. Testimony of Alexander Falconbridge, *HCSP*, 72:316.

55. Testimony of John Fountain, *HCSP*, 68:278–79.

56. Letters of Archibald Dalzel, 1762–1807.

57. Paula Giddings pushes this particular argument concerning bondwomen and the emotional ties to their children. For further discussion, see *When and Where I Enter: The Impact of Black Women on Race and Sex in America* (New York: W. Morrow, 1996), 45; see also Wilma King, *Stolen Childhood: Slave Youth in Nineteenth-Century America* (Bloomington: Indiana University Press, 1995).

58. Testimony of James Towne, *HCSP,* 82:22.

59. Martin and Spurrell, *Journal of a Slave Trader,* 104. For another primary example of the mistreatment of enslaved children, see Testimony of Captain John Ashley Hall, *HCSP*, 72:27.

60. For further discussion of the abolitionist activities of Moses Brown (Rhode Island) and William Rotch (New Bedford, MA), see Mary Ricketsen Bullard, *Robert Stafford of Cumberland Island: Growth of a Planter* (Athens: University of Georgia Press, 1995), 34.

61. Moses Brown Papers, John Carter Brown Library, Providence, Rhode Island.

62. Testimony of Isaac Parker, *HCSP,* 73:124–25; 129–30.

63. For further discussion of this idea, see Winston McGowan, "African Resistance to the Atlantic Slave Trade in West Africa," *Slavery and Abolition* 11 (May 1990): 19.

64. David Richardson, "Shipboard Revolts, African Authority, and the Atlantic Slave Trade," *William and Mary Quarterly* 58, no. 1 (2001): 76.

65. Peleg Clarke Papers, Newport Historical Society, Newport, Rhode Island.

66. David Barry Gaspar, *Bondmen and Rebels: A Study of Master-Slave Relations in Antigua, with Implications for Colonial British America* (Durham, NC: Duke University Press, 1993), 171.

67. John Atkins, *A Voyage to Guinea, Brasil, and the West-Indies* (London: Ward and Chandler, 1735), 72.

68. Ibid., 72–73.

69. Scarry, *Body in Pain,* 61.

70. Louis P. Maher, *Rites of Execution: Capital Punishment and the Transformation of American Culture, 1776–1865* (New York: Oxford University Press, 1989), 26.

71. Earle Collection, National Maritime Museum, Liverpool, England.

72. Testimony of Richard Miles, *HCSP,* 68:86.

73. Lorenzo J. Greene, "Mutiny on the Slave Ships," *Phylon*, 5, no. 4 (1944): 348.

74. Richardson, "Shipboard Revolts," 71.

75. Raynal, *Slave Trade*, 23.

76. John Newton Manuscript Journal, 1750–1754, National Maritime Museum, Greenwich, England.

77. John Savage, "'Black Magic' and White Terror: Slave Poisoning and Colonial Society in Early Nineteenth-Century Martinique," *Journal of Social History* 40, no. 3 (2007): 646.

78. Ship Logs, Sloop *Dolphin,* 1795–1797, D'Wolfe Family Papers, Rhode Island Historical Society, Providence, Rhode Island.

79. Peter Wood, *Black Majority: Negroes in Colonial South Carolina from 1670 through the Stono Rebellion* (New York: Knopf, 1974), 289.

80. See Judith Carney, *In the Shadow of Slavery: African's Botanical Legacy in the Atlantic World* (Berkeley: University of California Press, 2011).

81. Winthrop Jordan, *White over Black: American Attitudes towards the Negro, 1550–1812,* (Chapel Hill: University of North Carolina Press), 392.

82. Carol E. Fick, *The Making of Haiti: The Saint Domingue Revolution from Below* (Knoxville: University of Tennessee Press), 66.

83. Darlene Clark Hine and Kate Wittenstein originated the concept of "gynecological resistance." For an expanded discussion, see "Female Slave Resistance: The Economics of Sex," in *The Black Woman Cross-Culturally,* ed. Filomina Chioma Steady (Cambridge, MA: Schenkman, 1981), 289–300.

84. Certificates of Slaves Taken on Board Ships, House of Lords Record Office, London, England.

85. Marie Jenkins Schwartz, *Born in Bondage: Growing Up Enslaved in the Antebellum South* (Cambridge, MA: Harvard University Press, 2001), 58.

86. Series of Mortality Lists, House of Lords Record Office, London, England.

87. Several scholars have considered slaveholder's recognition of bondwomen's knowledge on how to terminate unwanted pregnancies. See D. White, *Ar'n't I a Woman?* 84–88; J. Morgan, *Laboring Women,* 114; and Barbara Bush, "Women, Childbirth, and Resistance in British Caribbean Slave Societies," in *More than Chattel: Black Women and Slavery in the Americas,* ed. David Barry Gaspar and Darlene Clark Hine (Bloomington: Indiana University Press, 1996), 204–205. Ken Marshall also offers further discussion of spiritual mediums that some African women explored within West African societies. See Marshall, "Powerful and Righteous," 34. These knowledge systems could have presumably bestowed some of these women with expertise in various areas that they carried aboard slave ships and into enslaved communities.

88. Darlene Clark Hine, *Hine Sight: Black Women and the Reconstruction of American History* (Indianapolis: Indiana University Press, 1997), 33.

89. See Katherine Verdery, *The Political Lives of Dead Bodies: Reburial and Postsocialist Change* (New York: Columbia University Press, 2000).

90. Stephanie Smallwood, "African Guardians, European Slave Ships, and the Changing Dynamics of Power in the Early Modern Atlantic," *William and Mary Quarterly* 64 (Oct. 2007): 682.

91. Wilma King, "Suffer with them 'til Death: Slave Women and Their Children in Nineteenth-Century America," in *More Than Chattel: Black Women and Slavery in the Americas,* ed. David Barry Gaspar and Darlene Clark Hine (Indianapolis: Indiana University Press, 1996), 152.

92. Eric Taylor makes this same assertion with respect to African insurgency. See *If We Must Die: Shipboard Insurrections in the Era of the Atlantic Slave Trade* (Baton Rouge: Louisiana State University Press, 2006), 5.

93. Darold D. Wax, "Negro Resistance to the Early American Trade," *Journal of Negro History* 51, no. 1 (1966): 2.

94. Herbert Klein, "African Women in the Atlantic Slave Trade," in *Women and Slavery in Africa*, ed. Claire Robertson and Martin A. Klein (Portsmouth, NH: Heinemann, 1997), 29.

95. Walter Johnson makes a rather critical point on the issue of dehumanization and slavery, positing, "Terror, torture, rape, and exploitation are activities which are elementally human and which depend upon the sentiment of a suffering human object to produce the effect desired by their (all-too) human perpetrators." See Johnson, "On Agency," *Journal of Social History* 37, no. 1 (2003): 116.

Chapter Five. Battered Bodies, Enfeebled Minds

1. Log of Slave Brig *Ranger,* Liverpool Record Office, Liverpool, England.

2. This argument takes a cue from Terri Snyder, who writes, "Little attention has been given to the meanings of self-destruction" bondpeople acted out. See "Suicide, Slavery, and Memory in North America," *Journal of American History* 97 (June 2010): 40.

3. On Igbo and their perceived suicidal tendencies, see Daniel E. Walker, "Suicidal Tendencies: African Transmigration in the History and Folklore of the Americas," *Griot* 18 (1999): 12; Michael Mullin, *Africa in America: Slave Acculturation and Resistance in the American South and the British Caribbean, 1736–1831* (Urbana: University of Illinois Press, 1992), 24; Kenneth E. Marshall, "Powerful and Righteous: The Transatlantic Survival and Cultural Resistance of an Enslaved African Family in 18th-Century New Jersey," *Journal of American Ethnic History* 23 (Winter 2004): 40; Leslie Owens, *This Species of Property: Slave Life and Culture in the Old South* (New York: Oxford University Press, 1976), 94.

4. Add. MSS 48590 ff. 29–31.

5. John Guerard Letter Book, 1752–1754, South Carolina Historical Society, Charleston, South Carolina.

6. T. Aubrey, *The Sea Surgeon; or, the Guinea Mean's Vade Mecum* (London: John Clark, 1729), 104.

7. Testimony of Robert Norris, *HCSP,* 68:9; For an interesting discussion of the role of trauma and behavior, see L. Stephen O'Brien, *Traumatic Events and Mental Health* (Cambridge: Cambridge University Press, 1998), 2.

8. Testimony of James Towne, *HCSP,* 82:16.

9. Testimony of Thomas Trotter, *HCSP,* 73:86.

10. Ibid., 73:85–86.

11. Bernard Martin and Mark Spurrell, eds., *The Journal of a Slave Trader (John Newton), 1750–1754* (London: Epworth, 1962).

12. Anonymous, *A Treatise of Diseases of the Head, Brain, and Nerves* (London, 1727).

13. Testimony of Alexander Falconbridge, *HCSP*, 72:315.

14. Testimony of Thomas Trotter, *HCSP*, 73: 98–99.

15. Testimony of Robert Norris, *HCSP,* 68:12.

16. Testimony of Thomas Trotter, *HCSP*, 73:98–99.

17. Testimony of Isaac Wilson, *HCSP*, 72:282.

18. Wilma King is one of the few scholars who offers a close view of the notion of "madness" with regard to bondwomen's resistive behaviors during plantation slavery. "'Mad' Enough to Kill: Enslaved Women, Murder, and the Southern Courts," *Journal of African American History* 92, no. 1 (2007): 37–56. Leslie Owens makes an important point that among the range of diseases that affected bondpeople, "scholars have been adamant in the near exclusion of one—mental illness." See Owens, *This Species of Property*, 44.

19. Testimony of Clement Noble, *HCSP,* 73:114.

20. Testimony of Isaac Wilson, *HCSP*, 72:287. For a discussion of fixed melancholy, see John Blassingame, *The Slave Community: Plantation Life in the Antebellum South* (1972; New York: Oxford University Press, 1979), 7.

21. Aubrey, *Sea Surgeon,* 132.

22. Testimony of Isaac Wilson, *HCSP*, 72:281.

23. Testimony of John Fountain, *HCSP,* 68:270.

24. Testimony of Thomas Trotter, *HCSP*, 73:86.

25. For a discussion of African ties to land, see John Mbiti, *African Religions and Philosophy* (New York: Praeger, 1969), 35.

26. Testimony of Isaac Wilson, *HCSP*, 72:281.

27. Testimony of Clement Noble, *HCSP*, 73:117.

28. Testimony of Isaac Parker, *HCSP,* 73:138–39.

29. Testimony of John Ashley Hall, *HCSP,* 72:275.

30. Testimony of Isaac Wilson, *HCSP,* 72:282–83.

31. Mbiti, *African Religions and Philosophy*, 6.

32. Testimony of James Towne, *HCSP*, 82: 21.

33. Testimony of George Millar, *HCSP,* 73:393–94.

34. For further discussion of the female slave networks, see Deborah Gray White, *Ar'n't I a Woman? Female Slaves in the Plantation South* (1985; New York: W. W. Norton, 1999), 119–41.

35. For another example of a black female captive cast as "insane," see Testimony of Clement Nobles, *HCSP,* 73:112.

36. Ibid., 73:32.

37. Alexander Falconbridge, *An Account of the Slave Trade on the Coast of Africa* (London: Printed and sold by James Phillips, 1788), 32.

38. Testimony of Thomas Trotter, *HCSP*, 73:86; For a discussion of hysteria, see Elizabeth Waites, *Trauma and Survival: Post-Traumatic and Dissociative Disorders in Women* (New York: W. W Norton, 1993), 5; Joan Acocella, *Creating Hysteria: Women and Multiple Personality Disorders* (San Francisco: Jossey-Bass, 1999), 29–30.

39. Testimony of Alexander Falconbridge, *HCSP*, 72:305.

40. Daniel Mannix and Malcolm Cowley, *Black Cargoes: A History of the Atlantic Slave Trade, 1518–1865* (New York: Viking, 1962), 117.

41. The higher incidence of "madness" illustrated through the previously mentioned cases of bondwomen seems to disprove William D. Piersen's theory that women withstood the Atlantic crossing slightly better than their male counterparts. See Piersen, "White Cannibals, Black Marytrs: Fear, Depression, and Religious Faith as Causes of Suicide among New Slaves," *Journal of Negro History* 62 (1977): 151.

42. Testimony of Thomas Trotter, *HCSP*, 73:88.

43. Testimony of James Fraser, *HCSP*, 71: 28.

44. Aubrey, *Sea Surgeon,* 132.

45. On the role of dance as a communicative art form within various aspects of African culture, see Omofolabo S. Ajayi, *Yoruba Dance: The Semiotics of Movement and Body Attitude in a Nigerian Culture* (Chicago: African World Press, 1998), 1; Jacqui Malone, *Steppin' on the Blues: The Visible Rhythms of African American Dance* (Urbana: University of Illinois Press, 1996); and John Chasteen and Lyman L. Johnson, *National Rhythms, African Roots: The Deep History of Latin American Popular Dance* (Albuquerque: University of New Mexico Press, 2004).

46. Monica Schuler offers a provocative discussion of music and religion among Central Africans in St. Thomas. See Schuler, *Alas, Alas Kongo: A Social History of Indentured African Immigration into Jamaica, 1841–1865* (Baltimore: Johns Hopkins University Press, 1980), 72–83. For a discussion of call-and-response practices, see Frances Aparicio and Candida Jacquez, eds., *Musical Migrations: Transnationalism and Culture Hybridity in Latin/o America* (New York: Palgrave Macmillan, 2003), 102. The collaborative opportunities these cultural practices created among different groups of slaves prompted their refusal within many mainland American colonies. Richard Cullen Rath, *How Early America Sounded* (New York: Cornell University Press, 2005), 176.

47. For discussion of the role of drummers and drumming, see Schuler, *Alas, Alas Kongo,* 77; John Generrai, *Blowing Hot & Cool: Jazz and Its Critics* (Chicago: University of Chicago Press, 2006), 139–40; Winnie Tomm, *Bodied Mindfulness: Women's Spirits, Bodies, and Places* (Waterloo, ON: Wilfrid Laurier University Press, 1995), 105; Steven Friedson, *Dancing Prophets: Musical Experience in Tumbuka Healing* (Chicago: University of Chicago Press, 1996), 131; Tracy D. Snipe, "African Dance: Bridges to Humanity," in *African Dance: An Artistic, Historical, and Philosophical Inquiry*, ed. Kariamu Welsh-Asante (Chicago: Africa World Press, 1997), 63; Dena Epstein, *Sinful Tunes and Spirituals: Black Folk Music to the Present* (Urbana: University of Illinois Press, 2003).

48. Testimony of Capt. John Ashley Hall, *HCSP,* 72:231.

49. Falconbridge, *Account of the Slave Trade*, 23.

50. Ibid.

51. Testimony of Henry Ellison, *HCSP*, 73:376.

52. On the production of pan-ethnic bonds, see Schuler, *Alas, Alas Kongo*, 66. For a discussion of the importance of song and the role of bonding, see James Wilson Jr., "Political Songs, Collective Memories, and Kikuyu Indi Schools," *History in Africa* 33, no. 1 (2006): 370. On the role of song as a part of collective mourning, see Eliyana R. Adler, "No Raisins, No Almonds: Singing as Spiritual Resistance to the Holocaust," *Shofar: An Interdisciplinary Journal of Jewish Studies* 24, no. 4 (2006): 50.

53. Testimony of Robert Norris, *HCSP*, 68:7.

54. Frances Henry discusses how musical practices, particularly singing, helped to carry words forward to a mystical world where spiritual forces dwelled. See Henry, *Reclaiming African Traditions in Trinidad: The Socio-Political Legitimization of the Orisha and Spiritual Baptist Faiths* (Kingston, Jamaica: University of the West Indies Press, 2003), 144.

55. Testimony of James Towne, *HCSP*, 82:22. William D. Piersen characterizes slave songs in the Middle Passage as "blues like songs of sorrow." See Piersen, "White Cannibals, Black Martyrs," 150.

56. Testimony of Henry Ellison, *HCSP*, 73:276.

57. Testimony of Ecroyde Claxton, *HCSP*, 82:36.

58. For a discussion of intentions with self-destruction, see Andy White, *Going Mad to Stay Insane: The Psychology of Self-Destructive Behaviors* (London: Gerald Duckworth, 1996), 120–22.

59. Scholar Gordon Lewis writes that matters of adjustment for bondpeople, "short of poisoning, suicide, permanent escape, and rebellion," represent the various factors "that the social historians of slavery must look [at] for the more characteristic and common exemplifications of slave protest." *Main Currents in Caribbean History: The Historical Evolution of the Caribbean* (Baltimore: Johns Hopkins University Press, 1987), 178.

60. Darlene Clark Hine and Kate Wittenstein, "Female Slave Resistance: The Economics of Sex," in *The Black Woman Cross-Culturally,* ed. Filomina Chioma Steady (Cambridge, MA: Schenkman, 1981), 289–300. For further discussion of suicidal behaviors among enslaved Africans, see Owens, *This Species of Property*, 93–96, and Blassingame, *Slave Community*, 7–10.

61. This statement is based on rare accounts mentioned in historical records of the Middle Passage. William D. Piersen makes the case that hangings were the most common methods of suicide. See Piersen, "White Cannibals, Black Martyrs," 153. Conversely, Louis Perez Jr. posits that self-sabotage was a common practice acted out by bondpeople, particularly within Cuba. See Perez, *To Die in Cuba: Suicide and Society* (Chapel Hill: University of North Carolina Press, 2007).

62. Testimony of Isaac Wilson, *HCSP*, 72:279–80.

63. See Michael Gomez, *Exchanging Our Country Marks: The Transformation of African Identities in the Colonial and Antebellum South* (Chapel Hill: University of North Carolina Press, 1998), 120.

64. Testimony of Isaac Wilson, *HCSP*, 72:279–80.

65. For more on "psychological hurt," see Nell Irvin Painter, *Soul Murder and Slavery,* Charles Edmondson Historical Lecture Series 15 (Waco, TX: Baylor University Press), 20.

66. Walter Johnson, "On Agency," *Journal of Social History* 37, no. 1 (2003): 116. Elizabeth Fox Genovese makes an important point regarding women and resistance. "The extreme forms of resistance—murder, self-mutilation, infanticide, and suicide— were rare." Yet, in going further she posits, "If they were abnormal in their occurrence, they nonetheless embodied the core psychological dynamics of all resistance." *Within the Plantation Household: Black and White Women of the Old South* (Chapel Hill: University of North Carolina Press, 1988), 329.

67. Franny Nudelman, *John Brown's Body: Slavery, Violence, and the Culture of War* (Chapel Hill: University of North Carolina Press, 2004), 44–45.

68. Falconbridge, *Account of the Slave Trade*, 31.

69. Testimony of James Fraser, *HCSP*, 71:45.

70. Testimony of Thomas Trotter, *HCSP*, 73:82–83.

71. See Marcus Rediker, *The Slave Ship: A Human History* (New York: Viking, 2007), 288.

72. Martin and Spurrell, *Journal of a Slave Trader*, 75.

73. Testimony of James Towne, *HCSP*, 82:21.

74. Testimony of Isaac Wilson, *HCSP*, 72:281.

75. Testimony of George Millar, *HCSP*, 73:393.

76. Testimony of Ecroyde Claxton, *HCSP*, 82:35–36.

77. Ibid. For recent discussion of the terror inflicted upon bondpeople through violent means, see Vincent Brown, *The Reaper's Garden: Death and Power in the World of Atlantic Slavery* (Cambridge, MA: Harvard University Press, 2008).

78. "Maritime fugitives" is a concept originated by Charlie Foy to describe bondpeople who escaped slavery by running away to work within the American maritime trade. See "Ports of Slavery, Ports of Freedom: How Slaves Used Northern Seaports' Maritime Industry to Escape and Create Transatlantic Identities, 1713–1783," PhD dissertation, Rutgers University, New Brunswick, New Jersey, 2007. Michael Gomez makes the point that suicide was only one form of rebellion and that another involved absconding. See Gomez, *Exchanging Our Country Marks*, 120.

79. See Julius Scott, "The Common Wind: Currents of Afro-American Communication in the Era of the Haitian Revolution," PhD dissertation, Duke University, Durham, North Carolina, 1986; Rediker, *Slave Ship*; David Cecelski, *The Waterman's Song: Slavery and Freedom in Maritime North Carolina* (Chapel Hill: University of North Carolina Press, 2001); Emma Christopher, *Slave Ship Sailors and their African Cargoes, 1730–1807* (Cambridge: Cambridge University Press, 2006); Kevin Dawson, "Enslaved Swimmers and Divers in the Atlantic World," *Journal of American History* 92 (March 2006): 1327–55; Richard McKinley Mizelle Jr., "Backwater Blues: The 1927 Flood Disaster, Race, and the Remaking of Regional Identity, 1900–1930," PhD dissertation, Rutgers University, New Brunswick, New Jersey, 2006; Sowande' Mustakeem, "She Must Go Overboard & Shall Go Overboard': Diseased Bodies and the Spectacle of Murder at Sea," *Atlantic Studies* 8, no. 3 (2011): 301–316; Jeffrey Bolster, *Black Jacks: African American Seamen in the Age of Sail* (Cambridge, MA: Harvard University Press, 1997); Foy, "Ports of Slavery."

80. See Mbiti, *African Religions and Philosophy*, 71; Marshall, "Powerful and Righteous," 39.

81. See Walker, "Suicidal Tendencies," 12.

82. For a discussion of the symbol of water by bondpeople, see M. Mullin, *Africa in America*, 204.

Chapter Six. The Anatomy of Suffering

1. Medical Log of the Slaver *Sir Lord Stanley*, 1792, kept by Christopher Bowes, Royal College of Surgeons, London, England. Along with the bondman discussed in

the above story, 386 of his fellow shipmates also perished from medical illnesses, allegedly believed to be dysentery.

2. This perspective departs from the work of noted scholar Kenneth Kiple. In his article "Nutritional Link with Slave Infant and Child Mortality in Brazil," Kiple relies on "present day medical knowledge on the past" to analyze the manifestation of disease among bondpeople although recognizing that "presentism of this sort is sometimes frowned upon by medical historians." Kenneth Kiple, "Nutritional Link with Slave Infant and Child Mortality in Brazil," *Hispanic American Historical Review* 69, no. 4 (1989): 677–90. There have been a number of historiographical debates concerning the slave trade and statistical queries, causes of mortality, duration of vessels at sea, and stowage of slaves on ships. For further reference, see Philip D. Curtin, "Epidemiology and the Slave Trade," *Political Science Quarterly* 83, no. 2 (1968): 190–216; Charles Garland and Herbert Klein, "The Allotment of Space for Slaves aboard Eighteenth-Century British Slave Ships," *William and Mary Quarterly* 42, no. 2 (1985): 238–48; Herbert S. Klein and Stanley Engerman, "Slave Mortality on British Ships, 1791–1797," in *Liverpool, the African Slave Trade, and Abolition: Essays to Illustrate Current Knowledge and Research*. ed. Roger T. Anstey and P. E. Hair (Liverpool: Historic Society of Lancashire and Cheshire, 1976), 113–25; William Darity Jr., "The Numbers Game and the Profitability of the British Trade in Slaves," *Journal of Economic History* 45, no. 3 (1985): 693–703; Paul Lovejoy, "The Volume of the Atlantic Slave Trade: A Synthesis," *Journal of African History* 23, no. 4 (1982): 473–501; Kenneth F. Kiple and Brian T. Higgins, "Mortality Caused by Dehydration during the Middle Passage," *Social Science History* 13, no. 4 (1989): 421–37; Joseph E. Inikori, "Measuring the Atlantic Slave Trade: An Assessment of Curtin and Anstey," *Journal of African History* 17, no. 2 (1976): 197–223; and Philip D. Curtin, "Measuring the Atlantic Slave Trade Once Again: A Comment," *Journal of African History* 17, no. 4 (1976): 595–605.

3. Kenneth Kiple, ed. *The Cambridge World History of Human Diseases* (New York: Cambridge University Press, 1993), 16.

4. John Duffy, *Epidemics in Colonial America* (Baton Rouge: Louisiana State University Press, 1971), 23.

5. See Franny Nudelman, *John Brown's Body: Slavery, Violence, and the Culture of War* (Chapel Hill: University of North Carolina Press, 2004), 46.

6. For further discussion of this concept, see Debbie Lee, "Yellow Fever and the Slave Trade: Coleridge's *The Rime of the Ancient Mariner*," *English Literary History* 65, no. 3 (1998): 676.

7. Kenneth Kiple, ed., "Scurvy," *Cambridge World History*, 1000–1001; R. S. Allison, *Sea Diseases: The Story of a Great Natural Experiment in Preventive Medicine in the Royal Navy* (London: John Bale Medical Publications, 1943), xix. Scurvy continues to garner its own body of literature. See Stephen Bown, *Scurvy: How a Surgeon, a Mariner, and a Gentleman Solved the Greatest Medical Mystery of the Age of Sail* (New York: St. Martin's, 2004); Alfred Hess, *Scurvy, Past and Present* (London: J. P. Lippincott, 1920); Kenneth J. Carpenter, *The History of Scurvy and Vitamin C* (New York: Cambridge University Press, 1986.)

8. James Lind, *A Treatise of the Scurvy in Three Parts Containing an Inquiry into the Nature, Causes, and Cure, of That Disease Together with a Critical and Chronological View of What Has Been Published on the Subject* (London, 1753), 61.

9. Ibid., 117, 119.

10. Anonymous, *The Ship-Master's Medical Assistant; or, Physical Advice to All Masters of Ships Who Carry no Surgeons; Particularly Useful to Those Who Trade abroad in Hot or Cold Climates, Containing a Brief Description of Diseases, Especially Those Peculiar to Seamen in Long Voyages with a Concise Method of Cure, the Result of Many Years, Practice and Experience in All Climates* (London: J. Wilkie, 1777), 6.

11. Ibid., 7.

12. Ibid. Addington added, "The most proper Diet for Seamen, much afflicted with the Scurvy, is the vegetable Part of their Provisions." See Anthony Addington, *An Essay on Sea-Scurvy Wherein Is Proposed an Easy Method of Curing That Distemper at Sea; and of Preserving Water Sweet for Any Cruize or Voyage (* London: Printed by C. Mickleright, 1753), 31.

13. Lind, *Treatise of the Scurvy*, 115.

14. In 1795, due to the persistent efforts of Sir Gilbert Blane, the British Admiralty passed a ruling concerning the use of citrus juices, particular lemon juice, as a daily ration requirement for sailors while at sea. See William McNeil, *Plagues and People* (Garden City, NY: Anchor, 1976), 268; Bown, *Scurvy,* 74–76, 197; Carpenter, *History of Scurvy,* 95, and his chapter examining scurvy within the British Royal Navy. As a result of this regulation, by the early nineteenth century it was estimated that those in the Royal Navy consumed close to 50,000 gallons of lemon juice annually. See Bown, *Scurvy,* 198–212. To understand the evolution of the term *limeys* as it was applied to nineteenth-century sailors, see David I. Harvie, *Limeys: The True Story of One Man's War against Ignorance, the Establishment, and the Deadly Scurvy* (Phoenix Mill, UK: Stroud, 2002).

15. Testimony of Robert Norris, *HCSP,* 71:10.

16. Lind, *Treatise of the Scurvy*, 147.

17. *Ship-Master's Medical Assistant*, 180.

18. Ibid., 180–81.

19. Addington, *Essay on the Sea-Scurvy*, 1.

20. *Ship-Master's Medical Assistant*, 181.

21. Addington, *Essay on the Sea-Scurvy,* 40–41.

22. Lind, *Treatise of the Scurvy,* 63.

23. *Ship-Master's Medical Assistant*, 181.

24. Addington, *Essay on the Sea-Scurvy,* 2.

25. Certificates of Slaves Taken on Board Ships, House of Lords Record Office, London, England.

26. Aubrey, *Sea Surgeon,* 116.

27. "Ship *Crescent*," James Rogers Papers, Duke University Special Collections, Durham, North Carolina.

28. Bernard Martin and Mark Spurrell, eds., *The Journal of a Slave Trader (John Newton), 1750–1754* (London: Epworth, 1962), 38. John Newton endured the losses

of twenty-four captives ("12 Men; 5 Women; 2 'Men-Boys'; 1 'Woman-Girl'; 6 Boys; and 5 Girls") to the flux aboard the *Duke of Argyle*.

29. Aubrey, *Sea Surgeon*, 116, 118.

30. *Ship-Master's Medical Assistant*, 36.

31. Aubrey, *Sea Surgeon*, 117.

32. *Ship-Master's Medical Assistant*, 38.

33. Ibid.

34. Ibid., 36.

35. Testimony of Isaac Wilson, *HCSP,* 72:291–92.

36. *Ship-Master's Medical Assistant*, 36–37.

37. Aubrey, *Sea Surgeon*, 118.

38. Certificates of Slaves Taken on Board Ships.

39. William Douglass, *A Practical Essay Concerning the Small Pox* (Boston: D. Henchman, 1730), 3. Beyond the slave trade, smallpox has been considered a historically devastating disease. For further reference, see A. M. Behbehani, *The Smallpox Story: In Words and Pictures* (Kansas City: University of Kansas Medical Center, 1988); Ian Glynn and Jenifer Glynn, *The Life and Death of Smallpox* (New York: Cambridge University Press, 2004); Peter Razzell, *The Conquest of Smallpox: The Impact of Inoculation on Smallpox Mortality in Eighteenth-Century Britain* (Sussex, Eng.: Caliban Books, 1977); Donald R. Hopkins, *Princes and Peasants: Smallpox in History* (Chicago: University of Chicago Press, 1983); Elizabeth A. Fenn, *Pox Americana: The Great Smallpox Epidemic of 1775–82* (New York : Hill and Wang, 2001); and Jennifer Lee Carrell, *The Speckled Monster: A Historical Tale of Battling Smallpox* (New York: Penguin, 2004).

40. *Ship-Master's Medical Assistant*, 192.

41. Aubrey, *Sea Surgeon,* 107.

42. Francis Bellinger, *A Treatise Concerning the Small-Pox in which a Plain and Easy Method of Curing that Disease under its most direful Symptoms, is discovered and the Case of Women with Child at that Time particularly consider'd; and so stated, as to be render'd even safer than that of other Women* (London, 1721), 18.

43. Thomas Dimsdale, *The Present Method of Inoculating for the Small Pox to which are Added Some Experiments, Instituted with a View to Discover the Effects of a Similar Treatment in the Natural Small-Pox* (London: W. Owen, 1771), 24.

44. *Ship-Master's Medical Assistant*, 194, 199.

45. Ibid., 196–97.

46. Bellinger, *Treatise Concerning the Small-Pox*, 18.

47. *Ship-Master's Medical Assistant*, 196

48. Douglass, *Practical Essay Concerning the Small Pox*, 14.

49. *Ship-Master's Medical Assistant*, 197

50. During the same year of this case, noted scientist Stephen Hales published his findings with respect to an experiment he conducted with the use of tar water. See Hales, *An Account of Some Experiment and Other Observations on Tar-Water: Wherein is Shown the Quantity of Tar That is Therein. And Also a Method Proposed, Both to Abate That Quantity Considerably, and to Ascertain the Strength of Tar-water* (London: Printed for R. Manby and H. S. Cox, 1745).

51. Ibid.

52. Slavery Collection, 1709–1864, New York Historical Society, New York City.

53. *Ship-Master's Medical Assistant,* 3.

54. Ibid.

55. Ibid., 4.

56. Ibid.

57. Sir Francis Millman, *Animadversions on the nature and on the cure of the dropsy* (London: J. Dodsley, 1786). Two scholars in their study of the health of bondmen and bondwomen contend that dropsy evolved to become a virtual "forgotten disease" within the historical record. See Anne S. Lee and Everett S. Lee, "The Health of Slaves and the Health of Freedmen: A Savannah Study," *Phylon* 38, no. 2 (1977): 170–80.

58. Millman, *Animadversions.*

59. Richard Wilkes, *An Historical Essay on Dropsy* (London: Printed for B. Law and G. Ray, 1777). Sir Francis Millman echoed Wilkes's medical sentiments in 1786, writing, "The female sex is more liable to this disease than the male: hence too it happens that young women labouring under the Chlorosis, or obstructions, are extremely prone to the Dropsy." Millman, *Animadversions,* 15.

60. Series of Mortality Lists, House of Lords Record Office, London, England.

61. Wilkes, *Historical Essay on Dropsy,* 131.

62. Ibid., 133.

63. Ibid., 134.

64. *Ship-Master's Medical Assistant,* 66.

65. Ibid., 67.

66. Wilkes, *Historical Essay on Dropsy,* 36.

67. Martin and Spurrell, *Journal of a Slave Trader,* 52.

68. Ibid., 73.

69. Henry Van Solingen, *An Inaugural Dissertation on Worms of the Human Intestines* (New York: T & J. Swords, 1792).

70. "Ship *James,*" James Rogers Papers.

71. Van Solingen, *Inaugural Dissertation,* 7.

72. Ibid, 7.

73. Ibid., 14.

74. John Huxham, *An Essay on Fevers, and Their Various Kinds, as Depending on Different Constitutions of the Blood* (London: S. Austen, 1750).

75. Certificates of Slaves Taken on Board Ships; emphasis in the original.

76. "Miscellaneous Documents," James Rogers Papers.

77. See Angela Davis, *Women, Race, and Class* (New York: Vintage, 1983), 6–7; Jennifer Morgan, *Laboring Women: Reproduction and Gender in New World Slavery* (Philadelphia: University of Pennsylvania Press, 2004), 114; Dorothy Roberts, *Killing the Black Body: Race, Reproduction, and the Meaning of Liberty* (New York: Pantheon, 1997), 23.

78. This phrase emanates from the primary source materials of the period. It is not used here to suggest that bondwomen complained, although it is conceivable they articulated feelings of medical pain during the trade.

79. F. Swediaur, MD., *Practical Observations on Venereal Complaints* (New York, 1788), 5.

80. "Ship *James,*" James Rogers Papers.

81. Certificates of Slaves Taken on Board Ships.

82. Ibid.

83. Thomas Gataker, *Observations on Venereal Complaints, and on the Methods Recommended for their Cure* (London: Printed for R. and J. Dodsley, 1755), 10–11.

84. John Hunter, *A Treatise on the Venereal Disease* (Philadelphia, 1791), 22, 30.

85. Ibid., 44, 59.

86. Ibid., 38.

87. Ibid., 41.

88. Physician Francis Swediaur offers considerable discussion on the origin of these complaints. See Swediaur, *Practical Observations*, 6.

89. Certificates of Slaves Taken on Board Ships.

90. William Rowley, *A treatise on female nervous hysterical, hypochondriacal, bilious, convulsive diseases; apoplexy and palsy; with thoughts on madness, suicide, etc., in which the principal disorders are explained from anatomical facts, and the treatment formed on several new principles* (London: C. Nourse, 1788), 184.

91. See Morgan, *Laboring Women*, 114; Kiple and Higgins, "Mortality and Dehydration," 677, 686.

92. For discussion of healthy pregnancy and its implication for black women during slavery, see Roberts, *Killing the Black Body*, 47.

93. Hugh Thomas shared, "It was not legally necessary to carry a surgeon, and many slave ships economized by neglecting to have one, including most of the ships flying the flags of the United States." *The Slave Trade: The Story of the Atlantic Slave Trade, 1440–1870* (New York: Simon and Schuster, 1997), 307–308.

94. For discussion of these morning attendances, see Testimony of William Littleton, *HCSP*, 68:295.

95. Testimony of Thomas King *HCSP,* 68:322.

96. Testimony of James Fraser, *HCSP*, 71:29–30.

97. For further discussion of surgeons' medicine chests, see Thomas, *Slave Trade,* 307–308; Testimony of James Fraser, *HCSP*, 71:40.

98. Ibid., 71:28.

99. For further discussion of African bilingualism, see Stephanie Smallwood, *Saltwater Slavery: A Middle Passage from Africa to American Diaspora* (Cambridge, MA: Harvard University Press, 2007), 118.

100. Aubrey *Sea Surgeon*, 131. The words "Yarry Yarry," according to Aubrey, meant sickness.

101. Testimony of John Knox, *HCSP,* 68:178.

102. Testimony of James Fraser, *HCSP,* 71:47.

103. Ibid., 71:28.

104. "Ship *Pearl*," James Rogers Papers.

105. Alexander Falconbridge, *An Account of the Slave Trade on the Coast of Africa* (London: Printed and sold by James Phillips, 1788), 28.

106. For a discussion of this idea of dead bodies as a "repository of mystery," see Nudelman, *John Brown's Body*, 52.

107. Testimony of Alexander Falconbridge, *HCSP,* 72:301.

108. Ibid., 72:338.

109. The availability of black bodies and their subsequent use by medical practitioners to better understand the implications of disease is based on the work of Todd Savitt in his article "The Use of Blacks for Medical Experimentation and Demonstration in the Old South," *Journal of Southern History* 48, no. 3 (1982): 331–48. For further discussion of the impact of the slave trade on the practice of English medicine, see Dott E. Noble Chamberlain, "The Influence of the Slave Trade on Liverpool Medicine," Atti del XIV Congresso Internazionale di Storia della Medicina, vol. 2 [Fourteenth International Conference of the History of Medicine], Rome-Salerno, 1954.

110. For further discussion regarding the quest to understand the proliferation of disease alongside theories of medical knowledge, see Julyan Peard, "Tropical Disorders and Forging Brazilian Medical Identity, *Hispanic American Historical Review* 77, no. 1 (1997): 1–44.

111. "Ship *Trelawney,*" James Rogers Papers.

112. "Ship *Pearl,*" James Rogers Papers.

113. Ibid.

114. Ibid.

115. Testimony of Thomas Trotter, *HCSP,* 73:95–96.

116. "Ship *Pearl,*" James Rogers Papers.

117. Ibid.

118. "Ship *Swift,*" James Rogers Papers.

119. "Ship *Pearl,*" James Rogers Papers.

120. Ibid.

121. "Ship *Daniel,*" James Rogers Papers.

122. An ongoing debate emerged in the eighteenth century that prompted some merchants to employ surgeons aboard the slave vessels they financed. Likewise, the surgeons themselves had to decide if they wanted to work on slave ships. See D.E.N. Chamberlain," Influence of the Slave Trade," 3–4; Richard B. Sheridan, "The Guinea Surgeons on the Middle Passage: The Provision of Medical Services in the British Slave Trade," *International Journal of African Historical Studies* 14, no. 4 (1981): 610.

123. Daniel Mannix and Malcolm Cowley, *Black Cargoes: A History of the Atlantic Slave Trade, 1518–1865* (New York: Viking, 1962), 122.

124. Emma Christopher offers a brief view of medical dilemmas sailors confronted at sea. See *Slave Ship Sailors and Their Captive Cargoes, 1730–1807* (Cambridge: Cambridge University Press, 2006). Leslie Owens discusses the inherent difficulty of trying to answer the question of what it felt like to be a slave by positing, "In truth we can never know this even when we try to see bondage from the slave's viewpoint." See Owens, *This Species of Property: Slave Life and Culture in the Old South* (New York :Oxford University Press, 1976), preface.

Chapter Seven. A Tide of Bodies

1. Slavery Collection, 1709–1864, New York Historical Society, New York City.

2. Letter Book of Robert Bostock, 1779–1790, Liverpool Record Office, Liverpool, England.

3. David Tuohy Papers, Liverpool Record Office, Liverpool, England.

4. For further discussion of the work expected of shipmasters upon arrival in the New World, see Emma Christopher, *Slave Ship Sailors and Their Captive Cargoes, 1730–1807* (Cambridge: Cambridge University Press, 2006), 167–223.

5. Phillip Hamer, ed. *The Papers of Henry Laurens* (Columbia: University of South Carolina Press, 1981), 1: 254–56.

6. James Dumbell Papers, University of Liverpool, Sydney Jones Library, Liverpool, England.

7. Testimony of William Littleton, *HCSP*, 68:210.

8. Testimony of George Baille, *HCSP*, 73:184.

9. Letter Book of Robert Bostock, 1779–1790.

10. Hugh Thomas, *The Slave Trade: The Story of the Atlantic Slave Trade, 1440–1870* (New York: Simon and Schuster, 1997), 429.

11. Bernard Martin and Mark Spurrell, eds., *The Journal of a Slave Trader (John Newton), 1750–1754* (London: Epworth, 1962), 67.

12. Testimony of Alexander Falconbridge, *HCSP*, 72:307–308.

13. Testimony of Clement Noble, *HCSP*, 73:119–20.

14. Testimony of Alexander Falconbridge, *HCSP*, 72:307–308.

15. Testimony of Hercules Ross, *HCSP* 82:258.

16. Testimony of Alexander Falconbridge, *HCSP*, 72:307–308.

17. Ibid.

18. Testimony of Clement Noble, *HCSP*, 73:119–20. For a similar discussion, see Testimony of Thomas Trotter, *HCSP*, 73:88.

19. Testimony of Alexander Falconbridge, *HCSP*, 72:307–308.

20. Ibid.

21. Testimony of James Morley, *HCSP*, 73:161.

22. Testimony of George Baille, *HCSP*, 73:184.

23. Ibid.

24. Testimony of Alexander Falconbridge *HCSP*, 72:307–308.

25. Testimony of Thomas Trotter, *HCSP*, 73:88.

26. Testimony of Alexander Falconbridge *HCSP*, 72:307–308.

27. Ibid., 72:308.

28. Testimony of Thomas Trotter, *HCSP,* 73:88.

29. Testimony of Clement Noble, *HCSP,* 73:119–20.

30. See Saadiyah Haartman, *Scenes of Subjection: Terror, Slavery, and Self-Making in Nineteenth-Century America* (New York: Oxford University Press, 1997.

31. Testimony of Hercules Ross, *HCSP*, 82:258.

32. Testimony of James Morley, *HCSP*, 73:161. For further discussion of vendue sales, see Stephanie Smallwood, *Saltwater Slavery: A Middle Passage from Africa to American Diaspora* (Cambridge, MA: Harvard University Press, 2007), 177.

33. Testimony of Hercules Ross, *HCSP*, 82:258.

34. Ibid.

35. Ibid.

36. Testimony of Alexander Falconbridge, *HCSP*, 72:307.

37. "Ship *Daniel*," James Rogers Papers, Duke University Special Collections, Durham, North Carolina.

38. Account Books of Ships of Thomas Leyland & Co., Liverpool Record Office, Liverpool, England

39. John Guerard Letter Book, 1752–1754, South Carolina Historical Society, Charleston, South Carolina.

40. "Ship *Diana*," James Rogers Papers.

41. "Ship *Daniel*," James Rogers Papers.

42. Martin and Spurrell, *Journal of a Slave Trader,* 69.

43. John Guerard Letter Book.

44. "Ship *Fame*," James Rogers Papers.

45. "Ship *Pearl*," James Rogers Papers.

46. "Ship *Fly*," James Rogers Papers.

47. "Ship *Fanny*," James Rogers Papers.

48. James Dumbell Papers.

49. For another example of woman and child sold into sales, see "Ship *Flora*," James Rogers Papers.

50. For an example, see the vessel *Othello,* Slavery Collection, 1709–1864.

51. Hamer, *Papers of Henry Laurens,* 2: 277.

52. Leslie J. Pollard, "Aging and Slavery: A Gerontological Perspective," *Journal of Negro History* (Autumn 1981): 230. See also Smallwood, *Saltwater Slavery*, 158.

53. "Ship *Swift*," James Rogers Papers.

54. "Ship *Pearl*," James Rogers Papers.

55. "Ship *Daniel*," James Rogers Papers.

56. "Ship *Fame*," James Rogers Papers.

57. Certificate of Slaves Taken on Board Ships, House of Lords Record Office, London, England.

58. Slavery Collection, 1709–1864.

59. John Guerard Letter Book.

60. Robert Pringle Letter Book, 1742–1745, South Carolina Historical Society, Charleston, South Carolina, 223–24.

61. Ibid., 280–83.

62. John Guerard Letter Book.

63. Ibid.

64. Ibid.

65. Slavery Collection, 1709–1864.

66. "Ship *Fly*," James Rogers Papers.

67. Hamer, *Papers of Henry Laurens,* 1: 353–54.

68. "Ship *Fanny*," James Rogers Papers.

69. Paul Cross Papers, South Caroliniana Library, Columbia, South Carolina.

70. T. Aubrey, *The Sea Surgeon; or, the Guinea Mean's Vade Mecum In which is laid down, The method of curing such Diseases as usually happen Abroad, especially on the Coast of Guinea; with the best way of treating Negroes, both in Health and in Sickness* (London: John Clark, 1729), 110.

71. Anonymous (A Surgeon of the Royal Navy), *The Ship-Master's Medical Assistant; or, Physical Advice to All Masters of Ships Who Carry no Surgeons; Particularly Useful to Those Who Trade Abroad in Hot or Cold Climates, Containing a Brief Description of*

Diseases, Especially Those Peculiar to Seamen in Long Voyages with a Concise Method of Cure, The result of Many Years, Practice and Experience in All Climates (London: J Wilkie, 1777), 255.

72. R. Shannon, *Practical Observations on the Operation and Effects of Certain Medicines in the Prevention and Cure of Diseases to which Europeans are Subject in Hot Climate, and in these Kingdoms* (London, 1794), 372.

73. Anonymous, *Ship-Master's Medical Assistant,* 256.

74. Benjamin Moseley, *Medical tracts. 1. On sugar. 2. On the cow-pox. 3. On the yaws. 4. On obi; or African witchcraft. 5. On the plague and yellow fever of America. 6. On hospitals. 7. On bronchocele. 8. On prison* (London: T. N. Longman and O. Rees, 1804), 185; emphasis in the original.

75. "Ship *Fame*," James Rogers Papers.

76. On disability and slavery, see Jennifer Barclay, "Cripples All! or, the 'Mark of Slavery': The Invisible Links between Disability and Race in the Old South and Beyond," PhD dissertation, Michigan State University, East Lansing, Michigan, 2010; Dea H. Boster, "An 'Epeleptick' Bondswoman: Fits, Slavery, and Power in the Antebellum South," *Bulletin of the History of Medicine* 83, no. 2 (2009): 271–301; John Hughes, "Labeling and Treating Black Mental Illness in Alabama, 1861–1910," *Journal of Southern History* 58 (1993): 435–60.

77. "Ship *Mermaid*," James Rogers Papers.

78. Ibid.

79. Slavery Collection, 1709–1864.

80. Ibid.

81. Ibid. There is a discrepancy in the historical records of this girl's case. According to account sales, she received medical treatment for a year extending from May 1755 to May 1756. Yet sources state she remained under a physician's care for two to three months.

Epilogue

1. Nell Irvin Painter, *Soul Murder and Slavery*, Charles Edmondson Historical Lecture Series 15 (Waco, TX: Baylor University Press, 1995), 6.

2. Mary Shelley, *Frankenstein* (New York: Dover Publications, 1994).

3. Michel-Rolph Trouillot, *Silencing the Past: Power and the Production of History* (Boston: Beacon Press, 1995), 27

4. Elaine Scarry, *The Body in Pain: The Making and the Unmaking of the World* (New York: Oxford University Press, 1987), 64.

5. For more on the *Zong* massacre, see James Walvin, *The Zong: A Massacre, the Law, and End of Slavery* (New Haven, CT: Yale University Press, 2011); and Ian Baucom, *Specters of the Atlantic: Finance, Capital, Slavery, and the Philosophy of History* (Durham, NC: Duke University Press, 2005).

6. Marcus Rediker, *The Slave Ship: A Human History* (New York: Viking, 2007); Sowande' Mustakeem, "'She Must Go Overboard & Shall Go Overboard': Diseased Bodies and the Spectacle of Murder at Sea," *Atlantic Studies* 8, no. 3 (2011): 301–316.

Bibliography

Primary Sources
Manuscripts

BOSTON PUBLIC LIBRARY

Boston Weekly Newsletter
Boston Evening Post
Georgia Gazette
Virginia Gazette

BRITISH LIBRARY, LONDON, ENGLAND

Gentlemen's Magazine
The Country Journal or the Craftsman
Read's Weekly Journal or British Gazetteer
Add. MSS 48590 ff. 29–31
Add. 18272, Collections Relating to the Slave Trade, 1775–1788

DUKE UNIVERSITY SPECIAL COLLECTIONS, DURHAM, NORTH CAROLINA

James Rogers Papers

HOUSE OF LORDS RECORD OFFICE, LONDON, ENGLAND

Certificate of Slaves Taken on Board Ships
Extracts of Such Journals of the Surgeons Employed in Ship Trading to the Coast of
    Africa
Series of Mortality Lists

JOHN CARTER BROWN LIBRARY, PROVIDENCE, RHODE ISLAND

Moses Brown Papers

LIVERPOOL RECORD OFFICE, LIVERPOOL, ENGLAND

Account Books of Ships of Thomas Leyland & Co.
David Tuohy Papers
Log of Slave Brig *Ranger*
Letter Book of Robert Bostock, 1779–1790
Ship Log Entries for Ships *Count du Nord* and *Madampookata,* 1782–1790
Register of Certificates granted by the Medical Faculty of the Liverpool Infirmary to
    the Surgeons for the African Trade, 1789–1807

NATIONAL LIBRARY, KEW GARDENS, ENGLAND

T 70/2, Abstracts of Letters from 30 September 1707, to 22 July 1713

NATIONAL MARITIME MUSEUM, LIVERPOOL, ENGLAND

Earle Collection

NATIONAL MARITIME MUSEUM, GREENWICH, ENGLAND

John Newton Manuscript Journal, 1750–1754

NEWPORT HISTORICAL SOCIETY, NEWPORT, RHODE ISLAND

Peleg Clarke Papers
Newport Intendant of Trade, 1785–1790
Samuel King Papers

NEW YORK HISTORICAL SOCIETY, NEW YORK CITY

Slavery Collection, 1709–1864

NEW YORK PUBLIC LIBRARY, NEW YORK CITY

Boston Post-Boy
Newport Mercury
New York Gazette
New York Journal

RHODE ISLAND HISTORICAL SOCIETY, PROVIDENCE, RHODE ISLAND

DeWolf Family Papers
Ship Logs, Sloop *Dolphin,* 1795–1797

ROYAL COLLEGE OF SURGEONS, LONDON, ENGLAND

Medical Log of the Slaver *Sir Lord Stanley*, 1792

SOUTH CAROLINA HISTORICAL SOCIETY, CHARLESTON, SOUTH CAROLINA

Robert Pringle Letter Book, 1742–1745
John Guerard Letter Book, 1752–1754

SOUTH CAROLINIANA LIBRARY, COLUMBIA, SOUTH CAROLINA

Paul Cross Papers

UNIVERSITY OF LIVERPOOL, SYDNEY JONES LIBRARY, LIVERPOOL, ENGLAND

James Dumbell Papers
Letters of Archibald Dalzel, 1762–1807

WELLCOME MEDICAL LIBRARY, LONDON, ENGLAND

Certificate of Tar Water Concerning a Guinea Slaver (1745)

Published

Addington, Anthony. *An Essay on Sea-Scurvy Wherein is Proposed An Easy Method of Curing that Distemper at Sea; And of Preserving Water Sweet for any Cruize or Voyage.* London: Printed by C. Mickleright, 1753.

Anonymous (A Surgeon of the Royal Navy). *The Ship-Master's Medical Assistant, or Physical Advice to All Masters of Ships who carry no Surgeons; Particularly Useful to those Who trade abroad in Hot or Cold Climates Containing A brief Description of Diseases, Especially those peculiar to Seamen in long Voyages with A concise Method of Cure, The result of many years, practice and experience in all climates.* London: J. Wilkie, 1777.

Anonymous. *A Treatise of Diseases of the Head, Brain, and Nerves.* London, 1727.

Anonymous. *A treatise upon the trade from Great-Britain to Africa: Humbly recommended to the attention of government by an African merchant.* London: Printed for R. Baldwin, 1772.

Atkins, John. *A Voyage to Guinea, Brasil, and the West-Indies.* London: Ward and Chandler, 1735.

Aubrey, T. *The Sea Surgeon; or, the Guinea Mean's Vade Mecum In which is laid down, The method of curing such Diseases as usually happen Abroad, especially on the Coast of Guinea; with the best way of treating Negroes, both in Health and in Sickness.* London: John Clark, 1729.

Bellinger, Francis. *A Treatise Concerning the Small-Pox In which a Plain and Easy Method of Curing that Disease under its most direful Symptoms, is discovered and the Case of Women with Child at that Time particularly consider'd; and so stated, as to be render'd even safer than that of other Women.* London, 1721.

Cugoano, Quobna Ottobah. *Thoughts and Sentiments on the Evil of Slavery.* Edited and with an introduction and notes by Vincent Carretta. 1787. New York: Penguin, 1999.

Dimsdale, Thomas. *The Present Method of Inoculating for the Small Pox to which are Added Some Experiments, Instituted with a View to Discover the Effects of a Similar Treatment in the Natural Small-Pox.* London: W. Owen, 1771.

Douglass, William. *A Practical Essay Concerning the Small Pox.* Boston: D. Henchman, 1730.

Equiano, Oladuah. *The Interesting Narrative of the Life of Oladuah Equiano or Gustavus Vassa, the African, Written by Himself.* London: Printed and sold for the author, 1789.

Falconbridge, Alexander. *An Account of the Slave Trade on the Coast of Africa*. London: Printed and sold by James Phillips, 1788.

Gataker, Thomas. *Observations on Venereal Complaints, and On the Methods Recommended For their Cure*. London: Printed for R. and J. Dodsley, 1755.

Hales, Stephen. *An Account of Some Experiment and Other Observations on Tar-Water: Wherein is Shown the Quantity of Tar That is Therein. And Also A Method Proposed, Both to Abate That Quantity Considerably, and to Ascertain the Strength of Tar-water*. London: Printed for R. Manby and H. S. Cox, 1745.

Hamer, Phillip, ed. *The Papers of Henry Laurens, 1724–1792*. 9 vols. Columbia: University of South Carolina Press, 1981.

Hunter, John. *A Treatise on the Venereal Disease*. Philadelphia, 1791.

Huxham, John. *An Essay on Fevers, and Their Various Kinds, as Depending on Different Constitutions of the Blood*. London: S. Austen, 1750.

Lambert, Sheila, ed. *House of Commons Sessional Papers of the Eighteenth Century*. 73 vols. Wilmington, DE: Scholarly Resources, 1975.

Lind, James. *An essay on the most effectual means of preserving the health of seamen, in the Royal Navy. Containing directions proper for all those who undertake long voyages at sea, or reside in unhealthy situations. With cautions necessary for the preservation of such persons as attend the sick in fevers*. London: D. Wilson, 1762.

———. *A Treatise Of the Scurvy In Three Parts Containing an Inquiry into the Nature, Causes, and Cure, of that Disease Together with A Critical and Chronological View of what has been published on the Subject*. London, 1753.

Martin, Bernard, and Mark Spurrell, eds., *The Journal of a Slave Trader (John Newton), 1750–1754, with Newton's Thoughts upon the African Slave Trade*. London: Epworth, 1962.

Millman, Sir Francis. *Animadversions on the nature and on the cure of the dropsy*. London : J. Dodsley, 1786.

Moseley, Benjamin. *Medical tracts. 1. On sugar. 2. On the cow-pox. 3. On the yaws. 4. On obi; or African witchcraft. 5. On the plague and yellow fever of America. 6. On hospitals. 7. On bronchocele. 8. On prison*. London: T. N. Longman and O. Rees, 1804.

Raynal, Abbe. *Slave Trade: A Full Account of This Species of Commerce; With Arguments Against it, Spirited and Philosophical*. Southwark, England: T. Cox, 1792.

Rowley, William. *A treatise on female nervous hysterical, hypochondriacal, bilious, convulsive diseases; apoplexy and palsy; with thoughts on madness, suicide, etc., in which the principal disorders are explained from anatomical facts, and the treatment formed on several new principles*. London: C. Nourse, 1788.

Shannon, R. *Practical Observations on the Operation and Effects of Certain Medicines in the Prevention and Cure of Diseases to which Europeans are Subject in Hot Climate, and in these Kingdoms*. London, 1794.

Sierra Leone Company. *Substance of the report of the court of directors of the Sierra Leone Company, delivered to the general court of proprietors, on Thursday the 26th of February, 1795*. Philadelphia: Printed by Thomas Dobson, 1795.

Smith, William. *New Voyage to Guinea: Describing the Customs, Manners, Soil, Climate, Habits, Buildings, Education, Manual Arts, Agriculture, Trade, Employments,*

Languages, Ranks of Distinction, Habitations, Diversions, Marriages, and Whatever Else is Memorable Among the Inhabitants. London: Frank Cass & Co., 1744.

Snelgrave, William. *A New Account of Some Parts of Guinea and the Slave Trade*. 1734; London: Frank Cass & Co., 1971.

Swediaur, Francis. *Practical Observations on Venereal Complaints*. New York, 1788.

Van Solingen, Henry. *An Inaugural Dissertation on Worms of the Human Intestines*. New York: T & J. Swords, 1792.

Wilkes, Richard. *An Historical Essay on Dropsy*. London: Printed for B. Law and G. Ray, 1777.

Secondary Sources

Aberth, John. *The First Horseman: Disease in Human History*. Upper Saddle River, NJ: Pearson Prentice Hall, 2007.

Acocella, Joan. *Creating Hysteria: Women and Multiple Personality Disorders*. San Francisco: Jossey-Bass, 1999.

Adler, Eliyana R. "No Raisins, No Almonds: Singing as Spiritual Resistance to the Holocaust." *Shofar: An Interdisciplinary Journal of Jewish Studies* 24, no. 4 (2006): 225–30.

Ajayi, Omofolabo S. *Yoruba Dance: The Semiotics of Movement and Body Attitude in a Nigerian Culture*. Chicago: African World Press, 1998.

Alagoa, E. J. and C. C. Wrigley. "Cannibalism and the Slave Trade." *Journal of African History* 25 (1984): 463–64.

Allison, R. S. *Sea Diseases: The Story of a Great Natural Experiment in Preventive Medicine in the Royal Navy*. London: John Bale Medical Publications, 1943.

Andrews, Kenneth. *Trade, Plunder, and Settlement: Maritime Enterprise and the Genesis of the British Empire, 1480–1630*. New York: Cambridge University Press, 1984.

Anstey, Roger. *The Atlantic Slave Trade and British Abolition, 1760–1810*. Atlantic Highlands, NJ: Humanities Press, 1975.

———. "The Volume and Profitability of the British Slave Trade, 1767–1807." In *Race and Slavery in the Western Hemisphere: Quantitative Studies*, edited by Stanley Engerman and Eugene Genovese, 3–31. Princeton, NJ: Princeton University Press, 1975.

Aparicio, Frances, and Candida Jacquez, eds. *Musical Migrations: Transnationalism and Culture Hybridity in Latin/o America*. New York: Palgrave Macmillan, 2003.

Aptheker, Herbert. *American Negro Slave Revolts*. New York: International Publishers, 1943.

Bailey, Anne C. *African Voices of the Atlantic Slave Trade: Beyond the Silence and the Shame*. Boston: Beacon Press, 2005.

Bancroft, Frederic. *Slave Trading in the Old South*. Columbia: University of South Carolina Press, 1996.

Baptist, Edward E. "'Cuffy,' 'Fancy Maids,' and 'One-Eyed Men': Rape, Commodification, and the Domestic Slave Trade in the United States." *American Historical Review* 106, no. 5 (2001):1619–50.

———. *The Half Has Never Been Told: Slavery and the Making of American Capitalism*. New York: Basic Books, 2014.

Barclay, Jennifer. "Cripples All! or, the 'Mark of Slavery': The Invisible Links between Disability and Race in the Old South and Beyond." PhD dissertation. Michigan State University, East Lansing, Michigan, 2010.

Barker, Anthony J. *The African Link: British Attitudes towards the Negro in the Era of the Atlantic Slave Trade, 1550–1807*. London: Frank Cass & Co., 1978.

Baucom, Ian. *Specters of the Atlantic: Finance, Capital, Slavery, and the Philosophy of History*. Durham, NC: Duke University Press, 2005.

Bauer, Raymond, and Alice Bauer. "Day to Day Resistance to Slavery." *Journal of Negro History* 37 (1942): 388–419.

Baynton, Douglas. "Disability in History." *Perspectives* 44, no. 8 (2006).

Beckles, Hilary. *Centering Women: Gender Discourses in Caribbean Slave Society*. Kingston, Jamaica: Ian Randle Publishers, 1999.

———. *Natural Rebels: A Social History of Enslaved Black Women in Barbados*. New Brunswick, NJ: Rutgers University Press, 1989.

Behbehani, A. M. T*he Smallpox Story: In Words and Pictures*. Kansas City: University of Kansas Medical Center, 1988.

Berlin, Ira. *Many Thousands Gone: The First Two Centuries of Slavery in North America*. Cambridge, MA: Harvard University Press, 1998.

Berry, Daina Ramey. *Swing the Sickle for the Harvest Is Ripe: Gender and Slavery in Antebellum Georgia*. Urbana: University of Illinois Press, 2007.

Blackburn, Robin. *The Making of New World Slavery: From the Baroque to the Modern, 1492–1800*. New York: Verso, 1997.

Blassingame, John W. *The Slave Community: Plantation Life in the Antebellum South*. 1972. Reprint, New York: Oxford University Press, 1979.

Bly, Antonio. "Crossing the Lake of Fire: Slave Resistance during the Middle Passage, 1720–1842." *Journal of Negro History* 83 (1998): 178–86.

Bolster, Jeffrey. *Black Jacks: African American Seamen in the Age of Sail*. Cambridge, MA: Harvard University Press, 1997.

———. "Putting the Ocean in Atlantic History: Maritime Communities and Marine Ecology in the Northwest Atlantic, 1500–1800." *American Historical Review* 113, no. 1 (2008): 19–47.

———. "'To Feel Like a Man:' Black Seamen in the Northern States, 1800–1860." *Journal of American History* 76 (March 1999): 1173–99.

Boster, Dea H. "An 'Epeleptick' Bondswoman: Fits, Slavery, and Power in the Antebellum South." *Bulletin of the History of Medicine* 83, no. 2 (2009): 271–301.

Bown, Stephen. *Scurvy: How a Surgeon, a Mariner, and a Gentleman Solved the Greatest Medical Mystery of the Age of Sail*. New York: St. Martin's, 2004.

Brooks, George E. *Eurafricans in Western Africa: Commerce, Social Status, Gender, and Religious Observance from the Sixteenth to the Eighteenth Century*. Athens: Ohio University Press, 2003.

Brown, Vincent. *The Reaper's Garden: Death and Power in the World of Atlantic Slavery*. Cambridge, MA: Harvard University Press, 2008.

Brueggemann, Brenda Jo, Sharon Snyder, and Rosemarie Garland-Thomson, eds. *Disability Studies: Enabling the Humanities*. New York: Modern Language Association of America, 2002.

Bullard, Mary Ricketsen. *Robert Stafford of Cumberland Island: Growth of a Planter*. Athens: University of Georgia Press, 1995.

Burch, Susan. *Signs of Resistance: American Deaf Cultural History, 1900–1942*. New York: New York University Press, 2002.

Burnard, Trevor. *Master, Tyranny, and Desire: Thomas Thistlewood and His Slaves in the Anglo-Jamaican World*. Chapel Hill: University of North Carolina Press, 2003.

Bush, Barbara. "Women, Childbirth, and Resistance in British Caribbean Slave Societies." In Gaspar and Hine, *More Than Chattel*, 193–217.

Byrd, Alexander X. *Captives and Voyagers: Black Migrants across the Eighteenth-Century Atlantic World*. Baton Rouge: Louisiana University Press, 2008.

Cable, Mary. *Black Odyssey: The Case of the Slave Ship*. New York: Viking, 1971.

Camp, Stephanie M. H. *Closer to Freedom: Enslaved Women and Everyday Resistance in the Plantation South*. Chapel Hill: University of North Carolina Press, 2004.

Camp, Stephanie M. H. and E. Edward Baptist, eds. *New Studies in American Slavery*. Athens: University of Georgia Press, 2006.

Carby, Hazel. *Reconstructing Womanhood: The Emergence of the Afro-American Woman Novelist*. New York: Oxford University Press, 1987.

Carney, Judith A. *Black Rice: The African Origins of Rice Cultivation in the Americas*. Cambridge, MA: Harvard University Press, 2001.

———. *In the Shadow of Slavery: African's Botanical Legacy in the Atlantic World*. Berkeley: University of California Press, 2011.

Carpenter, Kenneth J. *The History of Scurvy and Vitamin C*. New York: Cambridge University Press, 1986.

Carrell, Jennifer Lee. *The Speckled Monster: A Historical Tale of Battling Smallpox*. New York: Penguin, 2004.

Carretta, Vincent. *Equiano the African: Biography of a Self-Made Man*. Athens: University of Georgia Press, 2005.

Cecelski, David. The *Waterman's Song: Slavery and Freedom in Maritime North Carolina*. Chapel Hill: University of North Carolina Press, 2001.

Chamberlain, Dott E. Noble. "The Influence of the Slave Trade on Liverpool Medicine." Atti del XIV Congresso Internazionale di Storia della Medicina [Fourteenth International Conference of the History of Medicine]. Vol. 2. Rome-Salerno, 1954.

Chambers, Douglas. "Ethnicity in the Diaspora: The Slave Trade and the Creation of African 'Nations' in the Americas." *Slavery and Abolition* 22, no. 3 (2001): 101–120.

Chasteen, John, and Lyman L. Johnson. *National Rhythms, African Roots: The Deep History of Latin American Popular Dance*. Albuquerque: University of New Mexico Press, 2004.

Christopher, Emma. *Slave Ship Sailors and Their Captive Cargoes, 1730–1807*. Cambridge: Cambridge University Press, 2006.

Clark-Pujara, Christy. *Dark Work: The Business of Slavery in Rhode Island*. New York: New York University Press, 2016.

Cohn, Raymond. "Death of Slaves in the Middle Passage." *Journal of Economic History* 45 (1985): 685–92.

Coleman, Peter J. "The Entrepreneurial Spirit in Rhode Island History." *Business History Review* 37, no. 4 (1963): 319–44.

Conrad, Robert Edgar. *World of Sorrow: The African Slave Trade to Brazil.* Baton Rouge: Louisiana State University Press, 1986.

Cooper, Afua. *My Name Is Phillis Wheatley: A Story of Slavery and Freedom.* Toronto: Kids Can Press, 2009.

Coquer-Vidrovitch, Catherine. *The History of African Cities South of the Sahara: From the Origins to Colonization.* Princeton, NJ: Markus Wiener, 2005.

Corbin, Alain, and Jocelyn Phelps. *Lure of the Sea: Discovery of the Seaside in the Western World, 1750–1840.* New York: Penguin, 1995.

Coughtry, Jay. *The Notorious Triangle: Rhode Island and the African Slave Trade, 1700–1800.* Philadelphia: Temple University Press, 1981.

Craton, Michael. *Testing the Chains: Resistance to Slavery in the British West Indies.* Ithaca, NY: Cornell University Press, 1982.

Curtin, Philip D. *The Atlantic Slave Trade: A Census.* Madison: University of Wisconsin Press, 1969.

———. "Epidemiology and the Slave Trade." *Political Science Quarterly* 83, no. 2 (1968): 190–216.

———. "Measuring the Atlantic Slave Trade Once Again: A Comment." *Journal of African History* 17, no. 4 (1976): 595–605.

D'Arcy, Paul. *People of the Sea: Environment, Identity, and History in Oceania.* Honolulu: University of Hawaii Press, 2008.

Daniels, Christine, and Michael V. Kennedy, eds. *Over the Threshold: Intimate Violence in Early America, 1640–1865.* New York: Routledge, 1999.

Dantzig Albert van. *Forts and Castles of Ghana.* Ghana: Sedco Publishing, 1980.

Darity, William, Jr. "The Numbers Game and the Profitability of the British Trade in Slaves." *Journal of Economic History* 45, no. 3 (1985): 693–703.

Davies, K. G. *The Royal African Company.* London: Longmans, 1957.

Davis, Adrienne. "Don't Let Nobody Bother Yo' Principle: The Sexual Economy of American Slavery." In *Sister Circle: Black Women and Work,* edited by Sharon Harley and the Black Women and Work Collective, 103–127. New Brunswick, NJ: Rutgers University Press, 2002.

Davis, Angela. "Reflections on the Black Women's Role in the Community of Slaves." *Black Scholar* 3 (1971): 2–15.

———. *Women, Race, and Class.* New York: Vintage Books, 1983.

Davis, Lennard. *Enforcing Normalcy: Disability, Deafness, and the Body.* London: Verso, 1995.

Davidson, Basil. *The African Slave Trade: Pre-Colonial History, 1450–1850.* Boston: Little, Brown, 1961.

Dawson, Kevin. "Enslaved Swimmers and Divers in the Atlantic World." *Journal of American History* 92 (March 2006): 1327–55.

DeWolf, Thomas. *Inheriting the Trade: A Northern Family Confronts Its Legacy as the Largest Slave-Trading Dynasty in US History.* Boston: Beacon Press, 2009.

Diouf, Sylviane A., ed. *Fighting the Slave Trade: West African Strategies.* Athens: Ohio University Press, 2003.

Donnan, Elizabeth, ed. *Documents Illustrative of the Slave Trade to the America.* 4 vols. Washington, DC: Carnegie Institute of Washington, 1930–1935.

Dowd Hall, Jacqueline. "'The Mind That Burns in Each Body': Women, Rape, and Racial Violence." In *Powers of Desire the Politics of Sexuality*, ed. Ann Snitow, Christine Stansell, and Sharon Thompson, 328–49. New York: Monthly Review Press, 1983.

Downs, Jim. *Sick From Freedom: African American Illness and Suffering during the Civil War and Reconstruction.* New York: Oxford University Press, 2012.

Du Bois, W. E. B. *Suppression of the African Slave Trade to the United States of America, 1638–1870.* New York: Longmans, Green, and Co., 1896.

Duffy, John. *Epidemics in Colonial America.* Baton Rouge: Louisiana State University Press, 1971.

———. "Slavery and Slave Health in Louisiana 1746–1825." In *Medicine, Nutrition, Demography, and Slavery,* edited by Paul Finkelman. New York: Garland, 1989.

Egerton, Douglas. "A Peculiar Mark of Infamy: Dismemberment, Burial, and Rebelliousness in Slave Societies." In *Mortal Remains: Death in Early America*, edited by Nancy Isenberg and Andrew Burstein, 149–62. Philadelphia: University of Pennsylvania Press, 2002.

Elkins, Stanley M. *Slavery: A Problem in American Institutional and Intellectual Life.* 1959. Chicago: University of Chicago Press, 1976.

Ellison, Mary. "Resistance to Oppression: Black Women's Response to Slavery in the United States." *Slavery and Abolition* 4 (1983): 56–63.

Eltis, David. *The Rise of African Slavery in the Americas.* Cambridge: Cambridge University Press, 2000.

Eltis, David, and Stanley Engerman. "Fluctuations in Sex and Age Ratios in the Trans-Atlantic Slave Trade, 1663–1864." *Economic History Review* 46, no. 2 (1993): 308–323.

———. "Was the Slave Trade Dominated by Men?" *Journal of Interdisciplinary History* 23, no. 2 (1992): 237–57.

Eltis, David, Frank D. Lewis, and David Richardson. "Caribbean Slave Prices, the Slave Trade, and Productivity." *Economic History Review* 58 (Nov. 2005): 673–700.

———. "Mortality and Voyage Length in the Middle Passage: New Evidence from the Nineteenth Century." *Journal of Economic History* 44, no. 2 (1984): 301–308.

———. "The Volume, Age/Sex Ratios, and the African Impact of the Slave Trade: Some Refinements of Paul Lovejoy's Review of the Literature." *Journal of African History* 31, no. 3 (1990): 485–92.

———. "The Volume and Structure of the Atlantic Slave Trade: A Reassessment." *William and Mary Quarterly* 58, no. 1 (2001): 17–46.

Emery, Lynne Fauley. *Black Dance from 1619 to Today.* Princeton, NJ: Princeton Book Company, 1972.

Ephirim-Donkor, Anthony. *African Spirituality: On Becoming Ancestors.* Trenton, NJ: Africa World Press, 1997.

Epstein, Dena. *Sinful Tunes and Spirituals: Black Folk Music to the Present.* Urbana: University of Illinois Press, 2003.

Fage, J. D. "African Societies and the African Slave Trade." *Past and Present* 125 (Nov. 1989): 97–115.

———. "Slavery and Slave Trade in the Context of West African History." *Journal of African History* 10, no. 3 (1969): 393–404.

Farr, James. *Black Odyssey: The Seafaring Traditions of Afro-Americans*. New York: P. Lang, 1989.

Fenn, Elizabeth A. *Pox Americana: The Great Smallpox Epidemic of 1775–82*. New York: Hill and Wang, 2001.

Fett, Sharla. *Working Cures: Healing, Health, and Power on Southern Plantations*. Chapel Hill: University of North Carolina Press, 2002.

Fick, Carol E. *The Making of Haiti: The Saint Domingue Revolution from Below*. Knoxville: University of Tennessee Press, 1990.

Finch, Aisha. *Rethinking Slave Rebellion in Cuba: La Escalera and the Insurgencies of 1841–1844*. Chapel Hill: University of North Carolina Press, 2015.

Foster, Herbert J. "Partners or Captives in Commerce? The Role of Africans in the Slave Trade." *Journal of Black Studies* 6, no. 4 (1976): 421–34.

Foster, Thomas. "Sexual Abuse of Black Men under Slavery." *Journal of the History of Sexuality* 20 (Sept. 2011): 445–64.

Fox-Genovese, Elizabeth. *Within the Plantation Household: Black and White Women of the Old South*. Chapel Hill: University of North Carolina Press, 1988.

Foy, Charlie. "Ports of Slavery, Ports of Freedom: How Slaves Used Northern Seaports' Maritime Industry to Escape and Create Transatlantic Identities, 1713–1783." PhD dissertation. Rutgers University, New Brunswick, New Jersey, 2007.

Franklin, John Hope. *From Slavery to Freedom: A History of African Americans*. New York: Alfred A. Knopf, 1994.

Franklin, John Hope, and Loren Schweninger. *Runaway Slaves: Rebels on the Plantation*. New York: Oxford University Press, 1999.

Friedson, Steven. *Dancing Prophets: Musical Experience in Tumbuka Healing*. Chicago: University of Chicago Press, 1996.

Fuentes, Marisa. *Dispossessed Lives: Enslaved Women, Violence, and the Archive*. Philadelphia: University of Pennsylvania Press, 2016.

———. "Power and Historical Figuring: Rachael Pringle Polgreen's Troubled Archive." *Gender and History* 22 (Nov. 2010): 564–84.

Fyfe, Christopher. "West African Trade A.D. 1000–1800." In *A Thousand Years of West African History*, edited by J. F. Ade Ajayi and Ian Espie. London: Nelson, 1965.

Fyle, Magbaily. *Introduction to the History of African Civilization*. Vol. 1: *Pre-Colonial Africa*. Lanham, MD: University Press of America, 1999.

Garland, Charles, and Herbert Klein. "The Allotment of Space for Slaves aboard Eighteenth-Century British Slave Ships." *William and Mary Quarterly* 42, no. 2(1985): 238–48.

Gaspar, David Barry. *Bondmen and Rebels: A Study of Master-Slave Relations in Antigua, with Implications for Colonial British America*. Durham, NC: Duke University Press, 1993.

———. "With a Rod of Iron: Barbados Slave Laws As a Model for Jamaica, South Carolina, and Antigua, 1661–1697." In *Crossing Boundaries: Comparative History of Black People in Diaspora*, edited by Darlene Clark Hine and Jacqueline McLeod, 343–66. Bloomington: Indiana University Press, 1999.

Gaspar, David Barry, and Darlene Clark Hine, eds. *More Than Chattel: Black Women and Slavery in the Americas*. Bloomington: Indiana University Press, 1996.

Gates, Henry Louis, Jr. "Preface." *William and Mary Quarterly* 58, no. 1 (2001): 3–6.
———. *The Trials of Phillis Wheatley: America's First Poet and Her Encounters with the Founding Fathers*. New York: Basic Civitas, 2003.
Generrai, John. *Blowing Hot & Cool: Jazz and Its Critics*. Chicago: University of Chicago Press, 2006.
Genovese, Elizabeth Fox. *Within the Plantation Household: Black and White Women of the Old South*. Chapel Hill: University of North Carolina Press, 1988.
Genovese, Eugene D. *Roll Jordan Roll: The World the Slaves Made*. New York: Vintage Books, 1974.
Giddings, Paula. *When and Where I Enter: The Impact of Black Women on Race and Sex in America*. New York: W. Morrow, 1996.
Gigliotti, Simone. *The Train Journey: Transit, Captivity, and Witnessing in the Holocaust*. New York: Berghahn Books, 2009.
Gilroy, Paul. *The Black Atlantic*. Cambridge, MA: Harvard University Press, 1988.
Glymph, Thavolia. *Out of the House of Bondage: The Transformation of the Plantation Household*. New York: Cambridge University Press, 2008.
Glynn, Ian, and Jenifer Glynn. *The Life and Death of Smallpox*. New York: Cambridge University Press, 2004.
Gomez, Michael. *Exchanging Our Country Marks: The Transformation of African Identities in the Colonial and Antebellum South*. Chapel Hill: University of North Carolina Press, 1998.
Greene, Lorenzo. "Mutiny on the Slave Ships." *Phylon* 5, no. 4 (1944): 346–54.
Gross, Kali. *Colored Amazons: Crime, Violence, and Black Women in the City of Brotherly Love, 1880–1910*. Durham, NC: Duke University Press, 2006.
Gutman, Herbert. *The Black Family in Slavery and Freedom, 1750–1925*. New York: Vintage Books, 1976.
Haartman, Saadiyah. *Scenes of Subjection: Terror, Slavery, and Self-Making in Nineteenth-Century America*. New York: Oxford University Press, 1997.
———. "Venus in Two Acts." *Small Axe* 26 (2008): 1–14.
Hall, Gwendolyn Midlo. *Slavery and African Ethnicities in the Americas: Restoring the Links*. Chapel Hill: University of North Carolina Press, 2005.
Halsted, Charles H., and Robert B. Rucker, eds. *Nutrition and the Origins of Disease*. San Diego: Academic Press, 1989.
Hancock, David. *Citizens of the World: London Merchants and the Integration of the British Atlantic Community, 1725–1785*. Cambridge: Cambridge University Press, 1995.
Hancock, Ian. "On the Anglophone Creole Item Kekrebu." *American Speech* 60, no. 3 (1985): 281–83.
Harding, Vincent. *There Is a River: The Black Struggle for Freedom in America*. New York: Harcourt Brace Jovanovich, 1981.
Harris, Joseph. *Africans and Their History*. New York: Meridian Books, 1998.
Harvie, David I. *Limeys: The True Story of One Man's War against Ignorance, the Establishment, and the Deadly Scurvy*. Phoenix Mill, UK: Stroud, 2002.
Hawthorne, Walter. *From Africa to Brazil: Culture, Identity, and the Atlantic Slave Trade, 1600–1830*. Cambridge: Cambridge University Press, 2010.

Henry, Frances. *Reclaiming African Traditions in Trinidad: The Socio-Political Legiti-mation of the Orisha and Spiritual Baptist Faiths.* Kingston, Jamaica: University of the West Indies Press, 2003.

Hess, Alfred. *Scurvy, Past and Present.* London: J. P. Lippincott, 1920.

Heyerdahl, Thor. *Early Man and the Ocean: A Search for the Beginnings of Navigation and Seaborne Civilizations.* New York: Doubleday, 1979.

Higginbotham, Evelyn Brooks. "African-American Women's History and the Meta-language of Race." In *"We Specialize in the Wholly Impossible": A Reader in Black Women's History,* edited by Darlene Clark Hine, Wilma King, and Linda Reeds. New York: Carlson Publications, 1995.

Hine, Darlene Clark. *Hine Sight: Black Women and the Re-construction of American History.* Bloomington: Indiana University Press, 1997.

———. "Lifting the Veil, Shattering the Silences: Black Women's History in Slavery and Freedom." In *The State of the Afro-American Past, Present, and Future,* edited by Darlene Clark Hine, 223–49. Baton Rouge: Louisiana State University Press, 1986.

———. "Rape and the Inner Lives of Black Women in the Middle West: Preliminary Thoughts on the Culture of Dissemblance." In *Unequal Sisters: A Multicultural Reader in U.S. Women's History,* edited by Ellen DuBois and Vicki Ruiz, 292–97. New York: Routledge, 1990.

Hine, Darlene Clark, and Kate Wittenstein. "Female Slave Resistance: The Economics of Sex." In *The Black-Woman Cross-Culturally,* edited by Filomina Chioma Steady, 289–300. Cambridge, MA: Schenkman, 1981.

Holloway, Joseph. *Africanisms in American Culture.* Bloomington: Indiana University Press, 1990.

Hopkins, Donald R. *Princes and Peasants: Smallpox in History.* Chicago: University of Chicago Press, 1983.

Howard, Thomas, ed. *Black Voyage: Eyewitness Accounts of the Atlantic Slave Trade.* Boston: Little, Brown, 1971.

Hudson, Larry E., Jr. *To Have and to Hold: Slave Work and Family Life in Antebellum South Carolina.* Athens: University of Georgia Press, 1997.

Hughes, John. "Labeling and Treating Black Mental Illness in Alabama, 1861–1910." *Journal of Southern History* 58 (1993): 435–60.

Inikori, Joseph E. "The Import of Firearms into West Africa, 1750–1807: A Quantita-tive Analysis." *Journal of African History* 18, no. 3 (1977): 339–68.

———. "Measuring the Atlantic Slave Trade: A 'Rejoinder.'" *Journal of African His-tory* 17 (1976): 607–627.

Inikori, Joseph E., and Stanley Engerman. *The Atlantic Slave Trade: Effects on Econo-mies, Societies, and Peoples in Africa, the Americas, and Europe.* Durham, NC: Duke University Press, 1992.

Inyama, Emma C. "Religious and Political Culture in Igbo Traditional Society." In *Igbo and the Tradition of Politics,* edited by U. D. Anyanwu and J.C.U. Aguwa. Enugu, Nigeria: Fourth Dimension, 1993.

Jay, Bethany, and Cynthia Lynn Lyerly. *Understanding and Teaching American Slavery.* Madison: University of Wisconsin Press, 2016.

Johnson, Jessica. "Death Rites as Birthrights in Atlantic New Orleans: Kinship and Race in the Case of Maria Teresa v. Perine Dauphine. *Slavery and Abolition* 36, no. 2 (2015): 233–56.

Johnson, Walter. *Soul by Soul: Life Inside the Antebellum Slave Market*. Cambridge, MA: Harvard University Press, 1999.

Johnson, Walter. "On Agency." *Journal of Social History* 37, no. 1 (2003): 113–24.

———. *River of Dark Dreams: Slavery and Empire in the Cotton Kingdom*. Boston: Harvard University Press, 2013.

Jones, Howard. *Mutiny on the Amistad: The Saga of a Slave Revolt and Its Impact on American Abolition, Law, and Diplomacy*. New York: Oxford University Press, 1987.

Jones, Jacqueline. *Labor of Love, Labor of Sorrow: Black Women, Work, and the Family, from Slavery to the Present*. New York: Vintage Books, 1985.

Jordan, Winthrop. *White over Black: American Attitudes towards the Negro, 1550–1812*. Chapel Hill: University of North Carolina Press, 1968.

Joyner, Hannah. *From Pity to Pride: Growing Up Deaf in the Old South*. Washington, DC: Gallaudet University, 2004.

Kaba, Lansine'. "The Atlantic Slave Trade was Not a Black-on-Black Holocaust." *African Studies Review* 44, no. 1 (2001): 1–20.

Katz, William. *Breaking the Chains: African-American Slave Resistance*. New York: Maxwell Macmillan International Publishing Group, 1990.

Kaye, Anthony. *Joining Places. Slave Neighborhoods in the Old South*. Chapel Hill: University of North Carolina Press, 2009.

Kimball, Eric Bartholomew. "An Essential Link in a Vast Chain: New England and the West Indies, 1700–1775." PhD dissertation. Pittsburgh: University of Pittsburgh, 2009.

Kincaid, Jamaica. *A Small Place*. New York: Farrar, Straus and Giroux, 2000.

King, Wilma. "'Mad' Enough to Kill: Enslaved Women, Murder, and the Southern Courts." *Journal of African American History* 92, no. 1 (2007): 37–56.

———. *Stolen Childhood: Slave Youth in Nineteenth-Century America*. Bloomington: Indiana University Press, 1995.

———. "Suffer with them 'til Death: Slave Women and Their Children in Nineteenth-Century America." In Gaspar and Hine, *More Than Chattel*, 147–68.

Kiple, Kenneth F., ed. *The Cambridge World History of Human Disease*. New York: Cambridge University Press, 1993.

———. *The Caribbean Slave: A Biological History*. Cambridge: Cambridge University Press, 1984.

———. "Nutritional Link with Slave Infant and Child Mortality in Brazil." *Hispanic American Historical Review* 69, no. 4 (1989): 677–90.

Kiple, Kenneth F., and Brian T. Higgins. "Mortality Caused by Dehydration during the Middle Passage." *Social Science History* 13, no. 4 (1989): 421–37.

Kiple, Kenneth F., and Virginia H. King. *Another Dimension to the Black Diaspora: Diet, Disease, and Racism*. Cambridge: Cambridge University Press, 1981.

Klein, Herbert. "African Women in the Atlantic Slave Trade." In *Women and Slavery in Africa,* edited by Claire Robertson and Martin A. Klein. Portsmouth, NH: Heinemann, 1997.

———. *The Atlantic Slave Trade*. Cambridge: Cambridge University Press, 1999.

———. *The Middle Passage: Comparative Studies in the Atlantic Slave Trade.* Princeton, NJ: Princeton University Press, 1978.

Klein, Herbert, and Stanley Engerman. "Slave Mortality on British Ships, 1791–1797." In *Liverpool, the African Slave Trade, and Abolition: Essays to Illustrate Current Knowledge and Research,* edited by Roger T. Anstey and P. E. Hair, 113–25. Liverpool: Historic Society of Lancashire and Cheshire, 1976.

Kolchin, Peter. *American Slavery, 1619–1877*. New York: Hill and Wang, 1993.

Lane, Harlan. *When the Mind Hears: A History of the Deaf*. New York: Random House, 1984.

Law, Robin, and Kristin Mann. "West Africa in the Atlantic Community: The Case of the Slave Coast." *William and Mary Quarterly* 56, no. 2 (1999): 316–17.

Lawrence, Denise L., and Setha M. Low. "The Built Environment and Spatial Form." *Annual Review of Anthropology* 19 (1990): 453–505.

Lee, Anne S., and Everett S. Lee. "The Health of Slaves and the Health of Freedmen: A Savannah Study." *Phylon* 38, no. 2 (1977): 170–80.

Lee, Debbie. "Yellow Fever and the Slave Trade: Coleridge's *The Rime of the Ancient Mariner.*" *English Literary History* 65, no. 3 (1998): 675–700.

Lerner, Gerda. *Black Women in White America: A Documentary History*. 1972. Reprint, New York: Vintage Books, 1992.

Lewis, Gordon. *Main Currents in Caribbean History: The Historical Evolution of the Caribbean*. Baltimore: Johns Hopkins University Press, 1987.

Linton, Simi. *Claiming Disability: Knowledge and Identity*. New York: New York University Press, 1998.

Littlefield, Daniel C. *Rice and Slaves: Ethnicity and the Slave Trade in Colonial South Carolina*. Baton Rouge: Louisiana State University Press, 1981.

Longmore, Paul K. *Why I Burned My Book and Other Essays on Disability*. Philadelphia: Temple University Press, 2003.

Longmore, Paul K., and Lauri Umansky, eds. *The New Disability History: American Perspectives*. New York: New York University Press, 2001

Lovejoy, Paul. *Identity in the Shadow of Slaver*y. New York: Continuum, 2000.

———. *Transformations in Slavery.* New York: Oxford University Press, 1983.

———. "The Volume of the Atlantic Slave Trade: A Synthesis." *Journal of African History* 23, no. 4 (1982): 473–501.

Lovejoy, Paul E. "Autobiography and Memory: Gustavus Vassa, alias Oladuah Equiano, the African." *Slavery & Abolition* 27 (2006): 317–47.

MacDonald, I., and C. A. Williams. "Dietary Carbs, Health, and Disease." In *Nutrition of Health, a Perspective: The Current Status of Research on Diet-Related Diseases,* edited by Michael Turner. New York: Alan R. Liss, 1982.

Maher, Louis P. *Rites of Execution: Capital Punishment and the Transformation of American Culture, 1776–1865*. New York: Oxford University Press, 1989.

Malone, Jacqui. *Steppin' on the Blues: The Visible Rhythms of African American Dance*. Urbana: University of Illinois Press, 1996.

Manning, Patrick. *Slavery and African Life: Occidental, Oriental, and African Slave Trades*. Cambridge, MA: Cambridge University Press, 1990.

Mannix, Daniel, and Malcolm Cowley. *Black Cargoes: A History of the Atlantic Slave Trade, 1518–1865.* New York: Viking, 1962.

Marshall, Kenneth E. *Manhood Enslaved: Bondmen in Eighteenth- and Nineteenth-Century New Jersey.* Rochester, NY: University of Rochester Press, 2011.

———. "Powerful and Righteous: The Transatlantic Survival and Cultural Resistance of an Enslaved African Family in Eighteenth-Century New Jersey." *Journal of American Ethnic History* 23 (Winter 2004): 23–49.

Mbefo, Luke Nnamdi. *Theology and Aspects of Igbo Culture.* Onitsha, Nigeria: Spiritan Publications, 1997.

Mbiti, John. *African Religions and Philosophy.* New York: Praeger, 1969.

McGowan, Winston. "African Resistance to the Atlantic Slave Trade in West Africa." *Slavery and Abolition* 11 (May 1990): 5–29.

———. *Introduction to African Religion.* New York: Praeger, 1975.

McNeil, William. *Plagues and People.* Garden City, NY: Anchor, 1976.

Metcalf, George. "A Microcosm of Why Africans Sold Slaves: Akan Consumption Patterns in the 1770s." *Journal of African History* 28, no. 3 (1987): 377–94.

Miller, Joseph. "Mortality in the Atlantic Slave Trade: Statistical Evidence on Causality." *Journal of Interdisciplinary History* 11, no. 3 (1981): 385–423.

———. *Way of Death: Merchant Capitalism and the Angolan Slave Trade, 1730–1830.* Madison: University of Wisconsin Press, 1988.

Millward, Jessica. *Find Charity Folk: Enslaved and Free Black Women in Maryland.* Athens: University of Georgia Press, 2015.

Mizelle, Richard. *Backwater Blues: The Mississippi Flood of 1927 in the African American Imagination.* Minneapolis: University of Minnesota Press, 2014.

Morgan, Gwen, and Peter Rushton. "Visible Bodies: Power, Subordination, and Identity in the Eighteenth-Century Atlantic World." *Journal of Social History* 39, no. 1 (2005): 39–64.

Morgan, Jennifer. *Laboring Women: Reproduction and Gender in New World Slavery.* Philadelphia: University of Pennsylvania Press, 2004.

———. "'Some Could Suckle over Their Shoulder': Male Travelers, Female Bodies, and the Gendering of Racial Ideology, 1500–1700." *William and Mary Quarterly* 54, no. 1 (1997): 167–92.

Morgan, Phillip D. "British Encounters with Africans and African-Americans circa 1600–1780." In *Strangers within the Realm: Cultural Margin of the First British Empire,* edited by Bernard Bailyn and Phillip D. Morgan. Chapel Hill: University of North Carolina Press, 1991.

———. *Slave Counterpoint: Black Culture in the Eighteenth Century Chesapeake and Lowcountry.* Chapel Hill: University of North Carolina Press, 1998.

Mullin, Gerald W. *Flight and Rebellion: Slave Resistance in Eighteenth-Century Virginia.* New York: Oxford University Press, 1972.

Mullin, Michael. *Africa in America: Slave Acculturation and Resistance in the American South and the British Caribbean, 1736–1831.* Urbana: University of Illinois Press, 1992.

Mustakeem, Sowande'. "Blood-Stained Mirrors: Decoding the American Slave Trading Past." In Jay and Waverly, *Understanding and Teaching American Slavery,* 77–95.

———. "Breaking the Chains: Un-Silencing the American Slaving Past." In *Teaching Lincoln: Legacies and Classroom Strategies,* edited by Caroline Pryor and Stephen Hansen, 121–28. New York: Peter & Lang, 2013.

———. "Far Cry from a Fantasy Voyage: The Impact of the Middle Passage on New World Slave Societies." *ISLAS: Official Publication of Afro-Cuban Alliance, Inc.* 2, no. 8 (2007): 28–34.

———. "'I Never Have Such a Sickly Ship Before': Diet, Disease, and Mortality In 18th -Century Atlantic Slaving Voyages." *Journal of African American History* 93 (Fall 2008): 474–96.

———. "Make Haste & Let Me See You with a Good Cargo of Negroes: Gender, Power, and the Centrality of Violence in the Eighteenth-Century Atlantic Slave Trade." In *Gender, Race, Ethnicity, and Power in Maritime America*, edited by Glenn Gordinier, 3–21. Mystic, CT: Mystic Seaport Museum, 2008.

———. "'She Must Go Overboard & Shall Go Overboard': Diseased Bodies and the Spectacle of Murder at Sea." *Atlantic Studies* 8, no. 3 (2011): 301–316.

Norling, Lisa. *Iron Men, Wooden Women: Gender and Seafaring in the Atlantic World, 1700–1920.* Baltimore: Johns Hopkins University Press, 1996.

Northup, David. *Africans Discovery of Europe, 1450–1850* (New York: Oxford University Press, 2002.

———. *The Atlantic Slave Trade.* Boston: Houghton Mifflin, 1994.

Nudelman, Franny. *John Brown's Body: Slavery, Violence, and the Culture of War.* Chapel Hill: University of North Carolina Press, 2004.

Nwokeji, G. Ugo. "African Conceptions of Gender and Slave Traffic." *William and Mary Quarterly* 58, no. 1 (2001): 47–68.

O'Brien, L. Stephen. *Traumatic Events and Mental Health.* Cambridge: Cambridge University Press, 1998.

O' Malley, Greg. *Final Passages: The Intercontinental Slave Trade of British America, 1619–1807.* Chapel Hill: University of North Carolina Press, 2014.

Owens, Leslie. *This Species of Property: Slave Life and Culture in the Old South.* New York: Oxford University Press, 1976.

Painter, Nell Irvin. *Soul Murder and Slavery.* Charles Edmondson Historical Lecture Series 15. Waco, TX: Baylor University Press, 1995.

Parrish, Lydia. *Slave Songs of the Georgia Sea Islands.* 1942. Reprint, Athens: University of Georgia Press, 1992.

Peard, Julyan. "Tropical Disorders and Forging Brazilian Medical Identity." *Hispanic American Historical Review* 77, no. 1(1997): 1–44.

Perez, Louis, Jr. *To Die in Cuba: Suicide and Society.* Chapel Hill: University of North Carolina Press, 2007.

Phillips, Ulrich B. *American Negro Slavery: A Survey of the Supply, Employment, and Control of Negro Labor as Determined by the Plantation Regime.* Gloucester, MA: P. Smith, 1918.

Piersen, William D. "White Cannibals, Black Martyrs: Fear, Depression, and Religious Faith as Causes of Suicide among New Slaves." *Journal of Negro History* 62 (1977): 147–59.

Piot, Charles. "Of Slaves and the Gift: Kabre Sale of Kin during the Era of the Slave Trade." *Journal of African History* 37, no. 1 (1996): 31–49.

Pollard, Leslie J. "Aging and Slavery: A Gerontological Perspective." *Journal of Negro History* (Autumn 1981): 228–34.

Pope-Hennessey, James. *Sins of the Fathers: A Study of the Atlantic Slave Traders, 1441–1807.* New York: Knopf, 1968.

Postma, Johannes. *The Dutch in the Atlantic Slave Trade, 1600–1815.* Cambridge: Cambridge University Press, 1990.

Putney, Martha. *Black Sailors: Afro-American Merchant Seamen and Whalemen Prior to the Civil War.* New York: Greenwood Press, 1987.

Ramey, Daina L. "'A Heap of Us Slaves': Family and Community Life among Slave Women in Georgia." *Atlanta History: A Journal of Georgia and the South* 44, no. 3 (2000): 21–38.

Ransford, Oliver. *The Slave Trade: A Story of Transatlantic Slavery.* London: J. Murray, 1971.

Rath, Richard Cullen. *How Early America Sounded.* New York: Cornell University Press, 2005.

Rawley, James. *The Transatlantic Slave Trade: A History.* New York: Norton, 1981.

Razzell, Peter. *The Conquest of Smallpox: The Impact of Inoculation on Smallpox Mortality in Eighteenth-Century Britain.* Sussex, Eng.: Caliban Books, 1977.

Rediker, Marcus. *The Amistad Rebellion: An Atlantic Odyssey of Slavery and Freedom.* Penguin, 2012.

———. *Between the Devil and the Deep Blue Sea: Merchant Seamen, Pirates, and the Anglo-American Maritime World, 1700–1750.* New York: Cambridge University Press, 1989.

———. "History from Below the Waterline: Sharks and the Atlantic Slave Trade." *Atlantic Studies* 5, no. 2 (2008): 285–97.

———. "The Red Atlantic; or, 'a terrible blast swept over the heaving sea.'" In *Sea Changes: Historicizing the Ocean,* edited by Bernhard Klein and Gesa Mackenthun. New York: Routledge, 2003.

———. *The Slave Ship: A Human History.* New York: Viking, 2007.

Richards, W. A. "The Import of Firearms into West Africa in the Eighteenth Century." *Journal of African History* 21, no. 1 (1980): 43–59.

Richardson, David. "Shipboard Revolts, African Authority, and the Atlantic Slave Trade." *William and Mary Quarterly* 58, no. 1 (2001): 69–92.

Rinaldi, Ann. *Hang a Thousand Trees with Ribbons: The Story of Phillis Wheatley.* Boston: Graphia, 2005.

Roberts, Dorothy. *Killing the Black Body: Race, Reproduction, and the Meaning of Liberty.* New York: Pantheon, 1997.

Rodney, Walter. "African Slavery and Other Forms of Social Oppression on the Upper Guinea Coast in the Context of the Atlantic Slave Trade." *Journal of African History* 7, no. 3 (1966): 431–43.

———. "Upper Guinea Coast and the Significance of the Origins of Africans Enslaved in the New World." *Journal of Negro History* 54, no. 4 (1969): 327–45.

Rogers, Stanley. *Ships and Sailors: Tales of the Sea.* New York: George G. Harrap, 1928.

Rucker, Walter. *The River Flows On: Black Resistance, Culture, and Identity Formation in Early America*. Baton Rouge: Louisiana State University Press, 2008.

Ryder, A.F.C. "Portuguese and Dutch in West Africa before 1800." In *A Thousand Years of West African History*, edited by J. F. Ade Ajayi and Ian Espie, 212–32. Ibadan, Nigeria: Ibadan University Press, 1965.

Sandell, Richard. *Museums, Prejudice, and the Reframing of Difference*. London: Routledge, 2007.

Savage, John. "'Black Magic' and White Terror: Slave Poisoning and Colonial Society in Early Nineteenth-Century Martinique." *Journal of Social History* 40, no. 3 (2007): 635–62.

Savitt, Todd. *Medicine and Slavery: The Diseases and Health Care of Blacks in Antebellum Virginia*. Urbana: University of Illinois Press, 1978.

———. "The Use of Blacks for Medical Experimentation and Demonstration in the Old South." *Journal of Southern History* 48, no. 3 (1982): 331–48.

Scarry, Elaine. *The Body in Pain: The Making and the Unmaking of the World*. New York: Oxford University Press, 1987.

Schuler, Monica. *Alas, Alas Kongo: A Social History of Indentured African Immigration into Jamaica, 1841–1865*. Baltimore: Johns Hopkins University Press, 1980.

Schwartz, Maria Jenkins. *Birthing a Slave: Motherhood and Medicine in the Antebellum South*. Cambridge, MA: Harvard University Press, 2006.

———. *Born in Bondage: Growing Up Enslaved in the Antebellum South*. Cambridge, MA: Harvard University Press, 2001.

Scott, Julius. "The Common Wind: Currents of Afro-American Communication in the Era of the Haitian Revolution." PhD dissertation. Duke University, Durham, North Carolina, 1986.

Shelley, Mary. *Frankenstein*. New York: Dover Publications, 1994.

Shepherd, Verene, and Hilary Beckles. *Caribbean Slavery in the Atlantic World*. Kingston, Jamaica: Ian Randle Publishers, 1999.

Sheridan, Richard B. "Africa and the Caribbean in the Atlantic Slave Trade." *American Historical Review* 88, no. 1 (1972): 15–35.

———. *Doctors and Slaves: Demography and Medicine in the British West Indies, 1680–1860*. New York: Cambridge University Press, 1985.

———. "The Guinea Surgeons on the Middle Passage: The Provision of Medical Services in the British Slave Trade." *International Journal of African Historical Studies* 14, no. 4 (1981): 601–625.

———. "Resistance and Rebellion of African Captives in the Transatlantic Slave Trade before Becoming Seasoned Labourers in the British Caribbean, 1690–1807." In *Working Slavery, Pricing Freedom: Perspectives from the Caribbean, Africa, and the African Diaspora*, edited by Verene A. Shepherd, 185–205. Kingston, Jamaica: Ian Randle Publishers, 2002.

Smallwood, Stephanie. "African Guardians, European Slave Ships, and the Changing Dynamics of Power in the Early Modern Atlantic." *William and Mary Quarterly* 64 (Oct. 2007): 679–716.

———. *Saltwater Slavery: A Middle Passage from Africa to American Diaspora*. Cambridge, MA: Harvard University Press, 2007.

Smith, Antoinette, ed. *Thomas Clarkson and Ottobah Cugoano: Essays on the Slavery and Commerce of the Human Species.* New York: Broadview Press, 2010.

Smith, Gaddis. "Black Seamen and the Federal Courts, 1789–1860." In *Ships, Seafaring, and Society: Essays in Maritime History,* edited by Timothy J. Runyan. Detroit: Wayne State University Press, 1987.

Snipe, Tracy D. "African Dance: Bridges to Humanity." In *African Dance: An Artistic, Historical, and Philosophical Inquiry*, edited by Kariamu Welsh-Asante. Chicago: Africa World Press, 1997.

Snyder, Terri. *The Power to Die: Slavery and Suicide in North America.* Chicago: University of Chicago Press, 2015.

———. "Suicide, Slavery, and Memory in North America." *Journal of American History* 97 (June 2010): 39–62.

Stampp, Kenneth M. *The Peculiar Institution: Slavery in the Antebellum South.* 1956. Reprint, New York: Vintage Books, 1989.

Steckel, Richard H., and Richard A. Jensen. "New Evidence on the Causes of Slave and Crew Mortality in the Atlantic Slave Trade." *Journal of Economic History* 46 (March 1986): 57–77.

Stein, Robert. *The French Slave Trade in the Eighteenth Century: An Old Regime Business.* Madison: University of Wisconsin Press, 1979.

Stuckey, Sterling. *Slave Culture: Nationalist Theory and the Foundation of Black America.* New York: Oxford University Press, 1987.

Sweet, James. *Recreating Africa: Culture, Kinship, and Religion in the African-Portuguese World, 1441–1770.* Chapel Hill: University of North Carolina Press, 2003.

Tadman, Michael. *Speculators and Slaves: Masters, Traders, and Slaves in the Old South.* Madison: University of Wisconsin Press, 1989.

Taylor, Eric. *If We Must Die: Shipboard Insurrections in the Era of the Atlantic Slave Trade.* Baton Rouge: Louisiana State University Press, 2006.

Thomas, Hugh. *The Slave Trade: The Story of the Atlantic Slave Trade, 1440–1870.* New York: Simon and Schuster, 1997.

Thomas, R. Paul, and R. Nelson Bean. "The Fishers of Men: The Profits of the Slave Trade," *Journal of Economic History* 34, no. 4 (1974): 885–914.

Thompson, Katrina D. *Ring Shout, Wheel About: The Racial Politics of Music and Dance in North American Slavery.* Urbana: University of Illinois Press, 2014.

Thompson, Vincent Bakpetu. *The Making of the African Diaspora in the Americas, 1441–1900.* White Plains, NY: Longman, 1982.

Thomson, Rosemarie Garland. *Extraordinary Bodies: Figuring Physical Disability in American Culture and Literature.* New York: Columbia University Press,1997.

Thornton, John K. *Africa and Africans in the Making of the Atlantic World, 1400–1800.* 2nd ed. New York: Cambridge University Press, 1998.

———. "Cannibals, Witches, and Slave Traders in the Atlantic World." *William and Mary Quarterly* 60 (April 2003): 273–94.

Thorpe, S. A. *African Traditional Religions: An Introduction.* Pretoria: University of South Africa Press, 1991.

Tomm, Winnie. *Bodied Mindfulness: Women's Spirits, Bodies, and Places.* Waterloo, ON: Wilfrid Laurier University Press, 1995.

Trouillot, Michel-Rolph. *Silencing the Past: Power and the Production of History*. Boston: Beacon Press, 1995.

Turner, Sasha. "Home Grown Slaves: Women, Reproduction, and the Abolition of the Slave Trade, Jamaica 1788–1807." *Journal of Women's History* 23, no 3 (2010): 39–62.

Vahouny, George V., and David Kritchevsky, eds. *Dietary Fiber in Health and Disease*. New York: Plenum, 1982.

Verdery, Katherine. *The Political Lives of Dead Bodies: Reburial and Postsocialist Change*. New York: Columbia University Press, 2000.

Vickers, Daniel, and Vince Walsh. *Young Men and the Sea: Yankee Seafarers in the Age of Sail*. New Haven, CT: Yale University Press, 2007.

Waites, Elizabeth. *Trauma and Survival: Post-Traumatic and Dissociative Disorders in Women*. New York: W. W. Norton, 1993.

Walker, Daniel E. "Suicidal Tendencies: African Transmigration in the History and Folklore of the Americas." *Griot* 18 (1999): 10–18.

Walvin, James. *An African's Life, 1745–1797: The Life and Times of Oladuah Equiano*. New York: Continuum, 2000.

———. *Black Ivory: A History of British Slavery*. London: HarperCollins, 1993.

———. *Questioning Slavery*. New York: Routledge, 1996.

———. *The Zong: A Massacre, the Law, and End of Slavery*. New Haven, CT: Yale University Press, 2011.

Warren, Wendy Anne. "'The Cause of Her Grief': Rape of a Slave in Early New England Slavery." *Journal of American History* 93 (March 2007): 1031–49.

Watt, J., E. J. Freeman, and W. F. Bynum, eds. *Starving Sailors: The Influence of Nutrition upon Naval and Maritime History*. Bristol, Eng.: National Maritime Museum, 1981.

Wax, Darold D. "Negro Resistance to the Early American Slave Trade." *Journal of Negro History* 51, no. 1 (1966): 1–15.

———. "'A People of Beastly Living': Europe, Africa, and the Atlantic Slave Trade." *Phylon* 41, no. 1 (1980): 12–24.

———. "Preferences for Slaves in Colonial America." *Journal of Negro History* 58 (1973): 371–401.

Wheatley, Phillis. *Complete Writings*. New York: Penguin Classics, 2001.

White, Andy. *Going Mad to Stay Insane: The Psychology of Self-Destructive Behaviors*. London: Gerald Duckworth, 1996.

White, Deborah Gray. *Ar'n't I a Woman? Female Slaves in the Plantation South*. 1985. Reprint, New York: W. W. Norton, 1999.

———. "Mining the Forgotten: Manuscript Sources for Black Women's History." *Journal of American History* 74 (June 1987): 237–42.

White, Gavin. "Firearms in Africa: An Introduction." *Journal of African History* 12, no. 2 (1971): 173–84.

Williams, David M. "Humankind and the Sea: The Changing Relationship since the Mid-Eighteenth Century." *International Journal of Maritime History* 22 (2010): 1–14.

Williams, Eric. *Capitalism and Slavery*. Chapel Hill: University of North Carolina Press, 1944.

Wilson, Anne C., ed. *Waste Not, Want Not: Food Preservation in Britain from Early Times to the Present Day*. Edinburgh: Edinburgh University Press, 1991.

Wilson, James, Jr. "Political Songs, Collective Memories, and Kikuyu Indi Schools."
  History in Africa 33, no. 1 (2006): 363–88.

Winick, Myron, ed. *Nutrition and the Killer Diseases*. New York: Wiley, 1981.

Wish, Harvey. "American Slave Insurrections before 1861." *Journal of Negro History*
  22, no. 3 (1937): 299–320.

Wood, Betty. "Some Aspects of Female Resistance to Chattel Slavery in Low Country
  Georgia, 1763–1815." *Historical Journal* 30, no. 3 (1987): 603–622.

Wood, Peter H. *Black Majority: Negroes in Colonial South Carolina from 1670 through
  the Stono Rebellion*. New York: Knopf, 1974.

Index

SOWANDE' M. MUSTAKEEM is an assistant professor in the Department of History and the African and African American Studies Program at Washington University in St. Louis.

The New Black Studies Series

The University of Illinois Press
is a founding member of the
Association of American University Presses.

Composed in 10.5/13 Times New Roman MT Std
by Lisa Connery
at the University of Illinois Press
Cover designed by Jennifer Holzner
Manufactured by Sheridan Books

University of Illinois Press
1325 South Oak Street
Champaign, IL 61820-6903
www.press.uillinois.edu